P9-DNY-037

More praise for *Let Me Hear Your Voice*

"An engrossing account of a family's experience with autism . . . *Let Me Hear Your Voice* is the story of a mother's trials and triumph. Faced with losing her daughter, Maurice did what I imagine we all hope we can do when tragedy moves from nightmare to reality. She denied, cried, raged, read and finally took action. Then, when the worst was over, she made sense of an awful experience by writing about it so that others could understand. . . . In *Let Me Hear Your Voice*, the process of recovery is a sort of miracle, but documented, witnessed. One that can be duplicated. One that offers hope, not to all, but to some. And that is the best miracle of all."

—*The Women's Review of Books*

LET ME HEAR YOUR VOICE

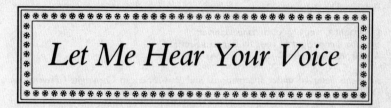

Let Me Hear Your Voice

A FAMILY'S TRIUMPH OVER AUTISM

Catherine Maurice

Fawcett Columbine • New York

Sale of this book without a front cover may be unauthorized. If this book is coverless, it may have been reported to the publisher as "unsold or destroyed" and neither the author nor the publisher may have received payment for it.

A Fawcett Columbine Book
Published by Ballantine Books

Copyright © 1993 by Catherine Maurice
Foreword copyright © 1993 by Bernard Rimland
Afterword copyright © 1993 by O. Ivar Lovaas

All rights reserved under International and Pan-American Copyright Conventions. Published in the United States by Ballantine Books, a division of Random House, Inc., New York, and simultaneously in Canada by Random House of Canada Limited, Toronto.

This edition published by arrangement with Alfred A. Knopf, Inc..

Grateful acknowledgment is made to the following for permission to reprint previously published material:
American Psychiatric Association: Excerpts from "Pervasive Developmental Disorders," in *Diagnostic and Statistical Manual of Mental Disorders*, 3rd ed. rev., pp. 33–39, copyright © 1987 by American Psychiatric Association. Reprinted by permission of American Psychiatric Association. *The Free Press*: Excerpts from *The Empty Fortress: Infantile Autism and the Birth of the Self* by Bruno Bettelheim, copyright © 1967 by Bruno Bettelheim. Reprinted by permission of The Free Press, a division of Macmillan Inc. *Macmillan Publishing Company*: Excerpt from "He remembers Forgotten Beauty," from *The Poems of W. B. Yeats: A New Edition*, by Richard J. Finneran (New York: Macmillan, 1983). Reprinted by permission. *Science of Mind Magazine*: Excerpt from "The Healing Power of Unconditional Love," an interview with Barry Neil Kaufman, copyright © 1988 by *Science of Mind Magazine*. Reprinted by permission. *Walt Disney Music Company*: Excerpt from "Once Upon a Dream," words and adaptation of music by Sammy Fain and Jack Lawrence, copyright © 1952 by Walt Disney Music Company. All rights reserved. Used by permission.

An adapted version of the "Do-It-Yourself Terminology Generator" is based upon an original design by Edward Fry, published in *Journal of Reading*, March 1968, International Reading Association, Newark, DE.

The lines of poetry on page 186 are taken from George Herbert's "Gratefulness," first published in 1633.

http://www.randomhouse.com

Library of Congress Catalog Card Number: 93-91090

ISBN: 0-449-90664-7

Manufactured in the United States of America

First Ballantine Books Edition: August 1994

20 19 18 17 16 15 14 13 12

FOR

Marilyn, Georgianna, Galina,
Robin, Leslie, Cindy, Lucille P.,
Lucille S., Joanne, Maureen,
Melissa, Donna, Joan, Paula,
Emmy, Amy P., Amy S., Elizabeth,
Wendy, Lalitha, Patty,
Cathie, and Lynn,

AND FOR THEIR CHILDREN

Come thou my love, my lovely one, come.
Show me your face, let me hear your voice.
For your voice is sweet,
And your face is beautiful.

—THE SONG OF SONGS

The author has written under a pseudonym in order to protect her children's privacy.

The names of doctors and psychologists referred to in the text have also been changed—except for the following, who appear under their own names: Dr. Steven Blaustein, Dr. Ira Cohen, Dr. Regina DeCarlo, Dr. Ivar Lovaas, Dr. Lilia Pasik, Dr. Richard Perry, Dr. Bernard Rimland, Dr. Vicky Sudhalter, Dr. Martha Welch.

Contents

Foreword

by

BERNARD RIMLAND, PH.D.

IN THESE PAGES Catherine Maurice graciously refers to me as her mentor. To some extent that is true, because while both of us, as parents of autistic children, walked strikingly similar paths, my struggles with the dragons of autismland began three decades before hers. My battles were fought from my background as a research psychologist; hers from training in literary criticism. Yet our paths converged. How pleasing it is to know that one's struggles and hard-earned lessons have served to make the path easier for those who follow. Other parents of autistic children know the sequence all too well—the first nagging doubts, the growing dismay and apprehension, the horror of finally identifying autism, the succession of additional horrors. . . . But let Catherine Maurice tell the story. She does it superbly well.

In some ways, Catherine is also *my* mentor. Her insightful dissection of the assumptions and presumptions of the psychoanalysts brings to light new and valid criticisms of that futile and archaic approach to therapy. Her discerning eye and keen intellect are also applied with great skill to a number of other treatment modalities, and to the pretensions of their practitioners. Her Chapter 33, a brilliant analysis and exposé of the therapeutic field, should be required reading for parents and professionals alike.

For many years I have urged the parents of autistic children to "press all the buttons"—to try all the various forms of treatment for which there is some positive evidence of efficacy. Each autistic child is different; each responds somewhat differently. Some autistic children improve, while others do not. It is clear to me that a child's chances for improvement increase substantially if the parents, like the Maurices, take an active, aggressive role in seeking and trying the various treatment modalities that others have found helpful.

Let Me Hear Your Voice demonstrates the value of such a dynamically positive attitude. Recovery from autism was almost unheard of a decade ago. More recently, within the past five or six years, there has been a sudden upsurge in published reports of autistic persons who now function within the normal range. In virtually all of these cases, however, there still remain some residual traits of autism. I am happy to say that I have visited the Maurice home and seen the children, *delightful* children, on several occasions, and did not (thank heaven!) detect any such residual signs. There are no guarantees in this life, but in the case of the Maurice children, their parents' efforts and good fortune appear to have achieved remarkably good results.

The one approach which appears to have been most effective in bringing about recovery in the Maurice children is the teaching procedure known as behavior modification. Soon after my book *Infantile Autism* was published in 1964, I learned that behavior modification might be helpful to autistic children and subsequently visited UCLA, where psychologist Ivar Lovaas was pioneering this method. My first-hand observations confirmed what I had read in the scientific journals—this simple-appearing technique not only helped autistic children; *it helped them a lot.*

"It's amazing," Dr. Lovaas told me. "All these years we've known how well it worked for Helen Keller, but no one thought to try it on autistic children."

The reason behavior modification had not previously been used with autistic children was simple: the overwhelmingly dominant dogma held that autistic children were biologically normal youngsters who had withdrawn from human contact because of supposed psychological mishandling by their "refrigerator mothers." They were thought to be emotionally disturbed and in dire need of psychotherapy and reassurance if they were to recover. The only two treatment options were psychotherapy and drugs. The scientific evidence showed that the former was useless and counterproductive, the latter harmful. I was so impressed with the potential of behavior modification that I founded a national parents organization (now the Autism Society of America, with nearly 200 local chapters) in order to bring this approach to public attention quickly and to provide a means for disseminating detailed information about it.

My plan worked. Within a few years behavior modification had replaced psychotherapy as the treatment of choice for autistic children. Hope replaced guilt, and the newly energized parents/advocates pressed Congress, in the mid-1970s, to mandate that the public school system provide for the education of autistic children. Prior to that, in most states autism fell within the purview of the mental health professions ("Tell me, Mother, just how did you make your child autistic?"). California, for one, had specifically excluded autistic children from the public schools on the grounds that their problem was considered "psychiatric," not educational.

Behavior modification, originally a rather crude method of training animals through the systematic use of rewards and punishments, has evolved over the past quarter century into a highly refined and effective pedagogical approach. The method relies primarily on the breakdown of tasks—even complex, abstract tasks such as communicative language—into a series of hierarchical steps, each step preparing the way for the next. Teaching through the use of "discrete trials," therapists and parents work as a team to create a highly structured and consistent learning environment. The child is rewarded for the mastery of each small step. Gradually, children learn not only the discrete bits of subject matter they are being taught, but, far more important, to focus their attention, to concentrate more effectively, and thus to learn more easily. All of this Catherine elucidates in her family's personal story. As she repeatedly emphasizes toward the end of this book, behavior modification must no longer be considered simply a way of "modifying behavior," but instead a scientifically validated, time-tested curriculum for the effective teaching of autistic and other learning-impaired children.

Several recent studies now suggest that if intensive behavior modification is started early enough, before age four or five, perhaps as many as fifty percent of autistic children may be expected to improve sufficiently to attend public schools with normal peers, and to have a reasonably bright outlook for the future.

Despite its outstanding success, however, behavior modification has more than its share of detractors, as Catherine Maurice's book amply demonstrates. Many professionals, as she observes, still counsel parents against this approach. Why? Some professionals appear to be quite ignorant about what a behavioral program entails. Some seem convinced that such an approach relies heavily on cruel and unnecessary

aversives, or punishments. Some, as Catherine points out, naïvely believe that even in the absence of any aversive, the mere imposition of
demands and structure on a handicapped child equates to abuse. A few
still cling to the vestiges of the old psychoanalytic view of the autistic
child. And there will always be those who consider *their* way to be the
only way, to the detriment of the children and their families. The empirical data, however, show clearly that strongly structured behavioral
programs have consistently yielded highly beneficial results for most
autistic children. And yet, despite the evidence, some people remain so
adamantly opposed to the enforcement of discipline that I refer to them
as advozealots—people who purport to be advocates for children but
instead are really advocates for their particular ideology.

As an ardent early proponent of behavior modification, I was frequently asked, "Since you believe autism is a *biological* disorder, how
can you advocate a behavioral approach as an effective treatment?" My
response was simple: "Behavior modification did not restore sight and
hearing to Helen Keller—her biological handicaps remained with her—
but it did permit her to learn the skills she needed to adapt to her
environment." (It is interesting to speculate on Helen Keller's fate had
Anne Sullivan believed that a firmly structured and disciplined approach would be too harsh and inhumane for her poor, severely handicapped charge, and so had refrained from using such an approach. I
am sure that would have been a mistake. I am equally sure that similar
mistakes are being made today, daily, by well-intentioned but poorly
informed parents and professionals.)

Yes, autism is a biological disorder, albeit the causes are as yet poorly
understood. For the past several decades I have devoted much effort
to a search for natural substances—not drugs—which will help nor-
malize brain function in autistic children and adults. Research, by myself and others (sixteen consecutive positive studies to date), has
established that almost half of all autistic persons improve in numerous
ways when given larger than normal amounts of vitamin B_6 and magnesium. There are other promising natural substances currently under
study. Behavior modification—and everything else—works much better in children whose brain metabolism has been at least partially corrected with these substances. Research along these lines is continuing.

Let Me Hear Your Voice will send a powerful and long overdue message to parents and professionals alike: if you want to help autistic
children, discard your biases and preconceptions. Find what has worked

for others, and give these approaches a wholehearted try. You will reap rich rewards in throwing aside dogmatism in favor of pragmatism. It worked for Catherine Maurice and her family.

Bernard Rimland, Ph.D.
Autism Research Institute
4182 Adams Avenue
San Diego, CA 92116

Acknowledgments

MARC, who is for me an unending source of strength, "is foremost of those I would hear praised." I hope that my children grow to emulate his kindness, respect his wisdom. One day they will know how much their father cherished their mother, and was her happiness.

I thank my family and Marc's family, Sister Damian and "Tante Carmel" for their constant support and their unceasing prayers. I am profoundly grateful to our friends who walked through the valley with us, and kept listening.

To Bridget Taylor, Robin Rosenthal Parker, Mary Beth Villani, Anne Marie Larkin, Kelly McDonough, I owe nothing less than the bright landscape that is my children's future. I can never thank them enough. May all parents who pass through this trial find themselves blessed with therapists of like commitment and intelligence and skill.

I am grateful to my children's classroom teachers—for their faith in my children, their patience and their graciousness. Gretchen Buchenholz and Rachel Cullerton deserve praise for their strong commitment to all children, healthy and handicapped.

For their encouragement to write this book, and for their sensitive and experienced reading of its first drafts, I owe much to my mentor, Dr. Bernard Rimland, to a friend, Debbie Attanasio, to my agent, Heide Lange, and to my editor, Corona Machemer. At the risk of sounding hyperbolic, I can't imagine a reader more intelligent and insightful than Corona. All of them—Dr. Rimland, Debbie, Heide, and Corona— believed in my ability to write before I did, and supported my efforts from the first chapter on.

And finally: If I have been able, in the course of this book, to point out any direction at all in the treatment of autistic children, it is not my doing. It's because some very gifted and farsighted people were there before me. Long before I came on the scene, Dr. Rimland took on the psychoanalytic Goliaths of the autism world and waged a one-man war against false expertise. Dr. Ivar Lovaas charted a path through new territory, and staked out the journey home. Whatever points of contention I may have with him over details of therapeutic style or substance, I am convinced that without the totality of his work we could not have rescued Anne-Marie and Michel. I am glad, and more grateful than I could ever say, that both of these scholars and teachers went before me, and showed the way.

PART I

Anne-Marie

I

"SHE'S SO SERIOUS!" said her father, with a puzzled laugh.

We were celebrating Anne-Marie's first birthday. At the party were gathered only her nearest and dearest: her mommy, her daddy, and her big brother Daniel, almost two and a half. She sat in her high chair, little feet barely touching the footrest, hands curled on her lap, dressed in a blue-and-white party dress. We had just paraded in with the cake.

Daniel joined in the singing with great excitement. We hammed it up, oohing and ahhing, blowing out the single candle. Anne-Marie's delicate face, with its porcelain skin and faint roses in the cheeks, was framed by wispy brown curls. Her blue-green Irish eyes gazed solemnly at the cake. Her baby body was still. Her mouth was unsmiling.

"Marc, that's her personality. You can't expect her to be just like Daniel."

My confidence, however, was a little forced. I myself had been somewhat preoccupied lately by this somber demeanor of Anne-Marie's.

"Anne-Marie. Look, sweetie, for you!" I handed her a present, some brightly colored balls, cones, and cubes that stacked together.

She glanced at them and moved them listlessly around the tray for a minute or two. One by one I opened her other gifts and gave them to her. She handled each for a little while, then lost interest.

She seemed almost sad, almost . . . a little anxious? I couldn't help making once again a silent comparison to her brother: At his first birthday, he had torn wildly into the wrappings, yelling and squealing with impatience and delight, eager to grab and explore whatever was inside.

And once again, I dismissed the comparison and the worry. It was a personality difference, that's all.

Who knows, really, what the first sign was, at what point Anne-

Marie began to slip quietly away from us. Was it during that first birthday celebration, or after, or before? The better question, I suppose, is: Who knows when we noticed the first sign? Things are so much clearer in retrospect than when you're going through them.

Earlier, when she was ten months old, I had observed some odd hand movements as she pushed around a bit of food on her high-chair tray. She couldn't seem to get hold of it with the normal "pincer grasp," but kept trying to pick it up with her thumb and pinky, of all things.

The subtlest, most fleeting hint of concern tugged at my consciousness: Problem here? . . . something wrong? . . . those splayed fingers, that odd employment of thumb and pinky, looked so . . . so . . . *bizarre*. A knot of anxiety constricted my heart for a moment, until I told myself to relax. Most likely she was just playing around with her fingers, a sort of tactile experimentation, or something . . .

Earlier still, Patsy, her baby-sitter, had remarked on how easy she was, how she could sit and play for such a long time by herself. "What a good little child!" Patsy exclaimed one afternoon. "She just sat and played in one spot for two hours!" I didn't know if I liked that. I too had noticed this stillness of Anne-Marie's, this quiet, almost too calm, solitary play.

She didn't crawl around a lot. She certainly didn't burrow into all the cupboards and drawers the way Daniel had, wreaking havoc wherever he went. We'd had to lock practically every drawer and door in the apartment to keep Daniel from killing himself. Whatever wasn't bolted down, locked up, or placed out of reach he tried to put straight into his mouth or pull over onto his head.

But sometimes I had the feeling I could leave ammonia under the sink and a matchbox on the floor and Anne-Marie, for lack of interest, would be in no danger. She seemed happiest holding and staring at one toy at a time, turning it in her hands, pushing it along the floor.

And all along that first year, we commented on her shyness, her sensitivity. "My supersensitive one," I told my mother. She cried easily, and it was not always evident to us why she was unhappy. For the first few months we had put it down to colic, but after that it seemed to be just part of her nature to cry frequently. When I tried to put her into the walker for the first time, her body stiffened. She seemed almost terrified. I began to wonder if at least part of her crying was due to a fear of unfamiliar things.

But in those early days of her life, it was easy to dismiss our occasional moments of anxiety. There was no pattern to anything yet. There may have been signs, but we didn't know what they indicated, not then.

Indeed, for every crying incident, there were as many scenes of charm and joy.

There was Anne-Marie, six months old, laughing with glee, eyes locked onto her daddy's, eagerly anticipating the next tickle, the next frolicking toss in the air, the next lip-smacking kiss.

And there she was at thirteen months, taking her first hesitant steps, then looking at me and smiling with delight at her new skill. She was so proud of herself, and wanted me to be just as proud of her.

Moreover, she was learning. Not only was she learning to sit up, to "cruise," to walk; but after she turned one, she began to learn words as well.

I have a memory of her toddling over to the door on her father's arrival home, holding up her arms and saying "Daddy!" She was fifteen months old, her father's darling girl-child.

And often, I remember, she would check into the kitchen where I was fixing dinner, wrap her arms around my legs, gaze up lovingly into my face with her big serious eyes and a little half-smile. I would pick her up and smother her with kisses: three because you're sweet, three because you're perfect, three because I love you! Satisfied that all was well in her world, she would toddle off again.

In her crib in the morning, whenever her father passed on his way to his early shower, up she would scramble, little baby face peeping over the top of the crib, baby voice piping "Hi Daddy!"

She was a beautiful doelike child, with her fair skin, dark hair, and an intense, graceful fragility. We loved her and delighted in her for who she was, with her shy hesitancy, her quiet demeanor. Her puzzling behaviors were due simply, we believed, to the uniqueness of her personality. After all, she was passing her regular pediatric checkups with flying colors.

As she entered her second year, Dr. Baxter and I would discuss language development, among other things, and we were both satisfied that she was well on target. In fact, I thought she was a little ahead.

"She's already combining two words," I told him in his office one day in June, when Anne-Marie was fifteen months old. I was thinking of the "Hi Daddy" that she said occasionally. I was a little surprised that a fifteen-month-old should be doing that.

"That *is* a little early," Dr. Baxter agreed. "Mostly what you expect to see around this age is a lot of babbling, and some single words."

"She does cry a lot, though," I said. "I keep trying to remember if Daniel cried this much at this age."

Dr. Baxter and I talked about how "the terrible twos" was a misnomer: how independent and cranky behavior often showed up well before the second birthday. Maybe that's it, I thought. Maybe she's just going to be more independent than the norm.

But we didn't have too much more time to dwell in this comfortable belief. Not long after that discussion with Dr. Baxter, the signs began to grow clearer, and although we still didn't know what they were pointing to, they were hard to ignore.

In that same month, June of 1987, Marc's brother was getting married in Paris and we had promised to attend the wedding. As the date approached, I found that I was becoming increasingly anxious about leaving Anne-Marie.

"What are you so nervous about?" asked Marc. "She'll have Patsy here, she'll be in her own home, it will be for just a few days. . . ."

Four days, to be exact. We had debated making a minivacation out of it, but in the end had opted for one of those weekend flights where you leave on a Thursday evening and come back on Monday afternoon. Still, I fretted and worried. Would she be all right? Should I ask my parents to come and stay? Why was I so worried about her, and not about Daniel? Well, she was so sensitive! Lately she had been crying more and more. Would she cry the whole weekend?

"No, no, no," friends and family assured me. "She'll be fine." Yes, of course. I knew of several children who had very nicely survived much longer separations from their mothers, whether for vacations or hospitalizations or whatever.

But during the flight over to France, and throughout the whole weekend, Anne-Marie nudged at the corners of my mind. I called home. "Oh they're fine," said Patsy. "But Anne-Marie misses her mommy. . . ."

"What do you mean?"

"Well, she wouldn't get out of the crib this morning. She just wanted to stay in there."

"Well, is she OK now?"

"Oh yes."

But I couldn't wait to get home.

We arrived on Monday afternoon, with little presents from Paris for both children. We walked in and threw Daniel into a tizzy of joy at seeing his mommy and daddy and getting a toy.

Anne-Marie sat on Patsy's lap and sobbed. Her mouth was trembling. "Sweetheart, come to Mama!" I implored, holding out my arms. But she wouldn't let go of Patsy. Finally, near tears myself, I took her from Patsy and went into my bedroom to try to calm her down and woo her back.

Marc and I had both heard of children getting mad at their mothers for "deserting" them. Our sister-in-law had told us of her two-year-old refusing to come to her after a week-long separation and then finally relenting and deigning to give her a kiss. But Anne-Marie didn't seem angry. She seemed more afraid than anything else. Although I couldn't bring myself to entertain this thought for more than two seconds, she actually seemed not to remember who I was! I was holding her, she was horribly upset, but she never once looked at me or cuddled. She seemed only to want to get back to the security of Patsy's arms.

I held her and rocked her and sang to her for an hour until she finally stopped crying and leaned against me.

After calm was restored I asked Patsy about the weekend.

"Oh, everything was fine, except Anne-Marie did something really funny."

"What's that?"

"Well, she just sat on my lap a lot of the time. But not only that: if I moved my arm, she cried. I had to sit in the same position, with my arm in a certain way across her back, and if I moved, she cried!"

I thought about this. I didn't understand it then, but I think I do now, now that I know about autism. My departure was not just a difficult separation for Anne-Marie. It was the disruption of a precious order in her world. She was trying, in her own way, to keep things the same: static, predictable. Sitting unmoving in Patsy's arms was a way for her to ward off any further changes.

At the time, however, I understood nothing. I knew only that something was wrong, and I didn't know what it was. I had sometimes the frustrating, almost frightening sensation that she was a stranger. "I'm worried about her," I blurted out once to my sister Debbie. But when she asked why, I couldn't say.

The summer wore on. The city was hot, I was halfway through another pregnancy, Daniel was thriving and active—and Anne-Marie was not happy.

The crying was getting worse. It seemed to me that it was change, the act of being intruded upon and made to do something, that caused her to cry. Being put into the bath. Being taken out of the bath. She would cry when I dressed her, when I undressed her, when I brought her to the table to eat. She would cry if I picked her up, and cry harder if I put her down. If anyone, whether stranger or family friend, came into the apartment, she would either cry or totally ignore him.

Mystified, Marc and I tried simply living through this unhappy period, expecting and hoping that it would all soon get better. I had mentioned her unhappiness to the doctor, once at our fifteen-month visit and once or twice over the phone, but he didn't seem unduly alarmed. This was, no doubt, a passing phase. Though many of our routines were punctuated by Anne-Marie's crying, we doggedly kept on trying to live normally.

"Let's all go to the park!" I would cheerily call. Then would come the ordeal of putting Anne-Marie into the stroller, in spite of her whining resistance. Daniel and Anne-Marie and Patsy and I would set off, one happy little boy, one miserable little girl, and two puzzled adults with frayed nerves.

Patsy invented reasons. I invented reasons.

"She's tired."

"She's hot."

"She's hungry."

"She doesn't want to go to the park."

"She doesn't want to leave the park."

It became impossible to take a bus or any public transportation, since Anne-Marie would cry even harder when surrounded by too many strangers. If we went into a store, she would either whine or become completely impassive, staring blankly ahead into nothingness.

Maybe she was bored. That was it: Her life was very boring and she needed stimulation. I searched around for little expeditions and adventures. One day I decided we would all walk across the park to the American Museum of Natural History. Daniel went wild over the elephants and dinosaurs. He loved it. Anne-Marie sat in her stroller, silent, expressionless, head down the whole time. "Well, of course she's not interested," I reasoned, more to convince myself than Patsy. "She's much too young. We'll just have to give her a little more time."

In August we all took off for a long-planned trip to Spain. We were to meet Marc's parents there, along with all his brothers, in-laws, and nieces and nephews.

We were looking forward to the children's spending some time with their French cousins. Marc had come to the United States from his native France when he was twenty-one, had earned an M.B.A. at Northwestern, and had gone on to make his career in investment banking. We had met at a "Bastille Day party" given by a mutual friend, when I was a graduate student in French literature at New York University. Ever since our marriage, we had tried to see his parents and our nieces and nephews at least once a year. His parents would come for our family festivities, such as the children's baptisms, or we would go there. This would be our first summer vacation spent with them.

The trip was a nightmare. We had to wake the children for a transfer in Madrid, stand on line with passports, walk miles to the connection, all at what was for us three o'clock in the morning. Daniel and Anne-Marie were both nearly hysterical and wanted only Mommy to hold them. There were no luggage carts to be seen, so Marc hauled four big suitcases around. We must have been a sorry sight as we straggled through the airport: two screaming children, one pregnant woman trying to hold both of them, and a husband laden with suitcases and with papers in his teeth. "Fun? Are we having fun yet?" I kept muttering.

But a few days later, everything had calmed down. We had settled into our lodgings and adjusted to the time difference.

We lounged on the beach, along with what seemed like half the population of France on their annual trip to the Costa Brava. Each person occupied his square yard of space and studiously ignored everyone else. Our family stood out a bit, it's true, being not only the palest people on the beach but also the most dressed. My voluminous maternity bathing suit especially looked like an evening gown next to the tiny monokinis on the bronzed bodies surrounding us.

One morning, lazily, we watched the children playing with their buckets and shovels. Anne-Marie picked up a red shovel, and held on to it for the rest of the day. As a matter of fact, she held on to it for the rest of the vacation. She would wake up in the morning and the first thing she would look for was that red shovel. Satisfied once she had it, she would carry it around with her, to the table, to the beach, even to bed. Her aunts and uncles, and we as well, thought that was so cute. "Here she comes with her red shovel!"

The shovel, indeed, seemed more interesting to her than her cousins. She never once approached any of them or initiated any contact. "It's astonishing," said Marc's mother, "how independent she is."

"Yes, she is independent," I responded, "but she loves us very much." I was watching her wander off again. No hesitation, no look-

ing behind to see who, if anyone, was following her, just going off by
herself. Once again I struggled up to follow her and bring her back.

It seemed to me that I had read in one of my baby books that children
are supposed to check in with their mother or father or baby-sitter
every now and then. They'll wander off, but they'll always keep coming back to touch base. Was it Spock who said that? It seemed like a
pretty logical thing to do. When was she going to start doing it?

A few days later, we all went to buy groceries. I sat in the car with
the children, waiting for Marc to finish shopping. It was hot, and we
were trying to fill up the time with some chitchat. Anne-Marie and I
were playing a little game. I said something, she repeated it.

> "Car" . . . "car."
> "Baba" . . . "baba."
> "Cookie" . . . "cookie."
> "Daddy" . . . "daddy."

I must have said about ten words, Anne-Marie's entire repertoire.
At the end of this game I thought: There, she can talk, I know she can
talk. I felt a bit defensive about her. Her French aunts and uncles kept
remarking on how silent she was.

But if she can talk, I thought, why am I sitting here trying to make
her repeat words? That odd disquiet, tinged with guilt, came stealing
over me once again. Did I think my daughter was slow? Was I comparing her unfairly to her brother? There was something about her that
. . . that was making me so uneasy. What was wrong with me? Where
was my joy in my child?

2

BACK HOME AGAIN, we picked up life in New York where we had left off. The summer was ending, so in between trips to the park, doctor, or grocery store I was preparing Daniel for his new play school in the fall, and searching for a mommy-child play group that had room for me and Anne-Marie.

I was reading more and more books on child development. Marc wasn't worried about Anne-Marie, but I was, and I was beginning to talk about her to anyone who would listen. I talked to my friends, I read books, I watched her. The hoped-for improvement was not happening. In fact, she seemed to be growing ever quieter and moodier. Lately, in moments of particularly intense crying or anger, she had begun to bang her head on the floor.

One day in the park I was pushing her in a swing. There was a woman nearby whom we saw there frequently. Anne-Marie, swinging back and forth, was smiling. The woman glanced over at us.

"That's the only time I've ever seen that child smile!"

These words, laughingly called out, hit me hard. Something in my mind took root: a thought, unformed as yet, but shot through with the first stirrings of fear.

"What is wrong with Anne-Marie?" I asked Marc that night.

"Wrong? What do you mean, 'wrong'?"

"She's so unhappy. She cries and whines so much. And why isn't she speaking more?"

"She has some words. She says 'hi' and 'bye-bye,' and 'juice' and 'no' and 'cookie' and 'baba' for bottle. She even says 'I love you.' "

Yes, it was true. She did say "I love you," in her own way. She said "Ah-oh-oo" when we picked her up and hugged her and said "I love you." That was good. And soon, I thought, very soon, she would begin to have some new words, different words, not these same few that we trotted out whenever the subject of her language came up. And then she would start combining words, and asking me for things and telling me things and . . . and something else: she would start letting me know who she was.

In the meantime, I resolved to spend more time with Anne-Marie—more "quality time," reading to her, playing on the floor with her. And I really had to get going and find some congenial play group where she could spend more time with other children. Yes, that was it. She needed more exposure to the world, not less. She needed to see other children, not just her brother. That would help her to be more flexible. I knew what the problem was! I had been coddling her too much, overprotecting her. I had been anticipating her every need, so that she felt no necessity to speak up for herself. Or maybe it was that Daniel was so exuberant and garrulous that we were giving him, in spite of our desire to be fair, the lion's share of attention. On and on I went, inventing all kinds of reasons for Anne-Marie's behavior.

Inevitably, a couple of our acquaintances asserted that this all came down to something quite self-evident: Anne-Marie knew that a new baby was coming and was upset with me and showing her anger. But here I shook my head impatiently. Freudian psychoanalysis of children had always irritated me, although at that point I had not yet reflected very deeply on it. It seemed to me, the little I had read of it, to be so arbitrary: Unhampered by the most rudimentary concern for empirical evidence, unencumbered by a verifiable methodology, or by any accountability at all for that matter, such psychoanalysis may assert anything it wants. What it wants, predictably, is to find a morose preoccupation with bodily elimination, or repressed sexual longings and lusts for parental death lurking deep within every young id. Its practitioners claim a curious omniscience about a child's inner life, her perceptions, feelings, and ways of structuring the world.

Anne-Marie was eighteen months old. Even if she had figured out that her mother's growing belly meant a new baby coming, by what advanced cognitive process had she then (fallaciously) surmised that this future event would mean her displacement? Had she ever before experienced a new baby in the house? Did she have a concept of future time, other than perhaps "waking-up time" or "nighttime" or "the time for having dinner/bath/story"?

Still, if I reacted defensively and with anger to other people's facile psychoanalysis, I nonetheless heaped guilt and blame aplenty on my own head. Intellectually, even at that early stage, I rejected the notion that I was such an extraordinarily bad mother as to have produced a chronically unhappy child; emotionally, however, things were not so clear. I began to feel burdened by a sense of failure. Something was going on, and I scrutinized our family life to try to figure out what it was.

The problem just had to reside with me. I was a stay-at-home mother, with Patsy providing lots of relief and help ever since Daniel's birth, so theoretically I should have been able to give my kids lots of wonderful, nonstressed motherly attention. But somehow, it seemed, I wasn't giving Anne-Marie enough. Maybe I didn't have the proper nurturing skills: It must be that I wasn't stimulating her enough. But this really confused me. Three of my six sisters were lawyers, and the two who were practicing now put in long, hard hours at the office, then arrived home, very tired, to children who wanted nothing less than 100 percent of Mommy's attention. It was an exhausting routine, and their kids saw their mother only a fraction of the time that Anne-Marie spent with me. And yet, Jean's little daughter and Theresa's little daughter, both of whom were younger than Anne-Marie, were leaping ahead of her in language, and seemed bright and happy children. Well, maybe my time spent with her was not "quality" enough.

I became reluctant to leave Anne-Marie, even for an hour or two. Whenever I did have to go out, I rushed back to quiz Patsy on how she had been, how she had passed her time. When I was home with her, I tried to spend as much time as I could on the floor, playing with her. The problem was, nothing I did with her held her interest for more than a few seconds. In vain I brought home new toys and books, in vain I sat down next to her and tried to engage her attention in reading a story with me. She would inevitably turn away, back to the same two or three toys with which she occupied herself, these days always in silence.

How powerful was the impetus to take the blame, even before I knew for certain that there was a problem. This was my child. She was born of my body. She had been raised and nurtured thus far predominantly by me. If there was something wrong, it had to be my fault. Not Marc's fault, not her fault—my fault. Whatever I thought intellectually was no match for that gut-level, entrenched, ultimately dangerous conviction that my child was somehow a product of, an extension of, me. Compounding that guilt were the negative emotions surrounding my every interaction with Anne-Marie these days: confusion, frustration, unhappiness. The question that had been haunting me since the summer just wouldn't go away: What was wrong with me that I didn't think of her with happiness, with pride?

I had been so happy watching Daniel thrive and grow through the lovely unfolding of his personality, a process that had begun practically on the day he was born. But Anne-Marie—here she was, almost a year and a half, and I was still waiting for her to show me who she was.

Nothing was clear. Something wrong with her, something wrong with me—the focus of "wrongness" kept shifting confusedly in my head. The only thing that was becoming obvious was that there was an intolerable difference in the way I felt about my two children. Daniel still filled me with delight and pride, while Anne-Marie inspired in me a gnawing anxiety. In response, I thought I should spend less time with Daniel. Drawn always back to the silent one, the unhappy one, I began to allow Patsy to take care of Daniel more and more, while I took care of Anne-Marie. But this shift of attention helped no one and only increased the pall of sadness that was beginning to settle over our whole family. I missed Daniel when I wasn't with him, yet would not allow myself my former joy in him.

I kept thinking that if I just could understand what was going on I would feel better about everything. The idea of "normalcy," the parameters of what was considered normal development and behavior, began to obsess me. I devoured books about early childhood. But nowhere in them could I find Anne-Marie. Most of them sternly cautioned me against comparing my child to other children. "If Johnny next door speaks in sentences while your child is still in the one-word stage, *relax*" was the general message throughout these popular works: "Do not be a competitive parent. Your child has his or her own timetable." Nowhere, not in one, was there even a hint that there might possibly exist in some children a developmental problem. Were the authors afraid of alarming parents needlessly? Afraid that any entry into the subject of abnormal development would be too much for the "average" parent to handle? I longed for a book that would spend less time dwelling on such scolding exhortations as "Do not trample on your child's self-esteem" and more time on, say, the normal stages of language acquisition.

But if I couldn't find Anne-Marie in any of these books, my friends provided dozens of examples of children who they swore had been just like her.

I craved these stories and would seek out people to tell me another one, and another one . . . about little Mary who didn't say a word until she was three . . . about Sam who cried all the time . . . about Jonathan who didn't speak until he was four, then opened his mouth and spoke in full sentences! . . . and one story about a teenaged prodigy who reputedly uttered his first word at age seven (that one, starved as I was for any reassurance, struck even me as apocryphal). And over and over again I heard about Einstein, who couldn't speak until he was . . . how old? The age varied with the teller, but Einstein was in any case practically proving the theory of relativity before he could speak.

Meanwhile, Anne-Marie was growing quieter and quieter. I couldn't coax words out of her anymore. I kept remembering the way she used to toddle to the door to greet her father. When was the last time she had done that? When was the last time she had said "hi" or "bye" to anyone? When was the last time I had heard "ah-oh-oo"?

Well, if I couldn't find Anne-Marie in any of the popular books on child development, and if all the stories of late talkers had stopped giving me much comfort, I would just have to do a little more serious research.

Ever since Marc's and my bout with a prolonged period of infertility (a first baby stillborn followed by three miscarriages), I had been an avid reader of medical texts. Books, articles, textbooks—whatever pertained to us and our situation I hungrily perused.

Somehow, though, it was with a certain furtiveness that I did my medical reading. In the back of a library, when I was still in graduate school and supposed to be writing my thesis, I would pore over *The New England Journal of Medicine*. I kept the *Merck Manual* by my bed, and would peruse it slowly and meditatively, almost the way I read my Bible. One day, with a certain indecorous haste, I purchased a thick textbook on obstetrics and gynecology. I felt as though I were buying something socially frowned upon, like some work by the Marquis de Sade. But no, anyone who has ever glanced at the gruesome black-and-white photos in such a clinical text will know that there is nothing further from the erotic. What embarrassed me, in truth, was my intrusion into a domain that was supposed to be reserved for the initiated, the licensed. I was not initiated. Not a doctor, I was presuming to usurp a certain authority, and thus breaking some subtle unstated rule of the social contract that exists between doctors and their patients.

Well, actually, I was a doctor. But my Ph.D. hardly qualified me to assume any expertise in the world of medicine. Moreover, and this was more complicated, I had absorbed some of our society's reverence for the M.D., and its marginalization of any Ph.D. in the humanities. In this country—not necessarily in France—doctors of philosophy do not stride with quite the same air of power and authority as do physicians. I never knew what I was supposed to do with my degree: print it in inch-high letters all over my stationery, as some of my former colleagues had done, or just take the years of analytical training for what they had given me, but forsake the title? The first option seemed affected and pretentious, especially since I was a "nonworking" mother now; the second seemed to mean caving in to a cultural tendency that I wanted to resist. Most of the time I just gritted my teeth in silence whenever a doctor—a physician—addressed me with that easy paternalistic familiarity that even the young ones assume by their third year of medical school: "Hello, Catherine? This is Dr. Jones."

Anyway, once able to decipher a good part of the medical lingo in these texts, I discovered that I did crave something they provided: Objectivity. Empirical research.

French literature and criticism, at the time I was in graduate school, were woefully obsessed with espousing the slippery uncertainty of any knowledge at all. After gamely agreeing to look at beloved works of poetry and fiction through the diverse lenses of structuralism, post-structuralism, phenomenology, feminist criticism, deconstruction, I pounced on medicine like some poor fact-starved rat. I was tired of truth as a relative term, a shift of one's perspective, a way of seeing. Information was what I wanted to try on for size. Science. A corpus of knowledge validated by whether its data held together empirically, not by whether its practitioners had the gift of gab. A bit more of the body, a bit less of the soul—or at least of what passed for soul among the French intellectual left.

"Knowledge is power," said a friend of mine when I told her of my pastime. She herself is of that rare breed of physician who genuinely seems to welcome the layman's intrusion onto professional turf and presumptuous questioning. Others of my friends were less accepting:

"You'll turn into a hypochondriac."

"You'll scare yourself silly."

"Why do you want to know every detail of every sickness that afflicts you? That's the doctor's business."

But I read my *Merck Manual* anyway. My daughter's health was manifestly my business, and I was going to pursue my questions about her until this aching anxiety went away.

And in bed next to Marc, on a night in September as the year was winding down and our time of innocence was waning as well, there I found it.

Under "Pediatrics and Genetics," subheading "Psychiatric Conditions in Childhood and Adolescence," subheading "Infantile Autism, or Kanner's syndrome."

It was a cursory definition, embodying just the salient features of the disorder, entering into none of the endless variations of behavior that have rendered diagnosis difficult for anyone attempting it.

Autism, I read, was a syndrome of early childhood characterized by extreme aloneness (lack of attachment, failure to cuddle, avoidance of eye gaze); insistence on sameness (rituals, resistance to change, morbid attachment to familiar objects, repetitive acts); disorders of speech and language (which vary from total muteness through delayed onset of speech to markedly idiosyncratic use of language); and markedly uneven intellectual performance.

The book didn't say much else. It didn't say what caused it, but hinted at some evidence for neurological dysfunction in some children and for a genetic cause. As to prognosis, over half the children had a "uniformly poor prognosis" and only about a quarter of them could do "moderately well," whatever that meant. Any mention of "cure" or "recovery" was conspicuously, ominously, absent.

My first reaction was one of bone-chilling fear. Something about Anne-Marie *might* correspond with something in each of those categories of behavior. I couldn't dismiss what I was reading about immediately and absolutely. No "Thank God it's not that!" rose up to my lips. Instead, something inside me recoiled, crouched down, in terror.

Then I went back, and read it again. You are crazy, Catherine. Will you please get real. Go on. Ask Marc what he thinks.

"Listen to this, Marc."

Marc's reaction was one of barely controlled exasperation. "Let me see that," he said. He read the page, then tossed the book away angrily. "That's not Anne-Marie!"

Of course that wasn't Anne-Marie. Oh Lord, I'd really done it now—here I was diagnosing my daughter as psychotic!

"You're right, Marc. This is ridiculous. I mean, what is this nonsense about 'extreme aloneness'? Anne-Marie loves us! She wants to be held all the time!"

We went through the four categories of behavior one by one. Extreme aloneness—no, patently false. She was a little shy around strangers, true, but she loved us deeply. Speech and language disorders—she didn't have enough language to have a disorder. She was just a late talker, that's all. Insistence on sameness—well, she might have a little of this behavior, but nowhere near to the obsessive degree they were implying! As to uneven intellectual performance, we didn't know what that meant. We didn't know what her IQ was, but she looked intelligent enough.

So we dropped the discussion, and I vowed once again to stop looking for trouble, to stop playing doctor.

The next day, however, I called Dr. Baxter. "Just wanted to bring her in for her regular eighteen-month checkup," I told him breezily.

A week later we sat in his office, and I went through my litany of worries. The crying, the fears, the head-banging . . . she's just so unhappy all the time. Would there be any possibility that she might be . . . autistic?

"No," said Dr. Baxter immediately. "Have you ever seen an autistic child?" No, I hadn't. In fact, as I reflected upon it, I knew practically nothing about autism, other than what I had just read in the *Merck Manual*. I had only a vague image, perhaps from some long-forgotten documentary, of a child sitting in a corner, mute and rocking, alone.

"They're usually completely indifferent. She wouldn't be clinging to you like this. She would allow a doctor to examine her without any reaction at all. She wouldn't care."

I felt almost giddy with relief. Also a little ashamed. When was I going to relax and accept my daughter for who she was? And who did I think I was, bringing up the word *autism* because I'd read one page in a book?

"Well, thank God. Sorry to be such a 'nervous mama' type."

I laughed, eager to have the doctor join me in a little self-deprecation. A little punishment, for creating problems where there were obviously none. But then I remembered about that other thing that had been bothering me—that thing that was a bit more concrete. Should I mention it?

"Just one other worry, Dr. Baxter. She seems to be speaking less. I think she has fewer words than she did just a few months ago. . . . Yes, I'm sure of it. . . . She's really not even babbling anymore. . . ."

Unbeknownst to me, I had just thrown a red flag into the discussion. However uninformed pediatricians might be about the early signs of autism, most are taught, I've since learned, never to ignore any hint of language loss.

"Now *that* has to be checked out. She should have a hearing test as soon as possible." He suggested the downtown branch of Hunter College, the School of Health Sciences. In the Center for Communication Disorders there, I could set up an appointment in the speech-language evaluation clinic.

"Of course, I'll get on that right away. I'm just glad that we can completely rule out autism." I looked at him expectantly.

He hesitated. "We can never rule out anything completely. But I would say that it is highly unlikely. Highly unlikely."

To be fair to Dr. Baxter, who is a good and smart doctor, nothing I had told him about Anne-Marie, other than the apparent loss of language, really did stand out as being extraordinarily odd. It was hard to sum up, in a twenty-minute visit, the true extent of how unhappy she was. "She cries a lot" didn't make it as an adequate description of what our days with her were becoming. And if his description of autistic children later proved to be fallacious in its overgeneralization, it was probably because those catatonic autistic people were the only ones he had ever seen. Medical schools don't seem to train pediatricians to be aware of and alert for the very early signs of autism, in children younger than five or six. Many cases are not diagnosed until the child starts kindergarten, where he stands out from his peers in a way that even the most insouciant parent and cavalier pediatrician cannot deny.

I called Hunter to set up the evaluation. I was anxious to have done with this whole question, and I was a little sick of myself constantly going on about Anne-Marie, who was obviously fine.

Fate, however, intervened before the evaluation could take place. Only a few days after this visit to Dr. Baxter, my own doctor ordered me into the hospital immediately. Third-trimester bleeding and a sonogram had revealed a dangerously low placenta—a marginal placenta previa that put both me and the baby at risk of a potentially catastrophic hemorrhage. The obstetrician wanted me in the hospital, that night. Worse, she wouldn't say how long I would have to stay. A week? A month? "I don't know yet."

"No," I said. "I won't go into the hospital."

I was close to panic. I raged, I argued, I even wept. The doctor was furious with me. She had never seen me act this way. "I want a second opinion," I announced. "This is ridiculous. I'm sure you're being over-cautious. I have two young children at home. What am I supposed to do, just leave them?"

I did go to the hospital, of course, but continued my histrionics for the first few days that I was imprisoned there. At one point the head nurse on the floor came to my bedside and lectured me on the need to leave my children every now and then because, after all, how else was I going to teach them independence? I nodded my head and said "yes, yes" to make her go away, then after she left I cried some more.

How could I explain to Marc, to my obstetrician, to these nurses, why I was so distraught, when I didn't understand it myself? It is not an exaggeration to say that I was close to panic at the thought of leaving Anne-Marie. Some murky part of my brain, the part that had been brooding over her for months now, knew something that my more lucid thoughts were not admitting: she was slipping away from us, and she was slipping away fast. There was a drumbeat quickening, the sound of a truth that needed to be heard. There was a child who was wandering into darkness.

And her mother had stood over her sleeping form, feeling her own heart contract once again with that strange fear, had asked God to bless her, and then had departed for the hospital for "an indefinite period."

My parents and my sister Burke had come into the city to care for the children in my absence. And Marc took time off from work each day to rush home, pick up the children, and bring them in for visiting hours. Every day they visited, and every day Anne-Marie would arrive crying, spend some whimpering time in the lounge with me, then depart, once again in tears. One day Marc took both children in his arms and entered a packed elevator. Daniel was crying because he had to leave me. Anne-Marie was screaming and crying too, but she, unlike Daniel, extended no arms to me, implored me with no beseeching look or word. She seemed, as usual, terrified, but unable to take comfort from either me or her father.

I was released from the hospital after about ten days, the obstetrical situation having resolved itself into one of less threatening urgency. As I walked in the door of our apartment, Anne-Marie came running around the corner and ran right past me.

"Boy, that kid is some shy," said my father over dinner that night. "She didn't look at me once the whole week long!"

When we were finally able to get our evaluation at the speech-language clinic at Hunter, it proved to be the first of many frustrating experiences in dealing with child-development professionals. We had a hearing test, whose results were fine, then the hour-long speech-language evaluation. Three earnest young women who were working on their degrees in early childhood education, and their clinical supervisor, sat on the floor with me and Anne-Marie and blew bubbles, played with balloons and a jack-in-the-box and other toys, attempting to elicit some speech from Anne-Marie. Finally, the supervisor announced her findings.

"Well, Mrs. Maurice, we think there's a problem, and we—"

"What problem?"

"Oh, we don't diagnose. We recommend that you see a psychologist. He will give you an official diagnosis. Meanwhile, we recommend that you bring Anne-Marie here twice a week for play therapy."

"But why? What is play therapy? And why should she need it?"

"Play therapy is what we've done here today, Mrs. Maurice. And we think she needs it because we think she has a problem. . . ."

Which you coyly won't divulge to me, but want to hold on to like some close-guarded secret, I thought.

"Now, Mrs. Maurice, shall we set up that play therapy schedule?"

"Well no, I want to talk this over with my pediatrician. And I would like to have a copy of your report."

"Oh no, Mrs. Maurice. We will send a copy of the report only to your pediatrician, and you can discuss it with him when he receives it. But we're very, very busy now, so he won't get the report for two or three weeks. Meanwhile, we hope you will decide to come in for play therapy."

Play therapy.

Across the jagged hole that autism rips in a child's future, these very serious and very, very busy people wanted to paste a couple of cute little Band-Aids. Two hours a week of play therapy—let's see if some more bubble-blowing and balloon-throwing will make her start talking!

I called Dr. Baxter. He agreed with my impatience at the idea of play therapy. "Look, she's getting enough stimulation at home from you and her brother. They're not going to offer her anything different from what you're already giving her. Let's wait to get their report, and then I'll decide if she really has a problem. If she does, you're not going to start any therapy without consulting Dr. DeCarlo."

"Who is Dr. DeCarlo?"

"She's a pediatric neurologist."

Every few days I called Dr. Baxter's office, wanting to know if the results had come in. Meanwhile, I was starting to mention "the word" again. "Autism." To my sisters and my friends, I was beginning to say it aloud, to bring it out into the open where we could look at it together, scoff at it, and declare it the furthest thing from an accurate description of Anne-Marie. "Those children are supposed to be completely withdrawn," said one of my sisters. "Anne-Marie is such a Mommy's girl. She's just a little shy around strangers."

It was almost as though the word had taken on a pulsing life of its own, and by our collective mocking and reviling of it we could somehow render it impotent.

Marc felt the same about it, only more strongly. He wanted not just to meet it head-on and disarm it, as I was trying to do; he wanted to stomp it out of existence altogether. "I don't want to hear any more of this autism stuff!" he declared angrily. "I see no relationship of this word to anything about Anne-Marie!"

But I was beginning to read a little more about it. Just a little, because everything I read was so appalling, and spelled such hopelessness. Inevitably, the words "severe, lifelong disability" would appear. It wasn't the "severe" that was so terrifying; it was the "lifelong."

Finally, in November, the evaluation from Hunter had arrived. Dr. Baxter got on the phone as soon as I called that day. "Yes, the evaluation has come and I've read it," he said. "I don't know if I agree with everything they're saying in it, though. I would like you to set up an appointment with Dr. DeCarlo. She's the only one qualified to make this sort of diagnosis."

"What sort of diagnosis?"

"I don't want to speculate on anything yet. Just come in and talk to Dr. DeCarlo. She's here on Friday mornings."

I made the appointment for December 18. The baby was due any day now, but I needed to make the appointment anyway. I couldn't stand waiting and wondering about Anne-Marie any longer.

The Christmas season was in full swing, but we had no tree, no wreath, and I had purchased not a single present. A powerful lethargy had seized me. Heavy and cumbersome, walking with difficulty, I waited for deliverance. As the year faded out and the days were growing shorter, I had become fixed on this one desire: deliverance. Deliverance from this pregnancy, certainly, but deliverance also from this whole year of burgeoning anxiety about my daughter. I wanted an end to it all, and I had suspended all movement forward, all plans and expectations about the future, until the yoke of this present time would be lifted from us.

A shining lovely moment broke through the gathering darkness: Michel was born.

Contractions began on the night of December 13, at around 10:30
P.M. In an hour, they were coming fast and strong, about every five
minutes. We got to NYU hospital at midnight, and by the time we
walked into the labor and delivery area I knew this baby was going to
waste no time. He wanted out, *now*.

My sisters and I, who love to "talk babies," agree unanimously on
one thing. We're not very happy campers when it comes to labor. We
want our epidural, thank you, and we want it preferably long before
the Sturm und Drang of transition hits us. I'm sure everyone feels labor
differently, and I do very much admire those women who can go from
start to finish undrugged, then emerge to pronounce the experience
"not so bad." But to me it feels as though some malevolent giant has
decided to calmly and slowly tear up a few abdominal muscles and
organs.

As each of those volcanic transitional contractions hit, I wondered
what on earth had ever possessed me to get pregnant again. "I want
an epidural!" I shrieked. But no, it was much too late for an epidural;
the baby was about to be born and we were on our way to the delivery
room. "Marc, please help me!" I moaned to the poor man in an excess
of self-pity, prompting him to inquire, not without some distress of
his own, what exactly I wanted him to do.

To make matters worse, I had a substitute doctor, not my own. This
person believed in the football-coach style of delivering babies—the
louder he yelled at me, the harder I was supposed to push. "Come on,
Catherine!" he bellowed at the top of his lungs. "When I say 'push,' I
mean 'push'! I'm not kidding around anymore!" By this point I was
weeping, but managed to stop long enough to explain to him, with a
kind of delirious politeness, that I had just decided that I wanted a
cesarean, and would he please go and fetch the anesthesiologist right
away?

Fortunately, a wonderful, gentle angel of mercy, in the form of one
of the delivery nurses, intervened at this point and somehow convinced
me to start pushing, and pushing efficiently.

A few minutes later, a baby's cry filled the delivery room.

One of the nicest things about labor is that it feels so blessedly,
blissfully good when it stops. To enter so abruptly into the land of No
Pain after one has been ripped into shreds for a few hours produces
what can only be described as instant euphoria. Add to that the placing
of a little wonderling in your arms, with the simple words "Here is
your son [or daughter]," and one slides over into ecstasy. Such hap-

piness I have never known as the happiness I have felt on the delivery table, as each of my children was placed in my arms, as I softly kissed each dewy cheek.

Michel was perfect. A beautiful, beautiful baby boy.

Marc and I looked at each other, spent. Somehow we highly flawed beings had managed to bring into existence this other life, perfect, lovely beyond words, a pure innocence entrusted to our care. The task of guarding him and guiding him was, we knew already, a daunting one, the hardest work that life would offer us. But we were thrilled nonetheless to have been permitted to share in his creation. This baby was entirely "unto himself," separate from me and Marc, and yet he reflected that which was highest and best in us, and called forth an ongoing effort toward perfection of ourselves. Mingled with the relief and the exhaustion and the joy in Marc's and my gaze was also an unspoken homage, a "thank you" each to the other, for opening up this bright hard path, for giving each other the gift of this baby.

Marc took his newborn into his arms and murmured a tender welcome: *"Michel . . . mon fils. . . ."*

In silence, I breathed a prayer of thanks and praise, then let myself go into this moment of pure joy.

It was a joy that was to last for a little while yet. Oddly enough, there was no letdown, not even a hint of postpartum depression or moodiness the next morning; only a milder version of that euphoric happiness. The first few days of Daniel's and Anne-Marie's life had been overshadowed a little by anxiety about whether I was up to the task. I had fretted about whether I could feed them enough through nursing, I had discussed each little sniffle and sneeze and body jerk. With Michel I was an old hand, confident, serene in my maternal role, knowing just what to do. I savored to the full his first days, cradling him to my breast in peace.

And I am glad I did savor them completely, because the darkness that had been looming close rolled in hard and fast just four days after his birth. The time for mourning was at hand.

On December 18, just two days after my return from the hospital, Marc and I and Anne-Marie and Michel set off for University Hospital again, to keep our appointment with Dr. Regina DeCarlo, the pediatric neurologist. Daniel stayed behind with Patsy. It was rainy and cold that day, and we didn't say much on the way down, just held our children and thought about them.

Dr. DeCarlo questioned us, calmly, kindly, and in exhausting detail, for about an hour and a half. Finally, she put down her pen and turned to look at me. Her voice was gentle, and serious.

"Well, I think I can assure you that Anne-Marie is physically healthy, and seems bright and alert enough. However . . ."

My heart began to pound; my palms were suddenly wet.

"I think there is some reason to believe your suspicions were correct, Mrs. Maurice. . . ."

I take it all back! I'm sorry I started this whole stupid farce! My thoughts, in silent terror, were scrambling to deflect this blow.

"Anne-Marie does fit the profile of a child with a developmental disability. . . ."

Oh my God. Let's not do this.

"She should see some other specialists right away, but I believe . . ."

Oh please don't say it.

". . . that her history and symptoms are suggestive of infantile autism."

The impact was almost physical. A fist was crashing into my chest. Immediately, in a reflex of self-protection, I tried to simply cancel out what the doctor was saying. If I shut my ears and eyes and then back-tracked through time, we wouldn't be sitting here and she wouldn't be saying this anymore. Crazy thoughts tumbled over one another: Come on, Marc, let's go home. What a bad idea to come here. Why had I done this? I had to go blathering on and on about autism and Anne-Marie and now I had created this monster! I promise, I'm not really worried about her, she's fine! I won't talk about this anymore, I promise!

The baby started to cry. I took him mechanically, staring at the doctor. Tears seemed to be welling up in my eyes. Where were they coming from? I felt no grief, only shock. And numbing fear.

Marc began to ask some questions. I turned slowly toward him. He had the look I'd seen him wear only one other time, when he held his firstborn son, lifeless, in his arms. His face was pale, his eyes shocked, his mouth set and stiff.

We knew a little something already about autism. And what we knew was very, very bad.

3

WE ASKED Dr. DeCarlo only a few questions, those that seemed most crucial at that moment:

"What is the prognosis?"

"No one can tell right now how severely afflicted she is. She's so young. I can tell you that she does not appear to be mentally retarded. Often children with this diagnosis have the complicating factor of severe mental retardation."

"What shall we do?"

"Get her into a program right now, before the diagnosis is confirmed. The sooner she gets therapy, the more progress she can make."

"Progress." There was that polite word again—the word that in the few articles we had read was always used, instead of "recovery" or "cure." What we already knew, sitting in Dr. DeCarlo's office, was that autism was considered a permanent handicap, and that our daughter, according to prevailing medical opinion, would never talk, or act, or love in any normal way.

We rode home in the cab with Anne-Marie and Michel. Neither Marc nor I could find anything to say. The gray cold day continued to unfold. Taxis honked, buses lumbered uptown, and people went about their business. Life—the buying and the selling, the rising and the working and the bustling—always does go on in that indifferent way.

But we weren't quite going on. Something was different. We had been jolted out of the mainstream and were entering into another time and place, one whose scope and boundaries were still unknown to us, but which surely resonated with the dark tones of grief. There are moments—only a few—that we experience as irrevocable leaps from the known to the unknown, when the normal smooth flow of time crashes into a flash flood; we are catapulted into a future that has sud-

denly become menacing, terrifying. "But I don't want to go this way,"
we cry, afraid. "I want to go back. Let someone else's child have leu-
kemia. Let someone else's mother die, someone else's husband leave. I
am not ready. Not ready to lose my day's sweetness, my night's
solace. My heart's desire cannot go over into absence, into death. I
don't *want* it."

This cry is our old habit of mind. We think we have some control,
even as the impassive, impossible truth sits staring malevolently at us.
"Whether you sink or whether you swim, you will deal with me,"
whispers the voice of catastrophe. "Whether you want me or whether
you don't, I am here, forever. You are impotent to change me. I will
change you."

Such now was this moment. I didn't know what Marc was feeling,
but I had entered into that time out of time. I couldn't go backward:
ahead, I knew, was some profound and dreadful loss. I willed myself
not to go forward. I clung numbly to the present, conscious that I was
moving in a muffled unreality, a suspended cocoon of nonfeeling, non-
response, yet dimly aware that outside my world was breaking apart.

We came home. I moved like a robot. I put the baby on the couch
to change him. I listened very carefully to something Daniel was saying
to me. It was very important that I answer him, using correct words
strung together in a correct sentence. Hold it back, hold it back. Don't
think about it yet, intoned my brain.

"What did the doctor say?" asked my sister Burke, who was there.

"She said she's probably autistic," I replied, forming the strange
words carefully in my mouth. There were those tears again—how odd
that they should come so easily when I had not even begun to let that
pain seize hold. Autism. Autism. Autism, banged a muffled drum. The
sound was still out there, all around me, moving in, but not yet pos-
sessing me.

Carefully I organized my household and my children. "Now Anne-
Marie and Daniel should have lunch, and Michel should sleep for a
few hours. I will be back soon. I have to go do some errands." I went
to the bedroom.

Marc followed me, irresolute, dismayed. "Catherine, are you all
right?"

"Marc . . . I . . ."

"What? Tell me."

"I'm sorry."

"What do you mean, you're sorry?"

"It's my fault. I did this to you."

"What are you talking about?"

"I wanted to have the children close together and now look at what I've done!"

It was I who had created this nightmare. I was sure of it. Either I had made Anne-Marie autistic by not giving her enough attention, or I had made everyone believe she was autistic by reading about it and talking about it too much.

Marc reached out to hold me, sorrowful and confused. "This isn't your fault, love. We'll fight this. There has to be something we can do. I can't believe there's nothing we can do!"

But I couldn't talk to him. I certainly couldn't talk about what we were going to *do* about Anne-Marie, since I couldn't right then even allow my daughter's name to come into my mind. I left the house to do my errands.

"Congratulations on the new baby, Mrs. Maurice!" called out the building manager in the lobby. "What's his name?"

"His name is Michel."

The man's face fell at my tone, indifferent and expressionless. I knew my voice sounded hollow and wooden, but I couldn't help it. He was out there, and he was calling these pleasantries to me across a wide space. I was in here, and it was a great effort to stay here. I had to push my words across that space. I had to fashion them together and push them out at him and I had to keep tight hold of normalcy.

Autism. A woman at the bank was talking to me impatiently. I was at the front of the line, just standing there. Oh, sorry. I moved forward.

Autism. Severe. Lifelong.

I summoned once again the fragments of dissolving reality and opened my mouth to speak to the teller. Again the words came out in an overly controlled, thickened effort. It was getting harder. My mouth, tongue, and vocal cords seemed muffled and frozen; the forming of sentences and the communication of mundane information was assuming the nature of a dream, elusive and unreliable. The world itself seemed fragile, about to implode. It was I who was keeping everything on course, who was maintaining the pleasantries and the busyness and the purposefulness of life.

"Oh, I see the baby arrived, Mrs. Maurice!" cried the pharmacist.

"Yes."

Silence.

"I need," I said, concentrating hard, trying to focus on her, "I need newborn diapers . . . and twelve nipples . . . and some bottles of formula, please."

"All right." She became businesslike instantly. Had I frightened her? She must think the baby has something wrong with him. I must reassure her. Yes, it was important not to upset her.

"The baby's fine. He's very beautiful."

"Oh. Good."

Beautiful, like his brother.

Infinitely precious, like his sister.

His sister . . . my daughter . . . my Anne-Marie. . . . Oh God!

The first sob rose, exploding out of my frozen throat. I ran out of the store, blind with hot tears. Don't think about it! Don't say her name! Hold it back! But the word had her now, had enfolded her already in a dark cloak of mystery and difference. Her sweet eyes. Autism. Her delicate mouth. Autism. My little one whose eyes had once upon a time smiled up into mine—where was she? Who was she? On a sidewalk in New York my last defenses crumbled, as I let the word come finally into my life, allowed it to reach out and take my daughter. Yes, she is autistic. And with that capitulation, my heart, stubborn with fierce resistance, began—at last—to break. Keening, weeping, I made for home, for my children. I needed to hold them. Let me hold them all. Forever. In the shelter of my arms could any harm come to them?

╔═══════════╗
║ **4** ║
╚═══════════╝

THE ENSUING DAYS were unreal, nightmarish.

We found it hard to keep track of time. We had entered a maelstrom, a whirlwind. Michel was born on December 14. On December 18 Anne-Marie was diagnosed. Christmas was coming. I remember that my parents and my sister Debbie's family visited on the nineteenth or twentieth, bringing gifts for Daniel and Anne-Marie and outfits for the new baby. Thank God someone is getting some presents for the kids, I remember thinking. Flowers arrived in celebration of Michel's birth. Someone sent a bottle of champagne. Someone else sent an enormous blue balloon: "It's a boy!" The phone rang incessantly: friends congratulating us, then listening in shocked silence as we tried to explain about Anne-Marie; Dr. Baxter, returning my frantic calls; relatives from Chicago, from Long Island, from California: "We're praying for you"; Marc's parents: *"L'autisme? Qu'est-ce que c'est? C'est sérieux?"*

We didn't know what to tell people. We had no information. We didn't know where to find information. We had a name for a disorder that had suddenly amputated Anne-Marie's future, but we knew next to nothing about it.

Recovering still from the birth, breasts swollen and aching as my milk surged in, eyes wrung dry with sleeplessness, I felt my world spinning out of control. There was too much happening: Christmas, and newborn Michel, and Anne-Marie, who seemed to be worsening daily. The phone, and nursing, and flowers, and autism. Questions upon questions, and no one to answer them. Daniel to be listened to and the baby to be held. Christmas lights and merriment all around and people to talk to and meals to be made and the wrenching sobs, late into the night.

Different forms of loss followed rapidly one upon the other. First to go was the past. Suddenly a retrospective light was cast on the year we had just come through, revealing a fearsome rift between the reality of that year and our cloudy perception of that reality.

Anne-Marie was different, not only from other children but from the little girl we thought we knew. Whom had we known? We had been thinking of her, in spite of our worries, as a normal child, filled with the needs and desires and even the pastimes of a normal child.

But those pastimes, now that we saw them in a new light, were so meaningless, so undirected, so bizarre.

Over and over she would use one object—her "Big Bird's" beak, for instance—to point at and touch something else. If she couldn't find Big Bird, she would pick up some other pointed thing—a stick, a spoon—and walk around the house silently touching the walls, the furniture, the piano leg. She gravitated often to the radiators, and would stand in front of them running her fingers back and forth over the grate. In her bedroom, we had often found her crouched under her crib, where she would spend endless moments mesmerized by the little spring on the bottom of the rail post. This she would lift and let drop, lift and let drop, over and over again.

Christmas came and went. The New Year dawned, gray and foreboding. I looked at my little girl and saw a child I didn't know, couldn't understand.

Stripped of our illusions, we found Anne-Marie to be suddenly alien. No, she was not just "shy," she had virtually no interest in or curiosity about anyone else, including her family. Now that it had been wrenched up to conscious level, I suddenly knew how a shy child would act. She would hide behind her mother's skirt and peer out at the stranger, fearful, yet still looking into his eyes. Her mother would be her safe haven. With wooing, smiles, and gentle touching, she could be coaxed out, and gradually won over.

But that was not at all Anne-Marie. Anne-Marie was not shy: she was largely oblivious to people, and would sometimes actually avoid them, including, a lot of the time, her own mother. She drifted toward solitary spaces: the corners of a room, behind the curtains, behind the armchair. If I was somewhere else in the apartment, she never sought me out but could spend hours just manipulating a toy or poking at the rug. When visitors came, she gave them at most a fleeting glance, then turned away with a blank expression, despite all their attempts to be friendly.

No, she was not just a late talker; she was a child who had had a few words, mostly nouns, and had lost almost all of them.

And she understood almost nothing. It was so frightening to realize this now—now that reality had come crashing in. Of course normal kids understand, I thought, berating myself for not having seen what was now so obvious. They understand so early, long before they can speak. They may not understand everything they hear, but they certainly understand phrases like "bath time," "lunchtime," "Do you want to go out?" My friends' children, my nieces and nephews, Daniel, all of them were showing evidence of this understanding well before they were two years old.

But Anne-Marie was not understanding. In vain would I take her by the hand and repeat my message in ever simpler terms: "Anne-Marie, do you want to go outside?" "Take a walk?" "Outside?" "Coat?" Nothing seemed to register anymore, not even the few food words that had piqued her interest once upon a time, like "juice" or "cake" or "cookie."

It was my father who gave me my first gut-level comprehension of the word "autism." "From the Greek for 'self,' " he said. "The same root as 'autonomous,' 'automatic': that which is self-contained, self-directed, self-motivated." It wasn't a medical or a psychiatric description, and it should have been obvious to me before, but it hadn't been. In any case, it somehow clicked with what I was discovering about Anne-Marie. For me, it gave some shape to her difference, a difference that seemed to be increasing at a terrifying rate. In essence, it came down to this: Daniel was reaching out to us, hungrily drinking in all the life and love and learning his spirit could absorb; Anne-Marie was curling in upon herself, silently, softly withdrawing from everyone, drifting ever deeper into a secret interior world.

It wasn't just that she didn't understand language. She didn't seem to be aware of her surroundings. She wasn't figuring out how her world worked, learning about keys that fit into doors, lamps that turned off because you pressed a switch, milk that lived in the refrigerator. Daniel, even as a year-old baby, had tried to put the nipple onto the top of his bottle. Had Anne-Marie ever demonstrated that she understood, remembered, carried over from day to day, such a simple aspect of the world she inhabited? We could see almost no evidence of that kind of learning. If she was focusing on anything, it was on minute particles of dust or hair that she now picked up from the rug, to study with intense concentration.

Worse, she didn't seem to be picking up anyone's feelings. I remembered "talking" with Daniel, well before he had any words—when he was still an infant, in fact. I remembered laughing with him, sharing pleasure with him, joining in his excitement when he saw his first bear at the Bronx Zoo. I remember his fear of sudden noises or strange faces, and his reaching out for my comfort whenever he needed me. When had Anne-Marie shared anything with me in the past year? When had she last responded to me, connected with me? If there was anyone there at all, behind that mournfully empty face, she was not reaching out to us in any way that I could see.

With a pang, I realized that she had never called me, never said "Mama" from across a room in order to get my attention.

For that matter, when was the last time she had even imitated the word, repeating it after me?

Our eyes were open now, and we saw so much more than we wanted to see: She seemed to have almost no nonverbal communication. No smile, no nod, no head shake, no gesturing or shrugging or mimicking of facial expressions. Once upon a time, she had waved bye-bye. Now, she rarely even imitated the gesture. Even pointing, which we could remember her doing quite frequently at ten or eleven months of age, was rapidly disappearing. If she wanted something—a toy, a piece of food, a bottle—she would take the nearest adult's hand by the back of the wrist, never looking up while she did so, and shove it at the desired item.

Worst of all, perhaps, was the lack of that primary connection: the sweet steady gazing into one's eyes that we began to see all around us in other toddlers.

Dr. DeCarlo had asked us about eye contact, and in the first days after her diagnosis we had suddenly become aware of how rarely she looked directly at anyone. As the days went by, she grew worse. In contrast to Daniel's eager, searching, curious stare, Anne-Marie's fleeting glance, her downcast eyes, became ever more obvious. Whatever eye contact she made had now dwindled to a brief flicker, without duration or interest.

Sometimes I would catch her gazing in my direction and would start up, eager to respond to her invitation, to meet her look. But her eyes, frighteningly, were focused on some middle distance, somewhere between me and the wall behind me. She wasn't seeing me at all. She was looking right through me!

Dr. DeCarlo had asked us if Anne-Marie imitated our behavior. The question had given us pause. Did she imitate us? Yes! . . . I mean . . .

We had glanced at each other, unsure. Come to think of it, maybe she didn't imitate a whole lot, not lately.

Could we think of *any* specific, recent examples of imitation, asked the doctor?

Well . . . not at the moment. . . .

Now, in the first weeks after her diagnosis, this lack of imitation became daily more obvious. Here she was, almost two, and I had yet to see her pick up the phone and babble. She had never "helped" me to wipe the table, never clapped her hands, never picked up my hairbrush to brush her hair, never tried to put on her shoes or her hat. I thought of Daniel, only a little over a year old, picking up a nail file and valiantly attempting to file his baby nails, the way he'd seen his mommy do.

I thought of every two-year-old I had ever known, and suddenly realized that that is indeed what they do: they imitate. They decide that this morning they will make pancakes, then throw flour in the bowl and drop the eggs on the floor, wrecking the kitchen before you intervene and allow them to terminate gracefully their very serious job. They are ecstatic when you ask them to "help" with the laundry; they joyfully throw the red shorts in with the white shirts and try to pour the entire gallon of laundry detergent over the load. They "shave" with Daddy in the morning, and put on Mommy's lipstick in the evening. They love to be involved.

Anne-Marie loved to be left alone.

This admission of Anne-Marie's affliction, this absorbing of the full gamut of her difference, alternated still with sporadic bursts of denial. Some days I would sit and look at her, mentally checking off in cold horror each instance of bizarre or asocial behavior. But Dr. DeCarlo's diagnosis had not yet been confirmed by anyone else, and there were still moments when I could look at Anne-Marie's beautiful face and almost convince myself that it was all some absurd mistake, promulgated by me and the credulous doctors. She didn't seem brain-damaged. She didn't appear to be mentally retarded. Just looking at her features, one saw only a sweet little-girl face.

One day between Dr. DeCarlo's diagnosis and a follow-up evaluation by another doctor, my mother called. Ever loving and supportive, she provided hours of patient listening as I careened through this mad time.

"Look, Mom," I explained carefully, "this is a diagnosis based uniquely on behavioral observations. There is no blood test or CAT scan or X ray that can absolutely definitively say she is autistic or she is not autistic. I've read descriptions of these children, and I still don't think Anne-Marie's behavior fits exactly into the syndrome. She doesn't rock, she doesn't scream or flinch when you touch her, she doesn't spin things or line things up. Maybe Dr. DeCarlo is wrong. Besides, you know it was I who put the word 'autism' in the doctors' minds. Maybe what happened is that I conditioned them to see autism in a child who is simply behind the norm."

Whenever we talked, my mother would listen and would allow me to say whatever I needed to say at the time. She would allow me my despair or my hope without pushing too much her own assessment or opinion. Only once did she gently and sadly correct some overly optimistic statement I had made about Anne-Marie.

"Well," she said with a sigh, "Daddy and I did think she looked very withdrawn the other night."

I could respond only with silence, knowing of course that "withdrawn" was a fairly accurate, even kindly description of Anne-Marie's social behavior.

Naïve expectations of professional help fell quickly by the wayside. Somehow I had thought that our pediatrician would rise up like a rescuing knight and tell us what to do. "Oh, she's received a diagnosis of autism?" I imagined him saying. "Well then, you must immediately take her to see Dr. X and Dr. Y; you must get her into this type of treatment. Here is a program that you can enroll her in. Here is a list of therapists to call. I will direct the handling of this problem. Have all reports sent to me." He was the authority; after all, he had "handled" all of Anne-Marie's other medical problems. We were to be quickly disillusioned.

I sent him a long letter, pathetically building a "for" and "against" case concerning Anne-Marie and autism. I waited by the phone, hoping for the favorable judgment that he would surely hand down on my exercise in logic; wanting him to tell me that, yes, I had amply demonstrated that it was all a case of misdiagnosis. Or, failing that, expecting him to tell me what I was supposed to do now.

He finally called, tired after a long day of dealing with ear infections, colds, chicken pox, and, for all I knew, terminal cases of childhood cancer.

"I read Dr. DeCarlo's report," he said. "Dr. DeCarlo believes she's autistic."

"Yes?" Was that it? Case closed?

"Well," he said, "we did discuss that possibility."

Yes! We did discuss it, and you dismissed it! The cry of protest rose to my lips, but I said nothing. What good could come of arguing about the past? I liked Dr. Baxter and wasn't looking to fight with him. He had been a gentle and considerate caregiver whose good sense and professional knowledge I had always respected. I couldn't understand why he was remaining so aloof from me in this crisis—so much graver than anything we had yet faced together, including Daniel's asthma. His manner on the phone now was reserved, distant, clinical. Yes, we had discussed that possibility, and Dr. DeCarlo was now confirming its reality. No sense in arguing. No room for a scream of fear.

Dr. Baxter was going on. He was telling me to watch a television program called "St. Elsewhere." Apparently there was an adolescent on the program who was autistic. He was recommending that I watch it in order to get a good sense of just what autism was. Was this the sum total of his message? Find out what it's like and start adjusting to it?

But I had another question, one that had been skirting around the edges of my mind. It concerned Anne-Marie's future.

"Will she have to be institutionalized?"

"Some children, when they grow older, eventually have to be institutionalized."

"I see. What . . . what can be done for her?"

"I don't know if there's anything that can be done right now. But don't give up hope. I believe that in ten, maybe twenty years' time they will have found something to help these children. Just look at what happened to all the manic-depressive patients after they discovered lithium."

I replaced the receiver gently. Oh, I see. Dr. Baxter's view of what constituted hope was a far cry from mine. It had nothing to do with the reality of the moment. And if I had wanted his role spelled out, it could not have been done more clearly. This was not his problem; it was ours.

In a diagnosis of autism, it is usual to consult at least three or four, or even five, specialists in order to assure a concordance of opinion. A normal child may appear particularly withdrawn one day in front of one doctor, and perfectly sociable and cooperative in front of another the next day. Professionals have to be pretty sure of what they're saying before mentioning the word "autism" to a parent. Psychiatrists and psychologists are not looking to be sued for mental anguish caused by a wrong diagnosis.

Moreover, diagnosis of a very young child, like Anne-Marie, is particularly delicate. The full range and severity of symptoms might not yet be as evident as in a four-year-old, for one thing. For another, a child's lack of language is not in and of itself a symptom of autism. Many two-year-olds don't have much of a vocabulary, and many two-year-olds are not very outgoing. Other symptoms had to be present, and seen by a number of people, for anyone to be certain of the diagnosis. Anne-Marie was very young still, and Dr. DeCarlo had strongly urged us to seek other opinions.

Dr. Berman, of New York Hospital's Payne Whitney Psychiatric Clinic, had been recommended to us by a friend who had heard, through an acquaintance of hers, that he was "a renowned expert," "one of the best in the field." (How often in the ensuing months were we to hear that assertion of *ne plus ultra*. "Dr. Smith is *the* best." "You mean you haven't heard of Dr. Jones?" "You must take her to see Dr. Brown. He's number one in this field.") So off we went one evening to see if the renowned expert could somehow help us, and Anne-Marie.

As we walked up the path to the doors of Payne Whitney, I dragged my steps. How was this possible, that we had come to this place and time?

"What is it?" asked Marc.

"I don't want to go in. What are we doing here, going into a psychiatric clinic with our baby daughter?"

"I know," said Marc, aware that the protest was rhetorical, a cry of helplessness only.

Inside, after an hour's discussion, Dr. Berman leaned back in his chair behind his big desk and hesitated. We hardly breathed as we waited for his verdict.

His verdict was not clear. He seemed to be saying that she could be autistic, but then again she might not be. She was, after all, so young. However, she did have several behaviors, in addition to the developmental delay, that caused him some concern.

As our friend commented afterward, "I could have been as ambiguous, and I wouldn't have charged you two hundred fifty for my opinion."

A little later the doctor asked us to leave the room while Anne-Marie stayed alone with him. He offered us no reason why. Perhaps he wanted to see if she would relate to him without her parents in the room, but the lack of an explanation bothered me. I had resisted this sort of paternalism since Marc's and my protracted experience with pregnancy losses. But this was a different problem, and in our fear we were slipping back into the old role of obedient patient doing everything the doctor ordered, accepting whatever he said.

After about fifteen minutes, we were invited back into the room, and found Anne-Marie hiding behind a chair. With no explanation as to what had transpired, the discussion limped forward.

What exactly is autism? we asked.

The doctor launched into a historical overview of the disorder. It was identified in 1943 by Leo Kanner as a syndrome that he had observed in a subgroup of children originally thought to be schizophrenic. . . . It was characterized by a particular set of behaviors . . . most notably extreme social aloofness and poor or absent speech development. . . . No one really knew its exact cause yet, but over the years, Dr. Berman concluded humorously, it had given many psychologists and psychiatrists an awful lot of business.

We stared at him. A lack of empathy we could perhaps understand: after all, one must become a little inured after twenty-five years in the business, after hundreds of diagnoses of autism. But try as we might, we couldn't bring ourselves to chuckle along with him.

"Well, if she is autistic, what should we do about it?"

There was, he informed us, a therapeutic nursery right there at Payne Whitney. He didn't know if we could get into it now, but if we talked to Mrs. Peters maybe she could get us in sometime next fall.

Next fall? Marc and I had the same reaction. We were not interested in next fall; we were interested in now. As ignorant as we were at that point about autism and its therapies, we were still possessed with a sense of urgency about starting Anne-Marie on something immediately. Hadn't Dr. DeCarlo said to get her into a program even before the diagnosis was confirmed? Next fall was nine months away.

And what exactly did they do in this "therapeutic nursery"?

Well . . . it seemed that there were several psychologists and psychiatrists . . . also a social worker. . . . The children's progress was followed carefully. . . . They were evaluated at regular intervals. . . .

I was asking about therapeutic practice; I was hearing about personnel and paperwork. Reams of assessments, evaluations, progress reports. "But what do they do?" I repeated. "What exactly is the 'therapy'?"

Once again, we got no precise answer. In truth, the doctor seemed not to know exactly what went on in that part of the clinic. He suggested that we talk to Mrs. Peters, the social worker, and make arrangements to visit the nursery.

Which I did, with Anne-Marie, two days later. There I was greeted by three women, one a teacher from the nursery, one a resident psychiatrist, and Mrs. Peters. No one said anything much, except Mrs. Peters, who took me into a side room and asked me many questions about how I was coping. The psychiatrist sat and observed Anne-Marie, while the teacher followed her around the room, attempting to play with her.

Again I tried to determine exactly what went on in the nursery. Was there a special curriculum for autistic children? How much one-on-one instruction did they get? Were there defined goals for each individual child? What exactly did they hope to achieve here? I knew one thing for certain that I wanted to find out: What could they offer her that she wasn't getting, or couldn't get, at home? What did their combined degrees of Ph.D, M.D., M.S.W., M.S. represent for Anne-Marie? And whatever their expertise was, could they teach it to me so that I could help her? She was, after all, still going to be spending most of her time with me.

But the response was mystifying and disappointing. In essence, they seemed to be promising a few hours a week of love, understanding, and "acceptance," accompanied by mounds and mounds of paperwork, and periodic important-sounding "conferences," where any progress would be "reevaluated."

I thanked them for their time and left. First decision made: Anne-Marie would not be going to the Payne Whitney Therapeutic Nursery.

5

IF DR. BERMAN wasn't quite sure of the diagnosis, we ourselves soon exhausted our last reserves of hope and denial. Day by day, Anne-Marie's condition grew rapidly worse. By mid-January, she no longer even looked up at anyone coming into or leaving the apartment. Seated on the floor, she would stare at a piece of dust, then slowly bring it up in front of her eyes and gaze at it, enthralled. She pulled little pieces of string off the rugs or the furniture, or a hair out of her doll's head. These she would twirl between her fingers, endlessly fascinated. At other times she seemed mesmerized by a combination of sight and sound, tapping two objects rhythmically in front of her face.

Her activities were becoming stranger, more bizarre. I watched her, feeling very close to panic, as she repetitively sorted through puzzle pieces, then held them up two by two, always at right angles to each other, and stared at them. Oh please baby. Please don't do that. Why are you doing that?

We had given her a teddy bear for Christmas, hoping that she might cuddle it and hold it the way a normal child would. Instead, she developed a strange ritual where she would push the bear through the bottom rungs of a certain chair, over and over again.

Her mannerisms increased as well. She had intermittently walked on her toes ever since she began to walk, but now she toe-walked almost exclusively. One day she added a new item to her repertoire: while seated on the floor and gazing dreamily into space, she extended her neck, held the position, and ground her teeth together. I was finding it hard not to cry out in terror at the sight of these strange behaviors. The sense of helplessness was overwhelming. Sometimes I would actually catch myself whimpering as I witnessed each new sign of her alienation.

One morning, without any preamble of frustration or anger, she raised both of her hands and calmly struck herself in the face: once, twice, three times before I rushed at her, trembling, and jerked her hands down.

We were finding it harder and harder to distract her at all. Either she spent endless moments staring at something in her hands or she wandered aimlessly from room to room, never focusing on the people there, only on things.

How long had it been since Michel's birth? A few weeks? It seemed like a lifetime. The days had become a series of long bleak hours, to be plowed through with grim determination. It was important to hold together, to do what I had to do for all three of the children. I was their mother, they still needed me to take care of them and to love them. I tried not to cry too much during the day. I didn't want to frighten Daniel.

One morning, however, he found me in the bedroom, wiping away the tears. He stopped still, afraid. Mommies aren't supposed to cry. His dark-brown eyes filled with tears.

"Mommy, you cry?"

"Yes, sweetheart, but I'm OK now."

He stood there, struggling to understand and to give words to his thoughts. I didn't know how much he had been picking up in this atmosphere of crisis and fear. We had been taking Anne-Marie here and there, talking about her on the phone, focusing on her in an obsessive and frantic way. He had seemed content and peaceful enough, as long as his routine wasn't too disrupted, but I knew that he was sensitive and vulnerable. I waited for him to speak.

"Mommy, you go to doctor?" His voice was anxious.

"Yes."

"You take Ammawee?"

"Yes."

"Ammawee sick?"

I knelt down and took him into my arms. "She'll be all right, my love. Don't worry. Mommy and Daddy will always take care of you, and Anne-Marie, and Michel."

He smiled up at me, happiness once again restored to his world.

I worried constantly about Daniel. There was simply too much to do, too much to find out and think about, to spend a whole afternoon or morning with him or to respond to his hundreds of three-year-old comments and questions. Moreover, there would be moments—when

the baby was screaming, Anne-Marie was off in a corner doing something strange, the phone was ringing, and Daniel was whining and
crying at me—when I would come dangerously close to lashing out at
him. I would feel a knot of fury begin in my chest, then travel outward
until my jaw, neck, and throat muscles had become clenched iron bands.
"Leave me alone!" I wanted to scream at him. "Stop asking me so
many questions! Stop needing me *all the time!* I can't do it! I can't think
about you now!"

I learned to recognize these moments as the flash points they were,
and force myself to walk away—to go into my room and shut the
door, to turn on a television cartoon to distract Daniel—anything to
buy a few moments of peace and silence in which to gain control. You
will not! cried some drowning voice of reason in me. You will not take
out your panic and rage on him!

But I felt the anger, and it was eating me up. This godawful thing
was turning me into a raging lunatic. I was evil, that's why such evil
had befallen me. Only an evil woman could feel rage against her own
child.

Some counterforce was needed, some defense against the ravaging
self-hatred, grief, rage, helplessness.

I had to learn how to stabilize, how to compensate, at least a little.
Each day, as a moment of solace for both of us, I tried to carve out
some time alone with Daniel.

It wasn't a long time, but I tried to make it as focused as possible.
Of necessity, I developed a new appreciation for that concept that I
had mildly scorned: "quality time."

We would go into my room, at an hour when Patsy or Marc could
take care of the other two children. I would close the door, and try to
empty my mind of its howling demons and turn my attention fully to
the joys and sorrows and questions of my little son. We would read a
story, or talk about something that was on his mind. Always I held
and cuddled him as much as possible, knowing even more than he did
just how often that day I had said "Not now, Daniel," "Later," "I'll
do that for you in a minute," "We'll bake cookies tomorrow," "Shh!
Mommy's on the phone."

These moments of love with Daniel brought a healing balm to a
wound that had opened up in my concept of myself.

A good mother was, in a secret part of my spirit, what I most wanted
to be: a patient mother, loving and gentle, knowing how to form and
guide a young life, how to teach wisely and well. While I thought of

work as a joy and a hard-earned right that all women should have access to, I knew that if I had to choose which way my happiness lay, it would always be for me in the gift of children. I had already borne the brunt of endless shocked commentary caused by our decision to have three (three!) children close together in age. On the streets of Manhattan's Upper East Side, I had weathered, though not particularly gracefully, many unsolicited comments by passersby at the sight of a pregnant woman with two little ones. "Social birth control" a friend of mine has called it, a kind of swooning horror, particularly prevalent among the refined classes. At cocktail parties I had learned not to be so vulnerable to the condescension of some Armani-suited, Gucci-shod twenty-five-year-old scrambling up the corporate ladder, not to flinch at that quintessential New York question:

"What do you do?" (Translation: "How glamorous, prestigious, and influential are you?")

Answer (a little self-consciously provocative): "I'm a mother."

"Oh." (Consternation. How interesting. How too too brave and noble. How boring.)

I had thought, after Daniel was born and I had worked through the hard adjustment to staying at home with him, that I had emerged into a broad green meadow of life, where I was comfortable with myself and with my choices. I was a mother—not a perfect mother, but a good mother. One who understood that boredom, isolation, and chaos were frequent occupational hazards, but who still reaped sweet reward from each day's small triumphs and joys.

Now, the fabric of my self had torn. How acutely these days did I feel that I was failing, not just Anne-Marie, but Daniel and Michel as well. Something was going wrong, I was confronting some terrible inadequacy in fulfilling precisely that motherly role. I could barely meet the needs and demands of my healthy children; I was completely helpless before my afflicted one.

So that hour I spent with Daniel was precious to me, maybe even more precious to me than to Daniel. I let him prattle on and on, marveling at his physical beauty, desperate to hold on to him in his passing loveliness. Your eyes are so happy, little son. Think no sad thoughts; fear no evil. We have each other, and you are happy.

Similarly, as this ominous postpartum period unfolded, I developed survival techniques with my newborn. I was physically exhausted, since he slept for no more than three hours at a stretch, day and night, then woke ravenously hungry and crying for food and holding. At night, I kept him in a bassinet next to our bed, and whenever he woke I would reach out and sleepily take him into bed with us. During most of the day, I took care of his physical needs mainly: feeding, bathing, and changing him with my mind racing in a thousand different directions, anxiety pulsing constantly through my body.

But then there would always come a period of time in the evening, with Anne-Marie and Daniel mercifully asleep and Michel at his most bright-eyed and alert. Then I would go to his bassinet, anxious to make contact with him, to hold him. As my footsteps approached, he would give me his first gift: his tiny head would turn toward the sound, an expression that I could almost swear was eagerness would light up his face. As I picked him up, supporting his floppy head, his eyes would stare into mine, with that astonished look that infants have in their first weeks of life.

Hollow-eyed, almost trembling with exhaustion, I would force my-self to take this moment and treasure it. I lifted him up, breathed in his pure sweet baby smell and touched my cheek to the indescribable soft-ness of his skin. His little fists were curled against his chest. His whole body could fit into one of my arms, he was so small.

You need me, littlest one. Thank you for needing me. Thank you for letting me give you milk and warmth and love. I held him while he nursed, and once again, as with Daniel, I was calmed by what he gave me. His eyes were half-closed now and his body was completely relaxed. He would drift off to sleep soon, warm and dry and fed and loved. You cry and I can comfort you. You are cold and I can warm you. You need me; I need you. *When my arms wrap you round I press/My heart upon the loveliness/That has long faded from the world.* My Michel. Lean your fragile head against me, and let me shelter you from all harm.

But if Michel and Daniel were providing both stress and comfort during this time, Anne-Marie had now become a source of unmitigated pain. She was going so fast into some shadowy space, and I didn't know how to reach her. As each day passed she seemed to fade more and more into herself, into a private dreamy world where she wan-dered alone. We were losing her.

"Do you remember when she used to say 'Hi, Daddy' to me?" asked Marc one night.

When was that? Had she really been that friendly, that verbal, that connected to us?

We traced it back, trying to pinpoint the moment when she had begun to turn inward. We dragged out photo albums and videotapes and spent an evening studying them, trying to understand.

There indeed were the baby pictures, several of them with Anne-Marie smiling directly into the camera. But as she grew, there were fewer and fewer where she even looked at the person taking the picture, let alone smiled.

And here was the videotape from our trip to Spain. All the children were being assembled on the beach for a group photo. Marc was filming while another uncle was taking still pictures.

Anne-Marie, alone of all the children, began to sob as the group was gathered together. At the time we thought she was just upset—about what, we didn't really know, of course. Was she tired, was she shy around so many cousins? Was she disturbed at the level of noise and activity? The whole sequence lasted a few minutes only, by which point she had stopped crying anyway.

Now we looked more closely at her image on the videotape and felt a cold stab of insight. She had not been "upset" for that brief moment, she'd been terrified: Her hands were up in front of her body, flapping away. Her mouth was open, looking almost ready to scream.

"Do you see that?" I said to Marc, my voice barely above a whisper. "Yes."

I took out some Polaroid snapshots. The children playing in the playground behind the Metropolitan Museum. Daniel with his shoulders scrunched up, his hands in his pockets, laughing right into the camera lens. Anne-Marie on a swing, her legs dangling listlessly down, her eyes downcast, her mouth in an upside-down U.

We felt enormous guilt for not having noticed immediately when Anne-Marie began to withdraw. How could we have gone out to dinner, gone to Denis's wedding in France, done *anything* while such a monstrous thing was happening to her? How could we have lived in the same house with her and not known? The doctors we were talking to told us that we had brought her in very early, assuring us that many children were not diagnosed before age three or four or five, when they were kicked out of nursery school or kindergarten. But we felt that we had somehow betrayed her. We hadn't seen it clearly for almost a year, we hadn't stopped it cold when it first started, whatever "it" was.

The problem was that now "it" was her, it was who she was. She "was" autistic, as someone "is" a man, or a woman, or short or tall. It was not like learning that your child has cancer or AIDS or some other terrible disease. I do not mean to diminish in any way those tragedies or to imply that they are less difficult to bear: they must carry their own measure of ferocious impossible sorrow. I mean only to say that this autism thing was taking over the very essence of who Anne-Marie was. She did not "have" autism; she was autistic. She was already so alien, so distant. When no light shone in her eyes as she glanced at us, no smile of recognition crossed her face, then no longer could we find a self in her. She was so cold, so indifferent now. I felt as though I were holding on to her by the tips of my fingers only. Each long day brought an ever fainter flickering of her spirit, "each slow dusk a drawing down of blinds."

My fitful sleep was punctuated by nightmares. Anne-Marie in a dark wood, Anne-Marie left alone in a house, Anne-Marie forgotten in a car. One night I dreamed that we were all at the beach, playing in the rolling surf. I had a growing sense of dread since I knew that I had to hold on to the three children or the current would take them. Daniel was clinging to my leg, I had the baby in one arm and with the other held Anne-Marie's hand. Suddenly she slipped. She was under the water! I couldn't find her! I was gasping and screaming. My free hand scrabbled across the ocean floor, trying to feel her body. *Baby love! Where are you?!* I screamed. I woke in a sweat, panting with fear.

Anne-Marie too had nighttime disturbances. A part of the syndrome sometimes is that a child's circadian rhythms become unpredictable and sporadic. She was sleeping less and less; there would be times during the night when I would go in to check on her and would find her awake, her eyes wide open at two o'clock in the morning, silent, staring straight ahead.

One night she woke with a cry—was it fear? Was she having a nightmare? I leaped out of bed and ran into her room. If she was afraid of something I wanted to be there instantly for her. I wanted her to be comforted by her mother. I reached out to pick her up. She stiffened, resisted my embrace, and turned her face to the wall. Then deliberately, staring into nothingness, she reached down for the cover and pulled it over her head.

The mornings brought no relief. She never called me. She no longer even babbled and made noises so that someone would come get her from the crib. She just sat there, expressionless, until I arrived to pick her up and change her. One morning I walked into her bedroom with

Marc. She was standing there, looking at the wall. "Good morning, sweetheart!" I called out. She didn't even turn her head.

Suddenly I sat down on the floor, back against the wall. "That's not Anne-Marie," I whispered. "I don't have to love her anymore because that's not Anne-Marie." I felt cold and angry. There. She negates me; I negate her. I was calm about it, very rational. This is better. This cold indifference is quite a relief. Better than walking around like some amputee, hurting to the point of madness. I truly do not have to care anymore about this strange child, because that's not my Anne-Marie.

This frozen hostile calm lasted for a couple of hours. Then it shattered under a storm of grief, doubly violent for having been denied. No, I could never turn away from her. She was lost in her own world, and I understood nothing of what she was feeling, except this one thing: she was not happy there. I had only to look at her mournful face, the downturned mouth and the empty eyes, to know that wherever she was wandering, this little two-year-old, it was neither a good nor a happy place. My peace and my happiness were inextricably bound up with her. Her future and mine were one. As she was drawn deeper and deeper into that dark wood, she carried in her small hands my broken heart. By no act of will or reason could I command my heart to disengage from hers. She was lost and alone, and she didn't know how to find us anymore. I couldn't turn away from her.

"What if," I sobbed in Marc's arms, "what if she never loves us again?"

He was silent for a moment.

"We'll learn to love without being loved in return," he said.

"But what if she suffers for the rest of her life?"

Again he answered as though he'd already given hard thought to the question. "She won't suffer. We'll do whatever we have to do to give her a good life."

With Marc alone could I let myself go fully over into the relief of tears. During the day grief and fear would build and build in me until by evening I could barely hold on. Every evening he'd walk in the door and I would pour out my obsessive anxiety before him. In the nighttime darkness he would hold me as, racked by sobs, I gave him the day's portion of pain. He listened, he held me, he mourned with me. He promised nothing, because he had nothing to promise except his faithfulness. We would go through this together, all of us, and we would hold on to each other, whatever came.

6

MORE AND MORE, we read—books, articles, anything that we could get our hands on. By now we knew better than to expect to find some magic cure in the literature, but we still wanted to find out as much as possible about the disorder. My desk and bedside table were piled high with books and articles on autism. I raced through texts, trying to discover what was happening to Anne-Marie, how she was experiencing the world.

Some of the material consisted of anecdotal accounts of living with an autistic child in the family. The rest could be divided into two major categories: the "coping" books and the "descriptive" books. The coping books were designed for parents and educators, and basically they let you know what to expect, in general terms, and gave suggestions for "handling the child's special needs." To me they all spelled hopelessness and resignation. I didn't want to know how to "handle" self-injurious behavior; I wanted to know how to blast it out of existence. I didn't want to know about options for group homes and respite care when the child grew older; I wanted to know how to keep her close to me, safe and beloved. The message of these books was clear: This is what's going to happen; here is how to adjust. One of the books was entitled *Autism, Nightmare Without End*.

The descriptive books and articles, aimed more at professionals, dissected the symptomatology of the autistic individual from every point of view imaginable. His biochemical and neurological makeup, his psychological, social, and linguistic behavior was described, categorized, and recategorized. It seemed to us an endless rehashing of a complex problem, with no clear solution emerging; a painstakingly minute analysis of thousands of bits and pieces of information; a huge jigsaw puzzle where individual pieces fitted together but no big picture was yet evident.

Someone over here had spent a year studying one particular aspect of one particular symptom: the echolalia that characterizes the speech of some autistic children. When did a subject echo another's speech in a parrotlike fashion? What made echolalia increase? What made it decrease? Was pronoun reversal—the tendency to say "you want apple" instead of "I want apple"—a function of echolalia?

Someone over there was looking at the role of certain neurotransmitters in autism. Another person was studying the abnormal patterns of states of alertness and drowsiness in autistic individuals. There was a new report about the levels of serotonin in the blood. One subgroup of autistic children had been found to have a chromosomal abnormality—the "fragile X syndrome." There were pages and pages devoted to diagnostic criteria, and endless attempts to devise new, more accurate, and "fail-safe" checklists for evaluations.

Much of this information probably represented the bricks and mortar that eventually, maybe in ten years, maybe in thirty, were going to yield a completed structure: a comprehensive and proven theory about the nature, causes, and even cure for autism. The biochemical research especially, although in its infancy, seemed promising in that respect.

But to us it was all essentially useless. None of it changed anything for us now. Whatever we were learning in these first days of the new year simply increased our sense of hopelessness and reinforced the certainty of the diagnosis. We began to recognize Anne-Marie everywhere in these clinical texts.

We learned, for instance, that no two autistic children were alike: If one ran his hands over any smooth or rough surface he could find, another might refuse to touch anything with the palms of her hands—lately Anne-Marie had begun to curl back the fingers of her hands and refuse to reach for things or hold things. If one hummed or clucked incessantly, another sat silently staring into space. If one lined things up repetitively, another might gaze at lights, or flick his fingers rapidly in front of his eyes, or run her fingers back and forth over a radiator grate.

These were all "self-stimulatory behaviors" and they had to do with the obsessive and bizarre stimulation of any one of the senses—touch, or taste, or sight, or hearing.

Some children rocked and twirled their bodies; others didn't. Researchers speculated that these activities might be an attempt to compensate for an impaired sense of movement and equilibrium. Toe-walking, teeth-grinding, and hand-flapping were common symptoms.

Activities that the child returned to again and again, to the exclusion of any social interaction, were termed "perseverative behaviors," and if they became highly patterned and routinized enough, they could develop into "stereotypical rituals." I thought of something I had seen Anne-Marie do many times, something that even before her diagnosis had tugged at my consciousness in an insistent and disquieting way. She would pick up her Big Bird in one hand and one of her "Golden Books" in the other. She would turn the book over, to the back cover, where there was a design of small figures and animals running all around the perimeter. With her Big Bird's beak, she would solemnly touch each figure, starting always at the upper right corner and slowly making her way down, around, and up the other side. I remember once just sitting and watching her do that, wondering, uncertain. . . . But back then I had never heard of or thought about anything called a "stereotypical ritual."

We learned too that many autistic behaviors—like toe-walking, hand-flapping, and rocking—are shared by normal children. In non-autistic children, however, these behaviors usually appear at a very young age, then fade away. In autistic children they are not transient but tend to lock in and become more pronounced as time goes on. It was suddenly clearer to us why it was so hard for an uninformed parent to "see" autism in a child of Anne-Marie's age. Many of the worrisome behaviors that had cropped up after her first birthday we had seen in other children at one time or another. Eager for reassurance, we had found it comforting to believe that if they occurred in normal kids then they were normal activities and so Anne-Marie must be normal.

One issue that was particularly confusing and distressing for us concerned Anne-Marie's earlier, seemingly normal period of development. She had had words. Why had she lost them? Where had they gone? How could she have been normal and now be abnormal? Didn't the presence of some language in the past mean that at least the potential to speak was still there?

It seemed that, in the general population of autistic children, researchers were attempting to identify different subgroups based on age of onset. Some children will, for a while, apparently develop apace with their peers, but sooner or later, often around eighteen months, they will slow, stop, and begin to decline. Another group is manifestly different from birth. In a third group ("late onset" children) the decline first sets in after the age of two. Some research-ers believe that there is no true period of normalcy, that the seeds of destruction are present in all autistic children from birth, even in the later-onset ones. Whatever the case, we found nothing to indi-cate any differences in prognosis among these subgroups. For all, it appeared uniformly bleak.

Thus day by day we grew more "expert" in autism, yet paradoxi-cally grew more helpless. We learned a lot of terminology for Anne-Marie's behaviors, but no one could tell us definitively what we could do about them. I was getting to the point where I would pick up a book, read the introduction and table of contents, devote fifteen min-utes to skimming through it, then toss it into the growing "useless" pile. "So many monuments to hopelessness," I muttered to Marc.

We discovered almost immediately that autism research, at least on the medical/biological front, was in its infancy. This was partly due to early fallacious assumptions about its cause. For about twenty-five years after Kanner's initial identification of autism as a diagnostic cat-egory, psychiatrists and psychologists, almost universally, had gone barking frantically and insistently off in the wrong direction. The con-sensus among the experts had been that autism was caused by—now who would have guessed it?—Mommy! Along with schizophrenia, mass murder, hyperactivity, and manic depression, it was only logical that mommies should take the rap for autism, thanks to the ever-vigilant and feverish Freudians.

Those witch-hunting days, the books assured us, were over. Most professionals now agreed that autism was a neurobiological and not a psychogenic disorder. Well, thank God for that, I thought, reflecting on those poor parents in the fifties and sixties who not only had to deal with their child's diagnosis but were informed in no uncertain terms that they were to blame. Thank goodness we lived in more enlightened times. Little did I know then how far from "over" those days really were.

It was scarcely a month since Anne-Marie's first diagnosis, but it felt more like six. Every single night, Marc and I would talk, incessantly and obsessively, of autism. We discussed Anne-Marie's behavior that day, her eye contact (if any), whether she had said anything at all, pointed at anything, approached anyone, whether she had played ap-propriately with any toys. We read together and summarized for each other, in quick, terse phrases, the pages and pages we were wading through. Both of us felt the most twisting urgency. We were racing against the days, racing to find some way of halting her inexorable progression backwards.

By that point, all of our reading and watching had prepared us somewhat for the next scheduled evaluation—meaning that we no longer expected to be told it was all a mistake. We knew Anne-Marie was autistic; our only hope now was that the next doctor would tell us she was very borderline, the mildest case he or she had ever seen. But even that hope, I was beginning to suspect, had no guarantee of fulfillment.

It was thus with a certain fatalistic calm that I headed off one morning to see Dr. Doubrovsky. Marc had to fly to Washington that morning, so I went alone with Anne-Marie. Someone had recommended Albert Einstein Hospital in the Bronx as a good place to find a therapeutic program, and when I called I had been told that Dr. Doubrovsky was probably the one I needed to see. She was the director of something called the Early Childhood Center of the Children's Evaluation and Rehabilitation Center.*

This interview/evaluation proved to be the low point in our dealings with doctors. If I had been disappointed thus far in the professional response to our problem, if I had found the doctors (with the exception of Dr. DeCarlo) to be unhelpful in our crisis, I was ill prepared for The Megalomaniac from the Bronx. "Unhelpful" was not the word. Dr. Doubrovsky's professional demeanor was nothing short of horrifying. With what lip-smacking glee, what barely concealed delight, did she seem to welcome this opportunity for narcissistic preening and self-aggrandizement.

I was waiting in the lobby when I heard her come into the office. "Is she here yet?" I heard her ask. "Send her in."

"Tell me, Mrs. Maurice," were her first words: "How did you hear of me?"

I stumbled over the answer. Well, someone had told me I should call Albert Einstein, and the operator passed me to another operator who thought I should talk to you.

She seemed miffed.

"Well, to whom have you been talking about your daughter?"

I started to tell her about Dr. DeCarlo and Dr. Berman. She interrupted.

"Who are these people? Did they mention me? Did they tell you to come to me?"

*Dr. Doubrovsky, whose name has been changed, has since passed away.

"No. I told you: I just called general information at Albert Einstein and through a series of connections I wound up with your name. . . ."

From the first moments of our hour-long discussion, it seemed clear that there was one principal subject, and that was Dr. Doubrovsky. Anne-Marie's diagnosis was a convenient topos through which she could draw the truly dramatic and important themes: Dr. Doubrovsky's expertise, her professional renown, her singular gift for diagnosis, her unchallenged authority. Whatever Dr. Berman, Dr. DeCarlo, or Dr. Baxter had said was greeted by a snort of disdain and a tirade about their lack of qualifications in the world of autism. She had a long checklist of questions about Anne-Marie, who had been taken off into a side room for observation by Mrs. Murphy, her colleague. But each time I tried to answer, I was cut off in mid-sentence (a bit of verbal aggression that is very high on my list of rhetorical offenses). At one point I simply gave up and fell silent. Seeming to remember that this was supposed to be a dialogue of some sort, she stopped talking about the incompetent young interns she was supposed to see the next day and fixed her gaze upon me.

"What are you here for, Mrs. Maurice?"

"I am here, Dr. Doubrovsky, to get a diagnosis, a prognosis, and a practical course of action to help my daughter."

"A diagnosis? Autism, of course!"

"I didn't know it was so definite."

"Of course it's definite! You're describing an autistic child."

These words, no matter how prepared I thought I was for them, still pierced with an icy intensity. I struggled against the tears that lurked these days always just below the surface. There was a box of Kleenex on the desk. I reached for one and angrily fought for control. I wasn't going to break down in front of this woman. There was a moment of silence.

"And whom did you say you were going to see next?"

"Dr. Cohen."

"Who's he? I've never heard of him."

"He's the head of the autism division of the Institute for Basic Research in Developmental Disabilities. It's part of the New York State Office of Mental Retardation." Dr. DeCarlo had given us his name.

"Well, I strongly recommend that you not see any more of these doctors. You should stop this running around and come to our parent workshop tomorrow night."

"What happens there?"

"The parents talk about the issues and problems that they're struggling with. Either myself or Mrs. Murphy leads the workshop. We counsel the parents on how to cope with the problems of autism and to understand their child. We meet every Wednesday night."

"I don't need counseling. Everyone wants to 'counsel' me! I need help for my daughter! I don't have time to go to your group therapy sessions!"

I was becoming truly frantic. So many people wanted to give *me* counseling, therapy, support. Having no notion of what to do with Anne-Marie, they still needed to feel needed and important, so they focused on me. I had been told by at least ten people during the past month to take some time for myself, get a manicure, go away for a weekend with Marc, etc. "You owe it to yourself and your family to stop thinking about this problem for a while." If I heard once more the sentence "Take some time for *you,* Catherine," I was going to explode. I didn't *have* time. Time was running out on us, and no one was telling me how to stop it! Please, someone, show me what to do! I don't have time; *she* doesn't have time for your verbosity, your jargon, your paralyzing pedantry, your useless expertise. I don't have time to be sidetracked into any seductive and lengthy contemplation of my coping skills and my emotions. I want to know how to help *her,* not how to help me! I have the rest of my life in front of me. She's falling off a cliff. Can't you offer anything better than a parent workshop? Let *me* deal with my grief and fear—you show me what to do with my daughter now, and every day, before she is gone completely! But of course, I'm forgetting. How gratifying it must be to have the desperate parents gather in your temple every week and implore, with beseeching eyes, your divine guidance.

"Who *is* giving you support, Mrs. Maurice?" Dr. Doubrovsky asked.

"My husband."

"Oh? And where is he today?"

"He's on a business trip."

"A business trip," she echoed heavily.

"And," I added, with a sudden desire to provoke her in this escalating sparring match, "my faith in God. My faith in God is giving me strength." I didn't care how pious the words sounded, and I offered no expansion on them.

"*I* ," she said, "do not believe in God . . ."

Well, of course you don't "believe in" God. You *are* God.

Anne-Marie   55

". . . but I do think we're here for a purpose, and that purpose is to help one another."

There. Case closed. That takes care of the God question. Dr. Doubrovsky was a psychologist who took her expertise very seriously. As a scholar of the soul, she had pronounced definitively on the meaning of life. An enlightened humanism, she had apparently decided, was the answer. She was, after all, the authority.

"Fathers!" she was muttering. I had reminded her of another of her pet peeves, and we were off into another tale of intelligence versus stupidity, keen insight versus blundering obfuscation. The central character and the repository of all learning was once again Dr. Doubrovsky, and the misguided fools in this tale were all the fathers she had dealt with who had refused to accept their child's diagnosis.

"And one," she concluded, "sat right there and said: "Don't you dare tell me there's anything wrong with my son.' "

She sat back, satisfied. We all knew what the end of that story was. Of course the child was autistic and the pigheaded father had been forced to accept reality. The doctor, flushed with her triumph, looked expectantly at me. I thought of that father, and his pain. . . .

I had had enough. I felt battered by this woman, and as usual I was trying to figure out if I somehow deserved her impatient bullying. I wasn't quite sure. Ingrained habits of compliance were telling me to do what I was told, to be obedient to authority and go to the workshop and listen quietly to the doctor. Ingrained patterns of social intercourse were telling me to give her what she wanted: compliments for an excellent diagnosis, thanks for her wonderful help. She was so strong, so sure of herself. Was she right? I wavered, in silence, then rose to go.

"Wait, Mrs. Maurice. Tell me one more thing. What do you think . . . of *me?*"

I felt very weary, overwhelmed with surging and conflicting emotions. I spoke slowly. "I think you're egocentric and overbearing. You've interrupted everything I've said. I resent your implication that my husband is not giving me emotional support."

She took the blow in stride, and turned it straight back at me. *"I* don't think your husband is failing you, Mrs. Maurice. Perhaps *you* feel that way, no?"

This woman was well defended. Her psychiatric schooling had no doubt conditioned her to interpret any attack against her as symptomatic of the "client's" pathology, not her own. She was impervious to criticism or rebuke. I could just imagine the write-up notes on my case: "Client exhibited marked hostility toward interviewer. She would most certainly benefit from counseling to help her deal more constructively with these inappropriate misdirected feelings of anger ... blah blah blah."

Mrs. Murphy appeared at that moment and proceeded to confirm Anne-Marie's autistic symptoms. Both women asked again whether I would be attending the workshop. "I don't know," I said, vacillating still between a desire to throw the ashtray at them and a terrified need to capitulate and accept their smothering therapeutic embrace. "Good-bye, Dr. Doubrovsky, Mrs. Murphy."

"Good-bye, Mrs. Maurice."

As the car wound its way back to Manhattan, I sat stunned. For the first time since Anne-Marie's diagnosis, I felt something taking root in me that was more powerful for the moment than grief or fear.

That something was rage. I didn't know what I was going to do, or who would help us. But I knew for certain that therapeutic nurseries, play therapy sessions, parent workshops, psychological counseling on stress management, were not the answer. The fury that was welling up in me over Dr. Doubrovsky's bullying had one salutary effect: it allowed me, dazed and swaying still with the impact of the diagnosis, to shake them all off—all the "helpers," the suffocating experts, the authorities who had built their careers and their egos around, precisely, the hopelessness of autism and the helplessness of parents. They counseled a resigned acceptance of a disorder that was stealing my daughter away; they pretended "understanding" of a condition to whose cause and nature they hadn't the foggiest clue. The help that they offered was nothing short of a death knell for Anne-Marie. As Dr. Berman had so lightheartedly put it, autism had given many people an awful lot of business for a very long time. As I drove away from Dr. Doubrovsky's office, one decision, at least, had become clear: I wasn't buying.

7

WITH AN IMPATIENCE born of despair I had slammed the door on the old order: it was truly a desperate decision, for I had no idea if there was any such thing as a new order.

I knew only that I had not yet resigned myself to anything. There was too much mystery here, too much darkness. I was stumbling around, lost in a black cave called autism. But it became evident to me early on that the "experts" I was consulting didn't know a whole lot more than I did. My crash course in autism had enabled me very quickly to throw the terminology around, just as they did. My frantic reading was bringing me to the point where I could pick out the abnormalities of behavior, just as they did. The only real differences were these: They, with their clinical distance, were comfortably resigned; I was torn apart. Worse, they could delude themselves, with their degrees and their windy verbosity, that they were "helping." I could afford no such pretensions.

I was in a race against time, and either I found someone or something that truly helped or I had lost Anne-Marie forever. It was as simple as that. There is something about autism that to me gave meaning to the phrase "death in life." Autism is an impossible condition of being there and not being there; a person without a self; a life without a soul.

I was brought to my knees.

How difficult it is for a woman like me—intellectually oriented, impatient, competitive, overly sensitive to criticism or disapproval— to write about prayer. In some circles I have frequented, there is such intolerance of traditional religious forms and rituals, such scorn for those who, in desperate childish wishfulness, need to posit the great Santa-in-the-Sky, the eternal Daddy who fixes everything, including evil, including death. I have spent years trying just to walk away from that cynicism, trying not to care. I've spent most of my adult life in a private battle against forces and attitudes which threaten the practice of my faith.

One such force is my own acknowledgment, born of twenty years of Catholic education, of the human failings of the Church that I love: the infighting, the claims by warring factions each to have the truth, the authority, the divine word. The conservatives and the liberals are equally shrill in their blanket condemnation of each other's politics. It's gone on for two thousand years, and it will go on for two thousand more. The Church, thank God, will survive it all.

Another attack comes not from within, but from without: the sophisticated, urbane environment in which Marc and I live, where practicing Catholics command about as much intellectual respect as dinosaurs.

Religion to me has meant many things, not all of them very virtuous or praiseworthy: an angry territorial stakeout in an antireligious culture; a personal solace when I was alone and unhappy; a testimonial to my ability to choose a direction, to define a purpose to life—a purpose that transcended the esteem of others, the embrace of power. Religion has served as a challenging creed for living and loving, as escape, as haven, as opiate, as structuring principle in a chaotic world.

But in rare moments my religion has brought me something more. And it is that something more that has sustained my imperfect faith, has transcended my defensive political stance, my frightened need for order and comfort. My faith has offered me nothing less than communion with God.

I mean that there have been moments, stealing over me in prayer, in silence, when I have been able to open up, to let go, and to apprehend—ever so fleetingly, so piercingly—a voice not mine, a presence of the Other. It is an experience impossible to render in its fullness. I can only attest, as others far more gifted and more holy have done before me, that it is not so much joy that seizes hold—though there is joy as well—but rather fear. One is so poor in spirit, so ill suited for so much light and beauty. Rudolph Otto has spoken of the *"mysterium tremendum"*—something so overwhelming and so mysterious that the soul bows down in awe, faints in fear and trembling before its Maker.

This light, this love, is so far beyond our reason, so charged with holiness. I have come to understand two things about it: The first is that I can never let go of that light. I will gladly spend the rest of my life waiting, hoping, to be drawn into its full illumination. The second is that I can never hold on to it. The moment of prayer will end, the church will be cold, and the hour will be late. I will have to run out to buy groceries, pick up a child, go back to all the day's anxieties, frivolities, pastimes, duties. Somehow, to be human and alive is never to possess the light, but only, if we are lucky, to know of it and to yearn for it—and then only from time to time, when we will our minds and our hearts to turn in that direction.

But now, in the face of this crisis, I did not rationally decide to turn to prayer: I threw myself into prayer. I held on to prayer as though it were one floating spar in a black tempestuous sea. My prayer was pure petition. I was far from any worshipful, contemplative love, far from any serene joy before the Almighty. My prayer was frantic, sobbing, desperate begging. "Lord, make it not be. Give me back my baby girl. Give her back to me. Don't let this happen. Stop it. Give her back!"

Every night, I would wake, several times, either because of Michel's cry, or because of fitful disturbing dreams. The stages of emergence into consciousness were the same, each and every time:

First would come an awareness of having been asleep, of swimming upward to a surface level. This stage lasted just a few seconds, a period of time when I was not yet fully conscious of who I was. Reality was still fragmented and fuzzy, dreams still held sway over thought. Then would come, suddenly, a physical sensation of intense disquiet. It would start with the skin of my face, a prickly crawling sensation. My hands would rise up and try to rub it away, in jerky spasmodic movements. Suddenly the feeling was in my chest, a thrill of pumping fear, a surge of adrenaline. Finally it was there, crashing down now just as I rose up to consciousness, the realization, the memory of *something wrong! What is wrong here?*

And then the full weight of "it." Oh yes. Anne-Marie. Anne-Marie is autistic. And I am drowning under this wave.

The only thing I could hold on to during these nights was prayer.

My prayer, however, was so poor, so needy. It was the whimpering reflex cry of a child who wakes from a nightmare, a repetitive demand for one thing only: Make it go away. I'm afraid.

The evening of the day that I visited Dr. Doubrovsky, I had had enough. I dreaded the next morning. I could find no solace anywhere, no reason to keep on going. Of course I knew I would go on; there was no choice really. But I didn't want to. Life seemed too painful, all joy drained out of it, all hope fading away. I couldn't resign myself to losing Anne-Marie, and yet all indications said that I would indeed lose her. I knew that I would get up and face the next day, but I didn't want to.

It was around one o'clock in the morning. I couldn't sleep. I couldn't cry. I had no tears left. I was spent, exhausted, but still wound to the breaking point with fear. There was a candle and an icon on my dresser. I lit the candle and gazed into its warm soft glow. Marc and the children slept on in the still night. I sat in that small circle of light and tried to feel the presence of God.

"Lord, I need your help, so badly. . . ." All along, I had been asking for reality to be changed: "Please make the diagnosis be wrong, please make her not be autistic. . . ." This night was different. I had to ask for something else. "Lord, send me . . . fill me with . . . Your strength . . . Your peace. . . . Give me Your strength and Your peace, and I will be able to go on."

But there was one more thing I needed to say, one hard and terrible thing. Gazing into the light, I raised my clasped hands and bowed my head, willing myself to trust in His love. Then I whispered the words that my heart hated, my soul decreed:

"Thy will be done"

—and was flooded, instantly, impossibly, with comfort.

I knew the stillness of a child who, trembling alone in the dark, suddenly feels herself enfolded in loving arms. I was rocked with love, soothed by peace. Through all the fibers of my being coursed a new strength, borne in on the wings of this nocturnal prayer. God is there; He knows, He hears. He watches over us; "He slumbers not, nor sleeps."

I blew out the candle, went to bed, and slept deeply, dreamlessly, for the first time in weeks. I had reached out in this black cavern, stumbling and weeping with fear, and had felt my hand grasped by nothing less than the hand of God.

I am not a theologian and have never known what to do with the most virulent forms of evil in the world, like the abuse of children, ravaging diseases, the suffering of the innocent, the triumph of injustice. But I don't think that God wills evil: as Rabbi Kushner has said, He suffers evil right along with us. "Thy will be done" did not mean to me that God wanted Anne-Marie and us to suffer. It was a way of saying to myself, of affirming, that if we trusted enough in His goodness and His love for us, we would not be swallowed up by this evil. Something good could come of it, if we turned it over to His will. He would give us the strength and the courage to deal with it and to grow through it. Whether that meant that we would find the courage to bear her condition or, instead, that we would miraculously recover her, I didn't yet know.

In the morning, I awakened refreshed, more serene than I had been since Michel's birth. There were eddies of fear and grief still swirling around the perimeters of my consciousness, and they would be there for many months yet. But at heart, I felt more peaceful. My hand was in the hand of God. He would lead me and my family through this fiery land; He would show us how to live again. And whenever the fear rose up, assumed too much dominance, I would stop and pray, remembering in Whose care and keeping I had placed my loved ones. "If God is for us, who can be against us?" What could crush us or annihilate us? We would find a way, we would place our trust in Him.

And then came the first sweet signs of hope. And everything began to happen very fast.

I was standing in the kitchen the next evening when my cousin Maria called from Chicago. I was holding Michel propped over my shoulder and stirring some pasta with the other hand. It was the children's dinner hour, always hectic and noisy. The phone rang.

"Catherine. Hi. It's Maria. How are you holding up?"

"All right."

"You sound tired."

"A little."

"Listen. Jack found an article in the dentist's office that he wants you to read. It's about a Dr. Lovaas, at UCLA. It says he's recovering some kids from autism."

"Recovering some kids from autism?"

"Yes. It says it right here. An experimental program. Forty hours a week of one-on-one therapy. The article is called 'Saving Grace.' Shall I send it to you?"

"Yes. Yes of course send it to me. Send it right away. But tell me what it says first." Recovering some kids from autism? No one we were talking to had mentioned the word "recovery." Could this be true?

Maria and I went over the article together. It had appeared in *Psychology Today,* in December of 'eighty-seven, just as Anne-Marie was being diagnosed by Dr. DeCarlo. The author, Paul Chance, described a little girl named Grace who had been part of Dr. Lovaas's experimental program for autistic children. Dr. Lovaas had bombarded the children with many hours a week of one-on-one behavioral therapy.

A crucial part of his approach was that everyone in the child's environment—parents, teachers, care givers—was trained to follow through on the instruction: to practice and maintain, with a high degree of consistency, the teaching programs specified for each child. There were nineteen children in the experimental group (one had dropped out early on), and twenty children in each of two control groups. The children in the control groups and in the experimental groups had all been diagnosed by independent evaluators. The main difference between the experimental group and the control groups was in the number of therapeutic hours. The experimental program tried to surround the children, almost every waking hour, with a therapeutic environment; whereas in the control groups the children had just a few hours of therapy a week, and the therapy was not carried over into their homes.

The results were unprecedented. Almost half (nine out of nineteen) of the children in the experimental program had achieved "normal cognitive functioning." By all standard measures of intelligence and reasoning, they were normal. But were they truly recovered? Did they have friends, did they relate normally to people? The article stated that the children were now in their teens, and that they had been passed from grade to grade by different teachers as they progressed through normal schools. In addition, preliminary data from some long-term follow-up studies indicated that they had indeed become indistinguishable from their peers, socially as well as cognitively. Grace, though shy, had friends of her own and was doing well in school.

I had heard of behavior modification but knew very little about it. From all our reading, Marc and I were beginning to understand that there were basically three mainstream therapeutic approaches to autism in this country: pharmacological, or drug-related; psychoanalytical; and behavioral. The pharmacological approach had so far not yielded very promising results, and in some cases had produced severe side effects. We had already decided not to put Anne-Marie on Haldol or Fenfleuramine, fearing the toxic potential of both of these drugs.

The psychoanalytical approach usually tried to understand *why* the children were psychotic. It saw autism as a manifestation of an ego problem. The psychoanalytic therapist, ever so gently and respectfully, led the child through sand play and water play and block play, all the while trying to communicate love, understanding, and acceptance of the child.

The behavioral therapist, on the other hand, was not concerned with the why of autism. Whatever the cause, it made no difference. The behavioral therapist worked in the present to eliminate undesirable behaviors and to teach more appropriate skills for living and learning. She looked at the child's conduct, not at his psyche. She taught in a highly structured, highly consistent way, breaking down learning into very small steps and "shaping" the child's behavior, much as one would shape, or train, a dog's behavior.

Steven Blaustein, Ph.D., a speech-language pathologist I had consulted, had confirmed the existence of these three approaches, and had been (blessedly) clear on which of them he recommended. All the data, he told us, consistently showed that a behavioral approach yielded the best results, the most progress.

Marc and I are grateful that early on one or two people like Steven raised their voices in support of behavior modification, because on the face of it, the idea was nothing short of appalling to us. Our vague idea of it—the very name seemed manipulative and cold—included images of Pavlov's dogs, trained seals, rats in mazes. "What are we going to do?" I asked Marc. *"Train* her to talk, to love us, to have feelings, to be human?" Already, I didn't like behavior modification, and I had yet to go through Anne-Marie's first sessions.

Nevertheless, if someone was recovering kids with behavior modification, we had better look into it seriously. I called the Lovaas Clinic, and spoke at length to someone named Joanne. She was very informative and courteous, but regretted that they had no space for us at that time. The article in *Psychology Today,* she told me, had generated an enormous amount of publicity, and they were struggling just to keep up with the influx of telephone calls. She did give me the ordering information for the teaching manual and invited me to write a letter requesting a two-day workshop with a clinic supervisor.

On January 20, we set off for the fourth of five evaluations. This one was with Dr. Ira Cohen at the Institute for Basic Research in Developmental Disabilities, in Staten Island. We arrived at the huge facility, a depressing institutional-looking place with tight security procedures for admission and exit. We walked down the somber corridor toward the autism unit, passing several children and adults who looked severely damaged. One man, who seemed to be around thirty, had his tongue hanging out as he shuffled along, vacant-eyed, with his caregiver. Hold it together, Catherine, I snapped to my sinking heart. Start learning how to look at these people with love, not horror.

Anne-Marie was so far gone by this point that she spent the evaluation period curled on the floor in a fetal position, refusing to open her eyes. We had to come back the next day. This time she was marginally better, but still cried off and on for the entire visit, refusing to look at anyone. We spent about two and a half hours with Dr. Cohen. He videotaped Anne-Marie through a one-way mirror, interviewed us, tried to engage her attention, and administered a screening test for developmental maturity, called the Vineland Adaptive Scales. At the end of all of this he looked grave and was silent.

"Go ahead," I told him. "You can say it."

"I believe she's autistic."

"Yes. We know."

Dr. Cohen would later write in his report that Anne-Marie had displayed "no appropriate verbal or gestural communication." By this time, we had not expected any.

"Do you have any idea how severe she is? Is she one of the worst cases you've seen? One of the mildest?"

He said that he couldn't really predict how the disorder would progress, and that she was a little young to be given any formal IQ test. He would, however, give us the results of the Vineland: Basically, she was functioning at about a one-year-old level in her communication and socialization skills.* In the areas of motor skills and daily living skills (eating with a spoon, drinking from a cup, etc.) she was somewhat more age-appropriate, but still below the norm. This uneven pattern of development reflected the common profile for autism, as did her history of some early language followed by regression and loss of function.

Dr. Cohen seemed objective and knowledgeable. I hesitated, then asked him what I had really come to find out. "Have you heard of a Dr. Lovaas, who says he's recovered some children?"

"Yes," he responded. "Yes, it appears that there is some hope in that direction. You've read the article? It only just came out in December."

I found that my heart was racing, so I tried to speak casually. Just a couple of academics discussing an interesting article. "I've only heard a summary of what must have been the layman's version, published in *Psychology Today.* Where was the scholarly article published?"

"In the *Journal of Consulting and Clinical Psychology.*"

"Can you send me a copy?"

---

*The Vineland is based on clinical observation and parental interview. Although Anne-Marie had displayed "no appropriate verbal or gestural communication" during the actual evaluation, the detailed questioning during the interview had revealed her marginally better functioning in her home environment.

"Certainly."

I found this conversation a little hard to believe. Was one professional actually offering to help us by sending us an article on *another* professional's work? This belied the tunnel vision and egocentric posturing that we had encountered in Dr. Doubrovsky and Dr. Berman. Had he said "Certainly"?

"Do you think he has actually recovered some children?"

"His data appear very solid, very careful: I think it's possible. . . ."

I was hanging on every word.

"Remember," Dr. Cohen continued, "his children were all very very young—under the age of three and a half, usually."

"That's important?"

"Well, neurologically, the brain is still forming. It still has a certain plasticity, malleability. The disorder has not progressed so far."

The idea was deceptively simple to me. Take a very young child, whose development was still unfolding. Bombard her, surround her with a very specific, very intensive therapy, and see what happened. The brain, Marc and I believed and were to remind ourselves often in the next few months, may have an untold, seldom-tapped potential for self-healing.

"What shall we do?"

Dr. Cohen did not mince words.

"Get the book, get the tapes, and get to work. You've taught before. Find out how to do this, recruit and train some student therapists, and set up a home program."

"OK." I swallowed hard, and fought back the wave of doubt and uncertainty. OK. We could do this. We could become overnight experts in whatever this therapy was, then go out and train some others to do it. No problem. Thank you. Thank you, God; thank you, Dr. Cohen; thank you, whoever you are, Dr. Lovaas, for just opening up this doorway to hope.

It took us a few days to begin to say the word "recovery" aloud, to begin to talk about it. It seemed impossible, given everything we had read and heard. Dared we raise our hopes? I needed to find other people who knew of Dr. Lovaas's work, who could confirm his data.

Mrs. Murphy, from Albert Einstein, called a couple of days later. "Yes hello, Mrs. Maurice. We were wondering if you had decided to attend our workshop."

What *is* this? I thought. They need warm bodies to prop around their conference table or their funding will be cut off?

"No thank you, Mrs. Murphy. But tell me, have you heard of a Dr. Lovaas and his recovery of some autistic children?"

There was a pause. "Oh yes," she replied. "But you know, everyone knows he preselected only very high-functioning children."

There was really no limit to the rage that these people could inspire in me. Who was "everyone" and how did they "know" that Dr. Lovaas had preselected only high-functioning children? The articles, both the scholarly one and the layman's version, had just appeared. Had "everyone" immediately flown out to California and interviewed the families of these children, demanded to see their intake evaluations and videotapes? And anyway, maybe Anne-Marie *was* "high-functioning." If Doubrovsky and Murphy truly were aware of the article, why had they not at least informed me of it so that I could know what my options were? We were only talking about the future of my child, after all.

I slammed down the phone, shaking with fury, and sat there, trying to collect my thoughts. Old habits die hard, I was beginning to realize. I was still operating under the naïve assumption that some "expert" should spell out the answer for us. I was taking my gift of hope and bringing it to the "authorities." I was asking for their stamp of approval. I was asking for their permission to believe.

But I didn't need their permission. If Doubrovsky, Murphy, and their ilk weren't going to guide us or even encourage us as we thought about setting up a home-based program, then we would simply leave them by the wayside and set off on our own.

I had an opportunity to try out this fledgling sense of independence a few days later. I was speaking to Dr. Perry, another psychiatrist, to whom we were scheduled to bring Anne-Marie the following week. I explained that we had heard about Dr. Lovaas's success and that it was our intention to set up a home-based program as soon as we could find the therapists.

"Autistic children don't recover," he said calmly.

I remember the reflex of fear, the feeling of caving in, being crushed by the absolute certainty of his voice. I bowed down at his word. But immediately I shook my head, struggled to rise again. No. He believes that, but that doesn't make it true. This is a man speaking, not God. I have been offered hope, I know that I have been infused with a strength not my own. I have the beginnings of an answer here, and God will show us how to make it happen. All things, all things are possible with God. How many times was I to intone that creed to myself in the ensuing months. Where there is life, there is hope; and all things are possible with God.

And once we had adjusted to hope, there was no turning back. There would be some deviation from the path, some false starts and some wasted energy as we felt our way forward. But the goal was there. It had become real and possible. We set our sights for the mountaintops, the very stars. Anne-Marie would be whole and normal. She would talk and smile and grow and love. She would recover.

8

RESOLVE WAS one thing; practical methodology was another. The beginning of the behavioral program was a trial for all concerned.

Marc ordered the book and tapes by overnight air express.* Dr. Cohen sent us the article from the *Journal of Consulting and Clinical Psychology*. Marc and I worked together in the evenings, poring over them, discussing them and analyzing them. I got on the phone as soon as the material arrived and began sending out job notices to the special-education and psychology departments in colleges and universities throughout the city.

The article sounded very promising. Marc, with his background in mathematics, deciphered the statistics for me. We read that article so many times we had it practically memorized. We discovered something that gave us an even more solid foundation for comfort: Most of the children in the experimental group, even those who had not recovered, had made very significant progress. Many of them had been placed in classes for "language-delayed" children. In fact, only ten percent had wound up in classes for the autistic/retarded. I wanted recovery for Anne-Marie, but it still comforted me to know that with this method she would at least communicate on some level.

Reading the article allayed my panic and buttressed my hope. But the books and tapes were another story. We hated them. We hated the

---

The Me Book, Lovaas's standard manual of behavioral treatment, along with a series of instructional videotapes, is available from

> Pro-Ed
> 8700 Shoal Creek Boulevard
> Austin, TX 78758-6897
> Tel. (512) 451-3246
> Fax. (512) 451-8542

way the children looked, so somber-faced and wooden. We hated the way the therapists sounded. I remember one scene of a therapist telling a young boy to match some cards. "Put with same," intoned the therapist over and over again, in a nasal singsong. "Put with same. Put with same." The boy, unsmiling, took each card and placed it in the appropriate pile. In another scene a mother was holding a little girl on her lap. A therapist was facing the little girl. I forget what command the therapist was giving, but it was something like "Clap hands." Each time the command was given, the mother would raise the little girl's hands and "prompt" her through the clapping. Then the therapist would spoon some gloppy food into the little girl's mouth. We were revolted. This therapy seemed the most manipulative and dehumanizing "treatment" we had ever seen a child subjected to. We also remembered that in Paul Chance's article in *Psychology Today,* there had been mention of an "aversive," a physical punishment meted out for inappropriate behaviors that were particularly tenacious. The punishment in the case of the experimental program was a single slap to the thigh.

"No one," I vowed to Marc, "is going to lay a hand on my daughter." The very idea outraged me.

He agreed, feeling as unenthusiastic as I did about what we were seeing and reading. In our late-night discussions, however, we had agreed that we had better give it a try, at least. After all, the sessions were going to be in our home. Surely we could have some control over what went on under our own roof.

Within a week or two after seeing Dr. Cohen, I began to get some call-backs from my job advertisements and started to interview a few students. They seemed good-hearted young women and men and they were enthusiastic, but none had ever worked with an autistic child before. We thought about hiring one or two, resigning ourselves to the inevitable fact that we, who did not know what we were doing, were going to have to teach them how to rescue our daughter. I gave them each a copy of Lovaas's manual of behavioral treatment, *The Me Book,* asked them to study it carefully, and told them that I would call them shortly.

Then through my door walked Bridget Taylor, a gift from heaven. At the time, of course, I didn't know she was a gift from anywhere. There was still so much darkness and stumbling around in those first weeks that I would not have known a gift of gold from a lump of coal, and it was only through the grace of God that I managed to keep making the right decisions. In the beginning I was to think of Bridget as a (barely tolerable) necessary evil.

She was twenty-three years old, long blond hair, blue jeans, high-top leather sneakers. She was finishing her master's degree in special education at Teachers College, Columbia University. She looked like a kid. I distrusted her instantly. What did this person, just barely into adulthood, know about children, let alone autistic children? I grilled her. She answered all my questions with a serious, reserved politeness. She was neither friendly nor hostile, but seemed just comfortable with who she was and what she knew.

And she did know about autism. She was the only one I had interviewed who had worked one-on-one with autistic individuals of all ages. She also knew behavior modification—"That's what I do," she informed me. I brought out *The Me Book* and launched into my summary of its approach and techniques. She interrupted me: "I know that book backwards and forwards. Anyone who works behaviorally with autistic children knows *The Me Book* and Lovaas."★ She furnished letters of recommendation from agencies she had worked for.

"Well," I said, "I need to make one thing clear." I was very frosty, very tense. "This is my house. I'm in charge of this program. No one will use any aversive on my daughter."

"That's fine," she replied calmly. "I don't use aversives. At least I haven't had to yet."

I was a little embarrassed. I hadn't expected to win in the matter of aversives so easily. I had been prepared for an argument but was meeting only cooperation.

"Have you heard of Lovaas's experimental program where he recovered children from autism?" I asked her.

"Yes," she responded. "But I haven't read the article yet. Do you have a copy?"

"Yes. I'll give you one."† I paused, then challenged her: "Do you believe that recovery is possible?"

She was silent for a minute. "I've never seen it," she said. "Some

---

★*The Me Book* was published in 1981. Behavior modification as a treatment for autism has been around much longer. The novelty of Lovaas's experimental program was to apply behavior modification at such a high level of intensity to children so young.

†O. Ivar Lovaas, "Behavioral Treatment and Normal Educational and Intellectual Functioning in Young Autistic Children," *Journal of Consulting and Clinical Psychology*, 1987, vol. 55, no. 1, 3–9.

children do become very high-functioning, but they still have some residual social deficits, in spite of their language ability."

"Well, I believe in recovery, and Anne-Marie is going to recover," I stated, handing her the "Saving Grace" article and the *Journal* article.

She didn't answer.

Marc and I decided to hire Bridget, based on her experience. I called her the next day and offered her the job, effective immediately. She graciously accepted, to my everlasting gratitude and astonishment now, because in her place I would have fled forever from such an angry, contentious potential employer as myself. She *was* a poor, struggling student at Teachers College; maybe she figured the job offered good experience and good pay that made it worth her while to put up with a bossy and delusional mother.

Bridget's first preparation for working with Anne-Marie was to confer with me about her behaviors.

She asked me to draw up a list of "behaviors I would like decreased" and "behaviors I would like increased." I found this an odd and disturbing way of thinking about Anne-Marie. I just wanted her autism to go away and a normal personality to blossom, the quicker the better. The idea of reducing her to a grouping of good and bad behaviors seemed cold and unnatural.

In addition, Bridget wanted me to draw up a list of "reinforcers"—things that we could use to "reward" Anne-Marie and motivate her for "good compliance." Obviously, Anne-Marie was completely indifferent to verbal praise, so we would have to start by pairing such praise with "primary reinforcers": bits of cookie, chocolate, sips of juice.

Right, I thought. We're going to rescue my kid from autism with a bunch of M&M's and some apple juice. Like a trained seal performing its stunts for a chunk of fish. What about love? Where was the place of love in all this? Reluctantly I prepared to write my lists, still convinced that we were going to give this awful therapy only a short trial period, just because we were so desperate.

I sat there in front of the blank sheet of paper, feeling absurd. What behavior did I want increased? "I want her to talk," I wrote. Did Bridget really need me to belabor the obvious like this? "I want her to play appropriately with toys. I want her to love us." Oh no. That last one was too affective, not behavioral enough. I crossed it out. "I want her to look at us—to gaze at us. I want her to smile." Let's see, what else? I wanted her to show some initiative, some joy in her world; how could I state *that* in behavioral terms? Also, at some point it would be nice if she displayed a little interest in her brothers, but I guessed it was too early to write that down.

What behaviors did I want decreased? I want all her autistic symptoms to go away! I thought angrily. But I picked up my pen and tried to think about what that meant specifically.

"I want her to stop crying so much . . . to stop twirling strings . . . grinding her teeth . . . sitting in a corner alone with her back to the room. . . ."

I listed every "stereotypical" and "self-stimulatory" thing I had recently seen her do.

Then I wrote my reinforcer list and handed it to Bridget with stern warnings about overfeeding her and giving her too much sugar and making her dependent on these cookies and goldfish crackers. "Yes, yes," said Bridget. She had obviously heard it all before, many times. "I'll give her only very small bits at a time. In a whole two-hour session, she'll eat maybe two cookies and ten goldfish crackers."

We made arrangements for Bridget to begin working as soon as she could, which would be in a couple of weeks. She would start by coming three times a week, for a two-hour session each time. She would quickly work up to five days a week.

The thought had momentarily crossed my mind that no two-year-old could possibly be expected to sit through two solid hours of therapy. But I dismissed it pretty quickly.

First of all, I had talked over that issue with Joanne from the Lovaas Clinic, and she had assured me that the children did adapt: as long as the activity was varied and the child could move periodically from table to floor and back again, two-hour sessions were tolerable.

But that was not the primary reason why I decided not to throw out a lot of arguments about the length of the session. The primary reason was that we had no choice. This was the only therapy around that allowed the possibility of something more than "progress." I felt the same resigned acceptance toward it that I would have felt if a surgeon had told me he had to carve open my child's body to correct a faulty valve in the heart. Would I want my child to be physically assaulted like that? Would I like the thought of giving her over to strangers with knives? Did I think she would enjoy the experience of being strapped to a table and drugged to oblivion? Hardly. But if that operation was going to save her life, there would be no question in my mind. Two hours, ten hours, forty hours of therapy inflicted on Anne-Marie—the amount of time made no essential difference to me. It was awful enough having to do this: we might as well do it right.

We were now in early February. Everything was coming together fast, so fast that I could barely keep track of what we were supposed to be thinking and feeling each day. Fear? Frustration? Anger? Hope? Fear again? In the drama that would become Anne-Marie's rescue, all the players were assembling in the wings. Bridget had just made her appearance. In another three weeks, the other major figures would come onstage and all the basic decisions would be made.

9

BEFORE WE BEGAN the actual behavioral sessions, we had to make another lightning trip to France. We had planned for a long time to baptize our third child in France, with Marc's family. All the preparations had been made months in advance.

"What shall I do?" I asked my friend Evelyne. "I know the trip over there will flip Anne-Marie out. But I can't stand the thought of leaving her. Which is worse, leaving her or taking her? Should we cancel the whole thing?"

"I don't know," said Evelyne. "I guess my choice would be to take her."

After much agonizing, Marc and I decided to take Anne-Marie and Michel on the four-day trip, and to leave Daniel home with his Aunt Burke. She planned an active weekend with him so that he wouldn't get too lonely.

On the flight over, Anne-Marie cried nonstop, as she had on the trip to Spain. This time, however, she was even more difficult to calm or distract. Marc and I took turns just holding her as she sobbed and sobbed. She buried her head in her father's shoulder, or my shoulder, and if we spoke or moved too much, she started sobbing again.

To top things off, the three of us—Marc, I, and Anne-Marie—had contracted some horrible virus that had our heads and throats pounding with pain and our chests racked by paroxysmal coughing. I remember sitting on the plane with tearful Anne-Marie, crying newborn Michel, sick Marc, every joint and muscle in my body throbbing. Marc and I glanced at each other across the aisle. He just shut his eyes and leaned his head back against his seat without saying a word.

This is one of those times, I thought, when you just have to hold on until it's over. Hold on to the conviction, if not exactly the comfort, that there is undoubtedly greater suffering going on somewhere in the world. I concentrated on getting away from my body, floating outside of time and space and just distancing myself from everything, myself included.

OUR FIRST DAY'S gathering with Marc's family was strained and quiet. The knowledge of Anne-Marie's diagnosis had cast a pall over what was supposed to be a celebration. One of the guests complicated the day's tension by pronouncing her opinion of what had happened.

"*Oui, c'était le choc psychologique.*"

"*What* psychological trauma?" I asked with consternation. What information did she have that I didn't?

That person was not the first, nor would she be the last, to assert that something in Anne-Marie's environment had driven her over the edge into madness. It turned out that she had been reading the French translation of psychoanalyst Bruno Bettelheim's *The Empty Fortress* and had decided that some emotional trauma had caused Anne-Marie's autism. Undoubtedly the birth of Michel.

This is just one of the minor trials that afflict the parents of autistic children. Suddenly our life is fair game for everyone's scrutiny, and everyone "knows" just what caused the problem. Friends, even casual acquaintances, feel compelled to pronounce their opinion as to cause and treatment. If you have a disturbed child, obviously you are in need of everyone's advice, no matter how uninformed.

And for everyone who discourses on cause or treatment, there are two more who will let you know that the problem is a figment of your imagination. My next-door neighbor, to whom I had incautiously blurted the whole story right after Anne-Marie's diagnosis, had decided that she could straighten out the silly misunderstanding. She had stopped me in the lobby the following day: "I told my husband the whole story, and he says it's utter nonsense. There's nothing wrong with your daughter." Considering that her husband had never laid eyes on Anne-Marie, I could only sigh and remind myself to be more discreet in the future.

"You want to know what I think?" said a friend of mine. "I think this autism business is a bunch of baloney. She looks just fine to *me!*"

"Oh that happened to a little girl I know," cried another acquaintance. "It was just after her mother had a new baby, and the little girl went into a fit of jealousy and really regressed. She completely gave up peeing in the potty and would wet her pants constantly, just to get back at her mother! Don't worry, she'll grow out of it real soon."

These remarks, of which I was to hear many more as time went on, became intolerable to me. Far from comforting me, they only increased my sense of isolation and difference. Minimizing or dismissing the problem may help other people feel more comfortable; the result for Marc and me was increased alienation.

But in France, it was important that we at least try to let Marc's family in on the complexity of the problem. Here I relied on Marc. I found that I was not capable of speaking objectively and rationally about the autistic condition. No matter how much I wanted to elucidate the subject for my in-laws, I found that I kept trembling with the effort of speaking clinically and calmly.

And God knows, it's not as though we had any proven and clear medical description to give them. How could we elucidate something that the doctors could not make clear to us? Marc did the best he could, explaining that research was going forward on several different fronts, biochemical, metabolic, structural; that researchers believed that there existed several different forms of autism, probably due to different etiologies; but that the general indication was that we were dealing with some as yet unspecified central nervous system disorder. What precisely had happened in Anne-Marie's case we did not know.

His parents and his ninety-year-old grandfather, Papari, listened with attentive sympathy.

"*Quel dommage,*" murmured Papari. He was gazing at Anne-Marie as he spoke, and I saw a look of sadness in his old and tired eyes.

THE FOLLOWING DAY, after Michel's baptism, we took a trip into Paris to visit Notre Dame.

Notre Dame, in its soaring beauty and cool vaulted solemnity, has always sheltered and strengthened me in times of confusion. I find in that cathedral something that uplifts my spirit: a symbol of a nation's homage to the Mother of God; an image of what men, committed to a high ideal, can give back to their Creator: highest artistry, astounding ingenuity, backbreaking labor, worship.

But more; Notre Dame holds for me a comfort more inexplicable and more personal than that: the presence, through the ages, of Our Lady—shining there, dwelling there, welcoming all who come to her: the heartsick, the angry, the broken, the lost.

We walked toward the cathedral that day, past the statue of victorious Charlemagne, through the main portals, into the dark interior lit by the glow of hundreds of candles and by the light filtering in through the richly colored windows, high above. We had left Michel with Marc's parents and had come with our little girl to make our petition.

Before the statue of Mary, I could barely formulate my prayer, not even silently. There was a floodgate, and if I opened it, even to myself, I knew a deluge of grief would follow.

I lit the candle, held on to one of Anne-Marie's small hands while her father grasped the other. Anne-Marie's face was softly lit by the flickering candles; she gazed quietly at their light.

I breathed the only words I could. It was a cry of longing, some broken words only. "Please . . . Mother of God . . . bring her home. . . ."

✱✱✱✱✱✱✱
✱ ✱
✱ **10** ✱
✱ ✱
✱✱✱✱✱✱✱

BACK IN NEW YORK again, and recovering from the trip and the flu, we took up the battle where we had left off.

By mid-February, we had had Anne-Marie evaluated by five professionals.

According to Regina DeCarlo, M.D., Ph.D., pediatric neurologist: "The child's history and symptoms are suggestive of infantile autism."

According to Richard Perry, M.D., psychiatrist:* "Anne-Marie impresses me as having pervasive developmental disorder: infantile autism."

According to Nina Doubrovsky, Ph.D., Associate Clinical Professor of Pediatrics and Psychiatry, Albert Einstein College of Medicine: "She impresses as a child with a pervasive developmental disorder with characteristics of the syndrome of infantile autism."

According to Ira Cohen, Ph.D., Head, Autism Unit, Institute for Basic Research in Developmental Disabilities, New York State Office of Mental Retardation: "Diagnostic Impression: Probable Autistic Disorder."

I felt, oddly enough, a paradoxical relief that four out of five experts had come up with the same diagnosis.† At least, the tearing uncer-

---

*Dr. Perry is Unit Chief of Child and Adolescent Services at a major New York hospital. It is important to note that each of these doctors, whether or not identified by his or her real name in this text, held an important position in a prestigious institution and had had extensive clinical experience in the diagnosis of autistic children. I emphasize this point because today it is frequently suggested—usually by people who know virtually nothing about the facts of our experience—that Anne-Marie was misdiagnosed.

†I was not to receive a copy of Dr. Berman's evaluation until I requested one three and a half years later while writing this book. At that point, Dr. Berman wrote that he had found Anne-Marie to have "Pervasive Developmental Disorder—Not otherwise specified." See Appendix I for a full discussion of diagnostic criteria and terminology.

tainty, the roller-coaster whipping from hope to despair, over and over again, was at an end.

Relief on one plane, yet continuous waves of terror on another. Anne-Marie was still sliding downhill. The only people who knew anything about recovering kids from autism, the Lovaas team, were unreachable. Did we really think we were going to abort this "incurable" psychosis by relying on an academic article and a twenty-three-year-old graduate student?

My mother had summed it up for me: "We have to pray as though everything depended on God, work as though everything depended on us."

We had help with the praying. My parents, Marc's parents, friends, and relatives—all of them spiritually closed ranks and stormed heaven with their prayers. In East Hampton, where we had a summer house, the sisters of St. Joseph, led by Sister Damian, tacked up in their chapel a photograph of Anne-Marie and knelt and prayed each morning for the return of the wandering little girl. In the south of France, Marc's aunt, a cloistered Carmelite nun, gathered the sisters together for daily prayer and murmured the name of a child they had never seen.

As to the work, that had not quite begun, aside from Marc's and my obsessive reading. Bridget was due to start the behavioral sessions in just a few days, but I was frantic to do something myself about Anne-Marie. I couldn't stand my sense of helplessness as I watched her decline. "Lord, please, please show me what to do," I would pray. "I don't know what to *do.*" It was all very well to have set up the behavioral program, but I still didn't believe it was anything I could or wished to be involved in myself.

One night, while going through some of my bedside pile of books, I stumbled upon one that opened up for me, quite suddenly, a new way of thinking about my daughter's condition. *The Siege,* Clara Park's book about her autistic daughter, enabled me, for the first time, to believe that I had some control, that I was not completely helpless.

The Siege was written at a time when psychoanalysis was still the dominant mode of thinking about autistic children and tolerant understanding was the recommended mode of approach. The symptoms of the autistic child were seen as signs to be interpreted, as deliberate messages sent to the world. There is in the book an emphasis on the idea of autism as a choice—a "willed blindness," "willed deafness," "willed weakness," "willed isolation." There are pages and pages devoted to a mother's poignant wondering about her daughter's world, an attempt to understand what was going on in her daughter's mind and heart.

Throughout, there is chronicled the mother's insistent, slow dismantling, bit by bit, of the walls around her child. The mother's siege, though tireless and tenacious, is a patient one. In one scene, Mrs. Park is trying to encourage her three-year-old daughter to throw rocks into a pool. For a while she hands the child each rock; then she decides to wait. The rocks are right there, in a pile. Will Elly stretch out her hand and pick up her own rock?

> No, she won't. Not today. I do not press. I know the answer is final. My immobility is a mirror of hers. I have learned to wait. [pp. 50–51]

From the beginning, my idea of a "siege" meant something more forceful and invasive than the kind of respectful, patient waiting portrayed in that scene. Nevertheless, it was in Mrs. Park's book that I first found the germinal concept for my part in the battle. As I read on that night, two concepts fairly burst into my consciousness: the notion of Anne-Marie as being "walled in," and the idea of assaulting those ramparts. Besieging Anne-Marie, not so much in the sense of waiting and wooing, beguiling and beckoning, but in the far more violent sense of storming the walls.

As though moving herself toward the more powerful connotation of the word "siege," Mrs. Park chose to quote near the end of her book a sonnet by John Donne, a beloved favorite of mine that has often resonated in my own life:

> Batter my heart, three-personed God, for you
> As yet but knock, breathe, shine, and seek to mend;
> That I may rise and stand, o'erthrow me, and bend
> Your force to break, blow, burn and make me new.
> I, like an usurped town, to another due,
> Labor to admit you, but oh, to no end;
> Reason, your viceroy in me, me should defend,
> But is captived, and proves weak or untrue.
> Yet dearly I love you, and would be loved fain,
> But am betrothed unto your enemy:
> Divorce me, untie, or break that knot again,
> Take me to you, imprison me, for I
> Except you enthrall me, never shall be free,
> Nor ever chaste, except you ravish me.

This sonnet, said Mrs. Park, sustained her many times in her lifelong battle for her daughter's love. I wonder if she ever dreamed that, twenty-five years after she wrote her book, another mother of another daughter would bow her head in gratitude at her perfect choice of image and song.

I let Donne's prayer become my own cry to arms; it did more than "sustain" me, it galvanized me to begin what was to become an assault on my daughter, an assault of love, with no holds barred.

I did not learn how to wait; I learned how to stalk and hunt, how to overpower.

I read that poem as a metaphor for Anne-Marie's voice, could she but speak to those who loved her. The violence of the imagery—the battering, the bending, the burning, the overthrowing, the final ravishing—was frightening. But no more so to me than was autism.

I had felt from the beginning that something was "taking over" my daughter, and that if she herself could know about and speak about what was happening to her she would cry out for rescue. There was a part of her that was still a lost and frightened baby girl, and if I had to batter her down, bend, break, and ravish her autistic self in order to get to that Anne-Marie spirit, I would do so.

She was "to another due," and unless we tore her out of the otherness of autism, she would never be free.

That very evening, I wrote some statements in my journal, the first draft of a battle plan.

"She will not sit in the corner. She will not play with strings. She will not not look at me. She will not be mute. She may want it. I will not have it. She will be dragged, kicking and screaming, into the human condition."

I KNOW I speak of a "self," a "part of a self," a "spirit," an "autistic self," and these are inexplicable and vague words, signifying nothing that can be demonstrated or validated. These are symbolic constructs only. I do not know what a self is any more than I know what a soul is. I live my life and I think my thoughts as though I knew what those things were. I have invested the words with meanings that change over time and will continue to change. When I speak of Anne-Marie's "self" as disappearing, it is partly because I thought that it was true—she had been a self-in-formation before she started to regress and fade away—and partly because I needed to think that there was still someone there, someone who would be there waiting as we fought our way through to her, someone, in fact, for whom all these tears were being shed.

Even at the beginning, I never entirely trusted the psychoanalytic idea of a normal child locked within a chosen autism, and today I actively decry that notion and believe it has caused great harm. But in a way, parents who are going to fight for their child do need the construct, however fictional, of that child imprisoned within, waiting to be reclaimed. That child has our committed love. What authority, autonomy, and choice we concede to that child, and when, is another story.

AFTER BRIDGET TAYLOR, the next player to enter was Robin Rosenthal, a speech-language pathologist whom Steven Blaustein had recommended.

Marc and I didn't know what a speech pathologist did, especially with a child whose speech was almost nonexistent. But I trusted Steven's advice, and at least it gave me the sense of doing something else concrete for Anne-Marie. I didn't think a speech pathologist was going to come in and magically make her start talking, but I thought any extra stimulation, especially if it was expertly focused, couldn't hurt.

Already, in late January, before our trip to France, I had interviewed three speech therapists, complete with degrees from respected universities. But they had no idea what to do with Anne-Marie! They followed her around the house, talking in paragraphs that floated way above her head, keeping up a running monologue whose primary structure was interrogative.

"What are you doing, Anne-Marie? Pushing your bear through the chair? Is that what you like to do? Oh, I like that too. Shall we do it together? What's the bear's name? I bet he's a really nice bear. How old is he? How old are you? Maybe we can find a blanket for the bear. Do you want to cover the bear?"

And Anne-Marie, in the middle of this discourse, would get up and walk out of the room, completely oblivious to the swirl of questions.

The speech therapists who did this were obviously nervous and uncomfortable, and knew they were not getting through to Anne-Marie. "I've never worked with an autistic child before," said one apologetically when I told her it wasn't working out. I felt sorry for her.

"It's OK," I said. "I'll find someone else."

She turned to look at me before she left. Her eyes were full of tears. She had told me that she had a baby daughter of her own.

"I just . . . I just want to wish you good luck," she blurted out, then left.

"Thank you," I whispered as the door closed behind her.

Then, just after we returned from Michel's baptism, we found Robin. She came over one evening after her day's work at Mt. Sinai Hospital Communication Disorders Center.

Like Bridget, she was a young woman—mid-twenties, I guessed. On the small side, with short dark hair and intensely beautiful dark eyes.

She came into the living room, sat down, and began to talk, knowledgeably, sympathetically. She leaned forward as she spoke, eager to listen as much as to inform. She didn't detour into any peripheral topics, such as how I had to take care of *me* now and think about *my* needs. She spoke first of all of what she did, what type of help she could offer Anne-Marie.

She explained that a speech-language pathologist was (usually) trained to help alleviate problems of both speech (the physical production of articulate sounds) and language (the communication of information and ideas). She managed to convey to me the message that yes, autism was a serious problem indeed, so we had better get going because we had a lot of work in front of us.

Most autistic children do have some rudimentary communication, Robin believed. Even screaming or nonsense phrases could be considered a form of intentional communication, especially if they increased in the presence of another person. A central role of the speech pathologist, Robin asserted, is to try to shape the communication into more useful and appropriate forms.

How would she do that? She would start, she explained, by setting up situations where Anne-Marie would feel highly motivated to comment or to request. Even if Anne-Marie did not say anything at this point, if she would point or reach or make any sound in order to obtain a desired object, or to call Robin's attention to something, that was to be counted as "intentional communication." Even if she looked meaningfully at Robin, to get Robin to blow a bubble, for instance, that would count as an attempt at communication: a kind of preverbal communication.

The overall goal, then, was to increase the frequency and the appropriateness of each communicative act. To that end, Robin would specify certain precise tasks that we would all work on each week.

For the first week we would start by modeling the sound "mmm . . ." for "more" every time Anne-Marie wanted some juice or food or a toy.

The idea was to *wait,* to withhold the desired object and clearly repeat the sound until Anne-Marie had at least made eye contact.

I said fine, that sounds fine, even though it seemed a bit like something I'd already tried with no success. But then, Robin was at least talking about specific linguistic goals. She seemed to have an overall plan, as well as detailed knowledge of the normal stages of language acquisition in very young children.

We had been talking for about a half hour. Then Robin asked if she could work with Anne-Marie right away. I agreed, and led her to Anne-Marie's room.

I watched as she brought out bubbles and windup toys. She set to work, trying to capture and hold Anne-Marie's attention. There was certainly not a whole lot of communication that I could see in that first half-hour session, but at least Anne-Marie was not resisting. She was staying in the room, even manipulating voluntarily some of the toys Robin had brought. She was quiet, not crying, though a complete stranger was intruding upon her. She didn't look at Robin or say anything or point, but she allowed Robin to be near her and to speak to her.

After a little while, Robin put a toy into the plastic container, then rattled it next to Anne-Marie's face. Anne-Marie, intrigued, gazed at the toy. Robin handed her the container. Anne-Marie tried and failed to open it. Frustrated, she began to whine. She grabbed Robin's hand and tried to put it on top of the container. Robin resisted until finally Anne-Marie glanced up into her eyes. As soon as she did so, Robin smiled at her and said "Open!" Then she opened the container and handed Anne-Marie the toy.

I stole out of the room and continued to listen from the hallway. No crying, no whining. Just Robin's continuous short sentences. Whatever Anne-Marie happened to look at, Robin would describe ("I'm blowing bubbles") or label with a single word ("truck"). She was clear, repetitive, concise. I realized suddenly that what she was doing was going back to the beginnings of language.

She was speaking to Anne-Marie as one would speak to a ten-month-old baby. Her intonation was high-pitched, similar to a mother's tone when talking to a very young child. Her language was focused and clear. The longest sentence she used was three or four words. But, differently from mothers, Robin eliminated from her discourse all questions and most pronouns, including the pronoun "you." Anne-Marie was not yet ready for them. Robin's vocabulary too was more limited than a mother's would be. A mother would speak in simple one-word labeling sentences to her preverbal child, but she would also use words and structures that she knew were beyond the child's immediate understanding. She would not edit her speech exclusively to her child's level but would likely, just in the course of normal chatting to her baby, throw in some words or phrases that were way beyond him.

One of my own first songs to Daniel (when he was only two months old) had been "I love my Daniel/My Daniel loves me . . . ," although of course I knew that he was not yet "understanding" the semantic transformations inherent in these pronouns "I," "my," "me," and that any concept of "love" that he was receiving was coming to him more through my tone of voice, my body warmth, the pressure of my arms, than it was through the word itself.

Robin's language was purer and clearer: mother-talk without any confusing extras. Mother-talk with a specific linguistic goal in mind. Mother-talk aimed at the simplest communicative unit: the one-word label ("doll"), or request ("more"). We seemed to have found someone who knew what she was doing.

And anyway, I felt so good about the professional caring demeanor of this young woman that I almost didn't care. Just to have someone have some success in keeping Anne-Marie occupied for a short while seemed like a major accomplishment. It *was* a major accomplishment.

Robin was the first one to be able to lift, for forty-five minutes at a time, an immense weight off my shoulders. When she went into that room with Anne-Marie, I felt as though I could breathe again. I could just put everything on hold. Someone else was taking care of her now, someone whom I could trust. I didn't know if Robin's speech therapy was going to make Anne-Marie start talking, but I knew at least that it was keeping her from sitting in a corner, tapping things together. On Monday, Wednesday, and Friday evening, when Robin came, cheerful and tender and charged with energy, I would take Daniel into my bedroom and just lie on the bed, utterly spent, holding on to him as he chattered away. I felt sometimes that Robin's forty-five-minute sessions with Anne-Marie were holding *me* together: that if she didn't come in and give me that relief, I would go flying off into a thousand broken, useless pieces.

"Are you sure you can't work twenty hours a week?" I asked her in all seriousness.

"No," she replied. "You really need to get Anne-Marie into a program, and have someone like me come in to supplement her therapy."

I told her about the Lovaas program that we had set up. She listened politely, but, like Bridget, was noncommittal on the subject of recovery.

Robin longed to be of service. It was obvious to me that she wanted to use whatever skill and learning she had to ease this crisis for our family. But she was not going to purchase our gratitude and love by promising us anything she could not deliver. That was OK with me, I realized. I still wanted her on our side, fighting for Anne-Marie.

So this was fine. I had one person I felt sure of, one type of therapy about which I had no immediate qualms or reservations.

BRIDGET WAS DUE to start working next. The plan was that she would spend two hours a day, five days a week, working with Anne-Marie while we looked for some other therapists to give us more hours. We ourselves meanwhile would learn the techniques from watching Bridget and would follow through on all the programs, maintaining them and practicing them throughout Anne-Marie's day.

On February 22 I led Anne-Marie into the bedroom for her first session with Bridget. I was very nervous. An assault, yes. A radical approach, OK. But by *me*. Not by some stranger. Not with this "behavior modification" business. Bridget set out many toys around the room: puzzles, push-button toys, stacking rings, a "shape-sorter box," a "speak-and-say" ring that made different animal sounds when you pulled a string.

I noticed that they were all toys geared toward the twelve- to eighteen-month age range. Logically enough, I conceded: Since Anne-Marie did not play appropriately with any toys, we might as well try to teach her first how to play with toys for younger children, rather than starting her off immediately on some complicated doll play. Again there was that notion of going back to the beginning: recapitulating, in a way, the stages of growth and development in specific areas, working up to her present age level.

Anne-Marie was whimpering and crying already. Bridget was very serious. She was scaring me. Unlike Robin, she did not try to woo

Anne-Marie and charm her with fun and bubbles and laughing peek-aboo games. She had work to do. About her there was an urgent sense of time speeding by. We had to get going. No time for chitchat or hand-holding sessions with Mother. There was not a minute to be wasted.

On the table she placed the reinforcers: apple juice, goldfish crackers, broken bits of chocolate cookie. She set out her notebook and her pens. She took off her watch and laid it face up on the table in front of her. She placed two chairs—one for her, one for Anne-Marie—close together, facing each other.

Watching her set up her materials, with Anne-Marie now crying on the floor and curled into a ball, I was starting to feel like some dazed and disbelieving survivor of a catastrophe. There was my daughter, hurt and terrified in front of me. And here came the paramedics, all cool control, all fast and sure decisions and motions, practiced a hundred times before. Getting hysterical will help no one, lady: just stand aside and let us do what we know how to do; please stay out of the way.

As soon as Bridget placed Anne-Marie in the opposite chair the crying broke out in earnest. Anne-Marie tried to get out of the chair; Bridget kept placing her firmly back in. She collapsed on the floor; Bridget picked her up and put her back in the chair. She tried to put her hands in front of her face; Bridget took them down and held them in her lap.

Anne-Marie was terribly fearful and distraught. She turned and looked directly at me, for the first time in weeks. Her mouth was trembling.

I was cold and clammy with tension. Was this right? Was I doing the right thing? But I had wanted an assault. Hadn't I decided that we were going to "drag" Anne-Marie out of autism? Oh God, what *did* I want?

It went against everything I had ever thought about child-raising to physically force a child against her will, especially one who seemed not defiant, but terror-stricken. What kind of message was I sending to Anne-Marie? She was looking at me for help. How could I refuse? I let out a long breath and held myself back, by force of all the reason I could muster, from rescuing her.

The first program was a simple one: "Look at me."

Bridget said it ten times in a row, holding a reinforcer at eye level, putting her other hand under Anne-Marie's chin to lift her head up. Each of the ten "discrete trials" was to be given a mark in the notebook. A plus if Anne-Marie looked spontaneously, a minus if she didn't look at all, and a "plus with prompt" if she looked with the physical promptings and the food reinforcers. I kept pacing in and out of the room. Staying there and watching was too hard, staying outside was too hard. I couldn't stand seeing Anne-Marie so upset and not being able to pick her up. But I had made a pact with myself, with Marc, and with Bridget that we would give this therapy a try, and if I was going to give it a try I had to at least let Bridget finish the session.

Bridget seemed completely unfazed by Anne-Marie's sobbing. How could she be so calm? She must not have a heart. She just kept prompting Anne-Marie through the trials, as though all this terror and distress were not happening. After each trial of "Look at me," she offered Anne-Marie a goldfish, and praised her. "Good looking, Anne-Marie!" or "I like that good looking!" Anne-Marie refused to accept the reinforcer. Bridget wasn't bothered by that rejection either, but still offered her food and praise, even though it was Bridget who was prompting the looking, not Anne-Marie doing it voluntarily.

"Poor child," said Patsy. Anne-Marie had been sobbing for close to an hour.

"I *know,* Patsy. But we have to . . . there's nothing else. . . . Bridget's not hurting her; she's just making her sit in the chair. . . ."

Finally Anne-Marie's crying began to subside. "Good quiet! I like that good quiet, Anne-Marie!" said Bridget, whenever it stopped. She named very specifically whatever action or behavior she was praising in Anne-Marie. It seemed an unnatural way of speaking to a child, and I had no idea at this early stage how quickly Marc and I would begin to exercise this reflexive praising and naming of Anne-Marie's actions.

I went back into the room.

The second hour passed a little better than the first. Anne-Marie began to accept some of the primary reinforcers* from Bridget, and her sobs had diminished to sporadic whimpering. Every minute of the two-hour session was spent in a directed, structured activity. There would be ten trials of "Look at me" in the chair, then a break to a floor

---

*"Primary" reinforcers are concrete rewards like bits of candy, sips of juice, even little wind-up toys. "Secondary" reinforcement is more abstract and includes social rewards like praise and hugs.

activity—a puzzle or a toy—then back to the chair. But even in the toy play, Bridget was right on top of Anne-Marie, putting a shape into her hand, guiding her hand to the corresponding opening on top of the shape box. "Good putting in the circle!" "Good putting in the square!"

At one point, a little calmer, Anne-Marie decided that she did want a piece of cookie. She grabbed Bridget's hand by the back of the wrist and shoved it toward the food.

Immediately, I saw Bridget jerk her hand away, grab Anne-Marie's hand by the back of the wrist, and push it forward.

"Here. *You* want it. Point." She shaped Anne-Marie's fingers into a point.

I drew in my breath sharply. I was acutely disturbed by Bridget's self-confident usurpation of Anne-Marie's will, Anne-Marie's bodily control. Should I let this woman handle my baby girl like that?

It was one thing to have decided in the abstract that I was going to adopt a certain stance toward Anne-Marie. It was another to watch a stranger force compliance out of her. I was agonized with ambivalence.

Bridget emerged after the session full of energy. I was drained. "It went pretty well!" said Bridget.

"But she hated it!" I said. "She cried for an hour!"

"An hour's worth of crying is to be expected. No one has ever forced her to pay attention before. These children are very resistant to intrusion, and much more so to the kinds of intensive demands we place on them."

It was because I had been charged up by the idea of an assault that I was able to even consider this behavior modification.

Anne-Marie was not going to be gently led out of autism. On one level, I knew that. If love and understanding could rescue a child from this psychosis, the disorder would not carry the hopeless prognosis that it did. Even if one were to assume that cold, unfeeling parents had not been able to convey enough love and tenderness to their child, there was an army of psychologists, psychiatrists, and social workers out there who had already tried that route and failed. They were still failing. "Autistic children do not recover" was their considered opinion.

I was already convinced that some radical force was necessary. But what kind of siege, what kind of force? I was very unsure that behavior modification was the right path to take. I felt such a heavy weight of responsibility. We *had* to make the right decisions. Anne-Marie's future depended on what Marc and I decided right *now*.

IT WAS in this frame of mind—anxious, unsure—that I found Martha Welch and holding therapy. I needed the idea of an invasion to be tempered by the idea of love, and became convinced that in holding therapy I had found that combination. I was so sure that holding therapy was our "cure," our "magic bullet," that I almost threw away my strongest ally, Bridget.

II

A FRIEND OF OURS called with news of a different kind of therapy: holding therapy. It's almost impossible to convey how quickly everything was happening. Robin began work, Bridget began work, I was reading *The Siege,* and I was first introduced to holding therapy and Dr. Welch, all within a two-week span of time, the last two weeks of February. Insights and reflections and decisions and revisions of decisions were toppling over one another, day by day, with dizzying speed.

Our friend mentioned a book by Niko and Elizabeth Tinbergen, *"Autistic" Children: New Hope for a Cure.* The Tinbergens were ethologists whose chief field of study had been birds, but they had become interested in autistic children and felt that there were many parallels between the bird behavior they had observed and autistic behavior in children.

The Tinbergens were scornful of the neurobiological research in autism that has gathered momentum in the last fifteen years, and dismissed it all in a few pages. Instead, they asserted, autism is an "anxiety-dominated emotional conflict," caused primarily by a failure of mother-child bonding in the first year or so of life, and most autistic symptoms were best understood as expressions of a fundamental "approach-avoidance" conflict: The child is caught between a strong desire to approach social interactions and new experiences, and an even stronger desire to avoid all such contact. Not properly bonded with his mother, he has no basis of security from which to make normal tentative sorties out into the world. The results are catastrophic. He becomes locked in an infantile state, somewhere between the ages of one and two years. Some infantile habits, like toe-walking or mouthing of objects, become formalized—so repetitive and obsessive that they assume permanence and ritualized status.

Armed with this approach-avoidance theory, the Tinbergens believed they had unlocked the mystery of autistic behaviors: For instance, they saw twirling as the first stage of approach succeeded by the first stage of avoidance/withdrawal. These motions are repeated over and over until the child is going around in circles. Rocking is similarly viewed as "a succession of intention approaches and intention withdrawals." Tapping objects is infantile exploratory touching, except that the autistic child does not dare to carry his exploration any further than a repetitive touch-withdraw, touch-withdraw. The curled-back fingers common to many autistic children is a frozen hand posture, illustrating both approach and withdrawal: the child wants to grasp, but dares not.

But what about the seizures that afflict some autistic children? Surely they are not willful approach attempts complicated by extreme anxiety. Yes they are, according to the Tinbergens. Most seizures can be understood as a "type of conflict behavior which is often due to strongly elicited but thwarted escape."

And the lack of speech? That was self-evident. Autistic children "refuse" to speak. They understand everything that is said and are perfectly capable of responding, but they dare not utter a word, so paralyzed are they by their terror.

On and on went the Tinbergens. The book was my first in-depth introduction to the psychogenic theory of autism. Bruno Bettelheim on the subject was yet to come.

But it was all very compelling to me! I believed that I had found the answer! Why? Wasn't this the same sort of fanciful unsubstantiated analysis for which I had previously professed a dismissive impatience? Was I not struck, even then, by the throwback to the tenacious ignorance of the bad old blame-the-mommy era?

None of that seemed to matter, suddenly.

The Tinbergens were talking about the only two things I wanted to hear: the first was a way of understanding my daughter, and the second was recovery—actually the word they used was "cure."

The idea of Anne-Marie as being almost paralyzed by fear was something that I could finally hold on to. It allowed me to make a kind of sense, for the first time, of many of her behaviors. I did think that a lot of her social avoidance had to do with fear, and I was ready to believe that all her other symptoms followed from that central one.

But even harder to resist was the Tinbergens' certainty about the possibility of recovery. The subtitle of their book was *New Hope for a Cure,* and their message was clear, unambiguous: You can "cure" autism by "rebonding" with the child. If a mother could succeed in this rebonding, she would reverse the downward spiral and the child would emerge from autism.

And how does she "rebond"? Through "holding therapy." The core of the Tinbergen book, the cure for autism, is holding therapy.

Martha Welch, a child psychiatrist, is the chief proponent of holding therapy in this country, and is the subject of much praise and discussion in the Tinbergen book. Dr. Welch's own paper on holding therapy appears in one of its appendixes.

Holding is to be done every day, an hour or more each day. The mother forcibly holds the child against her and lets the child know her true feelings, which could include the mother's own rage at being "rejected." Each holding ended when the mother had achieved a "resolution": when the child, molded to her body, looked at the mother, explored her face with his hands, and (theoretically) started talking to her.

The Tinbergen book was full of anecdotes about formerly autistic children and their miraculous cures through holding. I treasured those anecdotes. I read and reread them late into the night. I read them aloud to Marc. We agreed that if Dr. Lovaas was recovering some children, then recovery was possible, and maybe these Tinbergens had found an alternative way.

I didn't understand how forcibly bear-hugging anyone was able to result in emotional rebonding, but I willingly suspended all such logical questions. I skimmed over the parts in the book that harked back to the old psychodynamic excesses, and concentrated on the promise of a cure. Nothing could dampen my enthusiasm, my belief.

I explained the theory to my parents. Their response was a little too guarded for my taste. "Sounds interesting," said my mother.

Interesting? Didn't she understand that this was our miracle cure?

I read aloud passages to my sister Burke. "I don't believe that," she said flatly. "In what way didn't you 'bond' with Anne-Marie?"

Impatiently, I resolved not to try to explain to any of these doubting Thomases how a slightly flawed theory might possibly produce an effective therapy.

In any case, this mother-child bonding stuff was so much easier on the mind and heart than the behavior modification approach. I needed to believe that it was an assault of love that was going to save my daughter—my love alone—and not some rote and mechanistic training conducted by a stranger.

IF THE TINBERGEN book became my bible, Martha Welch became my high priestess: infallible, possessed of a higher insight into the souls of children.

"Hello, Dr. Welch? This is Catherine Maurice. My daughter has just been diagnosed as autistic and I was wondering if I could come over to see you. . . ."

"Take her to the Mothering Center in Connecticut. You'll find other mothers there who are doing holding therapy with their children."

"I don't want to do that. I need to talk to *you* about your work."

"I don't have the time right now. . . . How old did you say your daughter was?"

"She's almost two."

There was a pause. "All right. Bring her over."

Charming, charismatic, Dr. Welch was full of hugs and gentle spontaneous caresses. Without shyness or reserve, she would reach out to stroke my hair, or clasp my hand in hers, and then—disconcertingly for me—hold it there. Her office, a small room in her apartment on Fifth Avenue, was strewn with pillows on the floor and written messages on the walls from grateful clients. There was no receptionist, no paperwork other than a bill scribbled at the end of each session. She asked for no diagnosis, evaluation, or assessment of Anne-Marie.

"What a beautiful mommy Anne-Marie has," she murmured, smiling into my eyes, holding my gaze. And then, with a look of sadness: "What a terrible, terrible time this has been for you."

I felt the tears well up again, but this time I didn't try to hide them, not from this loving woman. How caring she was, how natural, unaffected, and how unbelievably concerned. I was reduced to a blob of jelly, all my angry defensiveness wafting away under this shower of warm sincerity.

As for Anne-Marie, of course she would recover! A thrill of exquisite hope ran through me. My breathing quickened.

"How do you know?" I asked Dr. Welch, almost in a whisper, hating myself for even posing such a cynical question, for even hinting that I doubted her.

"Oh, she looks like one of those smart ones."

Oh. OK. This Dr. Welch was very experienced. She obviously knew what she was talking about. I would ask her to explain what she meant . . . another time.

"How many children in your practice have recovered?" I thought it safe to venture that at least.

"Oh you . . . I can tell you're one of those people who are always into numbers and statistics. . . ."

Her warm smile as she said this belied any hint of criticism. Nevertheless, I dropped my eyes guiltily. It was true. I was always looking for the numbers and the data. I was so cold.

Dr. Welch was still gazing steadily at me and smiling reassuringly. "Anyway, to answer your question, I have about a fifty percent recovery rate. And I mean recovered! Talking! Thinking! Relating! Just like you and me!"

My heart leaped at her thrilling words. Oh God . . . I will do anything . . . anything. Just show me what to do, Dr. Welch.

"Let me show you a video of a holding. . . . You'll see a beautiful sight."

I watched the video of a mother doing a holding with a child. The child was quite verbal. "My hands! Let go my hands!" she screamed. After a few fast-forwards, the child now looked calmer and was telling her mother how beautiful the mother was.

"Yes," I concurred eagerly. "Yes, that looks very powerful, very moving . . . but . . . but tell me, how old is that child?"

"She's two."

"Two! . . . But she's talking! She's talking so well!"

Yes, Dr. Welch told me, she was quite advanced for her age.

"My God. Is she autistic? When was she diagnosed?"

"No, she's not autistic. I just wanted to show you a typical holding."

"I see," I said, but I felt slightly cheated. Why doesn't she show me a holding of an autistic child? That's what we're talking about, isn't it? I needed to hear an autistic child speaking that way, that normal self-assertive way. Quickly, I suppressed this overly critical line of thought. Well, she probably just doesn't have such a video right here, today.

"Next time you come, bring your husband. I'll see you on Monday."

"Of course. Thank you. Thank you so much."

As I left, Dr. Welch remembered that she had something she

wanted to show me. She came back to the door with an issue of *Life* magazine, and said that her work with an autistic child was featured in it, should I care to read it.

I did read it, with the faith of the newly converted. I was astounded, excited. The article described a young girl, Katy. She had been profoundly autistic as a child. Then she had met Dr. Welch, "the first person to treat me like a human being." The article asserted that under Dr. Welch's care, and through holding therapy, Katy was now beginning to "choose" the world of human contact over autism. Her progress had been so remarkable that she was now writing the most sophisticated and sensitive analyses of her own illness.

The statistics in the article were pretty terrifying, worse even than any Marc and I had read in the medical literature. And the article's allusion to behavior modification was none too reassuring:

> . . . the limited success that is achieved with either behavior modification or drug therapy . . . has led many to conclude that autism cannot be cured. With 95 percent of all autistic adults eventually requiring institutionalization, such a pessimistic view has not been unwarranted.

But through holding therapy, the article went on to say, Katy is breaking away from this bleak prognosis:

> . . . to judge from the progress of Katy—whose written eloquence redefines autism as a terrifying choice between safety and freedom—it [such a pessimistic view] seems premature.

I was thrilled to read these words. I was thrilled also to find a reiteration of that astonishingly high recovery rate: "Fifty percent of Welch's patients, she says, have managed to move into a normal life."

Fifty percent! Why, that was just as good as Lovaas was getting!

I immediately Xeroxed the article and sent it out to my mother. But when I spoke to her a few days later I was again disappointed in her response. She was so cautious, so reserving of judgment!

All right, so it wasn't *The New England Journal of Medicine!* Couldn't she see that this was how God was answering our prayers? She herself had told me many times that God worked in mysterious ways. Where was her faith?

And anyway, there were those scraps of paper, duplicated right there in the article, filled with Katy's mature and articulate poetry.

Marc's attitude toward the article was a bit like my mother's: neutral, reserved. Nevertheless, I did manage to persuade him to come along with me to my next meeting with Dr. Welch.

At that meeting, there was tension: Martha and I aligned in one theoretical corner, Marc in another, acutely uncomfortable with the whole idea of bonding and forced holding.

"Can you hold Catherine through anything she might say to you here?" asked Dr. Welch. "Can you listen to her feelings, and let her know your own feelings?"

In holding therapy, it is most important that everyone hold everyone else, or there can be no cure. Mother must hold child, father must hold mother, grandmother must hold mother, mother must hold father. If any person along the line doesn't give the proper support, the cure is seriously jeopardized.

"Anything she might say? Like what?" asked Marc.

What could Martha have in mind? I too wondered. I was nervous and fearful. I had to do this right. I had to show that I could be cooperative and good. If I confessed a grave enough sin, then I could redeem myself and get my daughter back.

"You remember, Marc?" I said, turning to him. "When Anne-Marie was born I said to you that I was worried that I could never love another baby as much as Daniel?"

"Yes? So what?" began Marc.

"Can you hold her when she tells you something like that?" interrupted Martha.

Marc complied, awkwardly. He wasn't exactly used to embracing his wife as part of a performance. I felt so torn. I knew how uncomfortable he was. He was such a private person, and here I was, making him discuss "feelings" and "bonding" with a complete stranger. Was this right?

Marc went on. "A lot of women feel that way about their second children. You said you talked to your sister Jean about it and she said that she'd gone through the same adjustment when Rebecca was born. It doesn't mean that Anne-Marie was loved any less than Daniel."

These children are so very sensitive, Martha told us. One has to be so careful, so very careful, around them. One of the autistic children she was working with had confided to her that she (the child) had overheard her parents' conversation about her when she was still in the womb! She had been deeply wounded by what she heard, and had become autistic.

"I don't believe a newborn baby can read her mother's mind! Or an unborn baby can understand speech!" protested Marc.

"What does Catherine say?" asked Martha calmly, turning to smile at me.

I was miserable. I didn't want Marc to argue with our savior. I *wanted* Anne-Marie's autism to be the result of nonbonding. That way I could do something about it. Maybe I *was* too intellectual and cold and had rejected too precipitately the psychoanalytical approach. Maybe I *hadn't* bonded properly with Anne-Marie when she was a baby. "I don't know," I said. "Maybe I didn't pay as much attention to her as I did to Daniel."

"I don't believe you were in any way neglectful of Anne-Marie," said Marc again, flatly. "I was there. I saw you get up in the middle of the night. I saw you hold her and sing to her. . . ." He stopped, frustrated.

He asked Dr. Welch for some documentation of her recoveries, some data to prove the effectiveness of her approach. After all, he told her, we had to decide between this and the Lovaas method, which had numbers and statistics all over the place.

"Oh, you." She laughed again. Again we got that gentle, affectionate teasing about our need for numbers. Dr. Welch, who was seated on a pile of pillows on the floor, leaned forward to clasp Marc's hand in hers as she explained that she was not a researcher. She was a doctor, and if other people wanted to keep data and records on her work, that was fine with her, but that was not her focus right now. She had to concentrate on these children, these poor children and their suffering parents.

Even Marc was disarmed, a little taken aback. We were both wondering at this point if our overintellectualizing of things might not indeed be at the root of Anne-Marie's problems. We didn't push the question very aggressively. It was such a fragile, impossible thing to have a psychiatrist talking about the possibility of recovery. We scarcely wanted to start any strenuous grilling and probing.

As to behavior modification, Dr. Welch was adamant. She was vehemently opposed to any stranger coming into our home and subjecting our daughter to this cold treatment. How on earth could I rebond with Anne-Marie if I sent her off to be mistreated by a stranger?

Weakly, we tried to defend the Lovaas experiment.

Well, said Dr. Welch, we really shouldn't ask her; she didn't know enough about that experiment. It was just that she had heard that those children were not truly recovered. In fact, she'd heard that they were functioning like high-level robots.

Dr. Welch's words carried tremendous emotional weight for me. Anne-Marie, she said, was only two years old, just a baby really. The only person she needed and wanted now was her mommy. Yes, yes, I thought, with a stab of pity for my little girl. "Just hold her" was Dr. Welch's repeated and insistent message. Just hold her and rebond with her and all else—all else—will follow. The only type of therapy she would allow—already she was speaking in strong authoritative tones— was some gentle play therapy, just because she knew that I could not spend every minute of every day with Anne-Marie. And be careful about Patsy, she warned me. Many of the mothers under her care relied too heavily on baby-sitters and nannies to take care of their child. Mommy was what Anne-Marie needed. Mommy to hold her. Mommy to bond with her. "Stick to her like glue," she enjoined, with the utmost gravity.

"But Martha!" I protested. "What about all the mothers I know who go to work and leave their kids with nannies all day long?"

"I know. Isn't it unfair?" she cried. "That must hurt you so much."

Well . . . yes. I guess I did feel hurt about that, but that was not exactly the point I was trying to make. I was trying to say something about how their kids seemed to be doing fine—well, never mind. I wasn't going to argue too strenuously about anything. I didn't want to jeopardize our chance at recovery. I was half in love with Dr. Welch. She had shown me another of the poems that the little girl Katy had written about her, and I was dumbstruck before the lucid, mature writing, the creative imagery, the words of love and praise for Dr. Welch. Here is *proof,* I thought. Here is a formerly autistic child's testimonial to her loving healer, her miracle worker.

"I believe that given your state of mind you should come to see me at least twice a week," she announced.

Yes. Of course. Anything you say. Anything.

Never had I met anyone who exuded such complete understanding, acceptance, and caring. She seemed so selfless, so truly concerned— with Anne-Marie, and with me. Whatever skepticism or hostility I threw at her in the beginning, she met with complete charm and disarming grace. She greeted my arguments (my feeble attempts to be objective about all this) not just with tolerance, not just with sympathy, but with outright flattery: Over and over I heard how smart I was to articulate so well all these doubts. How fascinating it was discussing

the complex interaction of biology and psychology with such an insightful person as myself. Flattery, and an absolute assurance that there
was only one end to our journey: Anne-Marie's complete recovery.

In contrast to the mainstream professional community, whose members could often convey an attitude not only of cool condescension but
also of resigned hopelessness, Martha Welch was an oasis of loving-
kindness. And, to dispel any possible residual doubts, my first holding
sessions seemed to work, if not perfectly, enough to lend credibility to
the Tinbergen-Welch hypothesis.

I began practicing holding therapy after my first meeting with Dr.
Welch. In the morning, while Daniel was in play school and Patsy
tended to Michel, I would take Anne-Marie into my room. There, I
would place her on my lap and hold her, her arms under mine, chest-
to-chest, face-to-face. I would hold her head so that she had to look at
me, and even though she kept averting her eyes I still persisted. "Look
at me, Anne-Marie! Look at me! Mommy loves you. Don't turn your
face away. Please, baby, Mommy needs you. Look at me." Ten minutes would pass. Fifteen. She began to struggle in earnest. Then she
would start to cry and lash out. If she could free her hands she would
go for my face. By the end of the first two weeks I had scratches over
my cheeks, forehead, and nose. A couple of times she succeeded in
biting me.

Our holding sessions lasted anywhere from a half hour to one three-
hour marathon session. The usual time was about an hour. During
holding, the mother is supposed to vent all her own rage and frustration on her child, but I never could bring myself to go that far. No
matter how often Dr. Welch assured me that Anne-Marie understood
everything I said to her, I couldn't bring myself to pour out my adult
angst into the ears of a two-year-old and feign an anger at her that I
didn't feel. Already, in physically forcing Anne-Marie into this close
embrace, I was at the limit of my own tolerance level.

After about thirty to forty minutes of strenuous struggling on both
our parts, usually both Anne-Marie and I would be reduced to frustrated tears. I was supposed to get a "resolution"—why wasn't one
occurring? It was taking forever.

After two or three unsuccessful attempts at achieving resolution, I
decided to make my own happen. When Anne-Marie had raged and
scratched and sobbed for a while, I began to change my tune. Instead
of the chest-to-chest restraining position, I would try to hold and cradle her more like a baby, across my lap, with her head in the crook of

my elbow. Then, instead of insistently commanding her to "Look at me!" I began to rock her, stroke her hair, and murmur endearments: "I love you, baby. I need you. Please look at Mommy." She seemed to grow calmer and quieter. I began to sing to her. For some reason I latched onto Bach's cantata "Sheep safely graze," and although my voice is neither strong nor sure, I would sing it to her over and over again. It became our anthem of hope.

> *Sheep safely graze where God is abiding;*
> *All his lambs he doth protect.*

Sometimes, when I sang this song to her, she would lie still and listen; and although she would not then or for many weeks afterward gaze at me, she would at least relax her body a little against mine, and not try so frantically to push me away.

And then, when I put her down finally, off she would run, obviously eager to get away. But—wonder of wonders—for the next hour or so she would indeed seem more alert. More in tune with her environment. She seemed more aware of me and other people, and would even glance up sometimes when I called her name.

I was hooked on holding therapy. This was the answer to my prayers, my miracle cure. God had led me to Dr. Martha Welch, who was going to teach *me* how to rescue *my* daughter from autism.

12

SO HERE WE WERE, just at the end of February, and the therapeutic program was officially launched.

Not that Marc and I were all that clear on what we were doing.

We had hired Bridget, but we distrusted both her and behavior modification. "I don't like it, Marc. I don't like giving her to Bridget. She's too harsh with Anne-Marie. I can't see treating a two-year-old like that."

"Give her a few more days. She just started. Maybe Anne-Marie will get more used to the drills."

We had hired Robin, and that was OK. There were no problems with the speech therapy. We only wished we could have more hours.

And we had contacted Dr. Welch and begun holding therapy.

"It's so much more natural that a mother should make the connection with her child, isn't it, Marc? This is the way to go after Anne-Marie. This is how we're going to get through to her. This makes more sense."

We were having dinner, and I could barely eat, I was so intent on making my point.

"More sense than what?" asked Marc.

"Than giving her over to a total stranger!"

"Do you see anything happening with holding therapy?"

"Yes. I really think so." Or maybe not, I thought with a flash of misery. Maybe I was making it up, because I wanted so much to believe. But no. There really was a difference in her after a holding.

"She looks at me more when it's over. She seems more alert. She seems more . . . awake and in tune, I guess."

"I trust your judgment, Catherine. If you think holding therapy is doing something, you're probably right."

"I do. And I'm crazy about Martha Welch." I knew Marc didn't share my feelings about Dr. Welch, and that was all right with me: I wanted him to form his own opinions about what was going on. I needed his objectivity. But I also needed his understanding. "I get such comfort from her, such hope. I really trust her, Marc."

Marc put down his fork and touched my hand. His face held only love. "If she's helping you, that's enough for me. I feel so helpless when I see you crying every night."

"She wants me to come in twice a week to her office, with Anne-Marie."

Whatever I needed, Marc assured me. Just do what I thought was best for Anne-Marie and for myself.

Bridget began the behavioral program under adverse circumstances, to say the least. Not only did I distrust her and her program, but I had fallen in love with a psychiatrist who informed me in no uncertain terms that behavioral intervention would be psychologically damaging to the "rebonding" process.

I remember the second week that Bridget came to work. Anne-Marie and I had just returned from Dr. Welch's office, and we were finishing lunch at the kitchen table. Bridget knocked and I let her in.

"Hi," she said.

"Hello."

Neither one of us smiled. "Come in," I said. "We're finishing lunch. Sit down."

Bridget sat down, a little reluctantly, I thought.

"We've just come back from Dr. Welch's office," I informed Bridget. I had already briefly described to her the Tinbergen book, holding therapy, and Dr. Welch.

"Oh? How was that?"

"Wonderful. We talked about some of her recovered kids. Do you want to see the *Life* magazine article on that girl I told you about?"

"OK . . . sure."

I went to get the article, then sat down at the table again, prepared to chat on about the miracle of holding therapy. "Do you want some coffee?" I asked Bridget.

She looked at her watch. "I'd really like to start working with Anne-Marie now."

"When she's finished lunch," I said, with some irritation. *I* will decide when Anne-Marie goes into that room, I thought angrily.

In silence, Anne-Marie and I finished our meal; then I carried her into the torture room. Once again, as soon as we sat her down in the chair, she began to sob and fall to the floor.

Bridget set out her toys, notebooks, and reinforcers. Without missing a beat, she picked Anne-Marie up, put her back into the chair, and pulled her hands away from her face. "Look at me," she commanded, and they were off for another two hours of no-nonsense work.

For those first few sessions, I wouldn't even stay to observe for more than a few minutes, partly because I hated watching the drills, partly because Anne-Marie's crying seemed to increase whenever I was there. I would usually just prowl around the apartment, furious with Bridget for being such a cold, mean, manipulative person.

My sessions with Dr. Welch, on the contrary, continued to be warm and reassuring. Anne-Marie and I visited her together, twice a week. There was no formality, no structure. We came in and sat down on the pillows or on the couch, and I would talk to Dr. Welch about my feelings while Anne-Marie played with some blocks on the floor. I had accepted the notion that Dr. Welch's role was primarily to hold me together, so that I in turn could have the emotional strength to pursue Anne-Marie, even in the face of her "rejection" of me. To that end, the discussion of my grief and anxiety was legitimate and logical.

I talked to Dr. Welch a lot about how the holdings were going. I described my frustration at never seeming to get a clear "resolution," and my excitement at what I felt was an increased level of alertness in Anne-Marie after each holding.

I talked to her a little about the behavioral program as well. Not a lot, because, in spite of my hostility toward Bridget, I wasn't quite prepared to let go of her. I didn't want to hear Dr. Welch attack her, or tell me again to stop that part of Anne-Marie's therapy—not just yet.

So when I did discuss behavioral therapy with Dr. Welch, I mostly talked about Dr. Lovaas's *The Me Book* and the videotapes illustrating his teaching method. I brought her one of the videotapes, and we talked about how dehumanizing and repulsive some of the images were.

From the beginning, I let her know as well of my difficulties with the theoretical underpinnings of holding therapy. One day I decided to risk a little aggressiveness and told her that I thought this "failure to bond" business was just another blame-the-mother theory and I didn't buy it.

"You're absolutely right!" she agreed. "It's not the mother's fault at all!"

Nothing I said could offend or fluster her. She was accommodating, conciliatory, admiring. And unfailingly reassuring about Anne-Marie's future. She told me about some of the other families she had worked for and the warm relationships she had developed with the children whom she had recovered from autism. In deep gratitude for her inspiration, and for her loving tolerance of my skepticism, I decided to repay her: I would reformulate the theoretical basis of holding therapy, and render it more plausible, at least for me.

"I think I understand something about holding therapy," I said to Marc one evening. "Listen. The Tinbergens and Martha posit that a failure to bond causes autistic withdrawal. And they are partly correct; they have uncovered part of a truth. They're only wrong in that they blame it on the mother. But failure to bond is not the mother's fault. It's the primary symptom of autism. Its source is neurobiological, chemical, whatever. The child is born with that deficit, that lack, and the other autistic symptoms follow from that central one."

"Yes. That could make sense."

"So then, you see, if you can rebond—or rather, bond for the first time—with the child, you can save her."

"Maybe," said Marc. "I'm just glad to see you so much better these days."

I explained my theory to Dr. Welch.

"Of course you're right. Of course no one is blaming mothers. How intelligent of you to see that subtle distinction."

That's right. No one is blaming mothers. This isn't something I did.

She wasn't blaming mothers, Dr. Welch assured me each time I brought up some point that had been bothering me in the Tinbergen book; she simply felt that it was mothers who were in the best position to rescue their children from autism.

Sometimes Dr. Welch would instruct me to do a holding with Anne-Marie in her office.

"You're too polite! Too civilized!" she would say. "How can she know how you *feel*, when you talk to her in such a sweet tone?"

"She doesn't understand what I'm saying."

"Of course she understands! Let her know how hurt you are. Let her know how angry you are."

"I'm not angry at her."

"Yes you are. Look deep down. Aren't you angry that she doesn't look at you, that she doesn't smile at you? Aren't you angry that she never says 'Mama'? Aren't you?"

"OK, you're right. Maybe I am angry. But not at her. It's not her fault. She can't talk."

"Stop telling her she can't talk! Don't you think she hears you? Don't you think she's hurt when you say things like that?"

"I don't know. . . . I just don't know! I don't understand what she feels or thinks!"

I held Anne-Marie and tried to obey Dr. Welch. Maybe she was right. How did I know that she wasn't right? Wouldn't it be wonderful if Anne-Marie *did* understand?

"Anne-Marie. Anne-Marie. I want you to look at me. Why don't you talk to me? Mommy's hurt. Mommy loves you."

Beside me on the couch, Dr. Welch crooned away: "Angry Anne-Marie. Scared Anne-Marie. Lonely Anne-Marie."

In Dr. Welch's presence, I was exhilarated with hopefulness, inspired to believe in Anne-Marie's potential, yet at the same time plagued by nagging guilt. One day in her office, when Marc was there as well as Anne-Marie, I was holding baby Michel in my arms, and trying to talk to Anne-Marie as Dr. Welch had instructed me.

"Look at Michel!" she interrupted urgently. "Don't you see that he's looking at you?"

I looked down at Michel. His dark eyes were fixed searchingly on my face. I felt almost panicked. "Hi, sweetheart," I murmured. "Mommy's here. I love you." I heard my own voice, sounding high and tight with nervousness.

"Be very, very careful," warned Dr. Welch sternly. "Never forget that he needs you too."

"I look at him and hold him a lot! I was just paying attention to Anne-Marie at that moment."

"I know that. You know that. But does a baby understand that? Does a baby understand that when his mother turns away, or doesn't meet his look, she's not rejecting him? You just never know how a baby can interpret a mother's actions."

I felt a flash of anger at Dr. Welch, extinguished immediately by fearful guilt. Don't do to Michel what you did to Anne-Marie, intoned that unforgiving voice in my head.

"I come from a family of five children; you come from a family of ten," Marc said later that evening. "Do you really think, Catherine, that our mothers gave us undivided attention all day long?"

"I know, Marc. I know a lot of this sounds extreme. But there may be a core of truth in it. It may be that some kids are born with just that much more sensitivity or vulnerability. A kind of predisposition to withdrawal."

Marc was silent.

"Do you mind," he said after a few minutes, "if I don't go with you to Dr. Welch's office anymore? She makes me really uncomfortable."

"No. I don't mind."

During the holdings that I did at Dr. Welch's office, Anne-Marie's reactions were not very promising. Most of the time she would whine and twist her body away. But the holdings at home were going somewhat better. I never achieved a "resolution," such as was described in the Tinbergen book—Anne-Marie never started suddenly looking at me and stroking my face and talking to me, etc., etc. But when she did relax in my arms, when she did make slightly more sustained eye contact, I was convinced that a kind of resolution was happening. Somehow she was becoming more responsive, more awake.

For the first two weeks of our combination therapy program, I woke up every morning telling myself that this was the day I would fire Bridget.

Finally, I decided to take action. Marc had assured me repeatedly that he trusted my decisions and my judgment. It was time that I did something to resolve this dreadful conflict. One day, after Bridget's session with Anne-Marie, I asked her to sit down for a few minutes.

"Bridget," I said to her, "I don't know if I should go on with this behavioral program. Martha feels strongly that it will damage the rebonding process." I was not happy saying this. Whatever animosity I may have felt toward Bridget and her methods, I did recognize that she had made her own commitment to Anne-Marie, and I was now suggesting that she pull out just as she had begun the battle.

But she did not protest. "You have to do what you need to, Catherine. It's your child. It's your decision."

I dropped my eyes. I hadn't expected such a professional, controlled response.

My gaze fell on the toys she had brought with her and laid around the room. Many were obviously new. Had she bought these for Anne-Marie and paid for them out of her own pocket?

"You've bought all these toys," I muttered.

Bridget spoke very clearly: "That is not a consideration. You have to feel comfortable with this program. You should not be thinking about these toys, or my feelings, or anything except what is best for Anne-Marie."

I looked at the notes in my hand. After every session, Bridget gave me the session notes and the data sheets. Every drill was described, the type and frequency of every autistic behavior was noted, Anne-Marie's performance in every discrete trial was scrupulously recorded. I thought of that parade of woefully inexperienced students I had interviewed and suddenly was not too certain that I was making the right decision. As a matter of fact, this might very well be the wrong decision. There was a cry of anguished confusion building and building in me. If only I could lay my head on someone's shoulder, someone I trusted, and give it all over: "What do I do?" I wanted to sob. "Please tell me what is the right thing to do!"

"I'll call you later," I said to Bridget.

That evening, after the children were in bed, I went to Marc.

"Should we stop the behavioral program? Martha thinks it's harmful to Anne-Marie."

Marc sat down at the kitchen table. He sighed and was quiet for a while.

"No," he said. "I don't think so." He got up and left the room, then came back after a moment with the Lovaas article from the professional journal. "Look," he said, "I don't understand what causes autism. I don't think anyone does yet, including the Tinbergens and Martha. But I do understand numbers. These numbers are good. They hold together."

Marc stopped. He wasn't really sure of himself either. He too had wondered if he was an overly intellectual, overly analytical person who had somehow contributed to, if not caused, Anne-Marie's withdrawal. Helpless before his daughter's condition, and knowing how desperately I was clinging to Dr. Welch, he hadn't wanted to say anything negative about her. In spite of his French reserve, he had consented to have his privacy violated, his marriage analyzed, his feelings probed by a stranger. But he wasn't going to be pushed too far. He wasn't going to walk completely away from reality as he knew it.

"This guy," Marc went on, putting his hand on the Lovaas article, "constructed a well-designed experiment. He had two control groups. He had independent intake evaluations and independent follow-up assessments. His control groups and his experimental group were matched for everything you could think of. He shows how he arrived at his results, and his results are good. No. They're more than good. They're great."

I was silent.

"I know how much you're relying on Martha, and I do believe holding therapy is doing something for Anne-Marie," he said. "But I don't want to pin all our hopes on holding therapy alone. Let's give Bridget and Lovaas's method a chance."

I put my head in my hands. I was so confused. Everything had happened so fast. Beliefs I thought I had held—that family privacy is important, that a lot of psychoanalysis is silly, that I was essentially a good mother—were dissolving and drifting away. Ideas of what was right and what was wrong for Anne-Marie kept shifting around, tumbling together in a scrambled blur.

Behavior modification was theoretically at antipodes to holding therapy. Who was right? Some madman out in California who tortured kids into robotic compliance, or Martha Welch, whose lovely message was that a mother's love alone (under Martha's guidance) could work miracles? My heart was telling me to follow Dr. Welch's direction, whether or not that entailed an admission that I had somehow failed to bond with Anne-Marie. My head was telling me to go with the Lovaas method, yet I hated to think that I could harm Anne-Marie emotionally by turning her over to Bridget.

I looked at the article Marc had placed before me. I looked up at him and remembered something. Something incongruous with the present moment, yet perhaps not. I remembered one of the reasons why I had fallen in love with him:

Marc had taught me that truth could be found not just in poetry, or prayer, or the heavens; but also in science, in nature, and in numbers. He was a logical thinker who calmly clung to facts even while surrounded by shrill ideologues of every political persuasion. He assuaged my thirst for the real—the thirst of one who had spent a lifetime in the realm of the ideal. He completed me, who hadn't even known how incomplete I was before he came into my life.

I looked at him, my fellow wanderer in this darkness. He was as lost as I was, as frightened and as uncertain. Yet he was making a decision. We would not turn back on a journey we had just commenced; we would not abandon the behavioral program.

I put my hand into his. He had trusted all my decisions thus far; I would trust his now.

"You're right," I said. "We'll only know in time, won't we? Maybe we'll keep Bridget on for now, and just see how it goes."

Whatever tension and confusion had been generated by this rapid decision-making process, whatever fear we tasted daily over the possibility of taking the wrong direction, we had somehow at least stumbled onto a path. Where it would lead we didn't know just yet. But we were very soon to find out. Anne-Marie was about to take her first tentative steps toward health.

13

"LOOK AT ME!"

All of us—Bridget in the behavioral drills, Robin through her vibrant, joyful pursuit of Anne-Marie, I in the holding therapy sessions, Marc when he was home on weekends—began demanding her gaze.

Since she didn't acknowledge our comings and goings, we went over, knelt on the floor within her field of vision, and, hands cupping her face, twelve inches from her eyes, forced her to notice us:

"Hi, Anne-Marie, I'm back."

"Anne-Marie, Daddy's going."

"Anne-Marie, look: Daniel's home."

"Patsy's here."

"Bridget's leaving."

"Robin's at the door."

We wouldn't desist until there was some spark, some acknowledgment, however fleeting, that someone was talking to her.

It was her gaze that came back first.

The thrill of watching those stirrings of a self can be compared in intensity only to the terror of losing her. She began to wake up to us and to the world. Each sign of this awakening was so powerful an experience for her father and me as to be almost wrenching.

I was walking up the street with her, on my way to pick up Daniel from nursery school. It was a mere two weeks after starting our combination program. We were on Fifth Avenue, just in front of the Metropolitan Museum. The fountains were turned on, sending jets of water up against the sunny winter sky of early March. Anne-Marie was riding in her stroller, silent and contained, as usual. But this time, she glanced over at the splashing water, already an improvement from her usual state of indifference to everything around her.

Then, suddenly, unbelievably, she stretched out her hand, pointed to the water, and turned around to look at me!

I was thrilled.

"Yes, water!" I practically yelled, laughing with delight. "What a good girl! Good showing Mommy the water!"

Passersby looked at me with some alarm as we stood and gave joyful homage to this lovely part of lovely creation. Thank you for this water, God. Thank you for bringing Anne-Marie to see and share this white and playful water!

She continued to look at me, a half-smile on her lips, her eyes wide and alert. Her hand was held out toward the water, her eyes were turned to me, inquisitively. No words could have been more eloquent: Do you see what I see, Mommy? Will you share this beauty with me? I felt as though I had looked into those clear blue eyes and seen, suddenly, unmistakably, hope made real. I had seen my baby girl look back at me. I knelt down beside her, took her face into my hands, and laid my cheek against hers. "That's water, my love, a fountain of water," I choked out, trying to hold together. Then I practically ran up to Daniel's school, so filled with happiness and hope that I couldn't stop grinning.

Whatever the inherent theoretical contradictions among the three therapies, Bridget and Robin and I had somehow managed to find at least one common goal: we were mounting, each in a different way, an invasion of Anne-Marie's world, a forcible disruption of her self-imposed isolation. In this respect, Robin was the gentlest of the invaders, but through highly focused skill and energy, she too was managing to draw Anne-Marie little by little out of her solitude.

As my own sense of purpose grew, I permitted Anne-Marie no quarter during the day. I was "on her case" constantly, bothering her, not letting her be. I set aside my sorrowful longing to have her just return to me of her own accord, and instead adopted a more tyrannical stance.

Whether inspired by *The Siege,* or holding therapy, or Bridget's behavioral approach, or all three, one central idea had crystallized for me:

My will, not yours, shall prevail here, little one.

By early March, I permitted no self-stimulatory behavior. If I saw her doing anything bizarre I would pick her up, take her someplace else, and, like Bridget, physically prompt her through more appropriate play. Often she would whine and resist, but I kept pressing her. Even her faraway, dreamy look was pounced on. It was too frightening to me. If I saw that spaced-out look in her eyes, I would do anything to snap her out of it: laugh and sing, become a clown, throw her up in the air a few times.

The physicality of this intervention was paramount. It did no good to sit six feet away from her and call, "Anne-Marie, what are you doing? Look at Mommy." No. I had to physically come into her space, by taking her on my knees, or sitting next to her with my arms around her, guiding her hands, or, very often, just carrying her around to try to make her pay attention to me and to the world.

Within the limits of the humanly possible, she was to have no prolonged period alone. "Prolonged" meant any more than a half hour, and "alone" meant not actively involved, somehow, with a person.

One-on-one interaction became the cornerstone of everything we did. I moved her crib into Daniel's bedroom, so that now, even at night, she would not be alone. When she was not in therapy she was with me and when she was not with me, she was with her father. To Patsy I turned over more and more of the running of the household, needing to conserve all my available time and energy for the three children.

Day by day we grew more relentlessly demanding of her. No gazing into space, no teeth grinding, no playing with her hands, no manneristic touching of surfaces, no *anything* that looked autistic. Since these behaviors were not as "locked in" as those of some older autistic children, it was not as difficult as it might have been to keep distracting her and redirecting her attention from inward to outward.

It was constant work, but our work yielded swift and sweet reward. Those bright and communicative glances were at first sporadic, then they gradually grew more frequent and reliable. My parents hadn't seen her since Christmas, just after her first diagnosis. She had at that time ignored them completely. But one day in March part of my numerous family had gathered for Sunday dinner at my sister Debbie's house in Oyster Bay. Anne-Marie came into the large gathering with some trepidation. I was expecting her usual tears and whimpering, or blank indifference. Instead, she hesitated at the threshold of Debbie's living room, surveying the scene of aunts, uncles, and children.

Seated on the couch were Grandma and Grandpa. Slowly, gazing straight into their eyes, she began to move toward them, recognition clearly in her gaze. "Hello, Anne-Marie," they both called gently, smiling back at her.

In everyone who was working with Anne-Marie there was this same paradoxical gentleness each time she reached out in any way to us. Paradoxical, because our own moves to her were becoming more and more forceful and intrusive and no-nonsense. But each time she, of her own volition, made one of those early tentative gestures outward toward the world, we instinctively responded with an outpouring of tenderness. There was something so fragile about Anne-Marie. Her self-in-bloom was so fearful. Perhaps one of the ways I can explain this for now is to say that we were murderously tough on her autistic self, but tried to handle the developing Anne-Marie self with infinite care, as one would handle a newborn.

From looking at family members and friends, she progressed to looking even at strangers. People had often made friendly overtures to Anne-Marie, as generally happens with a young child: "Hi, pretty girl!" "Bye-bye, sweetheart!" "Hello, big eyes!" Her response had always been to turn her face away in stony silence, or worse, to stare absently into space. As we walked into an optometrist's store one afternoon, the woman behind the counter came forward to greet us. "Oh, what a cutie!" she said. "Hello, little girl!"

Anne-Marie smiled shyly, tucking her head into my neck but continuing to gaze at the woman.

"She's looking at you! She's smiling!" I cried.

The woman looked at me oddly.

"Of course she's smiling. So why shouldn't she smile?" she asked with Brooklynese incredulity. Probably she was thinking: These yuppie mothers! They're so pathologically competitive about everything they even keep tabs on how often their toddlers smile!

One morning I woke to a sound—not a new sound, but one that I hadn't heard for many months: Anne-Marie babbling in her crib. I listened for a moment, scarcely believing. Then I rose, walked into her room, and sleepily embraced her.

"Good morning, love."

No response, no smile. Not yet. But that would come, I now believed. At least she graced me with a look, which I accepted for the gift it was. "Love you, sweetheart. Proud of you," I whispered into her fragrant hair. "Keep fighting, baby. You're going to make it." Her arms did not wrap round my neck, but she stood still in her crib, allowing, even seeming to want, the close embrace.

Two or three weeks into the therapy, I noticed that she put a train on the track and pushed it along. This was one of the first spontaneous indications of anything resembling normal play. A few days later, she began to imitate some common activities she had seen around the house. Just little things, like pushing the vacuum along the floor, or once even using a paper towel to wipe off the table. One evening at bath-time she did something she had seen me do many times. She picked up a bowl of water and tried to pour it over Daniel's head, in imitation of a shampoo. In all of these gestures, I thought that she was displaying more awareness of us, of our gestures and habits. Like a normal two-year-old, she had rather suddenly begun to imitate us—not to a normal extent, of course, but still, imitation was emerging.

Throughout most of that first full month of therapy, I was still distrustful of the behavioral program. I still thought it might very well be emotionally damaging to Anne-Marie, and it still seemed, even at best, far inferior to holding therapy.

Besides, Anne-Marie began to say some words, and neither Bridget nor Robin had taught them to her.

Bits and pieces of her language, both spoken language and understanding of language, began to emerge on their own. Every few days she would suddenly demonstrate understanding of a phrase or sentence that no one had taught her or practiced with her. And every few days she would say a word that we hadn't heard for months. I have no idea what was going on neurologically. It seemed as though somehow certain words and phrases had been stored somewhere, intact, and, as she got back on track, so to speak, and began to develop more normally, these words resurfaced to her consciousness. Some of the first to reappear in Anne-Marie's expressive vocabulary, as a matter of fact, were those she had had at fifteen months, those that had gradually died out as her second year progressed.

One of the earliest of these untaught words to reappear was "bye-bye," although the first time she said it again she mouthed it only, instead of saying it aloud. Still, "bye-bye" formed her lips, as her little hand hesitantly rose up to wave at her father.

Day after day, other words came back: "Ba-ba," "ju" (juice), "kee" (cookie). Every day I kept track of her words. I hung on to them like some kind of lifeline. If she said only two words one day, I was depressed and fearful. If she made it to five, I was elated.

I admit today to not understanding this phenomenon of flashes of understanding and expression; back then, I "knew" just what was happening. She was "rebonding" with me, and somehow her emotional rebonding was causing these cognitive leaps. How else would she be learning things, picking up new understanding and new words, outside of the formal therapy sessions?

I was prepared to let Bridget have her chance with Anne-Marie, but I was by no means ready to concede her much importance in this therapeutic program. Nothing that Bridget or Robin was doing was as essential as what *I* was doing through holding therapy. I was convinced of that. These words, this eye contact, this increased attentiveness— they were all due mainly to *my* intervention, not to theirs. I made certain that Dr. Welch knew of each step forward and assured her that in my opinion holding therapy occupied the most crucial position in our combination approach. Modestly, Dr. Welch accepted the credit as her due, occasionally teasing me about my initial doubts.

NEW WORDS too were beginning to come in. "More" was one of the first, which was to be expected, since Robin was working on it in every session. "Open" and "help" were two other early arrivals, as both therapists were targeting these functional verbs. But other new words began to appear outside of therapy as well. One day, while putting some toys away under the television cabinet, I heard Anne-Marie get up from the floor where she was sitting and begin to walk toward me. "Seh-seh-seh?" I heard her say. I turned.

"What, Anne-Marie? What did you say?"

"Seh-seh-seh?"

Her gaze shifted from me to the television, then back again, an expectant look in her face.

"Sesame Street!"

Wonderful! A new word! Eye contact! A request!

Hastily, I flicked through the channels, happy to grant her wish. Fortunately, the show was on. I let her watch it often after that. She had of course seen "Sesame Street" before, but she had always stared at it stonily, so I never knew whether she enjoyed it or not. Then, after her diagnosis, I had banned all cartoons and video-watching, fearing that they reinforced her spaced-out semisomnolence. But here she was asking for a specific program, and I was only too happy to oblige.

"It's working, Marc. Holding therapy is really working. I just can't believe it!"

I4

MY RELATIONSHIP with Bridget hung by a very slender thread throughout the first three weeks of March.

Fortunately, there had been some outside support for our tentative decision to retain her. Both Dr. Cohen, of the Institute for Basic Research, and Steven Blaustein, the speech-language pathologist who had recommended Robin Rosenthal, had told us that all the data consistently supported a behavioral approach to autism. And, as we continued our reading and telephoning and researching, we were finding more professionals who supported this approach. They tended to be the people who actually worked with children, rather than merely theorizing about them. They did not as a rule come from New York City, apparently a mecca for all diehard Freudians. We found that several of the more respected programs in New Jersey and Long Island had been using behavior modification for years, and were even now beginning pilot programs to try to duplicate the intensity and success of the Lovaas approach. Thank God for a few voices of reason in the wilderness.

But a battalion of psychiatrists all chanting "Behavioral therapy is the way to go" would not have convinced us, me in particular, that this method might be beneficial for Anne-Marie. What did convince me, finally, was watching Bridget work, day after day.

Once having committed myself to giving her method a try, I began to sit in more and more on her sessions. As each one unfolded, and as March turned into April, my suspicion and distrust started to melt away, to be replaced by a grudging respect. Maybe, just maybe, I might have been wrong about Bridget. Not that anything she was doing was as important as holding therapy, I continued to believe, but still, Anne-Marie was responding far better to the programs than I had dreamed possible.

Anne-Marie's crying had now diminished to a few token whines of resistance. In its place, Bridget was managing to obtain and sustain in Anne-Marie a state of alert and cooperative attention that to me was nothing short of astonishing.

How did she do it? I watched her, and I learned. Some instinct in me—some grace of God—was telling me to sit up, to keep quiet, and to pay attention, and what I saw impressed me not a little.

Bridget, more than anyone else, taught me that it was possible to be firm and demanding without being harsh. I saw, as I observed her day after day, that she could be rock-hard, *intractable* with a crying child, yet never let anger or even the pretense of anger become the dominant message. Nor did she dissolve into frightened distress herself.

I have since watched more than one autistic child who is being intruded upon, or forced to do something he doesn't want to do. It is a frightening and painful experience. He may quiver with silent panicky terror, or roll around on the floor in a screaming tantrum of rage. It's pretty easy to lose your cool. One wants above all else to rush in and soothe and love and comfort him. Or rather to *not* rush in, but to back off and promise never, never to disturb him like that again. It demands courage and training and self-awareness, all of which Bridget had, to take that step over the threshold and to say in effect, "I will intrude on you. I will touch you: your screaming will not drive me away, nor frighten me, nor anger me."

Bridget totally ignored Anne-Marie's whining resistance, repeating her request over and over in a calm voice, prompting Anne-Marie through all tasks. "She doesn't know how to pay attention," Bridget explained to me. "We have to help her learn that." She physically redirected all manneristic or inappropriate behaviors, prompting Anne-Marie to sit straight in the chair, to look up and keep her eyes on her. She constantly forced Anne-Marie's attention to her and only to her, narrowly focusing Anne-Marie's physical and mental presence, capturing her in a closed intense circle of Anne-Marie–Bridget. She used her whole body, her face, her hands, her voice, to keep Anne-Marie still and listening. She then filled up that created attentiveness with an impeccably organized and precisely paced curriculum—the individualized "programs." To motivate Anne-Marie, she used not only the primary reinforcers, the bits of cookies, but little windup toys and fun knickknacks and lots and lots of praise.

A behavioral program usually has two essential components: structured programs, most often taught in a drill mode, and "incidental teaching."

The first two months' set of structured programs had a double focus: to reduce certain behaviors—like perseverative repetitive activities, face-hitting, and throwing tantrums—and to increase other behaviors—like eye contact, paying attention, using language (including nonverbal language, like pointing), and play skills. Many of these beginning programs came out of Lovaas's *The Me Book*. His twenty years of research had laid the foundation for us. We were able to take his basic material and create our own variations and expansions of the programs.

One of Bridget's first goals in the area of receptive language* was to bring Anne-Marie to discriminate among the different names for different objects.

In behavioral therapy, all tasks are broken down into the simplest units. Bridget started with the visual and the concrete ("doll" as opposed to "happiness"), and with the smallest number of objects: one. As a prerequisite to discrimination training, she first had to teach Anne-Marie to respond consistently to the directive "Give me."

Bridget placed an object, a toy horse, on the table. She obtained Anne-Marie's eye contact and attention with the cue "Look at me." She then stated: "Give me horse." (Again, everything as simple as possible: she did not say, "Anne-Marie, could you please hand me that horse on the table?")

Bridget waited. Anne-Marie did nothing.

Bridget repeated the command, then picked up Anne-Marie's hand, placed it around the horse, and guided it to put the horse into Bridget's hand. She then praised her very specifically—"Good, you gave me horse!"—even though Anne-Marie had not willingly given her the horse at all.

Over and over they did this, session after session. Soon Anne-Marie began occasionally to give Bridget the horse without the physical prompt. Still they repeated it and repeated it, until the data (data were collected every single day) began to show a steady increase in unprompted performance. In twenty percent, thirty, fifty, eighty, ninety percent of the "discrete trials," Anne-Marie handed Bridget that one

---

*"Receptive language" is the understanding of language, as opposed to "expressive language," the spoken use of language.

object on the table. She was learning how to respond to the command "Give me."

Next, Bridget had to teach her how to discriminate between two verbal labels. A horse and a cup were placed on the table. Now the command was "Give me horse" with the cup as a distracter. Again, the beginning trials were all prompted; then the frequency of the physical prompts gradually decreased (or "were faded," in behavioral parlance) as Anne-Marie began to associate the sound "horse" with the correct object. When that particular task showed 100 percent performance over several days, they began all over again with the word "cup." When *that* association was mastered (many discrete trials later) Bridget began to randomize the two labels within the same drill.

Then, gradually, new objects were added to the group on the table, until Anne-Marie, several weeks into the therapy, was able to discriminate among seven or eight different objects, with no physical prompting. *Every single discrete trial, in every drill, week after week after week, was preceded by the imperative "Look at me."* Eye contact was the sine qua non of every interaction and every drill.

Bridget worked simultaneously on many other programs as well. Behavioral therapy, Marc and I had already figured out, didn't simply mean "correcting a child's behavior." The term refers more to a style of teaching: discrete trials, breakdown of tasks into small units, the systematic use of reinforcement. The actual *curriculum* was predominantly linguistic and cognitive.*

As this painstakingly arduous process unfolded, Anne-Marie's rate of learning the names of each new object increased. Gradually, we stopped expecting an overnight breakthrough from Anne-Marie and began to take more pleasure and hope from her mastery of each small step. She might have been learning in a different, "unnatural" way in these drills, but she was learning. How far she would progress we would only know in time.

In the second major component of Bridget's program, teaching was done in a less structured manner. Some therapists will concentrate only on the drills initially, since the children have such difficulty paying attention, but Bridget believed in incorporating incidental teaching from the start.

---

*See Appendix II for a summary of all the programs: behavioral, social, linguistic, cognitive, play.

"Incidental teaching" simply means that the therapist takes every natural opportunity in the environment—"natural opportunity" meaning anything that interests or engages the child's attention, even momentarily—to reinforce the goals she happens to be working on, or even to spontaneously introduce new concepts. If Bridget was helping Anne-Marie work with the shape sorter box, for instance, she took that opportunity to emphasize the preposition "in," even though it had not yet been formally taught: "I'm putting the square *in* the box." She could work as well on the names for the different shapes: "square," "circle," "triangle," etc.

Almost anything could be an opportunity for incidental teaching: "It's work time," "It's play time," "It's time for singing"—each transition of the behavioral session itself could be verbally described in a simple, consistent way. Incidental teaching could be done anytime, anywhere, by Bridget, by me, by Marc, by Patsy. It was a question of helping Anne-Marie to focus on some particular aspect of communication or social interaction or symbolic play, as the occasion arose, then verbalizing that experience for her. The act of taking a walk outside in the stroller could be used to direct her attention toward the phenomena and events of the world, and to verbally translate what we were attempting to make her aware of: "That's a bus. It's big. It's going fast."

Incidental teaching is what all parents do: With an autistic child, we had to do a lot more of it, and a lot more consistently. We had to learn how to counteract that withdrawal, that blank indifference, by a constant maximizing of Anne-Marie's awareness, of even her most fleeting interest in anything. Previously, it was as though she wouldn't notice things for herself; now we were all pushing her to notice things and to respond to people, and when she did, we seized the opportunity. We took the least flicker of attention and aggressively fanned it into something more prolonged and memorable, accompanying our intervention always with clear straightforward language: "You're putting the *bear* in the puzzle . . . the *tiger* . . . the *lion* . . ."; "Here's a *spoon* . . . here's a *plate* . . ."; "Shoes. We *put on* shoes."

THROUGHOUT MARCH and April Anne-Marie's expressive language continued to develop. On March 25 I listed twenty-five words in my journal. Since the beginning of March, she had gained on average one word per day, about half of them taught by her therapists, the other half picked up from the general environment. With the exception of "hi" and "bye" and "more" and "open" and "help," each of which we were specifically targeting, the rest were nouns.

Her receptive understanding of language, however, was still very limited, and would continue to be problematic for a long while. She seemed to me to be anchored in the concrete, the here and now. If I pointed to a book, obtained her attention, and said the word "book," she now was giving evidence that she understood that labeling function in language, and could even repeat the word "book" herself. But anything more complex, like "Put the book on the table"—an action-on-object command, Robin called it—still seemed beyond her. "Where's Daniel?" provoked no response from her, neither a glance nor pointing. I used to wince when strangers or even friends would ask, "What's your name?" or "How old are you?" Those standard conversation-starters with two-year-olds were still met by silence and a blank look. It would be a while yet before she understood even the most rudimentary abstractions, rationales, inferences, or projections. "We have to go home because it's cold," "What a scary monster!," "Daddy will be home soon"—these statements, which I could remember two-year-old Daniel understanding and reacting to, seemed far beyond Anne-Marie's grasp. She named things; that was all.

Dr. Welch kept telling us that Anne-Marie understood everything, but Marc and I found that assertion more and more difficult to believe. Some days, in fact, when Anne-Marie was particularly alert and responsive, she seemed actually to be *trying* to understand our words, but she couldn't. Something about the decoding process was just not working for her. The Tinbergen book kept insisting on this idea of a normal child locked within a chosen autism, unwilling to speak and willfully turning a blank stare when spoken to. But Marc and I felt more certain as each day passed that Anne-Marie's linguistic deficits were not voluntary at all, that she herself was struggling to understand the flux of sounds that bombarded her ears but just couldn't make sense of most of them.

By April, I was growing ever more skeptical of some aspects of the theoretical basis of holding therapy and daily more accepting of Bridget's work, no matter how rote and mechanistic the structured drills still seemed. I wasn't ready to abandon Dr. Welch, however, or holding, not by a long shot. I still went religiously to her office, still practiced holding therapy every day with Anne-Marie, still swore that I could actually see increased attentiveness and responsiveness after each holding.

But then back I would go to observe the daily session with Bridget, and I was finding it harder and harder to deny the power of this behavioral approach. I was amazed at what Bridget could get out of Anne-Marie, whether in the drills or in incidental teaching: more and more words in each session; smiles; eye contact; alertness; better play; more initiative.

Marc and I talked over the therapies constantly. Neither of us liked the feeling that we still didn't understand what we were doing.

"You know, Marc, let's put the emotional-bonding question aside for a minute. I still haven't figured that one out completely. Maybe there's something else at work here."

He waited.

"Something instead of, or in addition to, the rebonding," I went on.

"Like what?"

"Well, you know how I'm always saying that Anne-Marie seems more alert and awake after each holding?"

"Yes?"

"So I do a holding in the morning, either here or at Martha's office. Anne-Marie is then in a heightened state of responsiveness. *Then* we give her to Bridget, who fills up that attentiveness with a structured curriculum and nonstop teaching."

"I think I see your point," he said. "Holding therapy helps her to wake up. Bridget helps her to catch up."

"Maybe that's at least part of what happens." I thought for a moment, then went on. "It's like we're making her pay attention, but then maximizing that attention with some very specific lessons."

In any case, Marc added, the behavioral program didn't seem to be harming her, as we had initially feared.

"I don't think she's being emotionally damaged," I agreed. "Bridget's pretty good, Marc. She knows what she's doing."

"Bridget's 'pretty good'? You don't think she's a cold, mean person anymore?"

"Did I say that?"

"Yes."

"Well . . . I don't think that anymore."

As a matter of fact, Anne-Marie seemed if anything calmer, more awake, and friendlier after each of Bridget's sessions. But even though

Anne-Marie's "performance" made me happy, what calmed my fears the most was just watching her respond to Bridget. As I watched Anne-Marie both inside and outside of therapy, it did seem to me now that she not only tolerated, but some days actually even *liked* the highly predictable, stable, structured environment that Bridget was providing. She would still cry when Bridget came to the door, but within a minute of her going into the room with Bridget, the whining would turn to babbling and talking. She no longer had to be put in the chair, but willingly went over to the chair and sat, waiting expectantly as Bridget arranged her materials. One day she actually set up the little chairs herself, dragging them across the room and placing them opposite each other. When Bridget began the teaching she would come alive, eager and alert, visibly pleased when she got an answer right or performed a task correctly.

It was hard to keep thinking of behavior modification as some dreadfully damaging violation of Anne-Marie's personhood, no matter how many problems I still had with the rote quality of much of the learning.

One day, Bridget arrived for her session after lunch. The doorbell rang. I started to call, but stopped myself as I turned around. There was Anne-Marie, walking toward Bridget and looking her straight in the eyes, smiling.

My doubts about Bridget and behavior modification could find fewer and fewer grounds on which to thrive. I had tried to hate this therapy; I was now forced to recognize its efficacy. I had believed that it would further alienate Anne-Marie. She herself was now telling me, in many ways, that she needed it and she needed Bridget.

15

ANNE-MARIE had entered into her own springtime. April and May saw her blossoming, opening out to all of us who loved her. Day after day, she continued to improve in rudimentary language skills and social behavior. In retrospect, her progress was very fast, but as we lived it, it was gradual and uncertain. There was no overnight cure, no breakthrough or sudden revelation of a hidden child. Step by step she came back, but we never knew if she would hold on for the full distance.

Marc was steadily optimistic. "She's going to be fine," he assured me. "Look at how fast she's progressing. Look how far she's come in two and a half months."

I watched her in mingled disbelief, uncertainty, and hope. Sometimes I wondered if I were constructing some kind of fairy-tale miracle cure, and one day I would wake up to the reality that she was not going to make it. Sure, she was progressing, but her language and social interaction were by no means normal yet. There were many small triumphs, interspersed with persistent autistic behaviors. I sorely wanted to meet just one other recovered child, to talk to his or her parents and quiz them about every moment of this uncertain dawning, but I knew only of Lovaas's anonymous forty-seven percent. It was an intense time of prayer and vulnerability as well as work and hope.

Slowly, however, my panic was calmed. Amidst the doubt and the lingering anxiety, faith was holding fast, growing stronger. Each day Anne-Marie gave something to us, some sign that kept alive our hope. Whether it was a new word, slightly more sustained eye contact, a flash of interest in her brothers, or even an increased curiosity about the world she inhabited, she just kept getting better.

I loved to take her for walks in her stroller now. She made me so happy when she looked curiously into store windows or pointed out dogs on the street.

"Doggie," she said.

"Yes, love. That's a doggie."

A pigeon waddled in front of her stroller. "Wa-hoh!" she cried excitedly. I laughed. "Yes. *Oiseau! Bird!*"

Oiseau was the one French word she had learned. It had disappeared somewhere between sixteen and twenty months, along with her other words.

She still never initiated contact with her brothers, but I thought that she was at least becoming more aware of them. Occasionally she stared directly at Daniel, as he chattered away happily while playing or drawing. And she was beginning to respond to one form of play with him: chasing games. He would start running up and down the halls screaming and laughing. That really perked her up. She started running after him. Then he would turn and run after her. Marc and I never minded this loud roughhousing, for Anne-Marie, running and laughing with her brother, looked so happy and normal.

Michel she still ignored almost completely. She walked around his little baby seat on the floor as though he were simply not there. If I was holding him she never showed any jealousy or even awareness of his presence. One morning I was seated in the living room with the children. Michel was in the baby seat and Anne-Marie happened to walk directly in front of him. Suddenly his little arms and legs started to wave excitedly and he gave her a huge, joyful smile. He kept smiling at her and turning his head toward her until she walked out of his field of vision. Not that she noticed, of course. She didn't even see him. I thought he was too young to be bothered by this "rejection," but I felt bad for him anyway. I picked him up and smiled into his face, wanting him to know that *someone* had noticed what a loving baby he was.

Then, a few days later, Anne-Marie did notice Michel. I was holding him on my lap, and suddenly she got up, walked over to us, and tried to push him away and climb herself into my lap. I was elated. Any sign of normal sibling jealousy could only be healthy in a child who had been so utterly indifferent. I picked her up in one arm and held Michel in the other, then sat, blessed and happy as my two youngest nestled against me.

One evening I was carrying Anne-Marie up Madison Avenue. I had to dash to the grocery store to pick up some milk. I had left the boys with Patsy, and told her I would be back in fifteen minutes. Marc, meanwhile, had come home early and had gone out again himself to run an errand.

As I carried Anne-Marie along, my mind fixed on my own thoughts, suddenly I heard her start to laugh a little. I looked at her. She was peering up the street, darkening now as the evening fell. Her eyes were fixed intently on something, and she was smiling and laughing to herself.

"What is it, Anne-Marie?"

She pointed. I followed her gaze. Marc was walking toward us. He saw us and held out his arms. I put her down, and watched her run into her father's embrace.

Marc walked toward me, carrying her. We looked at each other.

"Did you see that?" I asked.

"Yes I did. She knows her daddy."

Marc put one arm around me and held her in the other. We stood still for a moment, our own circle of fragile peace on a city street as the night fell.

BY MID-APRIL, Bridget's influence on me was increasing day by day.

One morning I walked into the dining room and saw Anne-Marie in the corner, turning around in small circles, staring at the floor. On the spur of the moment, I grabbed her, threw her into the air, and shouted *"Up* we go!" Then as I let her down I shouted *"Down* we go!" I repeated this game a few more times, shortening my verbal cue to *"Up!"* and *"Down!"* She was really into it, smiling and squealing with excitement with each toss in the air. Finally, on the downward swing, I waited, holding her in my arms, leaning down over her and staring expectantly into her eyes. Something seemed to click. *"Pah!"* she shouted, her version of "up."

"Good, Anne-Marie! Good saying 'up'!"

On the next upward swing I waited again, suspending her in the air and gazing into her face. "D-d-d-d . . ." I prompted.

"Dah!" she shouted.

"Yay! Good girl! 'Down'!"

We did this over and over until my arms couldn't take any more. But I was excited. I was beginning to understand how to combine eye contact, fun, and reinforcement, and verbal prompts, just as I had seen Bridget do in the sessions. Once I picked up on this technique, I began to find dozens of ways of generalizing it throughout the day.

Bridget began to color my thinking in other ways as well. Right after Anne-Marie's diagnosis, I had started a journal. At first the entries were scattered and frantic thoughts: emotions spilling out of control, jotted down helter-skelter on the page. But as time went on, I became more objective. I began to keep track of Anne-Marie's symptoms and progress in a more systematic way. In play, language, social interaction, and imitation—in every area that I could delineate I trained myself to note her continuing disabilities as well as her growing strengths. While it hurt to keep ferreting out Anne-Marie's handicaps, I felt that unless I became clear-eyed and merciless about all her differences, disabilities, and lags, I could hardly help her to overcome them. It was ironic that I had mentally castigated Bridget for doing just this, when she had asked me to draw up my lists, but here I was learning how to look at my daughter's weaknesses and daily note all her autistic behaviors, just as Bridget did in the session logs. This clinical objectivity about something that a month or two before had caused me the most searing pain was rendered possible, I suppose, by the simple fact that she was making sure and steady progress on all fronts.

As to play, Bridget taught Anne-Marie the same way she was teaching her everything else: by breaking down the activity into small manageable units, then physically assisting her to complete each unit. If they were doing a puzzle, for instance, Bridget first guided her hand to put each piece into the appropriate place, then very gradually backed off as Anne-Marie herself gained understanding. *Everything* was prompted, physically and verbally. If this sounds contrived and forced, it's because it was. But it was better than watching her endlessly tap puzzle pieces together six inches in front of her eyes.

I was now doing this same sort of prompting with her outside of therapy. I remember sitting with her, guiding her hands to put her bear to bed, to cover him up, to put the toy bottle to his mouth. It didn't bother me quite as much as it had before that nothing was spontaneous. I had been watching Bridget prompt her through everything from expressive language to singing and dancing, and I had seen that after a while, Anne-Marie needed less and less active guidance. Once pushed and prodded, she would begin to take some of the initiative herself.

Gradually, I was moving away from the seductive psychoanalytical idea of trying to figure out *why* Anne-Marie was autistic, and had begun, like Bridget, to concentrate on what I could do to facilitate her progress in very specific areas of language and behavior and social interaction. I began, like Bridget, not just to stop her self-stimulatory behavior, but to prompt and shape more appropriate behavior.

This pushing and prodding took many forms. With a bit of coaxing, she began to try some different foods. I would put a little ketchup (which she liked) onto something new, and then put it to her lips. I wouldn't let her stay with any one food, toy, or activity for very long. At first she had strenuously resisted my every intrusion, but now she seemed to be growing gradually more flexible, moving from one activity to another with less distress and crying. Bridget was stressing flexibility a lot in the therapy sessions. She was demanding not just attention from Anne-Marie, but the ability to shift attention, to move from one activity to another without distress. They would do some drills at the table, then move to the floor, then do several programs there, then back to the table for some different drills. Sometimes Anne-Marie would become intrigued with a particular toy. Bridget would let her continue to play with it for a certain amount of time, then announce: "OK, time to do shape sorter now!" Whether Anne-Marie whined or not, on they would move to the shape sorter.

I too started pushing for change. Anne-Marie had always insisted on wearing the same clothes and shoes. Buying new shoes had become a major traumatic ordeal for all of us—me, Anne-Marie, and the salesperson, who had no idea why this child was sobbing and trembling and prostrate on the floor. If I bought her a new pair of pants or a new shirt I could be sure to expect protracted tears. Not knowing what to do, I had simply let her wear the same two or three outfits day after day. But now I began to put different clothes on her in a very matter-of-fact way, in spite of her crying. Once I started this, I did it with everything—sweaters, shoes, different-colored socks in place of her standard white ones, dresses instead of her uniform of pants and a T-shirt, new pajamas, etc. After a few weeks of this, she would accept anything I put on her.

I could remember our prediagnosis days in the park, when I had sat with her, confused and frustrated, because she wouldn't stop crying. There was Daniel, merrily and enthusiastically rushing to try everything at once. But whenever I tried to put Anne-Marie on the swing or the seesaw, she whined and resisted.

Now, after therapy on these fresh April afternoons, I would take her over to the park and, armed with more confidence, ignore her crying as I coaxed her to try new experiences. It seemed to me to be more and more like pushing her over a sill of fear, helping her physically with the first steps of something new, then fading back as soon as she was ready. The day that I could lead her from the swing to the slide to the seesaw in the park without her crying or stiffening up was a minor triumph.

If I thought that she was forming a habit, getting into a rut, developing an obsession, a routine, I would wean her away from her dependency immediately and get her into something different. She was a child who wanted an immobile, unchanging world. It was now much clearer to me how I had to respond to her. I had to take her into my arms, physically prompt her, push her, pull her into going with the flow. I had to teach her to rise and sink, bend and sway and dance with the dance of life. She wanted stasis. Under Bridget's guidance, I imposed not just love, but change upon change.

I was also learning how to impose upon her a greater degree of assertiveness, if such a statement can logically stand. One day at my father's house Anne-Marie approached a plate of cheese and crackers. She stood there, staring at the food, obviously wanting to try some. My father leaned forward at once. Most of our friends and family, knowing of Anne-Marie's diagnosis, always made a special effort of attentiveness toward her. They were trying hard to help her in the only ways they could think of. My father began to hand her a cracker.

"Wait a sec, Daddy," I said. I leaned forward and took Anne-Marie's hand. "Do you want a cracker, Anne-Marie?"

She said nothing, but looked up at me anxiously.

"Here, sweetheart," I said, taking her hand and extending it halfway toward the plate. "You take it. Go on. Take a cracker."

Looking as though she thought someone were going to bite her, Anne-Marie screwed up her courage and took a cracker.

"Good girl. You see? You can take the cracker. You did it. You took the cracker all by yourself."

I suddenly realized that I had made the same gesture of physical manipulation that had so disturbed me when I first saw Bridget do it in therapy. Now it had become routine. I was "shaping" her behavior in many ways, but the more I did so, the more courageous and outgoing she seemed to become. The moral scruples occasioned by the extreme authoritarianism of a behavioral approach were yielding to the practical reality that something here was working. Anne-Marie was progressing very rapidly. Bridget said it, Robin said it, even Marc and I were starting to believe it.

From looking at behavioral therapy as a radical stifling of Anne-Marie's self, her father and I were beginning to see it as a radical but necessary means of assisting her to form a self.

We were not imprisoning her, we were freeing her into normalcy.

We were not taking her over, we were helping her to break out of the bizarre behaviors and indifference of autism.

We were guiding her, as all parents have to guide their children, imposing direction, limits, motivation, and consequences—except that she was far more lost and in need than other children. There would be time for all kinds of freedom, autonomy, and choice. *Now,* while she was still so young, was the moment to wrench her into our way, our world.

16

"Do you still have that 'behavioral' person coming to your house?"

I was in Dr. Welch's office in late April.

"Yes."

"I hope you're not pressuring this child with those drills you told me about, are you? Is that person drilling her?"

"Bridget's OK," I muttered. "Anne-Marie is fine with her."

"Please, be extremely careful with what you expose Anne-Marie to. Always remember how fragile she is!"

I needed Bridget. I knew that now. Lately I had been arguing more strenuously with Dr. Welch that there was a place in autism therapy for Bridget's kind of approach as well as for emotional bonding.

But I still loved Dr. Welch. I loved what she had done for me—how she had made me feel—when the future was so black. I still felt vulnerable about disobeying her outright. I was hesitant about admitting to her that Bridget was now coming five days a week, and that I was allowing Anne-Marie to be drilled in the rote repetition of sounds and words and the matching of colors and shapes. I was loath to talk about how many of Bridget's techniques had seeped into my every interaction with Anne-Marie.

"She's OK," I said again, and changed the subject: "I think I might want to go to Connecticut one of these days. I'd really like to meet a few of the other families who are doing this."

"By all means," said Dr. Welch. "What about May 9?"

"Why May 9?"

The BBC, Dr. Welch told me, would be at the Mothering Center in Connecticut that day, filming a documentary on holding therapy. She had told the producer about articulate, intelligent me, and the producer would love to talk with me.

"Are you sure they want to hear my criticisms of the failure-to-bond theory?" I asked.

Dr. Welch assured me that whatever I said would be fine. Just recount our experience as it had unfolded. Tell them what I felt about holding therapy itself.

I agreed to go. Not so much because I wanted to be interviewed, so early in our battle for Anne-Marie, as because I did sorely want to meet and talk with other parents who were involved in holding therapy. I wondered, were any of them using a combination approach as we were? Were their children progressing as rapidly as Anne-Marie? More rapidly? Should I be doing anything else during the holdings to achieve a better resolution?

I was sure that I was going to meet many kindred spirits—people who believed in the practice of holding but had certain doubts about its theoretical foundations.

I could not have been more wrong. The people I met there were adamant, absolute in their belief in Dr. Welch, the Tinbergens, and failed bonding as the cause of autism.

The BBC crew was setting up when I arrived at the comfortable middle-class home on a wooded street in a Connecticut suburb. I walked up the driveway holding Anne-Marie, trying not to feel self-conscious as the cameramen snapped to attention and began filming me. I made my way into the house. There was Dr. Welch, looking excited and pretty, carefully made up, hair coiffed into a blond halo, her eyes bright. She was perfectly poised, gracious.

We kissed each other on the cheek, murmured greetings. She turned to introduce me to two women who were emerging from a sort of sun-room at the side of the house. The women were leading their children, a girl and a boy, by the hand. "Say hi to Catherine," they prompted. The girl, age ten or eleven, said "Hi, Catherine" without looking at me. The boy, sixteen or seventeen years old, said nothing.

"Martha, Desmond is waiting!" called a woman from the kitchen. Dr. Welch excused herself and went outside to talk to the BBC producer, Desmond Wilcox. One of the mothers explained that the woman in the kitchen was Dr. Welch's mother. This was her parents' home. They helped her to run the Mothering Center.

I walked into the sun-room, where there was almost no furniture but many pillows lined up against the walls. I started to chat, a little nervously, with some of the other parents. There were eight or ten mothers, the same number of children, and three or four fathers. The children ranged in age from the teenager I had just met to a couple of three-year-olds.

The first thing that struck me, so hungry for reassurance, was that none of the children looked cured. I saw hand-flapping and jumping and spaced-out staring. I heard some language from the older kids, but it sounded stilted and infantile. I saw no one who gave me a thrill of hope. My anxiety increased.

Discreetly, I asked the mother of one of the younger children where all the recovered kids were.

"Well, of course, they wouldn't still be here if they're recovered!"

Of course. Why hadn't I thought of that? But why were some of these other mothers still here after such a long time? Two of them had told me they had been coming for ten years. How long was holding therapy supposed to go on?

"Have you met any of the recovered kids?" I asked the mother I was talking to.

"No, but Dr. Welch told me about Mark H——."

I too had heard about Mark H——, many times. I was dying to meet him, and some of the other recovered children as well.

The parents all sat around chatting about their children. I listened with interest, then with growing dismay. Almost all the mothers were telling stories of how they had failed their children. Their stories carried an almost eerie cheerfulness: They were responsible, they knew it, and were most eager to talk about it. Oh, it was not their *fault,* of course, but they had done some things inadvertently that resulted in their child's going from normal to autistic. The fathers who were there concurred readily in everything the women said.

"I was depressed and I didn't even know it until I met Dr. Welch."

"I stopped nursing when she was only a year old."

"I never put my daughter in a Snuggli, the way I had with my first."

"I went on a trip, and when I returned she was gone . . . just gone."

"I was so busy with our move that I couldn't give him enough attention."

"Yes," chimed in this woman's husband. "She was very distracted and distant during that time."

"I let him cry in his crib at night because my husband said we should teach him how to sleep through the night."

I couldn't take much more of this.

"Failed bonding is a symptom of autism, not a cause!" I interrupted urgently. "The fault is not in us; it's not in our kids. It's in a damaged nervous system!"

Blank stares greeted me. I sensed a certain hostility. Who does she think she is? A doctor? A psychiatrist?

I tried again, less confidently. "Why can't we just try to bond with our children, and drop all this analysis of our wrongdoing in the past?"

Silence. Then a polite change of topic.

I understood them, since I had one foot in their camp myself. I'm convinced that the continuing resistance displayed by some parents toward the idea of a genetic or other organic cause of autism has to do with their despairing conclusion that if it is indeed a biochemical or metabolic disorder, they may as well throw in the towel because there is nothing that can be done about it.

As long as we don't see any overt damage, and one does not with the majority of autistic children, then we can still cling to our belief in the power of love, and love alone, to heal.

The hope offered to parents by the Tinbergens, by Dr. Welch, and by every psychotherapist who clings to the old psychodynamic approach to autism is that if we caused it, we can correct it. If we did it, we can undo it. Yes, I did it. I'm sorry. Just show me how to be a better mother. Please.

Every one of those parents, myself included, had embraced that guilt, because we believed that in that admission lay exoneration, and salvation.

But it was time for the group holding to begin. The BBC crew was in the room with us now. All the parents seemed to know what to do. They all took off their shoes and sat on the pillows on the floor. I followed suit. We gathered our children to us.

And then commenced a screaming and a shouting and a crying such as I have never witnessed. Anne-Marie and I were both so frightened we jumped up and ran to another room. But Dr. Welch's assistant followed us and firmly guided us back to the group.

I tried to concentrate on holding Anne-Marie and going through my usual "Mommy loves you, look at me" routine, but it was impossible to concentrate. Across from me the mother of the sixteen-year-old was screaming:

"One incident and you decide to withdraw forever? You've ruined our lives!"

Another couple sat with a newborn baby in the father's arms, a three-year-old boy in the mother's arms:

"Look at me!" screamed the mother to the boy.

"Look at her!" roared the father. The child writhed and sobbed. The newborn started to scream as well.

"You think you're the only one who should get attention?" shouted a mother to her sobbing daughter. "What about everyone else? What about *our* needs?"

I held Anne-Marie and tried to keep her calm. She was frightened and crying. I was torn between a desire to flee this crazy scene and once again that stubborn belief that if I could just let go of my intellectual inhibitions and believe, like these passionate parents around me, my daughter would recover.

Dr. Welch moved among us, calm and serene, smiling and encouraging us. Her constant exhortation was to express to our child our deepest feelings about him or her—to "let out the rage and the hurt." Only then could true bonding take place.

The BBC's camera followed her as she moved from group to group, with a word here, a smile there, a command to a particularly resistant child to look at his mother now!

Finally, it ended. People relaxed their holds, sat up, began talking more calmly to their children. I don't know why it ended when it did, whether because a certain amount of agreed-upon time had elapsed, or because some of the more experienced mothers were sending out "time-to-conclude" signals to the rest of us. It did strike me as bizarre that our holdings were all supposed to end at the same time. I looked around to see if anyone had achieved the longed-for "resolution," but saw no child engaged in heartfelt dialogue with his parent. The shift in attitude, in tone, and in noise level had emanated from the parents, just as it did in Anne-Marie's and my home holding sessions.

Smiles and sighs of relief and camaraderie all around. The children quiet and most indeed looking more relaxed in their parents' arms.

Then more group discussion, this time led by Dr. Welch. "Now listen, people. I've said it before and I'll say it again. These children are not dumb. They understand what is going on. . . ."

Outside afterward, I stood on the lawn for my interview with Desmond Wilcox. Sounding pedantic and oh-so-objective, I sketched out my doubts about the bonding business, my nervous reaction to what I had just witnessed.

Dr. Welch stood behind the crew, smiling at me.

"But," I said, catching her look, smiling back into her loving eyes, "this said, now let me tell you what Dr. Welch has done for us, for our family. . . ."

That month of May was to prove the high point of my adulation of Dr. Welch. I wanted to sing her praises, not only before the BBC cameras but before anyone who would listen. In fact, I considered it my duty to proclaim her message of hope to the world. I decided to write a letter to one of the most famous researchers in the field of autism, Dr. Bernard Rimland.

I had vaguely heard of Dr. Rimland or run across his name during the first few weeks of the year; I think I had read an article he had written on vitamin B_6 and the treatment of autism. But I hadn't focused on him until I happened to come across a quarterly newsletter that he published, the *Autism Research Review International*.

As I read through it, I was struck by how much material was crammed into its four or five pages. This Dr. Rimland had taken the trouble to comb through all the journals and periodicals that had recently published articles on autism. He had then summarized the research for easy, fast reading, had offered succinct commentaries on much of it, and had gathered the whole business into one newsletter. Now, as I reread the newsletter in early May, I decided to contact this person who seemed so knowledgeable and objective.

In a long, gushing letter, an extravagant hymn of praise to Dr. Welch—with a brief mention of Bridget and Robin, of course—I poured out the whole story to Dr. Rimland. I wrote of Anne-Marie's history and diagnosis, the therapies we were using, her remarkable progress so far, some of my confusion about how holding therapy worked, my hopes and fears for the future.

Beyond a shadow of a doubt, I wrote, the rapidity of Anne-Marie's progress was due to Dr. Welch. Bridget and Robin's work, I conceded, was very important, but the essential repair work, the heart of the matter, was being addressed through holding therapy.

BEFORE SENDING the letter to Dr. Rimland, I showed a copy to Bridget and then later to Dr. Welch.

"Well," said Bridget quietly after finishing the letter, "you do seem very enthusiastic about holding therapy."

"But I do mention how important your work is too, Bridget," I said defensively.

"Yes."

"And anyway, holding therapy *is* something that professionals should take seriously. It's recovering children from autism!"

"Have you met any of those kids?"

A lump of tension rose in my throat. I did believe in recovery, damn it! Martha had recovered some kids! I didn't care if Bridget believed that or not!

Bridget went on, breaking the faintly hostile silence that had developed.

"I think holding therapy probably has some emotional or physiological effect on both you and Anne-Marie," said Bridget. "I just don't know how much I would rely on it to teach a child appropriate behavior or communication."

"But I'm not. I have you ten hours a week."

"Yes, and you also have *you*, Catherine, carrying through this program a lot more than ten hours a week."

I showed the letter to Dr. Welch. She read it, was quiet for a moment, then suddenly looked up.

"Could I keep this copy?"

I agreed.

A few days later she told me that her father, who helped her run the Mothering Center, had been duplicating it and distributing it to various holding-therapy enthusiasts around the country.

"Oh?" I said. Something inside me contracted in nervousness. Did I really want those thoughts, and my name, and Anne-Marie's name, distributed like that? I was so grateful to Martha; she had saved my life. But couldn't she, shouldn't she, have asked me?

A first few insidious cracks of doubt snaked up the pedestal on which I had placed her.

That distribution of my letter bothered me more than I wanted to admit. I called a woman I'd met in Dr. Welch's office, a mother of a three-and-a-half-year-old autistic girl.

The woman had been practicing holding therapy for over a year. The child, while not recovered, had progressed to the point where she had some echolalic speech, and her screaming temper tantrums were down in frequency.

"Do you believe that holding therapy is going to fully recover your daughter?" I asked. "Do you believe in holding therapy?"

There was a silence, not very friendly.

"I've never believed in anything so much in my life," came the reply. "Don't you?"

"Yes. Yes," I said hastily. "Of course I believe that it's doing something. I'm just wondering how much of Anne-Marie's progress is due to holding and how much to the behavioral program."

"Why on earth do you *care?*"

"I do care! I want to know why she's getting better and how she's getting better! I want to know if her progress will continue, and how I can help it continue!"

"Well, I'm very happy with the progress my daughter has made, and I'd never do that behavioral stuff. There was a therapist who came here once and tried to do that nonsense with my daughter, and believe me, I never invited her back again!"

"No?" Maybe you should have, I thought.

"No, I didn't. A mother's instinct is always right. My instinct tells me that holding therapy is the only hope for my daughter."

In this woman, as in other holding therapy disciples, I was beginning to see something I didn't like—something that I recognized in myself: blind faith, idealization of a human individual, unwillingness to admit that we can make mistakes about what is right for our children.

But it would take a few more months for the truth to come clearly into focus, and for me to understand who really represented the God-sent gifts for my daughter. The two young women, Bridget and Robin, who were down on the floor, working with her hour after hour, day after day, producing no miracle cures out of a tophat, just painstakingly teaching her, step by step by step.

Before my relationship with Dr. Welch ended, I was to understand what it might be like to be seduced and drawn into a cult. To those who are frightened enough and desperate enough, it becomes harder and harder to hold on to sense and intelligence, reason and objectivity. Cast into an unknown land, uncertain of our bearings, we parents at the Mothering Center took enormous solace from the calm assurances, the sweet promises, of our savior.

17

DURING that three-month period of March, April, and May of 1988, Anne-Marie's vocabulary had exploded. When I started listing in my journal the more than forty words she had said on a particular day, I stopped keeping track.

But nothing about her was "normal" yet.

With the exception of the verbs we had specifically taught her, ninety-five percent of her spoken language consisted of nouns—nouns designating things, not people's names. She did say "bye-bye," and she was beginning to repeat "Mama" and "Daddy," because we had modeled these words for her over and over. But the rest were nouns. Moreover, many of these nouns were not spontaneously produced, but prompted by us.

Forty words, fifty words, still almost all nouns.

"When do children normally begin to combine words?" I asked Robin.

"When they have about ten to fifteen single words," responded Robin, who was always truthful with me.

Sixty words, seventy words, eighty words. Still almost all nouns. Anne-Marie now had a fascination with labeling things—anything and everything in the apartment.

"Shirt," she would say, grabbing hold of her father's shirt. "Shirt. Shirt. Shirt. Shirt."

"Shoe. Shoe. Shoe. Shoe."

"Pen. Pen. Pen. Pen."

At first encouraged, we soon realized the perseverative nature of this repetitive labeling, and would try to expand her thought a little. "Yes, Anne-Marie. This is *my* shirt. I'm *wearing* a shirt." The rote naming of things, I remembered from my reading, was a prime characteristic of autistic speech, and it made us nervous. All around us, among our friends and relatives, we heard two-year-olds expressing their thoughts, in two- or three-word combinations: "Want ball." "Daddy go." "Me want juice." "Doggy go outside." Would Anne-Marie ever say such things?

And it would be such a joy if she would one day greet me or her father spontaneously when we came into the apartment—or, impossible though it might seem, one day ask a simple question, like "Where coat?"

And, just once, *call* me from across the room: "Mama!"

Whatever she gave me, I wanted more. I was hungry, insatiable. I wanted a fully alive, loving, talking, laughing daughter, and at each step up, I raised my sights to the next level, and increased my tyrannical demands.

"Will she ever begin to combine words by herself and start to make sentences?" I asked.

"I think she will," said Robin. "We're working on two-word combinations a lot these days." Robin had been focusing on modeling very clear and contextually evident two-word combinations while playing with Anne-Marie: phrases such as "go car," "bye train," "more cookie."

But Anne-Marie seemed quite content just to go around naming things over and over again. She didn't even care very much if there was anyone within hearing distance. She didn't need a response. "Car. Car. Car. Hat. Hat. Hat."

Bridget too was working on two-word phrases and short sentences, through verbal-imitation drills. It was pretty easy to see where the term "robotic," applied to the effects of a behavioral program, came from. Anne-Marie's speech sounded very conditioned, very rote. Most of what Bridget had taught her came back exactly the same. No creative transformations to speak of. Feed the data into the tape recorder, back they come, unchanged: "Cookie." "Juice." And later: "I . . . want . . . juice." Marc and I did not believe this rote, inflexible, concrete language was *caused* by the behavioral program—it was one of the core symptoms of autism—but still we wondered: was the behavioral program reinforcing it? Anne-Marie was learning a lot through Bridget's drills, but would she ever have real communicative language? Would she ever be able to hold a conversation? What were we going to do, give her a stockpile of 500 sentences to take her through life? Linguistic and social skills are obviously not simply a set of learned responses, but require constant creative transformations on a set of rules.

I put these questions directly to Bridget and Robin. Not so much in a challenging way, as I would have a month or two before, but in genuine uncertainty.

Neither one ever having recovered a child from autism, they answered as best they could, relying on their experience of seeing children make at least some progress, some more, others less, toward higher levels of communication.

The task at hand, they helped me to see, went beyond this simple verbal imitation. In every way we could, we were to demand the functional use of Anne-Marie's words—what Robin called the "pragmatics" of communication. When Anne-Marie had learned the word "open," we were not to allow her to stand at a door and whine. She had to look at us and say "open." In many different contexts and in many different situations, all day long, Anne-Marie had to practice her words. Bridget would teach her a word through verbal imitation, then make her use it every chance she could. Robin and everyone else would work on generalizing every word she learned.

Pragmatic generalization included a constant modeling of the word in other contexts and in other semantic structures. Gradually, gradually, we moved from the concrete and simple: "Open it" to the more and more complex: "Open box." "Open up!" "Open your eyes!" "Is the store open?"

What we hoped would happen, said Bridget in a long conversation with me one day in May, was that Anne-Marie would begin to learn on her own, from the environment. She was picking up words and concepts so fast now; what we wanted to see was that she would start to pick them up more from everyone around her, not just in session, and that she would begin to generalize them faster and faster.

"We want her 'to learn how to learn,' " I reflected. "I think Lovaas said that in *The Me Book,* or in one of his papers that I read."

"Yes. I think that's a good way of saying it. She's learning how to learn."

Later that night I continued the conversation with Marc.

"Maybe what we're doing with all these rote drills is effectuating some kind of 'rewiring' or 'rerouting' in her brain. You know, by dint of pulling her through these programs, something starts to happen, neurologically."

Marc agreed. Somewhere, somehow, he thought, there was neurological damage. But we were helping Anne-Marie to override that damage, or to compensate for it, through external stimulation.

"Sometimes even stroke victims whose speech centers have been destroyed can learn to speak again through nonsurgical, environmental stimulation, can't they?" Marc said.

We recalled a PBS broadcast we had seen once, describing a girl who was born with part of her brain missing, yet was cognitively normal.

"The other sections of her brain sort of took over the work, in a way," I said. I thought that was what I remembered from that documentary.

Our speculations were founded on no empirical data, of course. But we needed to put a sense of order and process onto phenomena that we didn't understand completely, and probably never would. Our "brain-repairing-itself" construct kept alive our hope for full recovery.

On the twentieth of May, Anne-Marie injected a surge of new life into that hope.

Robin and I and Daniel and Anne-Marie were seated on the floor of the workroom after the speech-language session. Daniel and Anne-Marie were involved with one of the toys Robin had brought, and Robin and I were chatting about Anne-Marie's progress. Michel was napping in the next room.

The key turned in the door, and Marc entered the apartment. "Hello everyone," he called out as he made his way down the hall. Anne-Marie raised her head. Marc came into the room.

She turned to look at him, directly into his eyes. There was a pause, just a heartbeat, then she spoke. The words were soft, hesitant:

"Hi . . . Daddy."

There was a moment of silence. Then Robin and I both emitted a shriek of joy, and let ourselves go into a moment of giddy euphoria. Even Daniel, who didn't quite know what all the fuss was about, was laughing to see everyone so happy.

Marc knelt down and took his baby daughter in his arms.

"Hi, Anne-Marie, sweetheart," he whispered, his arms enfolding her, his voice catching.

A long moment passed. Father and daughter were welcoming each other home.

But the seesaw was in constant motion throughout that springtime. Each such sign of health and progress had its countersign of continuing illness. Every time we started to feel relieved about one area of Anne-

Marie's behavior, new worries would plague us about other areas. Even as her language improved, other symptoms of autism, both new and old, kept appearing and reappearing.

Throwing tantrums and crying certainly took a surge upward, not so much in the formal work sessions as in her daily life, when nothing much was happening and there was no clear antecedent for her crying. Bridget and I speculated that this increased negativity sprang from the increased demands made on her all day long.

Other symptoms blipped up as well. Toe-walking, teeth-grinding, and body-tensing became more noticeable. For a while, she made strange guttural sounds, what I called "growly-bear" sounds. These she would alternate with "squeaky-mouse" sounds, just out of the blue, with no rhyme or reason that I could discern. Were these some kind of self-stimulation with the sound and feel of her own voice? I could only guess. Who knows what goes on in the intensely interior world of autism?

One frightening behavior that increased for a couple of weeks was face-hitting. I actually broke out into a cold sweat each time I saw her do this. Of all her symptoms, this one panicked me the most. The sight of those little hands springing up to slap the baby-round cheeks created in me a fear that bordered on revulsion, a desire to flee the room, flee the apartment, run away from her.

Bridget's reaction was a lot calmer. This was just one more manifestation of the illness that we had to nip in the bud. "Now, about the face-hitting," she would say at the end of a session, and, in spite of my pounding heart, I would force myself to listen, to confer, to look at the problem as clinically as she was doing. Bridget kept daily track of the behavior's frequency, and tried to figure out if there was any pattern to it. Unlike the psychoanalysts, who attempt to trace autistic behaviors back to early emotional wounds, behaviorists look to the immediate environment for specific precursors to the child's actions. Then they try either to reshape the environmental stimulus in order to modify the behavior, or to reshape the behavior itself along more appropriate lines. Was there any antecedent to Anne-Marie's face-hitting each time it occurred? What provoked that response from her?

"She seems to hit herself every time she gets the slightest bit frustrated with a task," said Bridget. Almost always, the behavior occurred at the start of a new program or during a particularly difficult one.

"Well, we can't very well never introduce new programs," I said.

"No. And she will have to learn to deal with a certain degree of frustration without such an extreme response," replied Bridget.

If we dropped everything and allowed her to do something else every time she got frustrated, that would only exacerbate the problem, I concluded.

"Exactly. She hits her cheeks, we rush in to make her life easier—we end up by rewarding her for hitting herself!"

"She starts conditioning us, in a way." I was beginning to think like a true behaviorist.

Bridget laughed, a little ruefully. Unfortunately, she noted, she knew quite a few families who got into that rut. Every time their child had a screaming temper tantrum, one of the parents jumped up to love and cuddle him. Pretty soon the child was using the temper tantrum every time he wanted his own way.

"Well, I can understand not reinforcing a temper tantrum," I said. "We're all supposed to know that, at least . . . but what do we do when she hits her cheeks?"

We decided that our strategy for the moment would be to downplay it almost completely while redirecting her hands.

Every time she hit her own cheeks, we calmly took her hands, guided them to her lap, and held them there for two or three seconds, saying nothing. Then, after a couple of seconds, we would praise her, in the succinct specific language of behavioral reinforcement: "Good hands down."

Bridget explained that a behavioral program entailed a lot of trial-and-error intervention. If this redirection of Anne-Marie's hands did not work, we would think up something else, like firmly saying "No hitting" and immediately placing her palms flat on the table. Or, we could "put the behavior on extinction," to use the technical jargon, which means ignoring it completely: there is no reward, reinforcement, or attention given at all to the inappropriate behavior.

Although I was able to work cooperatively with Bridget, I continued to feel vulnerable about the rightness or wrongness of each day's difficult decisions. I was still prone to thinking that every autistic symptom was somehow my fault or Bridget's fault. Whenever a negative behavior increased, I would fall right back into blaming myself or even the behavioral program. Sure, Anne-Marie might be learning things, behaving more normally, even communicating more and more through language—but maybe our intervention was causing her further emotional damage.

Because one thing was clear: Her social/emotional progress was still an uphill struggle. Social interaction—what the psychologists called "relatedness"—was probably the hardest area for Anne-Marie.

How do we make her love us? That was the question to which I had no clear answer. It was a source of continuing sadness for me that she seemed so uninterested in those who loved her. She still almost never approached or greeted anyone spontaneously. Just because she had said "Hi Daddy" once did not mean that we could count on her to do it again. There were still days when she was almost as indifferent to everyone as when she was at her worst.

The expression on her face was still mainly bland, even sad. I could tell by merely looking at her face whether she was "with us" at that particular moment, or somewhere in her own world. Every time she smiled it was such an event that I noted it in my journal.

At night, I would put her to bed, cover her up, ask her to look at me, and whisper how much I loved her. Then I would leave, always with a pang of sadness that she never called me back. Will she ever need me or want me in her life, I wondered? Will she ever come to me, eagerly, needily, the way Daniel does? Is she just as happy when I'm absent as when I'm present? Daniel and Michel needed me so much. Their eyes were so full of joy when they looked into mine; they loved to be held and talked to and played with. Would she ever be like that?

But as I was to realize, over and over again, it was not up to me alone to figure everything out, to come up with all the answers. I was working with Anne-Marie, striving to connect with her, to teach her, to stimulate her. When it came to "making" her love us, however, I learned to rely less on myself and more on prayer. I did what I could, then gave that mystery over to God.

And then, finally, as that springtime ended and we turned to the growth of summer, came a moment I had been yearning for. She was sick one evening, feverish and congested and crying. I cuddled her for a longer time before I put her to bed, cradling her little sick body and trying to let her know some of the deep protectiveness I felt for her. I put her, half asleep, into bed, pulled the sheet around her, and began to walk out of the room.

"Mama."

I froze. She had called me. For the first time ever in her life, she had called me. The word reverberated in my heart. I sank down next to her and wrapped my arms around her. "Mama's here, baby. Mama loves you. . . ."

I stayed until she fell asleep, my cheek resting against hers, just as it had on the day she was born, when they placed her next to me on the delivery table. I held her, treasuring her fragile newborn need of me, beginning to believe. . . .

18

IT WAS EARLY JUNE. Anne-Marie seemed to be improving daily; the other two were doing well. Daniel was going part-time to his nursery school, where he seemed to be thriving. He still had his wide smile, so I felt that we were managing to keep his world safe and secure enough.

There were always a few crunch times of the day, when I would be trying to do some individual work with Anne-Marie and he would come running over to demand the toy or the game and the attention. Those were the impossible times: whichever child I turned to, I felt as though I were abandoning the other; Anne-Marie was not yet able to be drawn into any kind of shared play with him. My only recourse was to keep juggling the available adult help so that those times occurred as infrequently as possible. The problem was, even when another supporting adult was there—Marc, or Patsy, or one of the therapists, or my sister Burke—I still felt an urgent desire to hold and love each child myself. I lived in fear that I wasn't giving each one enough.

Michel was a happy little baby. He slept well, waking up now only once or twice during the night for brief periods of nursing. Then he would fall right back to sleep, often nestled between Marc and me in our bed. He was smiling a lot—a wide-open, brimming-with-joy, I-love-everyone smile that he bestowed on everyone he met during the course of his very busy baby day. His sister, his brother, Patsy, me, his daddy, the grocer, the elevator man, the UPS delivery man—one and all, indiscriminately, we were graced by Michel's unconditional blessing and approval.

And if she would not exactly interact with them, Anne-Marie was taking more notice of her brothers. One day I watched with bated breath as she reached out to Michel, seated next to her on the floor, and softly placed her hand on the top of his head. I noticed as well that she was beginning to bring whatever toy she was playing with over to where Daniel was playing. Instead of being content to sit by herself in her room, she was starting occasionally to seek us out.

To facilitate social awareness, Bridget was adamant that Anne-Marie should respond to *her,* and not simply to the goldfish cracker or the M&M. I've never heard anyone pour such enthusiasm and warmth into praise of a child's each small step. As I listened in the hallway or did my work throughout the apartment, Bridget's cries of encouragement became a familiar background noise.

"Yay! Anne-Marie! You did it!"

Although still naming the specific tasks Anne-Marie was performing—"Good saying 'want'!"—Bridget was adding more natural-sounding verbal encouragement as well.

"Who's a smart girl? You're a smart girl!" or "Fantastic!"

And Bridget made sure as well to keep in close physical contact with Anne-Marie. Hugging and kissing and tossing in the air were just as important as verbal praise, Bridget believed.

Needless to say, Marc and I had, by early June, an entirely different opinion of Bridget. Simply by observing how much Anne-Marie was learning with her, we were now nothing short of delighted that we had such a strong and committed warrior in our battle for our daughter. The behavioral program, we were convinced, was as necessary as holding therapy. Maybe, just possibly, it was even more important.

Unfortunately, however, we continued to hear attacks on Bridget and her method of teaching. It seemed as though our own initial prejudice was shared by quite a number of people, some of whom should have known better, to put it mildly.

A mother, Lucille, contacted me about finding some help for her autistic daughter. As I was to do often with other parents in the course of our own odyssey, I sent her all the literature I had and spent some time with her trying to help her find therapists. Meanwhile, as naïve as I had once been myself, she called Payne Whitney to ask their advice. A young resident psychiatrist listened to her explanation of what she was trying to do for her daughter. I had had occasion to meet this psychiatrist. Cool and aloof, she had listened to my description of our home program with barely concealed disdain.

"Behavior modification," she now coldly informed Lucille, "is morally reprehensible."

A friend of mine came over for coffee one afternoon and, during our conversation delicately hinted that a behavioral program was not in Anne-Marie's best interest.

"Why not?" I asked, thinking that she probably needed a little information about how it worked and how effective it seemed to be. I reminded myself that not so long ago I had been deeply suspicious of it and philosophically opposed to it.

"Well, I have a friend who has a Ph.D. in psychology, and she says no one who knows anything about children would ever subject them to behavior modification."

" 'No one who knows . . .' Does she have children?"

"No."

"Has she ever worked with autistic children?"

"I don't think so, but she's read a lot . . ."

"Tell me, what does *she* recommend?"

"Psychotherapy, of course."

I stomped around the house for a while after that conversation. Let the Ph.D. have a child, let the child be autistic, and let her psychotherapize him till the cows come home, I seethed. I want a recovered child.

Marc and I heard it all, and we heard it constantly: We heard that we were going to create a robot child, that we were addressing only the symptoms and not the root of the problem, that behavior modification stopped just short of child abuse. In New York City especially, the very word "behavioral" seems anathema. Other parents have since told me that in their states, they did not encounter this degree of animosity toward behavioral therapy, but here, the "best in the field," primarily Freudians, have clung to the same ideas for forty years.

We understood that part of this hostility was generated by the erroneous assumption that every behavioral program systematically uses a whole gamut of horrific aversives—everything from spanking to electric shocks to stun guns. In our home program, however, no therapist ever used any physical aversive. The most restraining thing we did was to keep Anne-Marie in the chair when she would rather have crumpled to the floor, although some people would consider that very aversive indeed. The forced holding of holding therapy was more aversive than anything that went on in our behavioral program.

I don't know what we would have done if Anne-Marie had been self-injurious, or self-stimulatory, to the point where we could not successfully redirect her, so I cannot pronounce a blanket condemnation on the use of aversives, especially where other approaches have consistently failed. Nor do I want to. There are cases on record of severe self-injury of several years' duration being permanently eliminated in a matter of days through the use of a mild aversive—a loud *no!*, a slap to the thigh. I suppose the issue revolves as well around what you consider aversive. One person may consider the infliction of any physical discomfort aversive, another would find unacceptable the use of a verbal reprimand, another would want no demands at all made upon an uncooperative child. Needless to say, there is a raging controversy on this subject, and a group of professionals who, convinced that they know best and care more for autistic children than do the children's parents, would ban the use of all such aversives.

But the hostility to behavior modification runs far deeper than the aversives issue. Its roots go deep into the essential conflict between two ways of looking at and working with autistic children, and even, in the larger context, with normal children. On the one side there is the behavioral approach, bent precisely on imposing many demands for change and conformity with standard acceptable behavior; on the other, there is a whole range of psychodynamic approaches, all heavily focused on "understanding," analysis, bonding, and "insight."

We were living and breathing this conflict. We were discovering just how persuasive and pervasive were the psychodynamic approaches, long after Bettelheim had supposedly been discredited. In time, we would understand just why their proponents were so furiously condemnatory of the method that was pulling our child out of autism.

19

By mid-June, Anne-Marie was beginning to use a few more two-word combinations: "Hi [plus name of person]," "Bye [plus name of person]," "More [plus noun]," and "All gone." Robin and Bridget had drilled her relentlessly in each of these phrases. Every time Robin put a puppet or an animal toy away, she modeled "Bye, Mickey!," "Bye, Pluto!," "Bye, Big Bird!" Marc and I as well targeted these phrases every chance we could. "Say hi to Blas!," "Say hi to George!"—the elevator operators and doormen in our building were now used to our constant prodding and prompting of Anne-Marie. She still never greeted them spontaneously. "She's so shy," remarked Blas one day. Dr. Welch was extremely pleased with her progress and urged me to take her back to the Mothering Center.

"All right," I agreed, somewhat reluctantly. I didn't really want to go back, but then again, I owed Dr. Welch at least the courtesy of another visit or two. Besides, I had struck up a friendship with two women I had met at the Mothering Center, mothers of young children who were keenly interested in doing a combination approach, as Marc and I were. I promised her that I would go back.

Our office sessions were not going very well. We were arguing more and more about the implications of a therapy based on maternal bonding. I was distressed by what I had seen at the Mothering Center and questioned Dr. Welch about some of the children I had observed there.

I was rereading the Tinbergen book as well, in a kind of last-ditch effort to hold together my crumbling faith. I had misjudged Bridget. Could I possibly have been wrong about the Tinbergens too? Had I exaggerated their cogency and insight? I was trying to understand how bonding fails and why the failure to bond should result in autism, but the more I read, the more the book's reasoning seemed to unravel into speculative and impressionistic accounts. Everything was interpreted in light of a theory that had already been decided upon, a priori. And it was all so simple. Too simple: Here is what causes autism. Here is what cures it.

One day I reread the section on self-injury.

Anne-Marie's face-hitting had disappeared by this point in June, but the memory was still fresh and terrifying. Other images of this grievous behavior haunted me as well. Marc and I had watched a PBS documentary on autism soon after Anne-Marie's diagnosis. The camera had focused on a severely impaired little boy, not more than four years old. His father had brought him to a treatment center in Boston hoping that they could stop the child from his almost continuous self-injurious behavior. The camera had lingered for an excruciatingly long moment on the child as he forcefully smacked each side of his head over and over. *Smack, smack, smack.* You could hear the blows as they landed. You could see the child's face, anguished, as though he himself wanted to stop but couldn't.

We had seen another boy, around eight years old, in another documentary film. He had already been institutionalized. His hands were swaddled in thick puffy bandages, apparently because no one could stop him from constantly punching his ears. His face was a mask of pure pain as his bandaged hands struck, over and over.

I know many autistic children are not supposed to feel pain normally, but some form of agony was written all over this small boy's face. It was the kind of image you just want to bring to God and sob, "Why, Lord? Why allow such suffering?"

The Tinbergens, of course, had an explanation. Such self-damage, in their view, was a kind of "redirected aggression," aggression elicited by frustration or humiliation inflicted by the *adults* in the child's environment—"for instance when they speak in a derogatory way within the child's hearing. . . . Since the child does not dare attack the person concerned . . . he directs [the aggression] against himself."

Such reasoning, even to someone who needed to believe because she thought her child's future depended on agreeing with these people, simply didn't hold up in the face of common sense. I have witnessed more than once a mother or a father belittling a child, berating him or her for being a sissy, a crybaby, a coward, a moron, whatever. I've seen children smacked around in public in a way that makes me deeply anxious about what goes on in private. I've seen them publicly and cruelly humiliated for peeing in their pants. I fear for the emotional health of these children and know that they are surely being wounded in spirit. But I have never seen any child, no matter what the abuse, be brought to inflict such continuous obsessive violence against himself. Moreover, the idea of blaming parents for such a sickening tragedy was beginning to sit poorly with me.

It was around this time, as I struggled to understand the roots of the psychogenic movement in autism therapy, that I picked up a book which Marc had brought home at the beginning of our research. The book was *The Empty Fortress,* by Bruno Bettelheim, probably the most famous book on autism ever written. I had never bothered to read it, because two or three psychologists we had talked to had assured us that it was passé. "No one believes it anymore," they said.

But I wasn't so sure. The Tinbergens and Dr. Welch seemed to place a lot of emphasis on maternal behavior in the genesis of autism. Wasn't that what Bettelheim had done? What was different? What had changed?

For decades, Bettelheim's word had been unchallenged, and what Bettelheim said was this: "Infantile autism is a state of mind that develops in reaction to feeling oneself in an extreme situation, entirely without hope."

The "extreme situation" is quite similar to that in the Nazi concentration camps of the Second World War: ". . . all psychotic children suffer from the experience of having been subject to extreme conditions of living. . . . they all share one thing in common: an unremitting fear for their lives." Like certain prisoners of the concentration camps, they suffer from "the conviction of imminent death," and this conviction results in "catatonia . . . regression to infantile behavior . . . total emotional depletion . . ."

Slowly, inexorably, the accusatory gaze is leveled at Mother:

> Turning to the origins of extreme situations in early childhood, it can be said that the mother's pathology is often severe, and in many cases her behavior toward her child offers a fascinating example of abnormal relation. . . .
>   I believe the initial cause of withdrawal is the child's correct interpretation of the negative emotions with which the most significant figures in his environment approach him. . . .

Not that it's her *fault,* Bettelheim hastens to add—she can't help it. She just does something slightly pathological, slightly wrong, clumsy, or incorrect—like leaving the child in a freezing room all night long, he offers as one example—and the child misinterprets this in a catastrophic way. The mother has her human shortcomings, her little failings and imperfections, which, alas, send her child into a state of catatonic terror. Bettelheim forgives both her and the child's father (sort of).

> The parents of autistic children simply lived their own lives, reacting to its conditions out of their own psychological makeup. True, they did so with little regard for the nature of their child, but this they did not know.

Well, he tries to forgive them. In a spirit of charity, he assures the reader that a particular couple he is discussing might very well have conveyed hatred toward their child, but "nowhere did parental attitudes suggest the idea of baking the child in the oven to eat her. . . .": Sometimes, however, Bettelheim cannot quite maintain his benign tolerance toward these sick, twisted parents, and really lets them—most often the mother—have it:

> I would stress that the figure of the destructive mother (the devouring witch) is the creation of the child's imagination, though an imagining that has its source in reality, namely the destructive intents of the mothering person. . . . Throughout this book I state my belief that the precipitating factor in infantile autism is the parent's wish that his child should not exist.

Months after reading this work I spoke to a vibrant woman whose daughter, now in her twenties and living in a group home, had been diagnosed in the heyday of Bettelheim's influence and prestige. *Everyone,* she told me, believed him. The parents believed what the professionals told them, and the professionals believed Bettelheim. No one questioned his authority. The psychiatrist had ordered her to bring her child in for "analysis" five days a week. The mother was not allowed to sit in the waiting room, so incensed with her was the doctor's staff. The nurses and receptionists informed her that she could drop the child at the door and wait for her outside. They never looked at the mother and refused to say hello or good-bye. She had caused this terrible condition in her child, and she merited no human courtesy. She told me that many a day she had stood there—whether in sunshine, in rain, or in sleet—weeping.

"How did you survive?" I asked her.

"I survived," she said softly. "Some others I know didn't."

"And later, did you feel rage?"

"Yes, I felt rage. But after a while I took my rage and flung it out to the universe. . . ." She paused, then added:

"You have to go on with your life."

She had concentrated on her daughter, had tried to make the best life possible for her, and was still trying to make sure she would be cared for after her own death.

I was silent. I had nothing to say to this woman. Nothing to say about suffering or courage that she didn't already know far better than I.

Needless to say, Bettelheim and the Tinbergens did not look kindly on behavior modification. According to Bettelheim,

> Conditioned-response regimes may turn autistic children into more pliable robots . . . autistic children are reduced to the level of Pavlovian dogs. . . . Better to let [an autistic child] decide what reactions she needs to feel . . . than to train her to live a conditioned-response existence because those around her find it more convenient.

The Tinbergens, for their part, make some derogatory remarks about how boring for the children is the "teaching of skills," and allude darkly to electric shock torture. Over and over they make the point that if one repairs the emotional damage, all these skills that parents are so obsessive about will fall into place.

I went to Dr. Welch. I was seeing connections—many of them—that I didn't like. "Why do you and the Tinbergens keep blaming parents?" I asked. "You don't sound that different from Bettelheim."

"We don't blame parents!" she snapped, momentarily losing her customary smiling charm. "No one is blaming parents!"

Was I misreading something?

I went back to the text.

It was with *great* regret that the Tinbergens were compelled to publish the painful evidence: "The behavior of the parents, in particular the mother," is at work in the "mainly psychogenic origin of autism."

> If we have to choose between hurting *some* mothers and refusing to rescue *many* children . . . we feel we have no choice but to be hard on mothers.

But how does Mother push her kids over the cliff into autism? The discussion of the mother's role has a Bettelheimian ring. There are some things that happen between mother and child, some things that the mother does or even unconsciously feels, that are . . . well, they're quite harmful. Mother may not think that her overly intellectual personality is going to have such a catastrophic effect; Mother of course does not intend for her child to become autistic, but really, aspects of her behavior reveal some troubling oversights and inattentiveness to her child's emotional well-being. The Tinbergens' list of "autismogenic" factors is gleaned, as they incessantly remind the reader, from their years of keen and patient observation. While they include some circumstances and events that are not Mommy-related—divorce, traveling too much, moving household, living in high-rise buildings— most implicate Mother directly. These maternal mishandlings include difficult nursing sessions, bottle-feeding rather than breast-feeding of babies, "overly intellectual mothers," depressed mothers, bored mothers, mothers who leave their child in the care of someone else (nanny or day care center), inexperienced mothers, overanxious mothers, mothers who read too many books on mothercraft, mothers who are too serious, too preoccupied.

Those who reject this psychogenic notion, by the way, do so for "nonscientific, nonrational reasons" arising from their own "feelings of guilt."

> These [feelings of guilt] make it almost impossible for parents of autistic children to accept the theory of a psychogenic origin of autism, even in the face of quite suggestive evidence. [Upon examination, the "quite suggestive evidence" turns out itself to be neither scientific nor rational; it stems solely from the Tinbergens' subjective (but extremely confident) interpretation of autistic behavior.]

Yes, but that was the Tinbergens. What did Dr. Welch have to say? Her paper on holding therapy appeared at the end of the Tinbergen book. "Autism," she writes, "is caused by faulty bonding between mother and child." She finds support for this firm declaration in the "fact" that children "cured" through holding therapy show no residual organic damage, which suggests that it is the mother–child interaction that plays the most significant role in the genesis of autism.

But once again, Mother is forgiven. Once again, the point is made that she just couldn't *help* it: She is a victim, just like her child, Dr. Welch charitably concedes.

Officially, then, Mommy is exonerated. In Dr. Welch's "case histories," however, Mother's peccadilloes are addressed somewhat more sharply:

"H.M.'s mother was cold, distant and intellectual."

"P.R.'s mother was punitive and cold toward him."

"In one severe case of autism . . . the child made twenty physical approaches to the mother's one."

My sense of unease with holding therapy could only keep increasing in the face of this ever-more-explicit evidence of what to me was its source in the Bettelheim model, the "blame-the-mommy" theory of autismogenesis.

I still needed to see and hear more, however. The promise of a miracle bonding cure is hard to give up, and a redeemer is hard to renounce. I stifled my nascent disloyalty to Dr. Welch and made the trip to Connecticut twice more—once with Marc and Anne-Marie, once with Anne-Marie only.

But some things happened there that were just too hard for us—too hard to rationalize, to excuse, to forgive.

The first episode involved Sean, a three-year-old boy. I was very anxious about Sean. He was one of the more severely impaired children I had seen at the Mothering Center. He was constantly in motion, dancing on his toes, flapping his hands, squealing, shaking his head, jumping up and down: a little marionette boy, completely locked into his own world. His mother upset me even more. I could barely look at her. She appeared quite literally exhausted with grief: gray skin, hollow eyes, mouth clenched into a tight line of pain. She and her husband were there, trying to do a holding with Sean. Nothing. No eye contact, no letup of the squealing and the shaking, no recognition of them at all. On and on it went. "Sean, look at me. Please. Please, Sean. Look into my eyes." Suddenly Sean's head cracked against a piece of furniture. His mother stopped, concerned now about the swelling bump. "Can I have some ice? I need some ice. He's hurt his head."

Dr. Welch was not there that day. The woman who seemed to function as her assistant came over. "Mary," she said, "that bump is insignificant compared to the damage you will do if you don't get a resolution from this child."

"I can't get a goddamn resolution!" shouted Mary, and she started to sob.

Everyone was quiet, concentrating on this painful drama, pretending not to. Then suddenly Dr. Welch's assistant turned to me: "Catherine, Mary believes that one of the reasons she can never get a good holding from Sean is that her husband is not giving her enough support. Perhaps you could tell us some of the positive ways your husband supports you. . . ."

One of Martha Welch's contentions is that if the father is absent, hostile to the idea of holding, or in other ways "nonsupportive" of his wife, no cure can take place.

"I don't think she needs a lecture on marriage from me!" I snapped. "I think she needs you to stop telling her she needs to get a resolution!"

How, I wondered angrily, could anyone allow this mother to think that the entire burden of helping such a severely disabled child rested on her shoulders alone? He should have been in an intensive therapeutic program. Why wasn't he? What if *we* had decided to throw out Bridget at the beginning, as I had been tempted to do? What if we had to rely on holding alone?

What is almost as pernicious as the idea of Mommy as cause of autism, I was suddenly beginning to feel, is the idea of Mommy as *cure* for autism. To put the entire burden of her child's progress on the shoulders of Mary, and pressure her to achieve a "resolution" with a severely impaired child, struck me as simply loading some additional guilt on her already breaking back.

The second incident, on our third and final visit, involved another boy, Tim, around ten years old.

As his mother began to do a holding with him, he resisted and they started to struggle together. The struggle escalated until they were both on the floor, the mother shouting at Tim, Tim silently fighting on. The mother, now visibly enraged, straddled him with her knees, and then, in order to keep his arms pinned to the floor, knelt with her full weight on his biceps. Suddenly Tim's face, impassive until then, twisted in pain, and he began, finally, to sob. "No!" he choked out.

I glanced up. Dr. Welch was there, observing the scene, smiling away as usual.

We left the Mothering Center, and never went back. We were disheartened, sickened by what we had seen: mothers lashing out not only against themselves but against their children. Though I was still susceptible to thinking this disorder was somehow my fault, I certainly didn't think it was Anne-Marie's.

Shortly thereafter, in early summer, Dr. Welch left the city. She was to be away for July, and then in August she was to take off for England, where the BBC would continue filming their documentary about holding therapy. Her fame was growing.

It was just as well that she was leaving, I felt. My most recent sessions at her apartment had been tense, argumentative to the point of anger, and punctuated constantly by calls from lawyers, agents, publishers, journalists. Whenever we did get around to talking about Anne-Marie, her advice was invariable.

"Anne-Marie is afraid to walk in the street," I would report.

"Hold her every night," came the response.

"Anne-Marie's language is still so limited and inflexible."

"Hold her and she'll talk when she's ready. I hope you're still not pressuring her with those drills."

"Anne-Marie still doesn't come to me when I get home."

"Just hold her a lot."

Compared to what we were doing in the behavioral program, this advice was beginning to sound a bit vague.

In spite of my growing disillusionment with Dr. Welch, however, there was a part of me that still wanted to believe in her. Not even so much in holding therapy per se, just in her. Whatever Dr. Welch's flawed beliefs, I thought, she was a sincere person, and she had held me together at a time when I needed her badly. Moreover, I still believed that holding therapy had some value. I decided to keep on with it (my own version). I would continue to refine it over the summer, while allowing Bridget to direct the arduous acquisition of all those "skills" which, I had to admit, I cared a lot about.

20

I'M NOT SURE I would know what a "normal life" is anymore, but one thing was certain: Marc and I were outside the pale. We were living, breathing, dreaming, talking, and thinking autism. Marc did have his work as a distraction, but even he admitted that between phone calls or meetings the obsessive thoughts on autism would come stealing back.

It was early June. We were still taking each day as it came, grateful for the gifts of the moment, trying not to be too anxious about what tomorrow held.

I craved silence and would treasure the quiet times that I could steal during the day, or late in the evening. I would sit on the couch or curl up in bed: not reading, not talking, just trying to let the day float away from me, easing myself into stillness and peace.

Some of my friendships disintegrated. Crises seem to have a way of shaking down your friendships. Some survive, some don't.

After our first child was stillborn, I rather naïvely expected a certain amount of understanding from my friends. I was in for one of the ruder shocks of my life, and was propelled into a more cynical adulthood than I had yet inhabited. After all was said and done—after all the "Don't worry, you'll have another" comments had stung once too often—I had resigned myself to a certain truth: Most people can't sympathize with what they don't have knowledge of. And unless they set themselves to consider a particular crisis or loss, unless they actively decide to put themselves into another person's sensitivities, they won't get that knowledge. They don't want it.

None of us, myself included, really wants to jump into another's pain. There are probably scores of other reasons that come into play as well: If we can't fix something in our friend's life, we feel helpless. If we can't make it go away, we want to pretend it's not there. We don't know what to say. We're at a loss for words. Our lives have their own aches and sorrows. If we see poverty, we try at least to help by giving some money away, even though we know that our money doesn't go very far. But if we see heartbreak, most of us are even less effective: we try to talk the person out of it. Maybe we have to learn that often there is no "solution" for suffering. Everyone has some of it, sooner or later. What helps is to have one or two people around who keep trying to understand, who are willing to just hold our hand as we walk on through it.

Throughout my catastrophic pregnancies I learned to turn to women—women who had gone through the same thing, or women who simply understood the powerful invasion of love that one can feel for a child one has never known, has only seen and held for a brief but terrible moment. Some women knew this because they had felt it themselves, because they knew what it was like to fall forever in love with a newborn, or to grieve the loss of a life just barely begun.

But for others, men and women, that which was visible, and easily understood—like, early in our marriage, my broken foot—inspired ten times the clucking sympathy and expressions of pity as all those messy, hidden, mysterious, and somehow shameful reproductive traumas. One day I am walking down the street with a big belly, greeting all the neighborhood friends and shopkeepers. A week later I walk around with no belly and no baby, and no one says a word. There is a polite turning away of the eyes. Did she have an abortion? Did the baby die? Better not talk about it; it'll just stir her up. She'll have another. There were times, in the weeks after that birth, that I wanted to carry a sign: *I had a baby. He was a boy. He was himself; irreplaceable; forever unique. He died.* The need to give voice to a shattered heart became overwhelming. This happened. This was real. This hurt. Please don't make me pretend that nothing happened.

During and after Anne-Marie's diagnosis a few good friends, like Evelyne and Daniela, did try to listen and to understand. My sisters not only listened; they also mourned with me.

But I had to find a way of defending myself against the others. Sometimes when I tried to share part of this struggle with autism with a friend or acquaintance, I encountered an almost hostile, certainly stubborn resistance to the idea that there was anything wrong at all.

"She looks fine to *me*" was a comment I was to hear fairly often. Or, "I'm sure she'll outgrow it. She's probably just shy."

On the one hand, I understood some of this resistance. Anne-Marie was young, we had caught her condition very early, and we seemed to be already turning it around. It was hard for anyone who didn't live with her to believe that there was anything wrong with a two-year-old child who was now combining some words. They had no immediate way of knowing what her history had been, or how far from normal still was her overall social and linguistic development. How could they be expected to know about frequency of spontaneous eye contact, inflexibility of language, paucity of social overtures to people? They judged by what they saw, and to a casual observer she now looked perfectly normal. They thought it helpful to diminish and downplay whatever problem I was rattling on about.

On the other hand, their attitude inspired a certain defensive paranoia in me. Did they think I had made it all up? Yes, life is very boring on the housewife-mommy track. Maybe I'll con a few neurologists and psychiatrists and various other professionals into diagnosing my daughter as autistic. Create a little excitement around here.

Of course, the incredulity I was encountering at this point was nothing compared to the outright skepticism we found as Anne-Marie got better and better. It is impossible. This cannot be. This child was misdiagnosed. Autistic children do not recover.

But that was still to come.

Back then, I held on to the handful of people who were willing to share some of the uncertainty and anxiety with me, and treasured their understanding. One spring weekend when Marc and I took the kids out to my sister Jean's house I was so grateful that she made no comment as I got up again and again to bring Anne-Marie back into the fold. Too often, other people could not accept this need to be vigilant and persistent. They would quite imperiously order me back to my chair.

"Sit down! Let the kids play in peace!"

"Relax, Catherine!"

"Leave her alone! She just wants to do her own thing!"

"Don't they understand?" I would ask Marc in despair. "Don't they see that the whole point is to go after her, *not* to leave her alone?"

There would be time enough to let her play in peace, to leave her alone. She had a whole lifetime in front of her to be a normal child and grow toward independence and autonomy. We had only this little window of opportunity, this slice of time that I figured was not more than a year or two in which to get her set in that direction. It wasn't the time yet for me to sit back and relax.

"No," Marc would respond matter-of-factly. "They don't understand. Either we sit them down and explain everything to them or we try not to let it bother us."

"Well, it does bother me. It's hard enough going after a withdrawn child all day long without being castigated as an obsessive-compulsive overprotective mother. Why can't they see that this is a crisis situation and we have to respond on red alert? Sit back, relax, take it easy, and somehow rescue our kid from a condition which we invented in the first place! Cretins! Imbeciles! I hate them all!"

"You hate them all!" Marc laughed.

I laughed too. "Yes! Stomp them! Jump on them! Boil them in oil!"

Walking around outside with Anne-Marie gave rise to a different sort of criticism. Ever since Daniel was a tiny baby I've realized that many people are made acutely uncomfortable by the sound of a baby or a child crying. I think some kind of instinctive reaction comes into play. A small child begins to scream or sob, the adults within hearing become uneasy and anxious, moving and shuffling around like a pack of elephants sensing danger. If Daniel started acting up in a grocery store, elderly women would rush over to jangle keys in his face. "Coo, coo! Baby! Stop crying!"

And then of course, everyone has his or her opinion about how the child should be cared for. When Daniel was little, he had a bad case of eczema on his scalp: "cradle cap," the pediatrician called it. I was supposed to rub an ointment onto his head, which had the unfortunate effect of turning his scalp pink. The second part of the doctor's recommendation was to expose his scalp to sunlight.

But the population of Greenwich Village, where we lived at the time, would have none of that. As I carried him to the park one day, my shiny-headed, pink-scalped baby, I was lectured by total strangers on every corner.

"Put a hat on that child's head!"

"He needs a sunscreen!"

My only consolation as I ran this gauntlet was the reflection that at least they cared!

When I tried to take Anne-Marie for a walk, I had a more acute problem. She wouldn't do it. She wanted to be carried or put in the stroller, but she refused to walk. Her knees would buckle under her; she would fall to the sidewalk in a sobbing heap. I didn't know it then, but apparently this is a fairly common problem with autistic children. A few mothers have since told me of having to lug their four- and five-year-old children every time they set foot outside.

I didn't know what to do. There was no question of waiting for her to grow out of it. I had already decided that I was not going to wait for her to grow out of anything. Problems only seemed to get worse if left untreated.

Bridget suggested that I make her walk.

"How do I *make* her walk?"

"Well," responded Bridget, "I would take her by the hand and just bring her along. If she collapsed on the sidewalk, I'd pull her to her feet. If she made any move forward at all I'd praise her a lot. I would completely ignore her crying. If she continued to cry I'd still go at least a block with her, then end the walk and take her back inside."

I tried it.

It was pure hell: Anne-Marie sobbing in the street, I pulling her to her feet, over and over, firmly repeating, "We have to walk. Come on, it's time to walk."

Passersby stared.

"Poor child."

"Oh, the poor little girl."

Drops of sweat beaded on my forehead. This was so awful. Did I really have to do this? And did I really have to do it in public?

"Come on, Anne-Marie. Time to walk."

Finally she took a few steps forward.

"Good girl! You're walking! Good walking!"

Miraculously, it worked. We walked half a block, Anne-Marie occasionally whimpering, but seeming a bit more calm and confident. I picked her up and carried her the rest of the way home. We would do this in increments, I decided. A half block today, a block tomorrow. The important step seemed to have been to get her at least to start, to try it.

Within a week, she was walking with me to pick up Daniel at his summer play school. My good-mother image was a mite tarnished in the neighborhood, but I did have a freely walking child, happy and calm.

So I was quite often to find myself between a rock and a hard place: chastised when I hovered around her; stared at stonily if I exercised the firm approach that a lot of her behavioral program demanded. I wish I were one of those people who have the knack of explaining difficult things easily without getting all tense and anxious. Failing that, I wish I knew how not to care what people think.

As time went on, the world of professionals, friends, acquaintances, and strangers became divided into two camps: those who rendered things more difficult, and those who helped. The first camp was far more heavily populated than the second. But notwithstanding the sometimes painful lack of sympathy Marc and I and Anne-Marie encountered, we were fortunate—indeed, blessed—in the people we did find who helped, each in his or her own way.

Dr. DeCarlo had given us an early diagnosis—no small gift when I consider the number of families I know today who have been strung along for years with "He'll be fine, just give him time." Autism seems to be progressive, at least in the first few years of life. The earlier you treat it, the more hope you have.

Dr. Cohen had been almost alone in allowing the legitimate possibility of recovery, and to speak of a fellow professional's work with objectivity. Now there are more professionals who will validate the occurrence of recovery, but in early 1988 they were few and far between.

As to therapy, we had been blessed with a couple of the best therapists around, Bridget and Robin. These two had just walked into our lives, a few weeks after Anne-Marie's diagnosis, and powerfully spearheaded every phase of her rescue. Knowing what I know now, I am sadly aware of how few good therapists there are, and how sorely they are needed by so many families.

For every friend's or stranger's insensitive remark or tacit disapproval of something I was or was not doing with Anne-Marie, there had yet been people who understood and who listened with intelligence and sympathy. And whenever I spiraled down into rage or sorrow or hopelessness, there was Marc, holding me up, enfolding me, knowing even how to laugh me into lightness.

In time, I would come to know many more good people: those who were to walk with us and talk with us on our journey, those who were truly to ease the burden. Several of them were psychologists.

Fortunately so, since even before Anne-Marie's diagnosis I had been well on my way to damning the whole lot of them as egocentric fools. I had thought of them all as preachers of a religion of the self, false priests and prophets imbued with an inflated authority, the gods of popular culture in America. Women's magazines especially annoyed me by the way they regularly turned to psychologists for the final word, the "expert opinion" on every subject under the sun.

But as the months went by, I was to find a few good psychologists: men and women humble about the limitations of their knowledge, yet possessed of enough theoretical or clinical expertise to be of genuine assistance; secure enough to discuss issues with me, instead of feigning knowledge they didn't have and lecturing pedantically to me; members of this "helping profession" who actually helped.

One of those in the ranks of the "good guys" was Dr. Bernard Rimland, who made me understand that when a psychologist is bad he is very bad indeed, but when he is good he is splendid.

He had received the letter I had written him about holding therapy and Dr. Welch, and sent a reply. It was a courteous, open-minded, and considered response. I was more than pleasantly surprised: I was almost shocked. Why should this man have taken the time and the trouble to respond with such eloquent thoughtfulness to a letter written by a complete stranger? Moreover, what was a cardinal, if not the pope, in the world of autism doing addressing a "lay person" with such evident respect, almost collegiality? His tone was not just courteous; it was lively and engaged, intellectually challenging, curious, probing: How did I account for this? What did I think of that? This guy was actually asking my opinion! In closing, he invited my continued correspondence.

And a rich and fruitful correspondence it proved to be. Bridget and Robin were in the front lines doing the hard work, the nitty-gritty fighting for Anne-Marie. But Dr. Rimland, as the months progressed, became an invaluable counselor and teacher. His knowledge was so broad, his objectivity so evident, that I felt as though I had finally found someone who could discuss in depth with me the whys and the wherefores of the different therapies we were trying.

His editorial on holding therapy in the Fall 1987 issue of *Autism Research Review International,* which he included in his first letter to me, shed much light on that complex and emotionally charged issue. Finally someone was giving me a credible context into which I could fit holding therapy. Someone very learned was allowing the possibility that it might indeed have some effectiveness, as I believed, but that the reasons why had nothing to do with Mother's lousy bonding skills.

Basically, Dr. Rimland's argument was that holding therapy, to the extent it was effective, was effective for physiological rather than emotional reasons. He hypothesized that, in line with years of research that pointed to a cerebellar dysfunction in autism, the forced holding of holding therapy may result in a type of cerebellar stimulation in the fiercely resisting child, rather than in any "psychic rebonding."*

I myself thought that there was probably an emotional attachment or interchange that went on between mother and child during holding—after all, Anne-Marie's and my holdings had evolved into something not very violent or fierce—in combination with the cerebellar stimulation that Dr. Rimland was hypothesizing.

In any case, his ideas broadened my thinking about the whole issue, and my subsequent long and rich telephone conversations with him helped finally to dissolve whatever feelings of guilt and confusion I still had. In the end, we agreed that if nothing else, holding therapy was an efficient way of getting some autistic children's attention, something that seems to be primary for any learning to take place.

The more I talked with Dr. Rimland, the more I learned about objectivity. He was the first to impress upon me the idea that psychology could actually aspire to the rigorous methodology of a science—verifiable data, accountability, controlled research, openness to peer scrutiny—rather than remaining the province of talk therapists collecting fees for their superior insight. These were some of the qualities he demanded of himself as a psychologist, and they were the qualities that he had spent a quarter century demanding of his colleagues.

Author of *Infantile Autism,* published in 1964,† Dr. Rimland had practically single-handedly rung the death knell of the Bettelheim hegemony. In the words of one journalist, "Rimland blew Bettelheim's theory to hell." After *Infantile Autism,* with its carefully reasoned, painstakingly factual analysis of just about everything that was known about autism at the time, the notion that the syndrome was psychogenic would never again dominate the professional consciousness. Although the diehards would linger on for years, as Marc and I had discovered, most mainstream professionals hailed Rimland as the profound and original thinker who had finally wrenched autism research onto the right track, cogently sketching out the more likely neurobiological basis of the autistic syndromes. His theories are being everywhere validated today. Not only did his prescience help to launch the search for

Autism Research Review International, vol. 1, no. 3, Fall 1987.
†Out of print today, unfortunately, but still available in libraries, and still known in the professional community as a seminal work.

true causes and cures, but his book was also a long-overdue cry of pity and justice for parents who had been blamed for years for their children's illness.

Dr. Rimland was a wise and generous teacher to me and, in the end, he became a trusted friend. If he had no direct hand in the rescue of Anne-Marie, his entire life's work certainly facilitated it, and his confidence in me continuously reinforced my strength of purpose and my own confidence in my choices for her. Torn by uncertainty and confusion when I first made contact with him, I gathered serenity and clarity of thought from every conversation I had with him. In strengthening me, he strengthened my whole family.

21

WE WERE STAYING in the city during that summer, in order to be near Bridget and Robin, and went out to East Hampton on occasional weekends. I had grown up out there, a hundred miles east of New York on the south shore of Long Island, and yearned to go back whenever I could for the blue waters, the quiet starry skies, the peace of the woods. Marc always called it paradise. However chic and crowded it had become, it was still to us the loveliest land in God's creation.

During the week in New York, Daniel went to play camp, and every day at noon I would walk up there with Anne-Marie to pick him up. In the morning I worked with Anne-Marie, taking her for walks, playing on the floor with her, trying constantly to involve her in whatever I was doing. I was beginning to be able to play more and more with her: I could hold her attention for longer periods of time than I had ever been able to. I was learning a lot from Bridget and Robin about how to maximize my time with her, how to reinforce and expand on her language.

Singing with her still seemed to be one of the best ways of getting her attention and working on language. Any song that entailed some physical play as well, like "the itsy-bitsy spider," or "little rabbit foo-foo," or "row-row-row your boat" really perked her up. Most of the time when I sang with her she had to be sitting right on my lap, facing me. That way I could get maximum eye contact and involvement from her.

Dancing was good too. I'm probably the world's klutziest dancer, but I have at least mastered the basic one-two-three of the waltz. I would pick her up in my arms and waltz her around the room to the strains of "Once Upon a Dream" from the Walt Disney movie *Sleeping*

Beauty. The lyrics expressed a tenderness and hopefulness that befitted our dance of awakening:

> *I know you, I walked with you once upon a dream.*
> *I know you, the gleam in your eyes is so familiar a gleam,*
> *And I know it's true that visions are seldom all they seem.*
> *Still if I know you, I know what you'll do:*
> *You'll love me at once,*
> *The way you did once*
> *Upon a dream.*

Play-Doh provided another good activity, especially for teaching the beginnings of imaginative play. We could do tons of things with Play-Doh: make snakes and have them hiss along the table and up her arm, make little hamburgers and pretend to eat them, stick candles in the Play-Doh cake and have a birthday party for one of the stuffed animals, make little people and have them walk around and talk to each other. . . .

We had fun with blocks too. Building a tall tower and having Anne-Marie knock it down never failed to get a laugh out of her. "Crash!" Then we would build it back up again, but this time we would turn it into a "my turn/your turn" game. "My turn to put on a block," I would say. Then, guiding her hand: "Your turn to put on the block." Then eventually "my turn/your turn" with only a touch to her hand, but always with eye contact.

So much of this play was influenced by my observations of Bridget and Robin. I was getting more adept each day at procuring Anne-Marie's attention, modeling contextually evident language, engaging her in interactive, rather than solitary, play. What fascinated me, though, was seeing that each one of us could work with Anne-Marie in our own style: Bridget, the most consistent and structured, could always get her interested in completing challenging cognitive tasks; Robin, affectionate and joyful, was often able to put her into a happy social mood, thereby encouraging verbal communication; and I, in spite of my pushing and prodding demands on her, my changing roles as tyrant and nurturer, could somehow still make her feel safe and loved. She wanted often now to be near me, and sometimes would tell Bridget so as soon as a session ended: "Want Mommy."

Coloring and drawing were rudimentary at this point, of course, but we handled them the way we were handling everything else. We started off by controlling and guiding her hand, forming her fingers correctly around the pencil, teaching her to imitate horizontal strokes, vertical strokes, circles, and squares. From there, we moved gradually to drawing circle-faces and showing her where to put in the eyes, nose, and mouth.* Over the course of many weeks, we gradually relinquished all control, praising and encouraging like mad her every initiative to create for herself. Fortunately, she loved coloring and drawing, and the activities themselves became rewarding for her after a while.

It seemed to me that once we had pushed so hard and forced her to *pay attention,* the rest was a question of filling up that attentiveness with anything that we could think of to sustain her interest, especially her interest in us and in communicative language. Once we had her attention, however, we had to do something else: we had to help her *shift* her attention. The programs had to be fast-paced. The activities in the outside world had to be varied. Even in working with her, we had to keep her from "locking into" any one toy or activity.

As she got better and better, our own language with her had to keep evolving. No longer could we speak in abbreviated telegraphic phrases like "Touch nose"; we had to become progressively more "normal" in our communication with her: "Would you give me that, Anne-Marie?"

All of us, Bridget in the structured curriculum, Robin and I in the more generalized play, had to keep asking ourselves the same questions: What are her weaknesses, both behavioral and linguistic? What is she ready for? How can we interest her? How can we challenge her?

Bridget came in for therapy every afternoon, and Robin came Monday, Wednesday, and Friday evenings, after the children's dinner. Life had settled into a fairly manageable routine. Marc and I actually went to a movie one night, the first in about seven months. We felt almost safe again. Our days were peaceful enough, our nights brought no more nightmares, our children were growing and thriving—all of them.

Michel was a happy smiling baby. He looked like a smaller version of his father: straight blond hair, full French mouth, dark eyes. Like Daniel, he was tall for his age, although he was still baby-round, not slender like his brother. Home videotapes show him scooting around in his little baby walker, grabbing things, babbling, curious about his world and responsive to the sound of our voices. His eye contact, of

---

*If we were working with Play-Doh or coloring or drawing, we tried to concentrate a little more on the representation of human faces rather than on inanimate objects. We wanted to increase her awareness of people over things.

which we were far more acutely aware than we had been with either Daniel or Anne-Marie, was lively, direct, and engaged. His smile was ready and full-hearted. Often Marc and I would breathe a sigh of relief when we looked at him or played with him. We knew that the probability of having two children afflicted with autism was very low, but still, we couldn't help feeling a little twinge of fear every now and then. We talked about his development frequently, compared him to what we remembered of Anne-Marie in her first year. What if . . . after all, Anne-Marie had had a late deterioration . . . Oh God, impossible. Thank heavens, there's no sign of that in him.

As the summer progressed, we caught and held on to fleeting happiness. Anne-Marie was doing so well, making such beautiful progress. We still didn't know how far she would go, but she was learning so fast, coming back so rapidly. People who hadn't seen her for a while saw her progress even more clearly than we, who lived with her every day.

One Saturday in July we were standing on the porch in front of the East Hampton house. My mother drove up, got out of her car, and began to walk toward the house. Anne-Marie, to our astonishment, dropped what she was doing and ran toward her grandmother.

"Gruh-gruh!" she said, her version of "Grandma." My mother's face lit up with joy. "Anne-Marie," she responded simply.

I happened to be putting together some Fisher-Price tricycles for Daniel and Anne-Marie. Anne-Marie began to whine and cry because she was impatient to try hers. My mother couldn't stop exclaiming over how wonderful that was.

"Why?" I asked.

"Don't you remember, a few months ago she would have been oblivious to anything like this!"

"That's true," I reflected. I remembered the Christmas right after her diagnosis. On Christmas Eve we had brought a large tree into the apartment, feeling that the children should still have some kind of celebration, even if the adults around them were in a state of shock. As we carried in the big green tree and set it up in the stand, Anne-Marie had not even looked up.

Bridget was becoming increasingly excited over Anne-Marie's progress in the therapy sessions. "She's just whipping through these programs!" she told me. But it wasn't only that Anne-Marie's rate of learning was so fast: She was becoming more socially responsive. Bridget didn't have to use the primary reinforcers quite as much as she had in the first weeks of the program. Anne-Marie now seemed to like an enthusiastic "Good job!" as much as the cookie or the windup toy. We were seeing a personality start to form. It was evident mostly in the expression on her face, when she would look inquiringly into our eyes or give her little half-smile when she got something right in therapy. We were seeing the beginnings of a self where we had seen only absence and indifference before.

Much later, Bridget confessed to me that at first she had found it quite difficult to work with Anne-Marie. "I can't get through to her," she had complained to her boyfriend, John. "She's learning, but there's no affect, no expression on her face." Now, Anne-Marie's bright eyes and curious look exhilarated us all.

I was sitting on the floor with her one day, playing, and the word "butter" came up.

"Ba-wa," she repeated.

"Butter," I corrected.

"Ba-wa," she persisted.

"But-*ter,*" I insisted.

"*Ba-wa!*" she yelled. The message was clear. All right already, Mom! I'm saying it the way I hear it!

I loved these sparks of independence.

After I had moved Anne-Marie's bed into Daniel's room, back in February, not wanting Anne-Marie to be alone even at night, her awareness of him and his interest in her as a potential playmate did seem to increase. Then, around the middle of June, she rather suddenly developed a much keener interest in her big brother. We were delighted. She started to seek him out, moving across the room to where he was playing. It was not quite interactive play, but it was certainly the seeds of parallel play, and day by day it increased dramatically. Soon, she was imitating his actions and gestures to a pretty extreme degree.

If he crossed his legs while sitting on the floor, she studied him, then crossed hers the same way. If he jumped up and down in excitement, she jumped up and down, then stopped as soon as he did. At the breakfast table it was simultaneously amusing, encouraging, and disconcerting to see her eyeing him keenly, observing his every movement and faithfully copying it. He took a spoonful of cereal. She took a spoonful of cereal, her eyes on him the whole time. He put down his spoon and picked up his cup of juice with both hands. She put down her spoon and picked up her cup. He put down his cup; she did the same.

"We'll just keep an eye on the behavior for now," said Bridget. "Let's see where it goes." We were pleased that Anne-Marie was tuning in to Daniel, after all. We didn't want to discourage her, even if she was going a little overboard.

Normal two-year-olds imitate other kids anyway, I thought. If she's carrying it to an extreme, maybe she's making up for lost time.

One day I brought Daniel back home from a friend's house. Anne-Marie must have heard the key in the door, because when I opened it she was standing there, looking expectantly up. (Even that small thing filled me with such happiness.) Daniel and I walked into the apartment. Before either of us could say anything more than hi, she reached out to him and put her arms around him.

"Ah-oh-oo," she said.

"I love *you!*" he cheerily responded, very matter-of-factly. Then the two of them were off, not noticing as their mother buried her face in her hands.

Daniel was a co-therapist of great commitment. *He* didn't consider that there was anything wrong with his sister. He wasn't mortally wounded by her lack of spontaneity or interest. If she didn't look at him, he yelled a little louder. Always an exuberant, demanding, happy, excitable child, he was hell-bent on getting his sister's attention, just as he got everyone else's attention. "Anne-Marie! Come here! Hold this!" He was always making something with Legos or wooden blocks or paper and glue. He wanted a playmate or a helper or sometimes just an audience, and he had no compunction at all about forcing his sister's involvement. "Look at me!" he would command her, apparently in imitation of all of us adults constantly asking for Anne-Marie's gaze. "Anne-Marie, *look!*"

Did she mind this tyrannical bossing around? She seemed to love it. She became almost inseparable from Daniel, looking for him as soon as she got out of therapy, more and more interested in his projects and his play.

Anne-Marie was in session with Bridget one afternoon in late July. We had been working on several different programs, including a naming program: we were teaching her to name everyone in her home, and to use the names whenever she wanted something. "Ee-yo" was her name for Daniel. I think she got it from the last syllable ("-iel").

Anne-Marie heard Daniel playing in the hallway and became agitated and whiny.

"What do you want, Anne-Marie? Use words."

"Ee-yo. Want Ee-yo."

"Great talking, Anne-Marie! Good asking for Daniel!"

And Bridget promptly invited Daniel in to finish up the session with them.

Maybe it was because he was little, like her, maybe it was because he made a lot of noise, maybe because he was just so aggressively demanding of her—whatever the reason, as Anne-Marie came out of the darkness, she stretched out her hand to place it in her brother's, and to this day she has not let him go.

ANNE-MARIE was making fast progress, but she was not home free yet. The worries still plagued us—partly because we had no model, not one other recovered child we could compare her to. Would she plateau at some point? Would she reach a certain level and simply stop developing? Her language was coming in, but it was still predominantly rote. Her social behavior was improving, but would she ever be as spontaneous, as curious, as communicative as normal kids? Would she ever in her life understand the rich subtleties of language, both spoken and written? Would she ever have a friend, ever cry over someone else's pain, ever fall in love?

Though I tried to be grateful—I *was* grateful—for the incredible gains she had made, I never knew if she would lose them the next week, or the next month, or, for that matter, the next morning. But she never did. She slowed down, she sometimes stopped. She still had days when she said almost nothing, or spent the whole afternoon without once reaching out to anyone for contact. She still had days when the "autism self" held sway over the "Anne-Marie self" and over and over she would return to the same sterile perseverative activity, and over and over I would have to drag her away from it.

But she didn't go backward. By that I mean that once she had learned something new she didn't lose it. Once she became interested in Daniel, she would never again be completely oblivious to him. Once she began to combine words, she continued to do so, at first sporadically and in imitation only, then more and more frequently.

However, there remained some hurdles to surmount. During this period of intense, accelerated learning, Anne-Marie did many things that normal children her age do, but to an extreme degree. Like echo-ing. Normal two-year-olds echo quite a bit. It's a linguistic behavior that peaks around thirty months, according to *The Me Book*. They be-come very interested in repeating verbatim what someone else has said. But they mix this echoing with more spontaneous and creative lan-guage as well. With Anne-Marie, echoing, which had begun in June, rapidly grew obsessive. Robin noted in one session that Anne-Marie had echoed approximately ninety percent of everything Robin said. Sometimes Anne-Marie would start to echo what we were saying even before we'd reached the end of a sentence. I thought of it almost as a kind of "verbal stim,"★ where she was becoming entranced with the sound of words, irrespective of what they meant. Her father came home from work one evening and walked into the bathroom, where I was bathing her.

"Hi, Anne-Marie."

"Hi, Anne-Marie," she responded.

"Say 'Hi, Daddy.' "

"Say 'Hi, Daddy.' "

"Could I have a kiss?"

"I have a kiss?"

He just kissed her anyway.

We tried not to draw any attention to the echoing, because in our weekly conference about Anne-Marie's program we had decided to ignore it. We had had enough difficulty getting her to repeat words; we didn't want suddenly to start telling her not to repeat.

But the problem grew worse and worse, to the point where the echoing completely dominated her speech. We decided to change tac-tics: Bridget would address it in session only, while the rest of us, in the "outside world," continued to ignore it. The "No Echo" program consisted of Bridget's saying "No echo" and placing a finger on Anne-Marie's lips every time she started to echo.

In time, the echoing did begin to fade as Anne-Marie mastered more appropriate communication, although I would estimate that in all it took about six to eight months to disappear entirely.

Prosody was another tricky area. As Anne-Marie's language came in more surely, she began to do something odd: she began to squeak. Instead of saying her words in a normal tone of voice, everything was

★The jargon becomes routine after a while. A "stim" is a "self-stimulatory behavior." Bridget, Robin, Marc, and I would talk about verbal stims, tactile stims, visual stims, etc., the way other people talked about the weather.

very high-pitched. "Do you want lunch?" I would ask. "Yes," she would squeak. "Want luntz." There wasn't a whole lot we could do about it, other than modeling an extra-low tone of voice. Sometimes I tried to involve her in a little game, where I would squeak something, laugh about it, then say the same thing in a deep voice. Back and forth I would go, trying to make her hear the difference between the two registers, trying to get her to imitate me. After a while we were able to use a verbal prompt: "Say it lower" (said itself in a low voice), and finally she became able to correct herself.

Fearfulness was still a big problem. She was prey to the most excruciating fears. I took her and Daniel for a walk one afternoon in the woods in East Hampton. Out of someone's driveway ran a little black dog, yapping excitedly. Anne-Marie began to cry, afraid. This excited the dog even more, and he began to jump up on her and Daniel. He wasn't dangerous, he was just a young puppy trying to play with them. But they both panicked and tried to run. "Don't run!" I called out. "He won't hurt you."

But it was too late. The children were screaming, the dog was going nuts, and the whole situation was out of control. I picked up Anne-Marie, took Daniel by the hand, and tried to walk calmly home. But the Hound of the Baskervilles kept jumping up on my legs, trying to get at Anne-Marie. She was practically hysterical.

Finally, I made it home and walked into the house with two sobbing children. Marc had to go out and chase away the dog, who insisted on yapping his head off and clawing on the front door. So much for our quiet walk.

Daniel cried for about five minutes, until we were able to calm him. Anne-Marie cried for the rest of the weekend.

Every now and then she would begin to quiet down; then she seemed to remember, and off she would go again, into a veritable fit of terror— trembling, sobbing, repeating "doggie, doggie" over and over again. I was beside myself. I held her, I talked to her, I tried to tell her about dogs and how they bark and jump when they want to play. Nothing worked. Indeed, any mention of the dog only seemed to increase her panic. Deep into the night she sobbed, until she finally fell asleep from exhaustion. The next morning she woke up and the tears and the trembling began all over again. This time, I tried ignoring the crying, just going about my business in a neutral way whenever she started up again. That was almost harder on me than it was on her, and didn't seem to help much anyway.

Finally, by Monday morning, I was at my wits' end. An idea suddenly occurred to me. Why not "dedramatize" it? Make it happen again, but this time give her some control? I took her on my lap, and retold "The Story of the Dog," hamming it up mercilessly.

"And *then* came the *dog!* And he made so much *noise! Yap, yap, yap, yap!* And Mommy came, and Daddy came, and Daniel came, and we all told that dog to stop! And Anne-Marie was the bravest of *all!* And she stood there and said, *'Go away, dog! Stop barking!'* "

She had stopped crying. She was listening. And she was understanding—at least the essence of the story.

"And Anne-Marie stood there. And Anne-Marie said, " *'Stop that, dog!'* "

I saw a little smile begin to form at the corners of her mouth.

"And *then!* Do you know what Anne-Marie did?"

She was listening attentively.

"She reached down and patted that dog's head!"

To be sure, this did not cure the problem instantly. But over the next couple of days, every time she began to cry about the dog, I would tell the story of brave Anne-Marie, and she would stop. Later, when we met dogs on the roads of East Hampton or the sidewalks of New York, the panic would start again. But each time, we stopped, turned and looked at the dog, and even reached out our hands to touch it. Marc and I are not advocates of throwing screaming children into the water, or forcing a panic-stricken child to touch an animal—we think that sort of thing is brutal. But there is something to be said for helping children take that first step over the threshold of what can be a paralyzing fear. Once we had pushed her a little to stop panicking and to make contact with dogs that frightened her, we were amazed to see how quickly she decided to like and trust them. She came around completely, going from quivering panic, to shaky courage, to laughing delight at their playfulness.

Anne-Marie had many fears as she emerged from her withdrawal. It sufficed for a person simply to look a little different—an extra-tall man, perhaps, or a woman who was wearing a very elaborate hat—to send her into another paroxysm of fear. A priest friend came to visit one evening. In walked Father Murray, six feet two inches tall, all dressed in black, with black hair. Anne-Marie took one look and shrieked. It was embarrassing trying to have a glass of wine and a cordial conversation while Anne-Marie cowered and sobbed every time she glanced at him.

"I hope you have an intact ego," I said apologetically.

"Shall I give her a blessing?" he asked.

"Well, let's wait till she goes to sleep."

Riding home on the bus one day, we were seated opposite a woman wearing a rather ostentatious red wig. Anne-Marie looked at her, buried her head against me, squeezed her eyes shut, and sobbed. Apparently she had some idea of a norm for physical appearance and couldn't stand any deviations.

The Tinbergen theory of an "anxiety-dominated emotional imbalance," whatever had caused it, really seemed valid to me in Anne-Marie's case. It wasn't until later, after I had met several autistic children who had never displayed this fearfulness, that I became convinced that while these phobias were one symptom in the autistic syndrome, they were not common to all afflicted children. Once when I was talking to a father about dealing with fears in his autistic son, he stopped me short when he asked, "What fears?" This was an intelligent man. I'm sure if his son had had the kind of fears Anne-Marie had, he would have been aware of it.

Along with debunking any overly simplistic theories about autism that might have seduced me, my many conversations with other parents made me aware of how different each autistic child can be, how individual.

ONE MORNING that summer my sister Burke called me. "Did you see the *Times* this morning?" she asked.

"Not yet. Why?"

"There's an article in the Science Section on autism. About someone out in California named Courchesne who's doing research. I didn't know whether I should tell you or not. It's sort of depressing."

I went to read the article. Eric Courchesne, Ph.D., had discovered an abnormality of the cerebellum in fourteen out of eighteen living subjects with autism. Previous studies of the brains of autistic subjects by means of X rays or even CAT scans had usually yielded negative results. Courchesne's work, facilitated by magnetic resonance imaging, was virtually the first clear-cut, visual suggestion of neurologic pathology in autistic people.

I called Burke back. "Why is that depressing?" I asked.

"Well, because if it's true, it makes her condition so final, so unquestionable . . . so real, I guess."

"Burke," I sighed. "I know it's hard to understand, but this news makes me happy!"

"Why?"

"Because there's so much nonsense out there about autism!" Every kook in the world had his pet theory about it, I told Burke. Everyone who thought he understood children thought he understood autism! I struggled to sound a little calmer, and went on:

"I like the fact that people are using MRI scans. I like the fact that those other people discovered a fragile x chromosome in some cases of autism." As a mattter of fact, I told her, I liked anything that would bring the cool light of reason and science to bear on all this mystery: I wanted more research on serotonin levels in the blood; the link between phenylketonuria (PKU) disease and autism; the connection between maternal rubella and autism. I couldn't wait for the day when we had some more answers.

I was surprised at the vehemence in my own voice. I hadn't realized what a tidal wave of impatience was growing inside me. I was angry. Not at Burke.

"But doesn't that make it more difficult for you, to know that something may really be neurologically wrong with Anne-Marie?" Burke asked. "Doesn't it make it more final?"

"No, not at all. I believe there was something wrong, but she's getting better every day. I believe she's recovering. I've believed from the beginning that the brain can sometimes heal itself, if given the right kind of stimulation."

"Yes, I can believe that too. And you're right. Anne-Marie is so much better every time I see her."

She was indeed. It was such a joy to see her blossoming before our eyes. It was impossible to remain worried for too long about any specific behavior or disability, because in all areas she just kept improving.

Even her odd mannerisms became less worrisome to me. Why should they devastate me, when I had a little girl who was learning how to talk with me, and look into my eyes, and smile at me?

Some of her mannerisms persisted far longer than others. She had always had trouble with the sense of touch. Sometimes she wanted to feel things too much, in an obsessive way, as when she would lay her cheek against any hard, cool surface she could find; or when she would spend many dreamy moments repetitively placing her palms flat against her own arms or legs.

At other times she had an aversion to touch. Those curled-back fingers that had been one of the earliest symptoms of her autism had become a familiar sight. It was as though she didn't want the palms of her hands to touch particular kinds of surfaces. One night she suddenly decided that she didn't want the soles of her bare feet to touch the granite floor in the kitchen. She stopped still each time she came to the kitchen doorway, dropped to her knees, and crawled awkwardly across the floor, hands curled into fists so that her palms wouldn't touch the floor either. She was "walking" on her fists and knees with her feet up in the air. It was astonishing to watch.

Along with trying to "desensitize" her tactile sense by running her hands and feet over different kinds of surfaces, Bridget and I would give her palms and soles deep massages. We didn't know exactly what we were doing; we had to feel (no pun intended) our way through this problem the way we had to figure out a lot of other issues. Now I hear that there are people who have more thoroughly researched the whole area of "sensory integration" and who know how to work with specific types of hypersensitivity.

But whatever the problem—prosody, echolalia, hypersensitivity, excessive solitude, lack of spontaneity or creativity in language, whining and crying—whatever it was, it just kept getting better. And it was getting better fast. Even I, who tended to worry the most, was beginning to feel more safe and sure as the weeks went by.

"Well, how did you expect your miracle to happen?" teased Marc one evening. "Pouf!—and she's cured? I don't think God works that way. I think you're seeing here everything you prayed for. I don't know if she could go any faster than she's going."

I wondered what Dr. Welch would say about her when she returned from England. I was starting to want to tell someone about Anne-Marie. I was beginning to be more than a little excited about what was happening in front of our eyes. Sometimes I would feel the joy as a physical presence, rising up inside and bubbling over in some unguarded moment, as a pure laugh of happiness. Day after day I watched her, and the gifts became innumerable.

Even in the small things, like her play, there was a purposefulness that had been lacking before. She had a truck with a little horse and cowboy that went inside. These days, instead of pushing the truck back and forth repeatedly over the rug, she would actually leave the room to search for that cowboy and horse. Then she would find them, bring them back, and go on playing. It seemed to me that she was thinking about what she needed in her play activities, planning things out more, taking steps to make her play more elaborate and imaginative.

With Daniel, she became more and more interactive. They were able to sustain their interest in each other's activities for longer periods of time, and it seemed to me that she was beginning to understand that he had some rights too—beginning, in a very rudimentary way, to grasp the concepts of sharing and turn taking. Once when he let out a howl because she had picked up something he was playing with, the train track set, she looked at him, then looked at the train in her hand, then gave him the train.

Even though she still cried a lot, Bridget and I rejoiced the first time we could bargain with her through language. A lot of her crying had become frustration crying: if she wanted something and didn't get it instantly, her automatic response was to burst into tears. But the day she seemed to understand and respond to "Anne-Marie, when you stop crying you can have the toy" was a breakthrough for all of us.

On August 30, Anne-Marie invited me into a game with her. She picked up a toy phone, walked across the room, extended the receiver toward me, and said: "Here. You. Me."

I practically jumped out of my chair. I almost frightened her, I was so excited. Everything—all the fast progress she had made in so many areas—was coming together in gestures and moments such as this one. This is great! I thought. This is wonderful! Look at her! She's inviting me into this interactive play! She's using language appropriately and spontaneously. She's using pronouns correctly, differentially.

Later that same day, she walked into the kitchen, where I was fixing a bottle for Michel.

"Mommy? Mommy?"

"Oh baby," I said, sinking down to take her in my arms. "Thank you for calling me. Anne-Marie, you are making Mommy so happy."

I could scarcely contain myself anymore. These moments of epiphany were almost overwhelming. That evening, I told Marc about her latest triumphs. He was as elated as I was. We needed to share our happiness with someone—someone official, who could validate this incredible progress and tell us where she stood in relation to her peers. We decided to make an appointment with Dr. Cohen.

It was September 29 when we returned to the big state Institute for Basic Research in Developmental Disabilities, in Staten Island. Marc drove; I sat in the back with Anne-Marie. It was a pretty day, with just a touch of coolness in the air and some white clouds floating high in a clear sky. "Boat," said Anne-Marie, as we drove by the Hudson. "Plane," she said, pointing at a helicopter. I held her hand. My mouth was a little dry. My heart was beating fast.

We waited for ten or fifteen minutes in the same waiting room we had visited eight months before. I was standing and holding Anne-Marie, who was looking at a bright calendar on the wall.

Dr. Cohen, accompanied by another psychologist, Dr. Vicky Sudhalter, walked into the waiting room. "Hello!" he called out.

"Hello," responded Marc.

Anne-Marie and I turned toward him.

"Hi," said Anne-Marie, looking straight into his eyes. She smiled shyly.

Dr. Cohen glanced at Dr. Sudhalter, then looked at Anne-Marie, then looked at me.

"Congratulations," he said softly.

I couldn't speak.

He knew. Even before we'd said anything, or gone through the videotaping, the parent interview, the Vineland test. He seemed to know at once. I think I understand this now. There is a quality to the gaze of a normal child. There is a connection, a recognition of the other as a person, an interest, that flashes out in the very first moments of a meeting. The autistic child lacks it so markedly that I believe some professionals can see autism within the first five minutes of an interview. I think that Dr. Cohen was seeing the absence of autism.

The evaluation went on for two hours. It was something out of a dream. Anne-Marie was in top form, actually seeming to enjoy the whole process. Dr. Cohen's written report of that reevaluation became one of my treasured documents:

> The child has made startling progress. . . . There was a marked contrast in Anne-Marie's behavior compared with our last observation. Then, she totally resisted reciprocal social interaction; engaged in perseverative behavior, had no eye contact, and was nonverbal. In today's evaluation, Anne-Marie had excellent eye contact; answered yes/no questions correctly; initiated "wanna draw" when seeing crayons; showed spontaneous labeling; imitated well; showed appropriate affect; identified body parts; knew colors; and differentiated "my" from "your."

Dr. Cohen obtained the following information from the Vineland Adaptive Scales:

In an eight-month period, Anne-Marie has moved into the clearly normal range in adaptive skills exceeding the ninety percent confidence interval predictions from 1/20/88. She has gained eighteen months in communication; thirteen months in ADL skills ["ADL skills" refers to daily living skills: eating with a fork, drinking from a cup, getting oneself dressed, etc.]; fifteen months in socialization; and sixteen months in motor skills.

The two doctors sat across the table from us at the end of the evaluation and summarized these findings. In all the skill categories, they told us—in communication, in social behavior, in motor skills, in daily living skills—she was functioning within the normal range.

Marc reached out to take my hand into his. I sat and stared straight ahead.

Dr. Sudhalter was smiling broadly. Dr. Cohen was asking Marc a lot of questions about the home program.

Don't cry! I said to myself with a mighty effort at self-control. *Don't start!*

But the tears welled up anyway, spilled over. I reached out for her, my lost baby come home, my lamb.

"Anne-Marie," I whispered as I buried my face in her hair.

Her arms came around my neck.

"Mommy."

* * * * *

A HALF HOUR LATER, we left the institute. Marc and I were moving somewhat cautiously, testing this new landscape. We were a little numb, a little dreamy.

We went to a mall we found in Staten Island to get a cup of coffee and to talk for a few minutes. In the lobby was a woman selling balloons. Anne-Marie noticed them and said, "Balloon?" I bought her one, heart-shaped, with "You're So Special" printed on it.

A balloon with "You're So Special." Total cost, $2.16.

How do I tell her what has happened, what she has accomplished? What gift or words or gesture would ever be adequate? How do I thank her for her own struggle as she made her way back to us?

We bought some Dom Pérignon for Bridget and Robin. I reflected on the absurd inequity of the exchange: Thanks for giving me back my daughter—here's a bottle of champagne.

Driving back to Manhattan, this time with Anne-Marie napping in the back and Marc and me up front, I turned to him and put words around what we both knew.

"God has answered our prayers."

"Yes."

"Why?"

Marc understood what I meant: Why us?

"Beats me!" He laughed.

Anne-Marie slept on. I thought of her future. I saw an opening into light, where I had seen only darkness before. I turned and looked out over the water.

Unbelievable. *Unbelievable.* Little miracle child, coming home.

> *Thou that hast giv'n so much to me,*
> *Give one thing more, a grateful heart.*
>
> *. . .*
>
> *Not thankful, when it pleaseth me;*
> *As if thy blessings had spare days:*
> *But such a heart whose pulse may be*
>   *Thy praise.*
>
> *Thou that hast giv'n so much to me,*
> *Give one thing more, a grateful heart.*

22

WAS ANNE-MARIE completely recovered? Was the battle over? For a while we didn't really know how or what to think.

In the week or so after the reevaluation we had some long conversations with Bridget, Robin, and Dr. Cohen. All three were in agreement: Her therapy should go on.

"It is highly recommended," Dr. Cohen had written in his reevaluation, "that her therapies be continued with a strong emphasis on generalizing her gains to other environments through modeling and continued mainstreaming."

Anne-Marie was only two and a half; we still had to see how well she would function at school, away from our intensive one-on-one attention. And we needed to see how well she would continue to develop linguistic and social skills.

As children move toward age three and beyond, all the questions come in: what, where, who, why, when, and finally, how. In addition, their conversational skills develop: they can speak more extensively on a topic and can converse with someone back and forth over several turns. They can respond to requests for clarification, like "What do you mean?," "Why did he do that?," "What did she say?" They understand nonliteral meanings in language: "We're going to have dinosaur stew for lunch" was a deadpan statement that Daniel would have greeted with a burst of laughter.

All of these skills were either absent or just barely emerging in Anne-Marie's language. None of us felt like pulling away all her supports just yet.

Dr. Cohen emphasized that the Vineland was a broad screening device, useful mostly to indicate whether a child was functioning within a statistical norm. It did not measure in any way whether she had any residual autistic traits; we all agreed she did. In expressive speech she still had echolalia and pronoun reversal, and in social conduct she could still be withdrawn.

These traits, in addition to some manneristic behaviors, made us all want to go on with the therapy until we were satisfied that she was perfectly safe without it.

To put it simply, our situation was not like some surgical operation where you have a diseased appendix one day and the next day you don't. We had reached a significant milestone on Anne-Marie's journey back, but we weren't quite sure if she would need our help for another two months or another two years.

We were out of the darkest woods of autism, that much was for certain. Whatever problems remained, Marc and I had a child with whom we could communicate. Moreover, every day we felt surer that she was learning to love and need us.

"I don't know what the future holds, Marc, but the present is fine."

"Yes. When you think of it, we don't know what the future holds for any of our kids, or for you and me either."

That was true, although I had to admit I was not one for divorcing myself entirely from the future. It seems to me it's just part of being human: to carry around our nostalgia for yesterday and our dreams for tomorrow.

One of the women from the Mothering Center with whom I'd become friendly had called the evening of Anne-Marie's reevaluation. Mother of a two-year-old boy who was just starting a home program, she generously rejoiced at our good news.

"Martha's back from England," she told me. "You should call her and let her know."

"OK," I agreed. Whatever my theoretical arguments with her, I really felt that I owed her something. I needed to thank her, the way I was thanking everyone else. She had given me hope.

I called her the next morning. She grew very excited when she heard the news, and asked if I would speak to the BBC crew.

"They're here again?"

Yes, she told me. They were in town, finishing up their documentary.

"I don't know, Martha. I've barely had time to adjust to all this. I feel a little numb. What do they want me to say?"

"Just tell them what happened. Just be yourself."

"Well, I'll talk it over with Marc and let you know."

But the BBC was in the city only until tomorrow, she told me. It had to be done before tomorrow at noon.

"Well . . . OK. But let me talk to Wilcox first"—Desmond Wilcox, the producer, with whom I had spoken already at the Mothering Center.

"Desmond's not here. I'll have the director call you."

Alex, the director, called that evening. "I want to be identified by my first name only," I told him. "And I want to talk about the two other therapies we used as well as holding, and I want to talk about my disagreement with the theoretical basis of holding."

"Fine, fine."

And off I went the next morning, fully confident, for some reason that is unfathomable to me now, that people who make television documentaries are keenly intent on being as objective as possible and solely interested in uncovering the truth, the whole truth, and nothing but the truth.

The repercussions of that ill-advised interview were terrible for me.

I was a little nervous when I came back, sensing that something was wrong, somehow.

"What's the matter?" asked Patsy, who had accompanied me there with the children.

"I don't know. I hope I didn't go overboard on praising holding therapy."

"But you did mention Bridget's and Robin's work as well."

"Yes. But I didn't dwell on them. It *is* a film about holding, after all. But I tried to be pretty clear that we had done a combination approach."

Amidst everything I had said, I remembered that I had had one clear summation sentence: " 'We did one hour a day of holding therapy, two hours a day of behavior modification, and three hours a week of speech therapy.' "

"Well? . . ."

"It's just . . . You know, Patsy, I could yakety-yak on about anything for any length of time; these people will use whatever *they* want." It was a little late suddenly to develop an insight into editing-room carnage.

I was nervous about the film, but just put the whole thing to the back of my mind. It wasn't due out in England until November. I had other things to think about.

Anne-Marie had started school. Phase Two of her recovery had begun.

For those who have backyards and a bunch of young kids from the neighborhood constantly visiting, it might be difficult to understand why so many city mothers put their children into play groups or nursery schools so early, at age two or three.

It's because the kids go stark raving bonkers if we don't. The morning spent in company with other adults and children breaks up their day and helps them to play somewhere besides the apartment. Daniel loved his mornings at "school."

With Anne-Marie, the only question was, Can she do it? There was no doubt in Marc's and my mind that she needed it, probably much more than Daniel. She had to let other people besides us into her world. She had to have as much preparation as she possibly could for the demands of real school, two or three years down the road, where she would be expected to follow directions given to a group, to play cooperatively with other kids, to participate verbally in group activities. So far, she had done well with optimum attention and one-on-one teaching. Could she now handle the more relaxed, less structured environment of a normal preschool? Would she listen to a teacher who wasn't constantly focusing on her alone?

We had decided to tell the teachers of her diagnosis and home program. Bridget and I had a couple of meetings with the directors and staff of the school, and we were very fortunate that they welcomed us and let us know they would be willing to work with us. Gretchen Buchenholz, the director of the Association to Benefit Children, the umbrella organization that ran the school, had an open-arms policy (space permitting!) toward all children, rich and poor, healthy and handicapped.

It was hard for the teacher, Annie, and her assistant, Celina, to understand why first Bridget, and then later I, needed to be in the classroom, since Anne-Marie looked so normal. After a while, however, they were able to see that she still needed some help. Every morning I would walk with her into the school and we would go through all the "hellos": greeting all the teachers with direct eye contact.

"Hi, Anne-Marie!"

"Hi," said Anne-Marie.

"Hi, Aaa . . ." I prompted.

"Hi, Annie," she complied.

Celina approached.

"Hello, Anne-Marie. How are you this morning?"

Anne-Marie did not respond.

"Anne-Marie," I said. "Look at Celina. Celina asked how you are."

"Fine."

She was completely cooperative, that was not the issue. Resistant crying was no longer a problem, and she had never been prone to violent temper tantrums. Nor did I think that her receptive language was seriously behind the norm any longer. She understood everything the teachers said when it was addressed specifically to her. But she still needed help in focusing on people; sometimes the teachers had to address her three or four times in order to get her attention. Lack of spontaneity and initiative was still an issue as well. Not as bad as it had been, but still not up to par.

Once when I was sitting to the side of the play area I watched a little girl just about Anne-Marie's age. "Jenny!" she called across the room to another little girl: "Jenny, look!" It was that sort of reaching outward—through a loud voice, through calling someone's name, inviting another into one's joy and activities—that was still hard for Anne-Marie. The spontaneous sharing of even a simple observation—"Look, raining outside"— was still infrequent for her.

I, and later the teachers, sometimes had to prompt her to ask so-and-so for something she wanted. She didn't always do it on her own.

"Juice," said Anne-Marie, seated at the table and looking down.

"Juice." "Juice." "Juice."

I put out my hand to stop one of the teachers from giving her juice.

"Anne-Marie, do you want juice?" I would ask.

"Yes."

"Ask Annie."

"Annie, I want . . ."

"Look at Annie."

She complied.

"Annie, I want juice."

"Could you say it louder?"

"Annie. I want juice!"

There would be plenty of time to teach "please" and "thank you." Right now, we were concentrating on the essentials of communication.

If another mother happened to stop in and heard me talking in this hyperdirective way to Anne-Marie, she would look at me oddly. I would squelch my oversensitive concern about her opinion of me, and just keep on with the task at hand. It doesn't matter, I would say to myself. Her little one is learning all of this naturally and easily. If only she knew how lucky she was. And anyway, Anne-Marie is learning too; she's just learning in a different way. I don't care how forced it seems.

Later, I taught her not only to look at the teachers, but to reach out and touch them in order to get their attention. I modeled for her how to put her hand on a teacher's arm, how to tap a teacher on the shoulder, how to speak a little louder. She was still prone to saying things in a very soft voice, almost in a whisper.

In time, Anne-Marie did start to initiate social contact by herself, once again demonstrating to her father and me that the mechanistic, programmatic quality to our intervention did not seem to preclude the development of spontaneity. She began to preface her requests with someone's name, to look directly into their eyes more frequently, and to speak more forcefully. Gradually, I tried to fade into the background, to minimize my prompts, to the point where a meaningful look, or a meaningful silence, or a simple "Anne-Marie" on my part was enough of a hint to get her to look up, or to speak up, or to respond to someone's question. And the teachers became very good at rewarding her for all these little steps forward: "I like the way you're looking at me, Anne-Marie!" "You said my name very well!"

Did she play with other children at school? She was still so young that the question wasn't really meaningful. There were flashes of interest in other children as people: from time to time she would smile at a boy or a girl, or spontaneously take turns with a toy, but I wouldn't say that she engaged in any extended cooperative play at school.

It didn't seem to matter very much. We saw that the beginnings of imaginative symbolic play were well established in her—she was now at the point where she could pretend that a block was a boat—and that she was capable of turn taking and sharing with her brother Daniel. So the template was there; that sufficed for the moment. I wasn't going to go nuts setting up extensive "play dates" for her, at age two years eight months. As long as we still saw progress, we remained hopeful that she would eventually achieve full social normalcy.

In October, we finally had a visit from the Lovaas Clinic at UCLA.

"Better late than never," said Marc.

We had contacted them the previous February. During the summer, meanwhile, a father who was doing a home program with his three-year-old son and who had visited the clinic had disabused us of any notion that it was some smoothly run well-endowed establishment with telephone operators, caseworkers, a large clerical staff, and an army of available therapists. "It's just an academic department," he told me, "strapped for money like every other academic department. There's a student who answers the phone; there's Lovaas, and a bunch of his graduate students, supervising a larger bunch of undergraduates." Not exactly sufficient to serve the entire country's population of autistic kids.

So we were grateful and excited when Doreen Granpeesheh, one of Lovaas's senior supervisors, called to say that she would be coming out. Bridget and Robin were eager to get her input, and I was anxious to discuss Anne-Marie's progress vis-à-vis the Lovaas children.

Doreen, like Dr. Cohen, seemed to know within five minutes of her arrival how well Anne-Marie was doing.

"She looks just wonderful!" she said warmly. "Thank God."

I liked Doreen instantly. She seemed genuinely to care about Anne-Marie and to be unconcerned about impressing us with her own expertise. She was also careful to recognize the amount of work we had already put in. One of the first things she said to us in our meeting was that we had done a splendid job so far on our own.

She observed Bridget working with Anne-Marie for an hour on her first afternoon. As I walked in at the end, she looked up at me.

"You've got a crackerjack therapist here, Catherine."

"I know that"—I smiled at Bridget—"now."

Doreen had a lot to offer us as well. She injected new life into our work, furnishing us with many of the "higher-level" programs that had been developed at UCLA. Among her program suggestions, which we were to incorporate over the next few months, were these:

• Work on reciprocal conversation. The adult states: "*I'm* wearing blue pants," then prompts Anne-Marie to say, "*I'm* wearing red pants." Or, "*I* had a baloney sandwich for lunch," prompting her to say what she had for lunch. Or, "*I'm* holding a red crayon," etc.

• Work on fine motor coordination with scissors.

• Work on identifying emotions in photographs of people. "Show me 'happy,' 'sad,' 'angry,' " etc. Work on understanding *why* characters in books are happy, sad, or angry.

• Work on identifying the functions of household rooms: "What do you do in the kitchen [bathroom, bedroom, etc.]?"

• Help her to express likes and dislikes. Work on spontaneity of such expressions of taste.

• Work on complete sentences with conjunctions, articles, correct subject pronouns, etc.

• Model and assist her to tell longer stories about a picture.

• Work on concepts of plural and singular, opposites, past and present.

• Model and assist her in the use of "before" and "after" in a sentence.

• Assist her in talking about things and events not immediately present: "What do you see at a circus?" etc.

• Social awareness: Set up situations with two people talking in front of Anne-Marie. Simple topic, simple sentences. Ask her, "What are we talking about?" Use Daniel to develop peer conversational skills.*

October and November saw another surge forward in Anne-Marie's language. In session, Bridget was working on action-labeling cards, and Anne-Marie was progressing from sentences like "Boy sitting" to "Boy sitting on chair" to "Boy sitting on red chair." Robin's symbolic-play sessions were becoming more and more verbally elaborate, with Anne-Marie now able to ask her "what" and "where" questions, and to enter into rudimentary dialogues with puppets and dolls.

But, perhaps most important, she was demonstrating to Bridget, to Robin, and to us that she was now capable of picking up more and more from the environment. She was coming up with many phrases and syntactic structures that no one had specifically taught her, but that she had heard instead from conversations around and with her.

In Bridget's session notes of November 2, the following spontaneous dialogue was noted:

Bridget: What happened?
Anne-Marie: Michel did it. (Anne-Marie is generalizing the past tense program begun in September.)
Bridget: Michel did what?
Anne-Marie: Throw books on floor.
Bridget: Who threw the books on the floor?

---

*This listing represents only about half of the programs that Doreen suggested. Appendix II, "Instructional Programs," includes many other program suggestions given to us by various members of the Lovaas staff.

Anne-Marie: Michel threw books on floor. (Anne-Marie self-corrects the tense to "threw" after hearing it once.)

By late November, I no longer had to accompany Anne-Marie to school. Whatever help she still needed could now be provided very competently by Annie and Celina.

In December, Michel celebrated his first birthday. I gathered the children around the supper table for the occasion. Marc was still at work. We had a chocolate cake and two or three presents to open.

I was happy; we were all happy. Our little world seemed to have regained its equilibrium. Anne-Marie kept getting better and better; Daniel had survived the year with grace; Marc and I had grown stronger in love.

"Happy birthday to you, happy birthday, dear Michel . . . !"

The childish voices of Anne-Marie and Daniel joined in the song. The kitchen was warm. The children were healthy and happy. Their faces around the table were beautiful. I took a long, shaky breath as I cut the cake. We had come through the struggle, and we had emerged into health and serenity. I handed a piece of cake to the birthday boy, who promptly attacked it with two hands. I laughed and planted two kisses on his head. One for your first birthday, and one for the year to come. God bless you, little man.

On January 30, 1989, thirteen months after the first diagnosis, I penned my last entry in my own black-and-white "composition book," my Anne-Marie diary.

The entry begins with the date. Then I list five sentences that I had heard her say that day:

"Do this for me, Mommy, I can't do it."
"Where Daniel?"
"What you doing?"
"Mommy, hold me."
"I fall down. Got boo-boo on arm. Kiss it."

"Just some examples from Anne-Marie's language today," I wrote.

All along, I had believed, and had not believed. Now my stubborn heart bowed down in fearful acceptance of this gift.

There would be other "tests" and reevaluations and trials for Anne-Marie: IQ tests, speech-language evaluations, her ongoing adaptation to this preschool and to other schools.

But we had come now into this place of peace, and the present was fine. More than fine. Shining with plenitude and joy.

All along, I had worried that we were re-creating her, forcing her into a mold of appropriate behavior and learned language; that our daughter had died somewhere between age one and age two and we had "remade" her out of the ashes and dust of what used to be our baby girl.

That worry was gone now; even to entertain the thought was to search for sorrow in the face of an enormous blessing. We had not, could not have, "remade" her. She was too much herself now, too joyfully full of her own life, her own thoughts and desires and creativity and intelligence, ever to have been made by anyone except her Maker. Just as she had been "knit together in my womb" without my controlling the miraculous process, so had she emerged from autism without our completely understanding or controlling her rebirth.

Whatever neurological processes had been reactivated in her brain, whatever chemical imbalance had been corrected, we would probably never know. Nor would we care, as she emerged into the light of human loving, and lifted her blue-green eyes to ours.

23

As November had come and gone, I had thought about that BBC film from time to time, wondering if it had been broadcast yet in England, and what it looked like. In December I had called Dr. Welch a few times, but she seemed oddly hesitant about discussing it with me. Finally I heard that she had had a little get-together for some people to watch the tapes. I called her and asked her if I could see them.

"Well, I don't have any extra tapes to give you," she said.

Now somewhat alarmed, and convinced that Dr. Welch was not that keen on my seeing the film, I set about procuring the tapes for myself.

They arrived sometime in February 1989. Two separate broadcasts, one aired on November 9, the other on November 16, 1988. Marc and I watched them one evening.

"Unbelievable," said Marc quietly.

I began to tremble.

A complete, unabashed puff-piece on Martha Welch. Holding therapy as the answer to desperate parental prayers. Martha Welch as a "fountainhead":

"But is it a cure?" asks the voice-over narrator.

The answer, over and over and over again, is yes. The narrator goes on:

For these parents, there is no doubt. They know many children have already resumed a full normal life, through holding. . . .

After holding, many children take their normal place in family, school and work. . . .

Her results, the number of children back in normal life, have made impressive evidence in America.

But where *was* the evidence? Where were the recovered children? Where were the cures, "the number of children back in normal life . . ."? What did that statement *mean?* I had asked over and over again to meet some of those children, and had not met one. Had Desmond Wilcox found a good sample of them? Had he found ten? Had he found five? Had he found one?

There was testimonial after testimonial from mothers claiming that their lives had been turned around, that they had been given hope, that they believed. . . .

But where were the cures?

There was a young boy who could recite the alphabet—along with half the rest of the autistic population. Number and letter recognition, precocious feats of memorization—many autistic persons have such splinter skills. These talents, which can, in the case of the people called "autistic savants," be nothing short of astounding, say nothing of the person's ability to communicate in flexible, animated discourse. The central character in the film *Rain Man,* whose producers consulted with Dr. Rimland in their depiction of his autistic condition, could do instant mathematical computations in his head, but his language remained infantile. What the BBC documentary on holding therapy lacked—the significance of which the public could not know—was even *one* sustained, interactive conversation with an autistic, or formerly autistic, child.

There was Katy, the young girl featured in the *Life* magazine article, she whose lengthy poems on Christ, redemption, and Dr. Welch had so moved me.

The documentary dwells for a moment on those astonishing poems. The narrator explains that a year ago, when she was ten, Katy had written a poem about Dr. Welch. She had, he informs us, already been to "a number" of holding sessions but had continued to remain "unresponsive." ("A number" of holding sessions, indeed. Katy had by that point had at least *eight years* of holding sessions.)

Dr. Welch then reads from one of the poems, a hymn of praise to . . . Dr. Welch:

> She enraged me and mortified me and challenged me.
> She respected me and fortified me
> and gave me a mother beyond my wildest dreams.

How much holding had Katy had before she got to the stage where she could write like this? asks Desmond Wilcox.

The question is wrongly put, responds Dr. Welch. Katy could have written like this for a long time. The reason she had not done so was because she was afraid, very frightened—and with good reason: "Her life was not at all secure." But, Dr. Welch continues:

> . . . once she got enough security to write, she began to write and she went from no communication to complete communication, writing at the college level at age nine.

To resolve any doubts, says the voice of Wilcox, now identified as the narrator, he was asked to join a literary session.

Cut to Katy and her mother sitting together on a bed. Her mother's hand is around Katy's. Together they write—in a big, childish hand across half the page—two words:

MOM
LOVE

I shut my eyes as these images unrolled, stung by something stronger than disillusionment: something closer to betrayal. MOM? LOVE? Where were the extended analogies, the theological musings, of the poems I had read? Where was the neat, precise, rather cramped handwriting of the "original" poems, supposedly written by Katy herself, that Dr. Welch had given me, and that had been reproduced as well in the *Life* magazine article? What relationship did any of those writings, whether in their physical formulation or in their conceptual maturity, have to this labored, wrenchingly childish, mother-assisted scrawl?

"I found it natural, amusing—and convincing," says narrator Wilcox. End of Katy sequence. All doubts resolved.

There was Anne-Marie and her mother. Anne-Marie's mother announcing the results of Anne-Marie's reevaluation. Anne-Marie's mother summarizing what Anne-Marie's therapy had consisted of.

"We did one hour a day of holding therapy."

Of course, if one listens really closely one hears, in the introduction to the Anne-Marie sequence, the narrator's parenthetical phrase ". . . as well as other therapies."

Not that that phrase would have registered with many in the British viewing public. After all, there is the mother of Anne-Marie, probably the only child in the film anywhere near recovery, saying: "We did one hour a day of holding therapy." Period.

On and on went the tapes, the same old Tinbergen-Bettelheim-Welch themes appearing throughout:

• Autism as a chosen withdrawal by a traumatized child: the "fortress" (Bettelheim's favorite metaphor) is "self-imposed," says Welch.

• Autistic children as brilliant little souls whose major problem is that they are emotionally blocked: ". . . these children," says Welch, "when they start to reveal their true potential, turn out to be exceptional, brilliant children. . . ." (These children? How many? Half of them? All of them?)

• Autistic children as needing only an accepting environment, an accepting adult presence, in order to finally reveal their pent-up emotions: Many of these blocked children, Welch lectures her audience, show their greatest emotion at her Mothering Center, "where they know there's support for it."

• Autism as a catastrophic response to a life event, especially that most horrendous of life events, the birth of a sibling: "But [his baby sister's] arrival triggered many symptoms in Michael," says Wilcox about the onset of autism in a three-year-old.

• And, most wearying, that same old theme of autism as a direct result of faulty mothering: One mother finally "admitted" to Welch that, because her own mother had not picked her up when she was a baby, the mother could not respond to her baby, couldn't pick him up when he cried. The "very normal baby" then just gave up and withdrew. This confession, Dr. Welch explains, gave her "new insight" into the origins of autism:

> This idea that the mother hadn't been held and wanted to was very ambivalent, the same kind of ambivalence in the children, it just hit me that "holding" would get over that avoidance behavior and allow the approach behavior to flower and then you would get normal development. So I set out to prove that.

How strange. I had always thought that researchers set out to test hypotheses, not to "prove" them.

So the mothers who had given birth to these "normal" babies, and then had emotionally abused them until they became autistic, now have the benefit of this second chance: holding will ensure that autistic children can now "take their normal place in family, school, and work."

But the benefits of holding, according to Martha Welch's testimony in this adoring film, go far beyond simply curing autism. Holding will cure just about everything! With holding therapy, says Welch, stages like the terrible twos and difficult teens just "disappeared"! Holding created "cooperative, affection-seeking" teenagers. Holding was the "perfect solution" for temper tantrums. Holding made sibling rivalry "disappear."

I called Dr. Rimland, struggling not to break down on the phone. "I know," he told me. "I heard about the film." The offices of the National Autistic Society in England, he said, were deluged by parents clamoring for this new "cure," screaming invectives at the "establishment" for refusing them information on this wonderful miracle treatment. The society was mounting a campaign of protest. Where were the controlled studies? they wanted to know. Where were all the recoveries? Where were the independent intake evaluations and the follow-up independent assessments?

I wrote, lodging a formal complaint with the Broadcasting Complaints Commission, in London. I was heartsick, devastated, that my testimony was being used to mislead parents of autistic children. I was furious with myself for having been so naïve and so intemperate in my praise of holding therapy, but I was doubly furious at all those responsible for creating this travesty of a documentary.

Back and forth went the letters across the Atlantic, throughout March and April, until finally Desmond Wilcox launched his own missive threatening me with legal action—I was, according to him, coming dangerously close to implying impropriety on his part.

Friends, family, my lawyer sisters, Marc, Dr. Rimland—all urged me to rattle the sabers right back. "Are you kidding me?" my sister Jean yelled at me one day. "You're going to withdraw your complaint because he starts huffing and puffing? You wouldn't survive for a minute in a legal career!"

But I couldn't bear to prolong the fight. Already I felt outnumbered, overpowered, and vulnerable. Martha Welch had given the BBC my letter to Dr. Rimland about her, and I had no idea whom else she might give it to, or whether my daughter's name would be dragged into the public forum.*

There was no way I could continue. To launch my own counter-suit against any of them—that way lay another type of madness and obsession, and I had had enough of warfare and high drama to last me a lifetime.

Already I was staying up till three o'clock in the morning writing those futile letters, trying to mitigate a disaster that had already happened. Already I was adding more anxiety and anger to a family life

*We had asked to be identified only by our first names for the documentary.

that had just barely regained some semblance of equilibrium. Before the end of April I withdrew my complaint.

But the pain lingered for a long time. "One more primrose path for parents," I remarked bitterly to Marc. "One hour a day of holding therapy: cure your child of autism."

No matter what I thought I had known about human egotism, the desire for recognition, the desire for fame, I still could not understand why Martha Welch had allowed this distorted view to be broadcast. I don't understand it to this day. I had praised her. I had validated her approach. I still think, in spite of all the anger, that holding therapy *did* contribute to Anne-Marie's progress. Why wasn't that enough for Dr. Welch? She knew about Bridget's and Robin's work; we had argued about it all the time. How could she allow anyone—any parent—to believe that one hour a day of holding therapy was going to rescue his child? How could she continue to propagate the "faulty-mothering" theory in one breath and deny it in the next?

Marc, usually such a calm counterpoint to my volatile temperament, was furious. He was not, however, shocked by the conduct of the producer and Dr. Welch.

"I'm not surprised," he said to me one day, trying to comfort me as I berated myself for the hundredth time. "The media charade certainly doesn't surprise me, and I've never trusted Martha."

He turned to face me.

"Look, sweetheart. Try to believe two things: The first is that it doesn't matter. People will not remember this film a year from now. What matters is that we're recovering our little girl."

I couldn't answer. I knew I should feel that way, but at the moment, I was torn up.

"What's the second thing?"

"The second thing is that truth survives. Nonsense doesn't."

He was probably right, but I couldn't be philosophical about it just then. It wasn't just the conviction that my words had been edited to serve someone else's ends, that our story of pain and triumph should now serve to mislead people, it was everything.

Everything that had been festering for the past year. All the frustration and anger generated by the scenes I had witnessed at the Mothering Center, the sanctimonious nonsense of the Tinbergen and Bettelheim books, the constant attacks against behavioral therapy, the therapeutic nurseries that offered little more than custodial care—it was all coming together for me in an almost unbearable way. There were nights when I couldn't sleep, lying in bed, going over and over all the idiocy rampant about autism, torn apart by my own participation in that idiocy. A sense of utter futility almost paralyzed me. The nonsense would go on and on forever, no matter what data were published, no matter how many scientific studies came out. The sensational and the simple would always prevail over the complicated truth. How naïve, how stupid I had been not to have fully understood the egotism, the *power* at play in the world of autism. Who gets to be the savior? Who gets the most media attention for being a savior? The stakes are high in this game. Who cares about objective truth?

Of course I was overjoyed that we were managing to pull Anne-Marie out of autism. But all around me, as I grew to know more and more families, I saw young autistic children sinking through the cracks as their parents were encouraged to spend months, years, in unproven therapeutic programs. Now I myself had contributed to the misinformation that assaults those parents.

There were moments during that April of rage that I was sick with remorse and fury at having been so taken in, so stupid.

24

IN MAY, we had another visit from the Lovaas Clinic. The arrangement is that one family, or two or three families, pay the cost of air fare and room and board plus a fee for the workshop. The fee is based on a sliding scale.

Anthony was the emissary this time—very sharp and articulate, filled with good ideas for high-level programs on expressive language and reciprocal conversation.

But I didn't agree with everything he said and I was not always comfortable with his therapeutic style.

This bothered me, since I now had such respect for the behavioral program and Dr. Lovaas's work.

"Catherine," said Marc, after Anthony's visit, "you want to think that there is a perfect therapy spelled out somewhere, and a perfect person who has all the answers."

"No I don't. Not anymore. But I still think the Lovaas people know a lot more about autism than we do."

"They do know a lot about autism, and about behavioral therapy. But we know our daughter, and what works for her."

"Yes . . . we do now."

"So if we don't agree with everything Anthony says, we don't do it. Modify it, adapt it, take what we can use. Nothing is written in stone. Anyway, I'm sure Lovaas would tell you the same."

Although Dr. Lovaas's work had given us part of the answer—by far the most important part—it was true that we had not done everything exactly as *The Me Book* said. Bridget was bringing us new programs all the time. Some of these had their evident source in *The Me Book*. Some, as she said, were "out there," culled from special-education curricula, books, articles, conferences on behavior modification. Some she invented herself, and some we invented by brain-storming together.

But it was not so much in the *content* of the programs that we marked out our own direction, as in the style of executing them.

The more I read about behavior modification, and the more therapists I had the opportunity to see, the more I realized two or three things that should have been self-evident to me.

The first is that therapists vary—from the good ones, to the well-meaning but not very experienced, to the ones who are downright harsh.

The second is that although behavioral therapy is, broadly speaking, founded on a principle of consistency—subjects have been shown to respond in a consistent manner to particular stimuli and structure—there will always be variation in the range and nature of that response. What works stylistically or substantially for one child might not necessarily work as well for another.

And the third is that behavior modification is a very potent tool. Its power can be astounding. It can also crush the human spirit.

Bridget was called in for consultation with a family once and came back to talk with me, distraught. She had been asked to observe another trained therapist working with a child. The therapist was young but extremely sure of himself. The child was a high-functioning, verbal boy barely four years old.

"The guy just kept screaming at the little boy!" Bridget told me. Usually so calm, she was visibly upset.

"What was he screaming?"

" 'Knock it off! Sit down in that chair! *Knock it off!*' "

The child, of course, was completely compliant in a matter of minutes. Every time he tried to cry came the "Knock it off!" again, as he was pushed with considerable force into the chair.

After a while, the therapist allowed the child to get up and go toward his mother. "Say hi to your mother!" he barked.

The child approached his mother, and began to whimper.

"*Quiet!* I said to say hi to your mother! Right now!"

Marc and I were as appalled as Bridget. Not that we are categorically against aversives. As I have indicated, all three of us believe in the necessity of some aversives, in some circumstances, with some children. We have heard of some devastating cases where a child's self-injurious behavior was so severe as to threaten his sight, his hearing, or even his life. One mother had told me that she had finally decided to try an aversive after her son had pierced his eardrums several dozen times. She had allowed her son's teachers to use an uncomfortable physical restraint every time he went for his ears, and that finally brought the behavior under control. We had read of a little girl who, over a period of five years, had hit herself so forcefully and so constantly that she had caused frontal-lobe brain damage, punctured her eardrums, and damaged her eyes so badly that she was legally blind. Her parents, unable to cope with what truly must have been a "nightmare without end," had given her over to her grandparents. After in her turn trying everything under the sun, the grandmother finally acquired a device, a helmet, that delivered a mild electric shock every time the child attempted to hit herself. The behavior was eradicated in a matter of weeks. The child, according to the grandmother's report and her teacher's corroboration, never attempted to remove the device during the times that it was on her head, and in fact became visibly upset when others tried to remove it. Nevertheless, an "advocacy" group was vigorously trying to ban the use of the device and to strip the grandparents of any say in the matter. "Maybe those advocates should live with the child for a few months," I told Marc upon learning about this controversy. "I wonder how long they could watch a child blind and deafen herself."

In another instance, closer to home, a mother asked for my help. Her autistic child, aged six, had been screaming since he was two. She had first ignored the screaming, then had tried saying "No screaming" every time he screamed. The screaming just kept getting worse and worse. At her latest count he was screaming up to eighty times a day. Once, in his school, he screamed sixty times in two hours.

It was clear to both of us, his mother and me, that he screamed anytime anyone intruded on him, asked him something, or placed any demand on him.

We two mothers sat down at the kitchen table and thought up an aversive.

Every time the child screamed, his mother would clap her hands loudly in his face and yell, really yell, *"No screaming!"*

Neither one of us liked it. But four years is a long time for a behavior to go on. The mother had tried love and understanding and gentleness and ignoring. She had seen psychiatrists and psychologists and therapists and doctors. The teachers in her son's school, she said, couldn't help her. They didn't know what to do.

She was afraid, she told me, that her son would never learn anything unless he stopped screaming. She was afraid that people would ostracize him or make fun of him forever if he kept on.

The first time she tried our aversive, the boy was shocked. He was quiet for a while, then he screamed again. Again his mother came down like a ton of bricks. And again, and again.

At the end of a week, the boy was screaming two or three times a day. At the end of five weeks, the screaming was gone, and gone for good. The boy was calmer, seemed friendlier, and was learning more. He smiled more often. Children in the park didn't run away from him, because he wasn't letting out bloodcurdling screams every few minutes. His mother had no doubt that she had done the right thing.

But this scene that Bridget had witnessed was different somehow. We tried to analyze why it troubled us so much. All of us were used to defending behavioral therapy against its detractors; now here we were, all outraged at this guy's arrogance.

"It's because he just met the child," said Bridget. "There was no analysis of the function of the child's crying: Was it task-avoidance? Was it fear? Was it attention-seeking from his mother? There was no behavioral analysis."

Such analysis of immediate precursors to a behavior is always the first step when you're trying to teach a child self-control, Bridget had often remarked to me. The next step, before you employ any aversive, is to try to gain the child's compliance through some other method: maybe praising for any evidence of calming down; maybe ignoring the crying and just working through some task, using a differential reinforcement for complying with that task. But there had been none of that in the episode she was describing. Instead there was the Sherman tank approach: Come in, plonk the kid in his chair, and, to use Bridget's words, "Verbally beat him up."

I shook my head, discouraged. If it wasn't one extreme, it was another. "Big macho man," I sighed. "If he really thought it necessary to suppress the crying right away, before trying anything else, why yell at the boy? Why not just firmly say, 'No crying'? And he's probably convinced the parents that they're complete wimps if they protest."

"The parents were sitting there looking as scared as their child."

While I have profound gratitude that Dr. Lovaas took the time and the trouble to publish his research, we certainly didn't follow to the letter every recommendation in his book. There were times when we had to use our own judgment. In *The Me Book* appears the following program for teaching the child to say "yes" and "no."

> Select two behaviors, one that your child definitely prefers and one that he does not prefer. For example, you may ask a question such as, "Do you want candy?", as contrasted to the question "Do you want a spanking?" Ask one of these questions, and then prompt the correct response. . . . [More specific instructions regarding the fading of prompts and the randomization of directions follow here.]
>
> It is probably wise for you to let the child experience the consequences of his using the terms yes and no correctly, as well as the consequences following an incorrect usage. That is, if the child says, "yes," when you ask, "Do you want a spanking?" then the child should probably be given a swat (just enough to make him feel a little uncomfortable). You can help the child formulate the correct answer by grossly exaggerating your gestures when you ask "Do you want a spanking?" That is, raise your arm so it is clear to the child what may be in store for him . . .

When Bridget used this program to teach Anne-Marie, she placed a bowl of ice cream and a bowl of spinach before her, asked her if she wanted one or the other, prompted for "yes" or "no," gradually faded her prompts, then randomized the two questions. The reward for a correct answer was praise or a bite of ice cream. The consequence for a wrong answer was, very simply, the lack of praise: silence.

Dr. Lovaas knows a lot more about autism than I do. He has had to deal with severely self-abusive, chronically self-absorbed and self-stimulatory children. Not only children, but teenagers and adults as well. It may very well be that some of the programs that Marc and I found too harsh as described in *The Me Book* were effective for other people in other situations. I myself spoke to a mother who, in spite of advice and counsel from a dozen different professionals, could not toilet-train her five-year-old autistic daughter until she tried Dr. Lovaas's program for toilet training in *The Me Book*. I also want to emphasize again the fact that Anne-Marie was very young, her autism perhaps not as far advanced as a four- or five-year-old's, her disabilities not as entrenched.

Dr. Lovaas himself, however, made the point to me once that nothing was absolute: every therapeutic program required constant adjustment and frequent brainstorming on the part of therapists and parents alike.

And that's precisely why I get so distressed when I see or hear of therapists using aversives without trying anything else; concentrating more on yelling than on praising; screaming "No!" at every mistake; punishing for every accident during toilet training. Nothing is written in stone. Judgments *are* called for, as are humanity, wisdom, temperance.

There is a fine line between firmness and harshness, and I suppose everyone defines that line differently. But there are some behavioral therapists whose general attitude goes over that line for me. There are therapists who are unmoved and strong in the face of tantrums, and those who *create* fear in the child and use intimidation as a first mode of approach. One could say that the ends justify any means, but one can't help but wonder, in some of these cases, if the ends, the results, are really all they could be.

Gradually, as time went on, Marc and I were learning how to take what worked, how to learn from those who could teach us, and how, finally, to trust our own instincts and reason.

25

ASIDE FROM the frustration and rage generated by the holding therapy film fiasco, the spring of 1989 was a time of rest and healing.

While the struggle for Anne-Marie went on, it no longer was a question of fierce relentlessness, hour by hour: She had taken over much of the learning herself; we had only to keep things interesting and challenging for her. She was no longer being dragged along crying and kicking. Our place was more behind her, pushing a little here, prodding there, giving her a nudge sometimes in a direction we wanted her to take.

Daniel was Anne-Marie's constant playmate. Around the house, I was beginning to have more extended periods of relaxation. As long as I could hear those two prattling away with each other, there was no longer need for me to be so constantly vigilant. For Anne-Marie was at the point where Daniel could understand her language and she could understand him. I have always found it astonishing the way very young children—three, four, and five years old—know how to adjust their language to a simpler level when they're talking to a baby or a two-year-old. I used to look at Daniel playing with his sister, hear his patient, clear explanations of some complicated game he had devised— "Anne-Marie, you hold this baby. I go get the daddy bear"—and inwardly bless him. If only he could know how much he was doing for his little sister.

At school, she was keeping up with her classmates as they all went on their way developing and learning and growing. Though she could still be somewhat shy, and occasionally unfocused and absent, she could also have moments of great alertness and friendliness. I would say that by March or April of 1989 she no longer stood out from her peers in any obvious way. I think that if someone had sat down and analyzed the frequency and duration of her eye contact he might have found it still below par, but this was something only we were conscious of, not anyone else.

Her language was becoming daily more creative, with longer sentences, more complicated questions—"Where Annie go?"—and more spontaneity. One day when I picked her up from school she told me herself, unprompted, something that she had done that morning. "Did you have a fun day at school?" I asked her. "Yes," she responded. And then, after a pause: "I made a puppet."

I checked with Annie. The class had made paper bag puppets that morning. Anne-Marie was beginning to talk more frequently and spontaneously about things that were not immediately present and concrete.

Robin and Bridget and I were beginning to wonder, by May of 'eighty-nine, if we had reached the point of searching for problems. We wondered if we could objectively judge anymore whether Anne-Marie's language was on target.

We asked around and found that Margery Rappaport had a respected name in the community as a good speech-language pathologist. We decided to ask her to evaluate Anne-Marie's language, in order to get an outsider's assessment of any subtle communication deficits or weaknesses. Anne-Marie was three years three months old in June, when the evaluation took place. We had informed Margery of her history.

Since there comes a time when handicaps and deficits are evident only in subtle areas of social communication, Margery's analysis of Anne-Marie's communicative abilities was especially significant for us. Our central question was whether Anne-Marie's language was simply "delayed," or whether it was "disordered":*

---

*For this book, I asked Margery herself to furnish me with a professional description of the distinction between "delayed" and "disordered" language. She writes:

"Language delay: A child with delayed language ability presents language typical of that of a younger child. One would expect to see in this child the features of essentially fully developed language but merely that of a younger child.

"Language disorder: *A child would be diagnosed as having a language disorder when atypical features are noted or certain skills are absent in his language.* [Emphasis mine.] The child may present a scatter of speech-language abilities, including age-appropriate skills in certain areas, along with the atypical or absent features. It is this atypicality that signals a disorder versus a delay. An example of a symptom of a language disorder is dysnomia, that is, difficulty in retrieval of words that are actually known to the speaker. This may exist in children with either good or poor vocabularies. Echolalia is another symptom which, when protracted, signals a language disorder. Immediate echolalia is seen as a rather brief developmental period in normally developing youngsters. When extended, marked or predominantly 'delayed' in nature [echoing of phrases

OBSERVATIONS

Anne-Marie separated effortlessly from her mother and was easily engaged in evaluation activities. She is an attractive child who was well related, somewhat shy, presenting a good, nondistractible attention span. Eye gaze was well established but maintained at levels slightly less than expected for age. Anne-Marie was fully cooperative for all procedures. She smiled and laughed, at times delighting in something discovered in the testing room or test materials. . . .

LANGUAGE

Anne-Marie's expressive language was characterized by the use of multi-word utterances often containing 4–6 words with a maximum of 10 words presented on one occasion (The boy playin' with a ball and a drum and a wagon). Mean length of utterance for a 3.3-year-old child is 4.3 words, placing Anne-Marie well above the mean. . . . Syntax-morphology was also judged to be near age-expectancy levels. . . . Occasional lags were noted: Anne-Marie tended to omit the articles "a" and "the." . . . Pronominal usage was well developed. Anne-Marie used compound sentences with *and*; *because* was often used to begin a sentence.

Anne-Marie initiated many utterances, used for a variety of functions: to label, to state facts and feelings, to describe, to acknowledge, to greet, to protest, to compare, to request objects and actions, to deny, to respond, to narrate and to a limited degree repair and respond to requests for repair of communication breakdown. Occasional ambiguous (*We have two dogs but there's only one dog*) or off-target responses were noted.

Receptive language was also judged to be near age-appropriate levels. Anne-Marie was able to follow 2-step commissions and to respond to various wh-questions (what, why, where, who, how and how many). Responses were occasionally off-target indicating lack of comprehension (E: Do you have any pets in your house? Anne-Marie: A couch). One instance of echoing was presented (E: Do you know what pets are? Anne-Marie: What pets are).

. . . Anne-Marie presents communication skills ranging from mildly delayed to significantly above-age expectations . . . .

Overall, Margery told us, she found that Anne-Marie's language could not be considered "disordered," only delayed in certain spe-

---

heard some minutes or hours before], echolalia is considered to be a feature of a language disorder. The absence of certain 'pragmatic abilities,' that is, the ability to use language appropriately in context, would also signal a disorder. Parents may be thrown off track when children present strength in vocabulary or grammar; it is important to assess the appropriateness of their language, not only its structure. Other features of language disorder might include absence of appropriate eye gaze or eye avoidant behavior. Aberrant vocal prosody, that is, inability to learn and use appropriate melody of speech, which is another way to convey meaning, is a further feature of a language disorder."

cific areas. In a matter of time, she assured us, these weaknesses would probably disappear—possibly over the course of the next six months.

Later that month, we decided to take Anne-Marie to see Dr. Perry as well. We had settled on Dr. Cohen as the professional who would monitor her progress at regular intervals, and Anne-Marie was scheduled to see him in July, so our visit with Dr. Perry was a bit redundant and was probably more for our benefit than for hers. I think that in a way Dr. Perry symbolized for us the professional community whom we had found unsympathetic to the idea of intensive behaviorism and recovery. However, of all the "unsympathetic" doctors we had seen, he still seemed intelligent and fair-minded. We were interested in hearing his reaction to Anne-Marie's progress.

Dr. Perry seemed almost shocked to see Anne-Marie chattering away, looking at us all, smiling at us, engaging in interactive play with him. He kept staring at her throughout the evaluation, with an expression of astonishment—and of pleasure. He seemed genuinely happy to see her doing so well. He was fairly quiet at first, and at one point I had the impression that he was struggling to find appropriate words. Our ensuing conversation with him was courteous: he asked about the various therapies we had employed and he listened to what we had to say with interest. All in all, Marc and I found his evaluation, which we received some weeks later, to be quite gracious and open-minded for a psychiatrist who had once stated, "Autistic children do not recover."

I first evaluated Anne-Marie on February 18, 1988. At that time my diagnostic impression was of infantile autism.

. . . Concerning my observations of Anne-Marie during the session, these began with my meeting Anne-Marie and her parents outside my office. Anne-Marie was between her parents holding their hands. She smiled and looked at me when I asked her how she was. She responded, "Fine." She continued to respond quite appropriately as the four of us made our way from outside into my office. Once in my office, Anne-Marie began looking at my toys. She became interested in a doctor's kit and said spontaneously, "Look, it's a suitcase." She then asked if there was anything in the kit and when she opened it she said, "Wow" in looking at the contents. I asked her what the stethoscope was for and she replied, "For tummy." Later, Anne-Marie played with a bear and a dog puppet. While she was holding one, I asked her if she had a teddy bear at home and she responded that she did and said that its name was "Bunny." My attention then shifted to Mr. and Mrs. Maurice and after several minutes of conversation with them I looked at what Anne-Marie was doing and she had taken some blocks and was building something. When asked, she replied, "I'm making a house for doggy." By doggy she meant the doggy puppet. At one point I gave Anne-Marie a pencil and paper and asked her to draw something. She drew a person which she said was her father. The drawing was advanced for her age. It contained eyes, nose, mouth, eyeglasses, hair, ears, arms and legs. Towards the end of the interview, Anne-Marie was asked if she would play with the dollhouse. She seemed to remember where the dollhouse was kept and went under a shelf to get it. Anne-Marie played out a scene in which the mother and the father were waiting for their child. The child came and gave the mother a kiss. Then Anne-Marie took out a table and some chairs and had the family sit down to a meal of french fries and "fish steak" [fish sticks]. After eating, the family played and then went to bed.

My impressions are as follows. I think Anne-Marie has made tremendous progress over the past year and one-quarter. I would not now diagnose her as having infantile autism. Her language relatedness and play do not now show the deviancies associated with that disorder.

I note several things that may be residua of autism. I emphasize that these things probably would not have impressed me and I may not have noted them if I wasn't familiar with Anne-Marie's past. On several occasions, Anne-Marie used the same phrases in response to questions. One phrase was the question "what these are called" and another was "I dunno," which she said in response to some questions. Anne-Marie's speech also seemed a little sing-song. Lastly, on two occasions, once when I was playing ball with Anne-Marie and another time when I was occupying her with the dolls, she seemed to rapidly move away from our shared activities back to what she was doing before I engaged her.

Concerning that which I have just noted, Mr. and Mrs. Maurice have told me that recently the speech therapist has been working with Anne-Marie on prosody. Also when I asked Mr. and Mrs. Maurice if they see any continuing problem areas, they responded that it is "subtle," but that Anne-Marie has a "tendency to be dreaming." This might be related to what I experienced as Anne-Marie detaching from me when she moved away from mutual play.

The above should not detract from the tremendous progress that Anne-Marie has made. In my own experience with autistic children, I have never followed one who over a period of a little more than a year could no longer be diagnosed as autistic. . . .

. . . It is my understanding that Mr. and Mrs. Maurice will continue Anne-Marie's therapy for as long as is needed. It is hoped that at some point Anne-Marie will not only be described as being indistinguishable from other children (as her teacher describes her) but as being simply a normal child.

Marc and I thought those "residua," if such they may be called, were fairly accurate descriptions of things Anne-Marie still did. But we weren't worried about them. Her prosody was already improving; her dreaminess has been diminishing for a year and a half, and would probably continue to do so; any repetitive phrases in her language were far outnumbered by the spontaneous and original expressions she was using every day. Time would take care of it all. Essentially, our daughter was a normal child.

PART II

Michel

26

IN THAT SAME MONTH of Dr. Perry's reevaluation, June of 1989, Michel was eighteen months old. His language was not coming in very fast. He had only a handful of words. Often he would scream when he wanted something, rather than reaching or pointing toward it.

For this book, I have unearthed the home videotapes I made in October of 1988, and later in December, at his first birthday supper.

Trying to see the beginning.

What do I see, in hindsight? Was there anything at all to see then, so early?

In the October tape, I see a ten-month-old baby taking his first steps. The big brown eyes staring at the camera; the pudgy legs, wide apart for balance; the determined drunken lurches from side to side—and then the *plop!* as down he goes on his well-padded rear.

I see whining and crying, but I see smiles as well.

Now he is a year old. I see a baby eating chocolate cake and wickedly ripping up the paper party tablecloth in front of him. He's on the floor now, walking toward me, more surely this time. His arms are outstretched. He is smiling.

My voice, on the tape, laughingly calls out to him. "Come, sweetheart! Come to Mama! That's it! Come on!" Proudly, I announce for posterity that he is one year old and he is walking and eating with a fork, and even talking!—he has one word, "no."

Watching the tape, I can remember listing those accomplishments. I remember the impetus behind my words: the need to reassure myself, over and over again, that he was fine. Everything was on track. Everything's OK, going smoothly.

I started to add that he was saying "Mama" and "Daddy" as well, but I stopped myself. I had heard "Mama" and "Daddy" only once or twice, when he was around ten months old.

I see something else on the October tape in the park. A friend of ours picking Michel up, talking to him, trying to get him to wave bye-bye. Michel has no response at all.

So what? He's only a baby. He doesn't have to respond to everyone's overtures 100 percent of the time. He's eating, sleeping, and growing well. He's babbling, looking, reaching, walking, smiling. And, at one year of age, he has one word.

I see one more thing.

In October and December of 1988, I occasionally have to call him three or four times before he will look up.

But so many things about him were different from how Anne-Marie had been. She had been so withdrawn; he was friendlier. He reached up his arms to be picked up. He smiled and laughed. His eye contact seemed fine.

Did he understand language? By the time he was eighteen months old, that had become an increasingly frequent subject of conversation. It seemed to us that he did understand certain phrases, like "bath-time," "come here," "sit down."

But the weeks and months were slipping by. If only his language would suddenly spurt forward, so that we wouldn't have to think about the dreaded possibility that he might be autistic. We just had to hang on until he was about thirty months old. Then we would all be out of danger.

"God in His wisdom has decided to give me a late talker," I said to my sister Debbie. I laughed, a little nervously. "Why?"

"I don't know. But he seems OK to me, from the little that I see of him."

"He seems OK to me too. I mean I could come up with a list of bad things and a list of good things about his behavior, but I think you could do that with any eighteen-month-old."

"Yes . . . what bad things?"

"Well . . . he's walking on his toes a little more these days. And he's pretty cranky. And he's not that interested in anyone besides me and his father. . . ."

"Mmm . . . I don't know. It's hard to know, at eighteen months."

No one, ourselves included, wanted to be too quick to pronounce him either totally fine or potentially at risk. I remembered the long-drawn-out period of uncertainty with Anne-Marie, and for the hundredth time, I wished fervently that there were some blood test, some definitive way of diagnosing or ruling out autism while a child was still very young.

We spent a weekend in East Hampton and saw my little niece Helen. Helen was six months younger than Michel. Already she was up and walking, babbling and pointing away. Just like Michel. Except that Michel wasn't really doing that much pointing. And Helen had a word that Michel didn't: "Mama."

In July, we took Anne-Marie, aged three years and four months, back to see Dr. Cohen. It had been almost ten months since he had last evaluated her. Without planning to, almost as a reluctant last-minute decision, we took Michel along with us.

Again, Dr. Cohen seemed thrilled with Anne-Marie's progress, and his evaluation provided a warm testimonial to how far she had come:

VIDEOTAPED OBSERVATIONS

Caretaker Interaction

Anne-Marie was a delight to observe during this interaction with her mother. Upon entering the room, her face lit up when she saw all the toys. She immediately went over to the table and played appropriately with them (a Mr. Potato Head; number blocks; girl doll). Verbally, her utterances were appropriate most of the time with well-formed questions and good pragmatic skills. Eye contact was excellent and accompanied by appropriate affect. Anne-Marie frequently made statements and asked questions with utterances of over five words. Some echoing did occur in context and intonation was sometimes inappropriate. Attention span was excellent.

During face-to-face interaction, Anne-Marie told an appropriate story about a "mean bear" who chased and ate a little girl and then described how the mommy "shot the mean bear with a gun." The story was clearly fitting for a three-year-old.

Stranger Interaction

Anne-Marie readily accepted interacting with Dr. Sudhalter and was quite charming. She kissed her mother good-bye and was perfectly cooperative. Problems with pronunciation were evident. She seemed to have problems with the "l" sound. Sentence completion tasks suggested a need to expand Anne-Marie's semantic network. For example, she couldn't finish the sentences "a girl sees with her ——" and "a flower grows in the ——." When asked who she loves, however, she promptly replied "Mommy."

. . . As before, attention was remarkable for a three-year-old and eye contact and affect were appropriate.

When Mrs. Maurice reentered the room, Anne-Marie looked over to her and smiled . . .

Comments

Anne-Marie continues to show remarkable progress. Her standard scores are now clearly in the average to above average range and her socialization score is one of these. Considering her rate of progress and her young age, I expect that she will continue to progress and, hopefully, show continued improvement in her communication skills. She clearly is no longer autistic although some subtle language deficits may remain. Anne-Marie has recently had a full language work-up which will deal with this issue. In any event, the only thing we can recommend at this point is continued work on expansion of Anne-Marie's knowledge base and continued exposure to other nonhandicapped children. Both Anne-Marie and her family are to be congratulated for this quite remarkable turn-around.

Marc was unable to share completely in witnessing his daughter's triumphant performance behind the one-way mirror. Michel was crying and whining so much that he had to take him into the hallway and pace up and down with him. But even there, Michel continued to create a disturbance. Finally, a doctor peered out into the corridor: "Uh . . . could you please take that child into a room somewhere? I'm trying to conduct an evaluation. . . ." Marc had to find an empty office where he could sit with Michel.

Later, all four of us, Anne-Marie, Marc, Michel, and I, joined Dr. Cohen in his office. We voiced some of our anxiety about Michel, although we hastened to assure Dr. Cohen that he was nothing like Anne-Marie had been. Nothing. His eye contact, for one thing, was very reliable.

"I can do a fast screening for abnormality of development," Dr. Cohen said. "Would you want that?"

"Well . . . yes," said Marc. "As long as we're here."

Another hour's worth of detailed questions from the Vineland, about Michel's verbal and nonverbal communication, social behavior, motor skills, adaptive skills, etc.

Dr. Cohen left the room to look over the results.

He came back in about fifteen minutes and sat down. He looked at his desk, adjusted his papers, picked up his pen.

Say something, please! I felt like a trapped animal: holding deathly still before some lethal threat; attentive, frozen.

"There appears," he said carefully—how I dread that careful tone of voice—"to be some cause for concern."

He paused. Marc and I were perfectly silent.

"Michel is currently functioning about six months behind his age level in communication and socialization."

"What does that mean?" asked Marc.

"It could just mean that he's delayed . . . ," said Dr. Cohen.

"Some children," I interrupted urgently, breathing a little too quickly, "some children don't say a word until they're two." How many times by now had I heard and repeated that sentence? How many times had I sought out people, before Anne-Marie was diagnosed, who would say just those same words to me about her?

"Michel is within the norm," Dr. Cohen responded.

"But he's on the low end?" asked Marc.

"Yes." Dr. Cohen paused. "The very low end."

"Is he autistic?"

"He doesn't look autistic today," said Dr. Cohen.

Always there was that careful choosing of each word. And why should there not be? A word too much and dreams are shattered. A word too little and the future closes down.

"I have not observed him enough to say anything definitive about him. Keep an eye on him. The next few months will tell us a lot."

We took the children home. I called Robin, then Bridget. I couldn't get the story out coherently. I was panicked.

"He's not autistic, Catherine," said Robin.

"I don't see autism in him," said Bridget.

"He's not, love. He's not he's not he's not," said Marc. He turned to pick up Michel. Michel squirmed, then relaxed and let his father hold him. Marc kissed each of his little chipmunk cheeks. "Daddy loves you, right, Michel? Tell Mommy how fine you are." Michel turned and reached out to me. "You see? He's fine. I know it. Just give him a couple of months."

We were due to go out with our friends Art and Evelyne that evening. A French-American couple like ourselves, and soon to be the parents of a third child, they were among our closest friends. Evelyne worked with Marc as an investment banker.

The conversation started out about work and the city but soon turned inevitably to our children. To my embarrassment, I broke down again—staring into the blurry wineglass, trying to control the terror.

Art and Evelyne were loving and comforting. We spent the next hour talking about their son Eric and comparing him to Michel. Eric was a month younger than Michel, and, like him, had only five or six words. Eric did not say "Mama" either.

By the end of dinner, I was breathing easier and smiling. Marc put his arm around me and I leaned back against his strength. All would be well. We were just so hyperconcerned because of what had happened to Anne-Marie. The chances of its happening again were too remote. What had Dr. Rimland told me? Only a two percent chance of autism occurring twice in the same family?

But over the next few months, I became driven by one central desire: to find reassurance about Michel. I discovered myself again talking to strangers in the park—obsessed by that nightmare question that had come to dominate my waking thoughts yet again: What is normalcy?

I would see a mother playing with a toddler who looked to be about Michel's age. Casually, I would stroll over to her.

"Sweet little girl." I would smile.

"Thank you."

"About twenty months?"

"Yes."

"Um-hm. My baby is a month older."

"Oh yes. I see him. Tall for his age."

"Yes. It's amazing how different they all are from each other, even at the same age, isn't it?"

"Definitely."

"My son hardly says a word. He's probably going to be a late talker."

"Oh yes. But that's pretty common."

"Yes. I know. How's your daughter's language?"

"She talks up a storm these days! Every day she comes up with something cuter."

On cue, the little girl toddles up and says, "Mommy. Wan bubboos."

"You want to blow bubbles? Sure, sweetie."

Little thrills of adrenaline shoot through me.

"Well"—I laugh gaily—"you know what they say about little girls."

"Oh, yes. Girls always talk a lot earlier than boys."

"Oops. Sorry, gotta go catch him! Take care!"

And jauntily, cheerily, I stroll out of the playground carrying crying Michel.

If I just play the script right, I tell myself, if I say all the lines I'm supposed to say now, the ending will turn out fine.

The running comparison with my niece Helen wasn't going too well either. Even in motor skills and adaptive skills and imitation, she was now running circles around Michel: drinking from a cup, walking up and down stairs while holding the bannister, even babbling at one point into a little toy telephone. Whenever I saw her I would watch her with a sinking spirit. Michel just didn't do any of those things as well as she, and she was only sixteen months old!

Out came the books again. It was no good. I couldn't find him in any of these bloody vague books.

What is an OK speech delay and what is a not OK speech delay?

I went down to University Hospital one day with Daniel, who had a sore throat. Dr. Baxter was on vacation. His partner examined Daniel.

"Do you have some late talkers in your practice?" I blurted out.

"Of course."

"Well, how late is late? When do they start putting words together, finally? My other son still has only a few words, and he's twenty-two months."

"I don't know if I can answer your questions specifically. One thing is certain, though. Children can always understand a lot more than they can speak, at the beginning."

"Maybe Michel has a problem. I don't know how much he understands."

"Oh, he's probably just a little behind. He'll catch up."

"How do you know there's not a problem? Maybe there *is* a problem!"

"OK, OK, there's a problem! You're talking about a child I've never met!"

"Sorry. You see, his sister was diagnosed as autistic and then she recovered and now I'm beginning to worry about him. . . ."

"His sister . . . ? Diagnosed as . . . ? Sometimes these diagnoses are erroneous, you know."

"The diagnosis was not wrong! She recovered from autism. Dr. Lovaas is recovering kids from autism! Haven't you read about him?"

I was about to launch into a summary of Dr. Lovaas's article when I had a flash of insight into how I must appear to this man: a complete maniac. Hurtling from Daniel's sore throat to my other son's "problem" to my daughter's "recovery from autism." Ready to jump down his throat if he said there was a problem and yelling at him when he said there wasn't a problem. And expecting him to be up on the latest research on a condition that afflicted probably one child per year in the entire group's practice of hundreds of children.

I muttered an apology and left.

Where could I find the words I wanted to hear?

Michel's language remained the same: static, unchanging. From week to week the same five to ten words. No "Mama," no "Daddy" among them. More screaming and crying. More frustration and temper tantrums. Up on his toes a lot these days. Looking at me, but not paying too much attention to anyone else.

One day I noticed him running up and down the hall, looking to the side. I followed him. Up and down he ran, looking not straight ahead, but off to the side, tracking the line of the wainscoting rail where it ran along the wall at eye level.

"OK, no more of that!" I picked him up and carried him off to play. See? He can play with me. Look at the way he's looking at me. I'm making Play-Doh snakes for him. He understands. He enjoys this!

Who would tell me he was fine? Not Dr. Cohen. But he was supposed to know! Where could I find someone who could tell me the answer today, now?

"Watch him for the next few months." No. Impossible. Go watch your child for the next few months and see if he develops cancer. It may come on slowly and insidiously, so be sure to keep your eye on him every day. Watch for changes. You know those changes.

No. I can't bear this anymore. Someone tell me he's all right.

I talked to Bridget and Robin. They didn't sound so sure anymore.

"I need to have this resolved. I can't stand not knowing."

Robin contacted a child psychologist she worked with, someone she respected who could do a good evaluation with a child as young as Michel.

The evaluation did not go well. Dr. Pasik tried, but Michel was fretful and angry throughout. He wouldn't do any of the little tasks she set out for him. I cut the session short.

Later she called.

"Look, I'm sorry I left," I said. "But you know, Dr. Pasik, I really think my anxiety is being communicated to Michel. Of course he won't cooperate. He feels all this tension!"

I, the avowed opponent of such vague imputations of cause, was coming up with every environmental "stress" reason in the book for Michel's increasingly disturbing behavior.

Dr. Pasik did not reply.

"Well, what do you think, anyway?" I pressed her. "I mean you're not going to tell me he's autistic, are you?"

The carefully chosen words were coming at me again, like knives.

"I was a little concerned that he never looked up when either of us called him."

"He was angry! He was purposefully blocking us out!"

"Perhaps. Perhaps that's what he was doing."

I spoke to Robin later.

"I don't think much of your friend, Robin. I really don't know if she has enough experience with a population of normal kids. All she knows is pathology, so she sees it everywhere."

Robin sighed. She was pained to be in the middle of this situation. I knew how I sounded. At some level, I knew that I was flailing around, seeking to attack any bearer of bad news.

I had an idea. "I know, Robin. Why don't I take him to see Margery Rappaport? She knows what she's doing."

Same scenario with Margery. Michel tunes her out, tunes me out, ignores all her toys, ignores her comments and requests, whines and cries and pushes her hand away without looking at her.

"Um, Margery, listen. I'm going to take him home. I'm sorry. I apologize for wasting your time. He's not himself. He's under the weather. He's just blocking us out because he feels all this tension. You go ahead and send me the bill for your time. But really, no need to write up any kind of report. He's fine. I'm sure he's fine. Sorry."

Just don't write anything down about Michel and send it to me. I can't take it. I'm sorry.

Michel.

Where are you going, little man? Golden-haired, dark-eyed baby. Oh please . . . please . . .

Night and day, he became our focus. Sometimes we talked about him. Sometimes we didn't. Sometimes we could pretend that all was well; at other times the landscape of our life seemed shockingly impossibly familiar.

No. Are we heading *there* again? Isn't this the place we passed through before? Those shadows of fear, that cavern of grief? We cannot be here again. That was a nightmare. This is daylight.

I went to Robin yet again. Insisted that she do her own evaluation of Michel.

One evening, after her session with Anne-Marie, she tried to engage him with some little toys she'd brought along.

She emerged from his room after a half hour and sat down with me in the kitchen.

"He wasn't too cooperative, Catherine."

"Robin, what is wrong with him?"

"I think . . . I believe that he may have a communication disorder. And maybe a socialization problem as well. He's so fiercely resistant, even to my presence in the same room with him."

"Communication . . . socialization . . ." I couldn't suppress the note of tense pleading in my voice. "Robin, these are the core symptoms of autism we're talking about."

"I don't know if anyone could give him that diagnosis today, Catherine. I just don't know."

Not today. Maybe next week? A long scream was building inside me. How much longer could this go on?

Robin left me some material to read. We were all trying to figure out if Michel had some other possible diagnosis. Some other label, not so terrible.

The people who write articles on speech disorders, communication problems, learning disabilities, are for the most part aware of how completely hopeless is the whole issue of accurate diagnosis. Two people named Fry and Spreen had made this point ironically when they provided these instructions for forming diagnostic labels:

> Choose any term from column I; combine it with one term from column II and one term from column III and you have an accepted diagnostic label. Those terms appearing in a box in column II may sometimes be used alone.

I	II	III
primary	language	disorder
secondary	linguistic	disability
specific	learning	delay
minimal	cerebral	deficit
mild	brain	dysfunction
congenital	perceptual	impairment
developmental	visual-motor	pathology
chronic	neurologic	syndrome
childhood	educational	handicap
psychoneurological	aphasia	problem
functional	dysphasia	injury
	dyslexia	

So much for scientific exactitude, I thought. Marc glanced at the list and figured out that there were 1,452 possible diagnostic labels. At this point, I would have taken any one of them.

One Sunday in December, we took a drive with the children into the New England countryside. Michel was almost two. We stopped at a McDonald's for lunch. I carried Michel in. Marc was holding Daniel's and Anne-Marie's hands.

Michel began to cry. Wrenching sobs.

People stared at us. I sat down in a booth with him and held him.

"Baby. It's Mama. I'm holding you. Why are you crying? See? It's OK. It's just McDonald's. We're stopping here for lunch."

On and on he cried. Full-throated sobs, welling up from some unknown source of fear and confusion in his young spirit.

"Love. Please. Don't cry. Look. Here's Daddy. Here's Anne-Marie. And Daniel."

"Don't cry, Michel," said Daniel.

"Don' cwy, Michel," said Anne-Marie.

Michel did not respond at all. It was as though he didn't hear us. His eyes were looking desperately around, right and left, but they never stopped on us. We were not there for him.

I stood up abruptly.

"I'll take him to the car," I said to Marc. "I'll wait for you in the car."

I carried him out and sat in the car. The last of the fall leaves blew and swirled around us. The air was cold. I held him while he sobbed.

Frantically, fearfully, his eyes stared to the right and to the left. They never settled on me.

Someone else in that car began to sob.

I wrapped my arms around his lost self and let in the truth once more. Rocked with the pain of the truth.

"Oh my God. Not again. Not my Michel."

27

I NEEDED TO WALK around with this knowledge for a while.

There were some things I had to do, and I didn't want to do them.

First of all, I had to tell Marc.

Marc is such an optimist—so determinedly cheerful. He refuses to cave in to anxiety until he has to.

Marc treasures his family.

"Where would I be without all of you?" he used to wonder. "Who would I be? I know. An aging bachelor, married to my work, coming home at night to frozen dinners and a chrome-and-steel apartment!"

"Um-hm. Decorated in basic man-colors: navy blue, brown, and beige. But just think. You'd have peace and quiet."

"Yeah. Maybe a little too much peace and quiet."

Marc had begun to make great plans for his kids: "One day I'll have a boat. I'll take them on the boat as crew members. They'll love it! You can stay home," he charitably offered. "I know you hate boats."

"I don't hate boats. I just hate spending two weeks in a rocking lurching hotel with no hot and cold running water."

He would ignore me and go on. "Let's see. The boys will be the gorillas, and Anne-Marie will be the galley chef."

"Sexist!"

"OK. Anne-Marie will be a gorilla-ette and Michel will be the galley chef."

"Michel will miss his mommy."

"See that? You have to come. I'm not leaving Michel behind."

Photographs of the three children were scattered all over Marc's office. He bragged about their every exploit and triumph, from Daniel's first smile to Michel's first steps. He was sure that they were all going to graduate first in their class from Yale, then go on to conquer the world.

"And will you still adore them if they graduate last in their class in high school?"

"Of course."

Marc talked so enthusiastically about his children that at more than one cocktail party I had to remind him that his captive audience of young associates and vice presidents included some single people who were beginning to look a little glassy-eyed with boredom.

"Marc. Stop bragging about us. People aren't that interested."

He would just laugh. "I'm interested. They're my kids, and they're fascinating."

But more than their future, it was their present that gave Marc joy. Always reserved and careful with his feelings, he had found in fatherhood an outlet for a long-dormant tenderness. He delighted in having their lives to guide and protect. Initially awkward when Daniel was an infant, he grew quickly adept at cradling his children close when they were ill or frightened. The first time he was able to soothe crying baby Daniel to sleep by walking with him, and cradling his head on his shoulder, he came back with a smile of quiet pride.

When Michel was still only around thirteen or fourteen months old, he was his father's chief welcoming committee. If Marc came home from work early enough, it was Michel who let out a scream of excitement when he heard the key in the door. Up the hallway he would come, toddling at ninety miles an hour, lunging at his daddy's knees in order to give them a baby-bear hug.

After a grueling day of high-pressure meetings; nonstop traffic in and out of his office; twenty phone messages, thirty phone messages, all to be returned as soon as possible; demanding clients and warring colleagues—you could see Marc melt under this onslaught of love.

Michel's smile was bursting with joy. His arms were around his father's knees. His head was tilted back so that he could gaze at his adored daddy.

Marc would gather him up for a mighty hug. The two of them would laugh into each other's eyes.

But that was . . . how long ago? These days Michel would hardly look up when his father came home.

One evening, a week or so after our trip to McDonald's, Marc found me in the bedroom, seated on the bed, doing nothing.

"What is it, Catherine? You look so sad."

"It's Michel."

"I know you're worried about him . . . but we've talked about this so many times. . . . He doesn't fit the syndrome . . . he's too well-related."

I stared at the floor for a while.

"Marc. He's not looking at me much these days. He's not saying his words very consistently. I think . . . he may even be losing some of his words."

Marc didn't say anything. The air was tense and still. I put the words carefully out into the space between us.

"The other day, Marc, I took him on my lap. I held his bottle up. I knew he wanted it. I said 'ba-ba.' I must have said it twenty times."

"What did he do?" asked Marc.

"He stared into my eyes. He just didn't seem to know what I wanted from him. He kept reaching for the bottle, but he couldn't say the word."

I stopped. Took a deep breath. Went on:

"He used to say that word. That used to be one of his words."

Marc sat down next to me and waited.

"Finally," I said. "Finally, both he and I started to cry."

Marc was pale.

"You'd better call Dr. Cohen. And Dr. DeCarlo. No?"

"I guess so."

I couldn't stand the thought of any of this. Dragging Michel back for those terrible, terrifying evaluations. Hearing those words. The happy ending to Anne-Marie's story could not even come close to mitigating the impact I knew those words would have on both his father and me: "He is autistic." Farewell to Michel. Farewell to the dream of who we thought he was: the perfect child, the blessed baby. Good-bye to that self, so newly born and blossoming toward life. Now he too, blighted at the root. He too, slipping away. This was no bright morning he was traversing, but a somber twilight.

I HAD MET another mother, Diane Meier, at Anne-Marie's school. Diane had become one of the few people in whom I could confide. She was a physician at a New York hospital, and used to dealing with illness and trauma on a daily basis; her intelligence and sensitivity had been a balm to my spirit. She listened so well, with such attentive sympathy, that she more than made up for the lack of understanding I had encountered elsewhere.

I called her.

"Diane. I need help. I need to take Michel to someone and get a definite answer once and for all."

"Tell me. Let me help."

I outlined my criteria:

First, I wanted someone whom we didn't know and who didn't know us. I didn't want to take him to Dr. Cohen or Dr. DeCarlo, not yet. I was worried that, having seen Anne-Marie at her worst, they might be prejudiced toward a positive diagnosis for autism in Michel. More than that, on a more primitive, less rational level, I wanted to avoid a reenactment of those nightmarish scenes of diagnosis. I was still desperately searching for difference.

Second, I wanted a professional who knew normal children as well as autistic children. I still held out hope that all he had was a language delay.

Third, I wanted someone who wasn't going to talk to me as though I were ten years old. I'd put in my time. I was in no mood to be condescended to by any "expert" in autism.

Miraculously, Diane found the right person. Dr. Maryann Gershwin, Ed.D., had had extensive clinical experience with different types of children: normally developing children with emotional problems, autistic children, children with speech delays.

Dr. Gershwin came to my apartment a few days later.

I trembled a little as I prepared some coffee for her. The spoon clattered on the counter.

"I'm a little nervous about this."

"I know."

We sat and talked. We played on the floor with Michel. Daniel and Anne-Marie moved in and out of our conversation. Three hours went by very quickly.

Dr. Gershwin walked with me into the living room and sat down.

"I think you know, don't you, Mrs. Maurice?"

I put my head back against the chair and closed my eyes, just for a second.

I opened them.

"Yes. I know."

We talked quietly for a while longer. Then she left. Later, I was to receive her report, a detailed analysis of Michel's strengths and weaknesses.

Diagnosis: probable infantile autism.

Marc was going to come home early that evening. I was going to have to tell him.

Michel. Golden child. Recompense for suffering. Oh please, hold on.

The fear kept rising up.

I fed the children, bathed them, got them into their pajamas. Their small bodies were so perfect, so whole.

Daniel and Anne-Marie wanted to hear a story after the bath. I sat and read to them. Michel played with his train in the library. Every now and then I trembled.

MICHEL. You smiled at me on days when I couldn't see for crying . . . Where has your smile gone?

MARC CAME HOME. There was nothing to do but go with this madness, do what had to be done. Let your heart scream its scream, and walk into the land of loss.

I told him calmly, standing next to him while we looked at the three children playing.

He crumpled. Just a little. Just momentarily.

He stood still and let out a long sigh. Then he walked into the library and sat down next to his little boy. His whole body drooped.

"Marc," I said. I could barely speak: "We will recover him. We can do it again." I didn't believe it myself. We had already had our miracle. We weren't going to get two.

"Yes," Marc said woodenly.

But his eyes held such pain.

He started to say something. Maybe he was trying to find the brave words, the strong words that had sustained me so many times through Anne-Marie's ordeal.

But none would come.

He sat next to his baby boy and looked at him.

Back and forth, back and forth fiercely, went the choo-choo train. The train stuck on something. Michel, never looking up, let out a high-pitched screech of impatience. He grabbed his father's hand by the back of the wrist. He shoved it at the train.

I saw Marc's face quiver for a second. He stood up. He walked out of the room. I let him go.

THE NEXT DAY, I took the necessary steps. I knew what I had to do. There was no sense in resisting anything anymore.

I called Dr. DeCarlo and Dr. Cohen. I set up appointments with both of them.

I called Bridget. I told her that I wanted to get Michel's therapy under way now, immediately, even before the diagnosis was confirmed.

"I'll come in on Friday and do a baseline session with him. We'll see how he adapts to the structure of the program."

"Thank you, Bridget."

I called Robin. She promised to come and begin working with Michel immediately, twice a week.

"Thank you, Robin."

Everyone was moving fast now, making quick decisions and rearranging their lives. The sense of urgency was increasing exponentially, as we all finally let the truth seize hold again.

We hadn't even stopped working with Anne-Marie. There was no closure to her program. We just immediately halted her therapy in order to use all the available manpower with Michel. For Bridget and Robin didn't have quite as much flexibility as they had had two years ago. Bridget especially was strapped for time. She had begun a doctoral program in psychology, she was working part-time at a school for autistic children, and she couldn't promise me unlimited hours. Robin was juggling private clients and her full-time job at Mount Sinai.

Never have I felt so dependent on two people. Where could I find two women of such talent and commitment again? When Bridget told me that she could come in, at least in the beginning, for four sessions a week, I wanted to throw my arms around her.

Setting up and launching the program was thus child's play, compared to what we had gone through with Anne-Marie. We knew what we were doing, and we each knew what roles we had to play.

But nothing could prepare us for Michel's reaction.

Bridget's first session with him was unbearable.

Anne-Marie had cried and trembled and fallen to the floor. She seemed above all petrified.

Michel threw a fit of uncontrollable fury.

All Bridget did, in that first session, was to set some toys before him and continuously call for his attention.

"Michel. Look at me. Michel!"

Michel started by blocking her out and pushing her away, but when she wouldn't desist, he began to scream.

His rage escalated. His sobs became paroxysmal. He began to roll on the floor, back and forth, kicking the chairs over, hurling anything within reach.

I had stayed to watch. I thought I could handle it. I thought I could handle anything by now.

A sound, a moan, escaped my mouth, as I watched him rolling on the floor, convulsed with near-hysterical rage. I left the room. I went to the far end of the apartment and sat with my arms around Daniel and Anne-Marie. They were talking to me, but I couldn't hear them.

Bridget came out after fifteen more minutes.

"Can you come in and calm him for a little while? I told him you would come in."

I went to hold him. I sat on the floor next to his sobbing body and stroked him. When he finally allowed me to, I held him and rocked him and told him how much I loved him, how much Bridget loved him. His sobs finally diminished to quivering silent spasms.

When he was calm, Bridget came in, and they started all over again.

Within two minutes came the screaming rage once more.

That scene was repeated the next day and the next day and the next. He wouldn't calm down.

Every day, I paced up and down the hallway. Unable to stay in the room, unable to remain too far away. He must calm down. He will calm down. Anne-Marie did. He will too. This can't go on.

And finally, he did begin to calm down. But what followed was almost worse. He sat in the chair the way Bridget wanted him to, his little feet square on the floor. His hands hung down at his sides. He no longer screamed. He cried as though his heart would break. Tears coursed down his cheeks, but he didn't even raise his hands to wipe them away.

With a camera set up on a tripod in the room, Bridget was video-taping everything for program planning and for tracking his progress. I would watch the day's session on tape, at night, after the children were asleep. But I couldn't get through any of them. "It's too painful, Marc. I can't bear this."

Dear God in heaven, he's only two years old! Why is this happening? Why do we have to do this?

Only one thought gave any comfort at all: Dr. Lovaas's people had mentioned to me, more than once, that it seemed to be the children with the most fire and fight in them who went the farthest. The hardest children were the ones who were listless, uncaring, unmoved, almost not there.

Michel was fighting us with everything he had.

Marc had taken a week off from work so that we could hold each other together as we started the journey again. Both of us were reeling. I was losing weight quickly, and my heart kept jolting into a frightening arrhythmia. Marc seemed achingly sad. I wanted to comfort him. I tried to seem optimistic. But I knew that it wasn't simply a question of promising him that Michel would recover. He was grieving for what was happening to his son now. Whether or not there would be a rebirth, some part of Michel was dying right now.

On February 5 we had an appointment with Dr. DeCarlo in the morning and Dr. Cohen in the afternoon.

The meeting with Dr. DeCarlo was calm and quiet and the evaluation as detailed as Anne-Marie's had been. There was no surprise at the end. Dr. DeCarlo's diagnostic impression was as we expected: "infantile autism."

"But I have every hope for him," she said to us as we left.

We drove to Staten Island in silence. The inexorable process continued.

At the institute, we waited in the too familiar waiting room. I stepped out into the hallway with Michel for a moment. I turned, to see Dr. Cohen and Dr. Sudhalter walking toward me. Their faces were grave.

"Hello," I said.

"Hello." Their eyes went from me to Michel.

I attempted to lighten the atmosphere a little.

"I can't say," I began blithely, "that I'm happy to see you." But my voice couldn't carry the joke through, and broke.

"No," said Dr. Sudhalter.

Same tests, same questions, same videotaping.

During the videotaping, I took Michel on my lap facing me and poured everything I had into getting the eye contact, the smile, the response.

He brightened up briefly. Dr. Cohen turned to Marc, standing behind the mirror. "That's good. That's a good sign. Does he do that often?"

"I don't think so."

In the taping room, I sat back, drained.

No one could know the concentrated energy it took to keep Michel that focused for five minutes. It was almost as though I had to hypnotize or enthrall him. Everything in me—voice, expression, eye gaze, smile, body posture, position of my hands—all were summoned to one purpose: keep this child focused on me, on my eyes. More: make it enjoyable for him.

Dr. Cohen's and Dr. Sudhalter's diagnosis: infantile autism.

Michel had actually lost ground since the Vineland Scales that had been administered the previous July, seven months earlier. He was now over two years old but was functioning at only ten months of age in communication and socialization. His motor and adaptive skills had remained unchanged.

His receptive language had diminished even further, and his stereotypical mannerisms were increasing. His eye contact was sporadic and unreliable.

He was falling off the cliff.

There was nothing to do but go through the grieving and get on with the work.

Bridget would start off by giving me four sessions a week, but she would be looking around for other therapists to come in as soon as possible.

Robin would start at two sessions a week and increase to three when his language got a little better.

I would do what I had done with Anne-Marie: keep after him during the day, never let him spend too long on any one activity, constantly demand his attention, try to reinforce and generalize whatever Bridget and Robin were working on.

During the first couple of weeks, I did some holding therapy with Michel, then let it go. I still thought that holding therapy had some real though limited worth. Good for making initial contact with some very withdrawn children—sometimes. One method among several for attempting to make eye contact; one method among several for momentarily "waking up" some kids. But not anything I was going to rely on to carry our child through to health. Not anything that was ever going to teach him all that he had to be taught. For that, we would rely primarily on the behavioral program, Robin's speech therapy, and our own knowledge of how to interest Michel, how to generalize the programs, and how to forcefully intrude on his withdrawal. In addition, Marc and I just tried to make sure that we continued to hug and kiss and cuddle him a lot, as we always had and as we would do with any normal child.

THE DIAGNOSIS had been made and confirmed. The therapeutic program was under way. We all knew what we had to do; we were all doing it already.

After that week of diagnosis and fear and marshaling of the troops, Marc went back to work. He had come through his shock and his initial grief and now was climbing back up toward hope. I knew he had confidence in me. Everyone had confidence in me. Dr. DeCarlo had said as much, and Dr. Cohen, and all our friends and family.

"You did it once. You can do it again. With a mother like you, and the same therapists you had for Anne-Marie, he has every chance in the world."

The only problem was, I didn't believe that Michel would recover.

```
┌─────────────────────┐
│ ✳ ✳ ✳ ✳ ✳ ✳ ✳      │
│ ✳ ┌─────┐ ✳         │
│ ✳ │     │ ✳         │
│ ✳ │ 28  │ ✳         │
│ ✳ │     │ ✳         │
│ ✳ └─────┘ ✳         │
│ ✳ ✳ ✳ ✳ ✳ ✳ ✳      │
└─────────────────────┘
```

I WAS SO WEAK in faith, and Michel was so strong in resistance.

The first month of his therapy was a nightmare. It became apparent that he was not going to be a carbon copy of Anne-Marie. She had adjusted to the sessions pretty quickly, in retrospect. His anger and resistance were double, triple, what hers had been.

Day after day, I would stand in the hallway outside the closed door listening to his sobs. I prayed for his adjustment and cooperation. I used to lean my head against the wall and cry inside. "Oh God, please please make him stop crying. Make him start learning the way Anne-Marie did."

I was a frantic nervous mess when therapy was going on. My mind and soul were in that room, and I couldn't stand any distraction or any interruption of my vigil. This had to work. It just had to. I didn't have any other aces up my sleeve.

No one was allowed to go near the therapy room or play loudly around it in the hallway. Bridget was in a day-by-day struggle to win Michel's cooperation, and if she didn't we had lost him forever, I was convinced of it.

I was in my bedroom one day, next door to the therapy room. Patsy was with Daniel and Anne-Marie in the library. Michel was sobbing while Bridget tried to work with him, and I was hanging on every sound emitted from the room, hoping against hope that he would just stop and begin to cooperate and to learn.

Suddenly I heard his bedroom door open.

I bolted into the hallway. Anne-Marie had walked into the therapy room.

I ran after her, picked her up, and carried her into my room.

"I told you no one goes into that room! Didn't you hear me? Didn't you hear Mommy? Answer me!"

I was shaking with fury.

Her eyes stared, shocked, into mine, then her face crumpled. She started to cry.

All the anger drained out of me. Shame took its place. I gathered her up.

"I'm sorry, baby. I'm so sorry. Mommy's sorry. I love you."

She cried for a little while; then suddenly she stopped and pulled away from me. Her cheeks were wet, but she managed to summon a smile.

"It's OK, Mommy. It was a assident!"

Children forgive us so completely.

DURING that first month, in many ways, Michel daily grew worse.

I don't know how this autism thing works. Especially in late-deterioration cases such as my children went through. I mean that even as you swing into full attack against the disorder, wrench the child into a listening, learning, looking, paying-attention mode, even as you begin to see some words come back and some attentiveness come back, you still see decline for a while. Parts of the syndrome are being aborted, but other parts are just coming into play. Someday someone will figure out what is going on neurologically. Most cases of autism are not diagnosed until the child is three or even four, when the symptomatic picture has come into full focus. Our children were diagnosed just as their deterioration began to accelerate visibly.

Michel was toe-walking and hand-flapping constantly now; tensing his body, shaking his head, gazing intently at objects that he held up to the extreme corner of his eye, trying to look at things upside down, screeching and throwing tantrums and daily more difficult to make eye contact with. He still seemed to have some rudimentary pretend play, as when he put a dolly into a bed, but he only did it if I set up the doll and the bed in his immediate visual range, then modeled the action for him.

His language, what little he had, was dwindling to nothing. And he was losing awareness of all of us.

On the day that he did not look up at me once the whole morning, did not react when I walked into the apartment with Daniel and Anne-

Marie, and actively tried to avoid my gaze when I got down next to
him on the floor, I lost it. I called Marc at the office and just sobbed.

"I can't . . . I can't do this anymore. . . . This isn't working. . . . I'm
losing him!"

I believed in nothing.

I prayed, but my prayer felt like empty words addressed to an absent
Being.

As I fingered my rosary or murmured my novenas, mocking laughter echoed in my head.

How do *you* rate?

Who do you think *you* are? You get not one miracle cure—you get
two! That's rich. That's funny! You think God is listening to you? You
think there is a God? Dream on.

Where my heart had harbored love and trust, there was only cynicism and terror.

"Oh Lord, I believe. Help Thou mine unbelief!"

It was the words of the Gospel that rose up to defend me against
this onslaught of despair. The words not only of that long-ago father
of an epileptic, pleading before Jesus, but of the faithful centurion whose
child was dying:

"Lord, I am not worthy that Thou shouldst come under my roof.
Only say the word, and my son shall be healed."

I had to become childlike.

Of course I couldn't make sense of it all: Who is worthy? Who is
not? Whose prayers are answered? Whose are not? Why? When I tell
my children that there is a God, and that He loves them beyond all
telling, they believe me without question. Could my spirit, battered
by too much knowledge, ever wend its way back to that childlike trust,
that fullness of faith? Could I really believe that there was a God who
was taking care of us? That either Michel would recover, or, if he did
not, that somehow there would still be peace in my heart?

Not through reason at all: fear overpowered any reason to trust in
God. Only through an act of will, an offering of a poor prayer, so
imperfect as to deny itself in its very unfolding:

"Lord, I believe. Help Thou mine unbelief."

I stood outside Michel's door, day after day after day. I prayed and
prayed, and the sobs continued. He did nothing but cry. "Tap table,"
prompted Bridget, "tap table," picking up his hand and tapping it on
the table.

Day after day the data remained unchanged. One hundred percent with a prompt; zero percent on his own.

Lord, give me one half hour. The last half hour. Let him be calm and quiet. Let him let Bridget in. Let him stop crying!

My hands are clenched into fists. I'm leaning against the wall of the corridor, listening to my son.

The sobs begin to diminish.

They stop. There is quiet.

Then there is Bridget, sounding excited.

"Yay! You did it! You tapped table!"

Then there is another sound, a new sound: babbling.

Then silence, then more babbling.

And finally, I hear the sweetest sound of all. Michel is laughing. He is laughing at something that Bridget is doing. My son is laughing because Bridget is doing something funny.

I cover my face with my hands. My whole body is shaking. Pain and joy come crashing together in a wave that threatens to engulf me.

The healing has begun.

29

SOMETIMES, GOING FORWARD, the way seemed very dark. I had hope, then I lost it, then I gained it again. One day Marc and I looked at each other and wondered if our journey through this different land was at last coming to an end.

Some memories stand out more than others: the turning points, the moments of confusion and those of triumph. There were times when the work seemed overwhelming and the decisions too difficult; other times when we felt surer of the way.

IT IS A FEW WEEKS into Michel's program. He and I are in my room. We are seated on the floor. He is playing with the wooden Brio train, which he loves. I gather all the little cars and hide them in the folded-over bottom of my shirt. He looks around for the train. I show him one of the cars in the palm of my hand. He tries to take it, but I close my hand.

"Choo-choo," I say.

He starts to whine. He tries to pry the car out of my hand.

"Choo-choo," I say.

His whining increases, escalates to screams. He tries to scratch my hand. I hide the car in my shirt, pick up his chin to get eye contact, and persist: "Choo-choo."

Fifteen minutes of rage ensue. No sobbing, thank goodness; just rage and screams and kicking.

I know how much he wants that train. I couldn't do this with just any old thing. In my shirt, I am holding a reinforcer far more effective than any piece of chocolate.

"Choo-choo," I say.

"Too-too!" he finally chokes out.

I let out a war whoop, smother him with kisses. "You said it! You said 'choo-choo'!"

There are eleven more cars. He says "too-too" to get each one.

EVERY MORNING, for the first five months or so of Michel's therapy, I work with him in my room, from 9:30 to 11:30. Daniel and Anne-Marie are in school.

I've learned to concentrate my work more, do more in less time. I have to. I need to spend more time with Daniel now, and I'm deeply anxious about not giving Anne-Marie enough attention. The after-noon will belong largely to them, while Michel is in therapy.

Tacked up in front of me is my list of songs, games, and activities, compiled from memory, from tapes we have of the singer Raffi, from books, from my own invention. A friend, Christine Allison, has sent me a copy of her beautiful book, and I comb through there as well, looking for any material that will help me with Michel.* On the inside cover is Christine's inscription: "Dear Catherine and Marc—with God's help we *can* outstare the darkness."

With the aid of my lists, I am able to keep Michel's attention on me for most of those two hours.

"Ring around the rosy": His favorite. During this song I can almost always get him to look up at me, in anticipation of the "All fall down!"

"This is the way the ladies ride": I bounce him on my knee. Great for eye contact.

"This little piggy": The words of this rhyme and the other rhymes aren't that important. What is important is that he gets pleasure out of the game, and the pleasure is associated with me, a person, his mother.

Pretending to eat each one of his toes: Much laughter and shrieking during this game. His reaction borders on fearfulness, as when we play monster games or chasing games. The pleasure/fearfulness has to be pushed just to a certain point, so that he doesn't get *too* afraid.

"Peek-a-boo": Not very successful at the beginning. We're too physically separated to keep his attention on me.

*Christine Allison, *I'll Tell You a Story, I'll Sing You a Song* (Delacorte, 1987).

"One-two-three-squeeze": Another anticipatory game. I count out one-two-three slowly, then give him a mighty squeeze, which he seems to love.

Blowing on his face: This always seems to get his attention, especially if I turn it into a game.

Rhythmic massages while singing to him: Music is one of the most powerful magnets for all three of my kids. I sing to them a lot, most often accompanying the song with dancing, or swaying, or rocking, or stroking.

Tickling: As long as he doesn't get too silly.

"Trot-trot to Boston": Another bouncing-on-knee song.

"Little rabbit foo-foo"/"Itsy Bitsy Spider": Any of the rhymes that use finger-play, like these two, help to keep him focused.

"Open/Shut them": A hand motion song, opening and shutting my hands. He has to be sitting on my lap, not across the room from me.

"Head, shoulders, knees, and toes": This song entails touching the various body parts as we sing. Every nursery school teacher knows it.

"Bumpin' up and down in my little red wagon": Another bouncing song, taken from one of our Raffi records.

"Row-row-row": Bridget had shown me how to do this; we face each other, rocking back and forth and holding each other's hands.

"Six little ducks that I once knew": Another Raffi song. Michel loves the "quack-quack-quack" part, especially when it's really nasal and exaggerated.

"The noble duke of York": Again, a body movement song. The lyrics are illustrated through physical movements.

Any other song or rhyme that uses dancing or rocking or bouncing or finger-play or hand motions.

In addition to playing these rhymes and games, we read books (baby books, one word per page); we play with dollies as much as Michel can understand, and we play with *any* toy that will lend itself to turn taking and requesting. One such toy is a cash register by Fisher-Price with big colored coins that fit into slots. As with the trains, I can hold these coins, and not give them to him until he looks at me and makes some sound for each one. The basic technique is always to get him interested in something—or to profit from his own interest in, for instance, a toy—and then to use that something to keep pushing the idea of language, communication. I didn't care what he said when he asked me for those coins—I think he said "gih!"—as long as he was grasping the concept: that is I (Michel) use sounds coming out of my mouth to communicate. I say something, and when I do, that bothersome mommy gives me what I want.

In April we added another therapist to the program, Mary Beth Villani. Bridget was starting to reduce her hours. In May, Anne Marie Larkin came for a few weeks, then had to stop. In June, Kelly McDonough joined the program.

Michel's program hours would, for the rest of the year, vary between a low of ten and a high of twenty-two hours of behavioral therapy per week. As soon as she could give us the time, in early May, Robin started to come for three hours a week.

Bridget's role became more of a director of curriculum as she cut back to one or two sessions a week, and let the other, less experienced therapists take on more of the work. My role was to manage and coordinate the program, to keep everyone working on the same goals, and, like Robin, to generalize Michel's linguistic gains during nonsession hours.

Mary Beth, Anne Marie, and Kelly proved to be therapists of talent and commitment. Each had distinct strengths and different levels of experience. Mary Beth could get a smile out of Michel on some of his stormiest days. Anne Marie rivaled Bridget in the creative originality she brought to her work. And Kelly turned out to be our most reliable, conscientious, and committed worker, never missing a session unless she was felled by the Hong Kong flu or some other disaster. They all learned how to grow and learn and work together, and I learned how to lean on them more and more, instead of clinging to Bridget as the only effective behavioral therapist in the world. (Though she still ranks up there with the God-gifted and the near-perfect, in my assessment.)

It was my decision to give Michel the extra hours of therapy. I trusted the behavioral program far more the second time around, and I didn't want to do it all myself: I mean that Marc and I had pretty much decided, after our experience with Anne-Marie, that it was crucial to keep an autistic child occupied and if possible engaged with people almost every waking hour of the day during the first year or two of therapy. With Anne-Marie, that burden had fallen primarily on me, whenever Bridget or Robin wasn't there. This time around, I was willing to share the work with any good behavioral therapist.

The down side was of course increased disruption of our home life and our privacy; the up side was I had more time to give to Daniel, to Anne-Marie, to Marc, and to myself. Entering our third year of crisis, it had become important to not play superwoman any more than necessary. The more I could share the work, the easier it was.

MICHEL was so different from Anne-Marie. She had been more socially withdrawn, and far more fearful. He was better-related. When he finally began to respond to secondary reinforcement, to praise, in his therapy sessions, he did so with a full smile and good eye contact. When Michel was "on" in those first six months of therapy, he was really on—happy, alert, so well related that we thought he must have already moved out of the realm of what any professional would call "classically autistic," in the sense of being withdrawn and lost in his own world. But in between his moments of burgeoning affection he was a terror. His temperament, his screaming crying tantrums, were horrific.

As for language, Anne-Marie's ability to communicate had come in more easily than his. Where she had needed more social pursuing—specifically by me, following her constantly around the house, never letting her be—Michel needed more-structured teaching sessions. We had to concentrate a lot on verbal imitation. Jackie Wynn, a therapist from the Lovaas Clinic, came out to give us some good intensive verbal-imitation drills.

For a long time, his articulation was terrible. Even as the number of words in his vocabulary increased, his articulation rendered those words almost unintelligible to anyone except his therapists and his parents. He said "Adoh" for Dumbo, "dis" for fish, and "guh" for bug.

In spite of all these differences between him and his sister, both in personality and in our overall therapeutic approach, Michel made rapid progress.

By April, he was repeating "Mama," "Daddy," "Deedee" for Bridget, "Wah-wah" for Robin and "Mmm-bah" for Mary Beth. He was still very confused over who was Daniel and who was Anne-Marie.

We had taught him five two-word combinations:

1. "No [name of food]."
2. "Bye-bye, [name]."
3. "Hi, [name]."
4. "Night-night, [name]"—which he pronounced "Nih-nih."
5. "More [name of food or game]."

Although he could now give an approximate imitation of virtually any two-word combination we modeled for him, these were the only combinations he would occasionally initiate himself.

Two months later, there were evident strides forward:

Articulation was better, to the point where he could now say "house" instead of "how"; "car" instead of "keh."

Spontaneous, creative language was beginning to increase a little. One day he picked up a small grape and said "baby grape," indicating a certain level of analogous reasoning and ability to express it in language. A few days later he repeated this comment with Play-Doh, picking up a small piece and saying "Baby Pay-Doh," then a larger one and saying "Mommy Pay-Doh."

We found that he responded well to little dramatic vignettes, illustrated for him either with Play-Doh or with drawing: I draw a big fish on his Magna-Doodle,* then help him to put in eyes, mouth, big teeth, and a tail. Gradually we add water, a boy, a boat, and a fishing pole. He loves the drama of the boy catching the big fish with the scary teeth. He wants the stories to be a little fierce, a little powerful. We make a big lump of Play-Doh into a mommy dinosaur, and a little lump into a baby dinosaur. He is delighted when the baby dinosaur falls off the edge of the table and the mommy has to jump down to his rescue. "Help, help!" He imitates the plaintive call. "Don't worry, I'm coming!" yells the mommy. The more dramatic the story, the more exciting the dialogue, the easier it is to keep his attention.

In therapy, the language drills were relentless. Verbal imitation, consonants, vowels, one-syllable words, two-syllable words, adjectives; labeling photographs with the appropriate action verb depicted (running, sleeping, walking, etc.); prepositions, the adverbs "down" and "up." Everything had to be *functional*. The goal was not just to have him repeat a word or phrase, but to have him understand and *use* language.

---

*A great toy, made by Tyco. Michel loved it. It consists of a metallic board and a magnetized drawing pen. It allows the child to draw and erase with considerable ease.

Bridget kept astounding me with her creativity. Finding that he was bored with the endless preposition drills, she decided to use Michel himself, instead of a toy, as a prop: she stands him on top of a chair.

"Where are you?"

She models the response: "On the chair."

She holds the chair over his head.

"Where are you?" She's laughing. They're making a game of it. She models: "Under the chair." They have practiced each of these phrases already, in many previous drills with toys.

"Where are you?"

"Next to the chair," he responds ("Neh do da dteh").

"Behind the chair."

"In front of the chair."

Marc and I felt that with respect to social/emotional attachment, Michel made perhaps even faster progress than had his sister. One day in May we all piled into the car to drive out to East Hampton. Anne-Marie was sitting in the middle seat, Michel was in the car seat next to her, and Daniel was in the very back seat of the station wagon, out of Michel's view. As Marc pulled out of the garage, suddenly Michel became very agitated, and began to cry. He seemed really distraught. I turned around.

"What is it, baby?"

"Michel! Michel!" He sobbed, staring into my eyes. His hands were reaching toward the window beside him. "Michel!"

"What? What? I don't understand. Marc, pull over. He's really upset."

"Michel!" He twisted around in his seat, trying to look out through the window at the garage we had just left.

"Oh Lord, he's calling Daniel!"

"Daniel!" Michel repeated, this time smiling through his tears.

The poor little one thought we had left his brother behind. He couldn't get the name right, since we had only very recently begun a name program with family members, but he did know one thing: He wanted his brother.

"There he is, love. Do you see him? He's right behind you!"

"Here I am, Michel!" laughed Daniel, popping up from behind the seat.

Michel began to laugh with delight and relief. We all began to laugh. Marc and I looked at each other, savoring one of those moments of happiness when we both knew that Michel, whatever his problems, could certainly not be described now as "indifferent" to his family.

In time, I gained more and more confidence in myself. Marc and I felt OK now, making our own decisions about Michel's program. Or I should say, Marc felt OK about leaving the decisions to me; and, where I would have quaked at such responsibility for my son's future a few months before, now I too felt that Bridget and I, and Robin and Mary Beth and Kelly, could carry him the rest of the way through.

```
*********
*       *
*  3 0  *
*       *
*********
```

ONE AREA where I wanted to use my own judgment was in dealing with Michel's crying. I still don't know if I handled it well. It seemed to go on forever. Maybe it would have stopped sooner if I had been tougher.

But I couldn't adopt—I mean I was emotionally incapable of—the 100 percent consistency that a behavioral approach demands.

It's seven o'clock in the morning. The children wander sleepily one by one into our bedroom. I drag myself out of bed—I'm not very good in the morning—and say: "Let's have breakfast."

With that, Michel throws himself to the floor and sobs. No rhyme, no reason, except perhaps that someone has put a demand on him. I sigh, Marc sighs, Daniel and Anne-Marie ignore him. We are all used to this.

I gird up for what I know will be the first of perhaps twenty-five such scenes throughout the day.

Here, I can be very "behavioral." I know what I have to do. I do not feed into his crying at all. I don't reinforce it by any attention whatsoever. I set the table and serve the other two children their breakfast. Then matter-of-factly, I pick Michel up, bring him to the table, and hold him in his chair. I hold his hand around the spoon, guide the spoon from the bowl to his mouth, ignore the yelling and the screaming, and hold the spoon at his mouth until he takes a bite. I push him verbally: "Mmm. Yummy. You're eating Cheerios. Good boy. Good eating breakfast."

Eventually, he always starts to eat, because I don't give up until he does. It's not like trying to get Daniel to eat vegetables. Daniel hates vegetables, and that's one power struggle that I don't even bother engaging in. But Michel is hungry and he does like Cheerios, and he's resisting because something in his makeup is compelling him to fall on the floor and cry rather than eat his breakfast. I'm trying to free him from that behavior. I'm trying to strip that activity of any external reward, so that he will stop it and get on to the normal childhood business of eating his cereal in the morning.

After many many similar scenes, yes, it does begin to work. Lo and behold, here he is, coming to the table, sitting down himself, picking up his spoon and eating. Miracle of miracles, he is enjoying every bite.

But! I don't know if I believe that there are any clear and absolute rules that apply to human behavior—mine or his or anyone's. There are times when he emerges from his fourth hour of therapy, late in the afternoon. He's tired, frustrated, his tolerance is stretched to the limit. Daniel or Anne-Marie happens to pick up a toy he's playing with. He throws himself to the floor, rolling around in a fit of wrath and tears.

This is when I pick him up and hold him and kiss him and sing to him until he has relaxed in my arms and the storm has passed.

I didn't *want* to reinforce his tantrum. It *was* an extreme reaction to frustration. But I did reinforce it, because another need took precedence at that moment: the need to convey to him that he was loved, that I understood how hard it was to be pushed so relentlessly all day long, that he had the right, as I had the right, to give vent from time to time to rage and grief and confusion.

So all along, he was getting pretty inconsistent, sometimes even contradictory messages from me about his crying. Often I "extinguished" his extremely tantrumous behavior, at other times I wound up rewarding it. Nor was there even any consistent rule of appropriateness that I could articulate about when he needed hugging and when he needed ignoring. It was something I decided on a running basis, depending on context and preamble and even mood of the moment— his and mine. It seemed to me that there had to be some latitude on our part, some flexibility in us as well. I thought that in time, with some more development of communicative skills and social awareness, the crying would begin to wane. I thought, in some vague way that I find hard to define, that he was not ready to stop this extreme degree of crying: he wasn't mature enough. He was nearly three, but in certain respects he was still much younger. To me, it was like trying to get a baby to stop crying. In most areas, I felt that it was OK to push Anne-Marie and Michel; in other areas, I felt that their emotional immaturity—in Michel's case, almost his "babyhood"—should be taken into account.

Although Bridget was able to accept my contention that judgment calls were appropriate, she was frustrated that Michel was getting such contradictory handling of a very problematic behavior. And problematic it was. Every outing, every therapy session, every bath time—most changes of activity—was accompanied by a shorter or longer period of crying (often complicated by anger or aggression). His crying and temperamentality lasted well into his second year of treatment. It was an intense strain on everyone, Daniel and Anne-Marie included. If he hadn't been advancing so well in linguistic and play and social skills, we might have had serious doubts, once again, about the appropriateness of behavioral intervention.

This is the dilemma you get into when you start defending behavioral therapy. You know it's effective, you know it's very powerful, you know that if pushed, the kids will do a lot better than anyone expected, so you want to preach 100 percent consistency. "Whenever he cries, do this." Period. No discussion. In practice, with my own child, however, in particular areas I was not 100 percent consistent, and relied more on subjective judgment calls.

But it's always a judgment call, isn't it? All of us parents have to keep balancing between the extremes of either psychoanalyzing our kids to the point of accepting any behavior, or shaping and forcing their behavior to the point where we crush their individuality.

A little girl comes to play with Anne-Marie one day. When her mother arrives to pick her up, the child shouts "No!" and runs in the opposite direction. Twenty minutes of begging, bargaining, and pleading ensue. I have to stand at my apartment door while this four-year-old sends her mother through the circus hoops. Finally, Mom persuades little girl to put on her coat. Little girl takes it off and throws it on the floor. Twice more we go through this performance. Meanwhile, Mom is sighing away about how "high-spirited," how "strong-willed" is her child.

Lady, I sigh to myself, are you that afraid of scarring her little psyche for life if you pick her up and actually carry her into the elevator? Pick up the coat, put it on her, and prove to her that her mother has a higher IQ than a jelly bean!

That sort of hyperconcern over denying a child what he wants to do, ever, drives me insane. I see constant examples, among "normal" families, with "normal" children: mothers dissolving in tears because their five-year-old refuses to put on his coat; fathers spoken to with intense sarcasm by ten-year-olds. The only thing that disturbs me more is seeing a child being smacked around.

Parental confusion over what is the "right" way of treating kids, either handicapped or normal, goes right back to that old conflict between the psychodynamic and the behavioral modes, both of which are pervasively enmeshed in our culture, and both of which can be carried to an extreme. I have been defending behavioral therapy throughout this book, because the field of autism has been dominated for so long by the most absurd excesses of the psychodynamic school of thought, and because many parents of autistic children whom I have met find it very difficult even to try behavioral therapy. But in the larger context, there is a possibility for excess on both sides of the spectrum.

On the one hand, there is the Biblical quotation, so beloved of Victorian moralists, "Spare the rod; spoil the child." I do believe that this extreme leads to child abuse. The rod, the belt, the paddle, the whip, the fist, the open palm—I don't care what is used, if we rely on any of these as our chief disciplining device, we're using something to beat our child into compliance.

Every parent I know, myself included, has lost control and given a whack across the behind. That doesn't make it good or right or particularly intelligent. It astonishes me that we do to children what we would never dream of doing to an adult. Convicted felons in this country have more legal protection of their bodily integrity than do "naughty" children. And does hitting have any practical worth in disciplining? I doubt it. I think most parents do it because "My father did it to me, and I turned out OK."

The Victorian mode of child rearing is like behavior modification taken to an extreme: The parent is absolute authority. He beats his child into absolute compliance (for a while). He believes that physical punishment is the "only way they'll learn." Mostly because he himself knows no other way to teach.

On the other hand, I believe that the love affair with psychology that has dominated the twentieth century directly contributes to the astounding "permissiveness" today that allows young children unlimited "freedom of expression," whether or not it's rude or hurtful to anyone else. Most books on child care give precious little practical advice on how to shape children's behavior. Indeed, the very words "obedience" and "behavior" have fallen out of favor, as though these concepts were somehow distasteful remnants of a more ignorant era. "Self-esteem" is in, "discipline" is out. Some parents of my generation seem so afraid of damaging their child's self-esteem that they literally cannot say no.

One result, in my view, is the booming business of child psychologists: all those distraught parents who wonder, Why why *why* is Susie hitting her baby brother so much? What did we do wrong? We prepared her for the birth. We took her to "Birth of a Sibling" classes. We encouraged her to express her feelings of jealousy and rage, over and over again. We understood, we sympathized. We gave her lots of love and attention whenever she struck out at baby brother. And *still* she keeps on doing it!

Seeking help, we turn, often uncritically, to psychologists, so many of whom will instruct us to seek out the "stress in the home," which is "undoubtedly" the cause of the problem. With our helper's guidance, we identify every life change as a source of "stress." We wonder, we scrutinize, we analyze, we excuse, to a nonsensical degree. We know when little Tommy decided he wouldn't take any more baths. It was when Mommy started her new job. We understand why Jennie is using those four-letter words: she's distraught at the birth of her brother. We can accept Michael's refusal to go to bed: he's angry that his father comes home late from work. We are led to believe that life events, any change, our adult needs and desires, are all the triggers for childish misconduct. Not our fault, of course, but still . . . so stressful for little Timmie. And the solution? Always and forever, those vague directives: Give him more attention. Talk it out. Be respectful of his feelings. Listen to him more. Have family conferences: "OK, children, time for our Saturday night conference on why you never obey Mommy and Daddy." Oh dear, they refuse to come to the conference table.

Enough already. We can be sensitive to the pressures and anxieties that children have without making them the constant excuse for poor behavior. We can understand that children's lives can be complicated and worrisome, as much as ours, but we can still teach them how to act according to some standards that we—yes we—get to decide upon.

Parents need practical advice, not moralizing lectures about the need to reduce stress in the home, not impatient commands to "give her a good smack." Practical advice. Techniques that work. Researched methods of shaping appropriate behavior.

While I certainly don't have all the answers—I wish I did!—I have come to believe that the behavioral program we went through had quite a lot to teach Marc and me about raising our kids. For one thing, we discovered that we could still be passionately antispanking without being antidiscipline at all.

That we are behaviorally oriented does not mean that we ignore our children's emotional life. On the contrary, we are humbled and awed before the rich complexity of their characters.

But we can still aim for order and calm in their home, and their lives, and their conduct. It's not just for our benefit, but for their happiness and stability as well. A bratty undisciplined child is not considered "exuberant" or "just being a kid" by his exasperated teachers and classmates; he's considered a pain in the neck.

Behavioral techniques are neither hard nor unfamiliar. Most of them are just common sense, techniques that parents have always employed, some with more consistency than others.

Like what?

• Like teaching kids by breaking down tasks into small, manageable units, and reinforcing for the mastery of each unit. This works for everything from getting dressed to making beds to mastering schoolwork. It also frees children from an overdependence on adult assistance. They take enormous pride in being able to do things "all by myself." We can take the time to teach how to button, how to zipper, how to hang up a coat; we can take the time to practice it until it is mastered. It isn't hard to show them how to scrape their plate and bring it to the sink. It's not hard, it's not child abuse; it's teaching them to contribute to the work of the family.

• Like spelling out our expectations for what we want our kids to do, while they are still learning what is appropriate conduct and what is not. If we want our kids to behave themselves at the table, this requires standing there, making the behavioral goals clear, praising and reprimanding as necessary, until they've learned what our standards are. People's standards at table may differ (as an American married to a Frenchman, I can attest to vast cultural differences in this respect), but our kids are not going to know what is expected at our table unless we are explicit about it, and pay explicit attention to their dinnertime conduct. Making our behavioral goals clear to the children is a whole lot better than ignoring them for an hour, and then exploding in rage when we can't take any more of their wild antics.

(Anyone who thinks children are going to eventually become civilized, caring, courteous, and industrious little creatures out of the innate goodness in their hearts believes too much in old Jean-Jacques Rousseau's thesis that children, if left to educate themselves, will tend naturally toward all that is highest and best and most noble. Spend an afternoon in a playground with a bunch of kids merrily bopping each other on the head and calling each other names, and ask yourself if you really believe that. Children may be born innocent and good, but the world and their own desires pull them relentlessly toward selfishness. Rousseau, by the way, left his numerous children to perish in France's most notoriously cruel orphanage.)

• Like praising for good behavior, and being very specific about what's being praised. If we praise enough for good behavior, we don't have to correct poor behavior nearly as much. "You put on your own coat so well, sweetie. Thank you." It's easy to fall into the trap of paying attention to our kids only when they misbehave, and ignoring them when they're good.

• Like physically prompting through a behavior. No yelling, no screaming, no hitting is needed. Just calmly walking a child through a task, in spite of his histrionics, is pretty effective. My friend Evelyne, a working woman with an extremely demanding career, is one of my role models. She never seems to raise her voice! But what she does do is *follow through*. Every time she tells her kids to do something, or not do something, she makes sure they comply. If she says, "Please don't eat that chocolate ice cream cone in the living room," she means it. She doesn't sit there and repeat herself fifteen times. If her little one ignores her, she gets out of her chair immediately, takes him by the hand, and walks him into the kitchen.

• Like having certain consequences (yes, aversives!) for disobeying the rules. We have to have clear rules, we have to praise for following the rules, and we have to have some consequence for breaking the rules. If we establish a rule, we establish a consequence and stick to it. Otherwise we shouldn't even bother yelling about rules. We announce what the consequence will be, and we follow through. And we *can* discipline without hitting. It helps to think of preschool teachers. They have to control up to twenty four-year-olds at a time, and they don't yell, they don't scream, they don't hit. If they can do it with twenty, we can do it with two or three. Being made to sit alone in a chair (time out), or being sent to their room are consequences that have worked well with my kids. I think also that when a strong basis of love and respect is there, explicit disapproval of children's conduct can be a powerful aversive—at least when they get to a certain age.

Loving parents don't expect or want perfect children. Children do make noise, break things, run around like demons, fight with each other. If they didn't do those things they wouldn't be kids: they would be forty-year-olds in five-year-old bodies. Nor can parents be expected to act like behavioral therapists. We can't be 100 percent consistent. We have to make exceptions and bend the rules from time to time. But when children's conduct is infringing on some basic rights of adults—like the parents' right to have some time in the evening for themselves, or the grandparents' right not to have their house destroyed when the darling angels come to visit—and disturbing the peace of the home, it's amazing what a little consistency can do. It's amazing how fast you can turn a behavior around by instilling a rule and a consequence, and sticking to the consequence. Children seem to crave order. They crave routine. Their world is safer when they understand its boundaries and its rules.

Nothing is simple. When does motivating turn into bribing? Guiding turn into nagging? Understanding into excusing? Just consequences into angry punishment? We parents have to keep adjusting our attitudes, figuring out what we're doing as we're doing it. It's on-the-job training, unfortunately without any practice sessions. From time to time we are all prone to self-deception, convincing ourselves that we are "fondly tolerant" when our kids are out of control; telling ourselves that we have exercised "firm discipline" when in fact it is we who have lost control. The only thing we can be sure of is that there is no single formula, no absolute in this task of raising the young—and if we are thinking in absolute terms, we probably need some correction in the other direction.

But there is perhaps *one* thing that Marc and I are now more firmly convinced of than ever: the value, the power of attention. We have seen what focused, directed attention can do with an autistic child: it is equally powerful with a nonhandicapped child. No behavioral rule, no psychoanalytic understanding is worth a hill of beans if we don't give our kids attention—and it's one of the hardest jobs in the world to truly pay attention to little ones. It requires setting aside all our own desires for intellectual stimulation, peer recognition, challenging adult conversation. It requires extraordinary patience: the ability to listen to a sentence started over six times by a little tongue fumbling for the right words; to break up and negotiate the endless tearful squabbles over rights and toys; to repeat for the umpteenth time, "Say please," "Use your words," "Pour the milk with two hands."

It is very easy to think that if we're in the same room or the same house with children we are giving them attention. We're not. Attention is attention. It means getting off the phone, getting away from our work, our reading, our conversation, even our thoughts, and looking at them, talking to them, playing with them.

And attention is more than the perfunctory "How was school today?" This is a charming question for an adult to hear—"How was work today, dear?"—but most kids find it yet one more demand to "perform," to say what Mommy or Daddy wants to hear. We can give attention by initiating something that gives them immediate pleasure, like, very simply, reading them a story.

I'll get off my soapbox and refer any interested reader to one of the best books on this subject of child-rearing that I have found: *Family Rules* (St. Martin's Press, 1990), by Kenneth Kaye, Ph.D. I like this book a lot because it gives equal time to both sides of the equation: building up a child's self-esteem, and imposing some clear limits on his behavior. The author, a psychologist, speaks with experience of children from two years old all the way through the teens—when I expect I'm going to need all the help I can get. As a friend of mine—a psychologist with whom I can laugh—said: "When they're little you have (with the exception of certain calamities) little problems. When they're big—watch out!"

ON A WARM SUMMER DAY in July I dress five-year-old Daniel and four-year-old Anne-Marie in shorts, sandals, and T-shirts and walk them up to Daniel's school. Anne-Marie's first school will no longer be open next year. She has been accepted into Daniel's school, to start prekindergarten in the fall. The directors of the school have allowed her to start early and attend "play-camp," along with her brother, for six weeks. There will be children her age in the group. Marc and I are pleased that she will have this short preamble to her new school.

We have decided not to tell them of her diagnosis, fearing that she will be stigmatized. The strong recommendation of the Lovaas people, who know far more about this subject of recovery than we do, is not to paste a label on your child as he enters a normal school system. Apparently there is always a factor of altered expectations and altered behavior on the part of the teacher toward a child with a label, especially a label like "autistic." However well-intentioned the teachers, we still fear that they will be inclined to look on Anne-Marie as different and handicapped.

This is Anne-Marie's first experience in a school where no one knows her history.

INITIALLY, for the first week in play-camp, Anne-Marie is fairly quiet. During free play, she likes to sit in a corner of the room, playing elaborate pretend games with a group of plastic animals. I see this when I drop her off and when I pick her up. In between, I don't know how she's doing, although I worry about her constantly.

One day, one of her teachers approaches me, with a friendly smile:

"Anne-Marie is so sweet! She reminds me of myself when I was a little girl."

"Oh really? How so?"

"I was just like her. I used to sit in the corner and play by myself a lot, just like her!"

I swallow hard.

"Yes. It does take her a while to warm up. Perhaps you could . . . well, maybe encourage her to participate a little more? . . . She's shy, you know. . . . She needs encouragement to make contact with other kids. . . ."

"Oh sure. No problem. We'll work on that. Everyone in this class is working on something."

I thank the teacher, kiss Anne-Marie and Daniel good-bye, and take my leave.

Outside, I meet Diane, who has just dropped off her little boy.

"Diane . . ."

"What is it?"

"She said . . . Wendy said . . . Anne-Marie sits in the corner, alone. . . ."

My voice is none too steady. Frightening images keep rising up. Images of Anne-Marie, a social recluse, forever alone. She is failing this first real test!

"Catherine. She just started! Give her time! She plays with Daniel. You know she can do it. I'm sure they've had other kids in the class who were shy!"

Diane calms me down, but still I have been badly frightened. The time has come, I feel, to begin setting up regular "play dates" for Anne-Marie.

THERE WAS A little girl in Anne-Marie's class who had come with her from her first school. Kelly was friendly and warm, and, at age four and a half, was one of the most outgoing and nurturing children in the class. Her mother agreed to a weekly play date.

Every Wednesday the two little girls got together after their morning at play camp. They had lunch together, chattering away, and then they played. I would prowl around, eavesdropping on their conversation.

"Anne-Marie, do you want to pretend fairy princess?"

"Yes. I can be the fairy princess and you can be the dragon."

"OK. But then I want to be the fairy princess."

"OK."

They could share together, pretend together, and quarrel together.

"I want to play with the bear now, Kelly."

"No. It's my turn."

"Mommy!" (Tears and high tragic drama.) "Kelly says it's her turn for the bear, but it's my bear!"

"Yes. But Kelly's your guest. Remember about sharing toys with guests. You can give Kelly her turn now. Then she'll give it back."

Five minutes later they're playing happily together again.

They are blessedly, perfectly normal.

Once on a Friday when Daniel was out of the house on his own play date and Michel was in therapy, Anne-Marie came to me with her lower lip stuck out and the big eyes overflowing with sorrow.

"What what what could make my precious child so sad?"

I didn't want to hurt her feelings, but her response caused me to smile with the purest happiness.

"I don't have nobody to play wif!"

TWO MONTHS LATER, in September, we go back for a reevaluation at the institute. The news is good. Very good. Michel has achieved a low normal rating in the most important areas, communication and socialization:

> Michel's scores in social communication have markedly increased over these past seven months and now fall into the low normal range. The child has gained eighteen months in communication and twelve months in socialization.

His adaptive skills still lag behind, mostly because we have not even started toilet training yet. It took so long with Anne-Marie that we have decided to start when he is closer to three. His motor skills are also behind—we don't really know why. But it doesn't worry us. As long as he is making such fast progress in communication and social-ization, we don't care if he doesn't ride a tricycle until age three and a half.

Again, as with his sister at her first reevaluation, there are residual mannerisms and limited interaction with strangers. The battle is not yet over. And this time around we are more impatient to get to the end. Both Marc and I are happy and grateful, but both of us feel weighted down with the work still in front of us. We feel as though we have been doing this forever.

Nevertheless, I call Dr. Rimland to share our good news.

We have a long conversation about the possibility of recovery for other children. The odds seem insurmountable. The diagnosis has to be made so early, the parents have to be able to find a good behavioral program, or set one up themselves, the child himself has to have the potential for recovery. Even in Dr. Lovaas's clinic, which has a lot more experience and manpower than anyone else around, the odds are still only about fifty percent. It's very daunting. "Do you think there's any reason for me to write this book I have in mind?" I ask him. "Is it worth it?"

"For those children who are diagnosed early enough, there's no question," he replies. "A fifty percent chance is better than zero, or two percent."

"It may cause pain to some parents."

"Yes, it may. But that's no one's fault. It might also help some other parents."

WE JUDGED that in certain areas Michel was ahead of Anne-Marie, and in other areas behind. Overall, we thought that he was probably at least halfway home.

But our next challenge with Michel was still before us. He was starting school.

32

MICHEL HAS BEEN ACCEPTED into Merricat's Castle, a school on the Upper East Side which tries to combine normally developing children with a certain percentage of handicapped children. Gretchen Buchenholz again is the director of this school. She has been told of Michel's diagnosis, since I believe he will need my presence in the classroom, just as Anne-Marie had. She and Rachel Cullerton, the director of education, agree to give him a chance.

I do, however, have to go through the regular channels, and my first step must be to call one of the school's social workers, Mary. I have to inform her about the diagnosis and Michel's progress to date.

"It's a long story," I begin. "Originally, his sister was diagnosed as autistic. We did a home program with her, and she got better and better, and now we think she's at a point where we can say she has recovered. . . ."

I am talking fast and nervously. I want her to hear me out. I know my story is incredible, and I want to give her all the facts in a nutshell.

"Obviously misdiagnosed," says Mary.

Something in me explodes. I have heard these words one time too many.

"What do you mean, 'misdiagnosed'? Do you know anything about her history? Do you know anything about us, or her? What do you know about . . . about autism? What . . . what do . . ."

I am scarcely able to talk. Too many people have had this knee-jerk reaction. Too many people—people who had never met either of our children—just took it as an absolute, a given, decreed for all time: autistic children don't recover.

My whole family had come through a war. We had been battered and torn, shattered over and over again, rocked and racked by a continuous onslaught of this enemy called autism. We were still uncertain of our safety, still trying to bind up the wounds. Now we were being informed, every time I turned around, that there really had been no war at all—we must have made it up. I had been stared at pitifully, nodded to, smiled at, patted on the head just one time too many. Uh-huh. Sure. If you want to believe your kids were autistic, that's OK. Whatever makes you feel good.

And it wasn't just my sensibilities that were at issue here. Far from it. If the professionals refuse to believe the evidence that Dr. Lovaas has published and that my children were validating; if they refuse to believe that any autistic children can recover, then we can be absolutely sure of one thing: none will recover. Why bother making the tremendous effort for a goal you don't believe in?

My conversation with Mary went downhill from there. She is actually a great person, whom I like and respect today. But that day, in our first phone conversation, I was ready to strangle her.

Later on, we were able to laugh about it.

"I really pushed some buttons in that conversation, didn't I, Catherine?"

"Yes, you did. And in my usual calm way, I responded with a controlled and reasonable explanation of where we seemed not to see eye-to-eye."

"Um-hm."

Mary at least was willing to listen, and eventually to accept the fact that with Anne-Marie, no fewer than four professionals—psychiatrists and psychologists and neurologists, all highly experienced in diagnosing developmental disorders—had arrived at the same diagnosis: infantile autism.

With Michel, the three* we had consulted had all concurred: infantile autism.

Dr. Berman had been alone in finding that Anne-Marie did not satisfy all the criteria for autism. His diagnosis was "Pervasive developmental disorder—not otherwise specified."

In a field where parents can get as many different labels as doctors they consult, it was not surprising that there was one difference of opinion. What was more surprising, and significant, is that four out of five professionals agreed with one another.†

---

*Actually four, but I am counting Dr. Cohen and Dr. Sudhalter as one team.
†See Appendix I for a discussion of the problem of diagnosis, and diagnostic terminology.

Before school began, I also had a preliminary conference with Patricia, the head teacher in Michel's classroom. She was a little nervous when she heard the word "autism," but accepted my assertion that recovery is possible, and expressed a willingness to help Michel in whatever way she could.

His first day at school was a disaster.

Anne-Marie had been quiet and shy and withdrawn. Michel, true to his own nature, reacted to the unfamiliar environment with the same anger and aggressiveness he had shown on his first day of therapy. Every time a teacher approached him he threw a tantrum.

I was aghast. I could see the look of unease on the faces of the assistant teachers. They had all seen a lot of different kids, but they'd never seen a child who could not be wooed or distracted at all. His screams would double if they so much as walked near him. Patricia kept looking at me for guidance. But I felt as helpless as they did. It was one thing to deal with this behavior at home. It was another to watch its full-blown resurgence at school.

How on earth were we going to do this? Michel cried and raged for the whole first morning. I couldn't ask the teachers to put up with such extreme behavior. I couldn't inflict such disruption on the other kids.

I had the same sinking feeling I had had when Anne-Marie's teacher told me about her solitary habits. We were in big trouble. He just wasn't going to make it.

Rachel, the director of education, met me in the hallway after the morning class. She took one look at my face and put her arms around me.

"Hang in there, kid. We'll all work on this together."

Can I ever doubt that God just kept opening doors? If you have to rescue a child from autism, it helps to have the therapists appear miraculously on your doorstep. It helps to have normal schools willing to work with a child who is not quite there yet, who still has significant behavioral problems. It helps to have teachers stepping forward when it comes time for them to join in the drama, and willingly offering their hands and their hearts.

They had promised to listen, and listen they did. I requested a meeting, and they gave me not one but many. Every three weeks for that first semester, Gretchen and Rachel and Patricia, as well as the assistant teachers and the special-education teachers, would gather together with Marc and me to confer about Michel.

I was nervous about offending them. After all, they were professionals, and they had many years of teaching experience among them. I was apprehensive that they would resent my coming in and, basically, telling them how to handle Michel.

But they were gracious and attentive. I decided to share as much of our experience with them as I could write or tell them, so that they would be able to understand the complexity of the situation. The hardest part for them, I knew, was hearing Michel cry day after day and not being able to comfort him. But I stayed in the classroom with him, and I insisted that Michel follow through on everything the other children did. Michel had to adapt to the routine; we were not going to bend the routine to Michel.

So "circle time," for instance, where the children sat around while Patricia sang some songs, was a trial for all of us. I held crying Michel on my lap, and would not allow him to go off and do what he wanted to do. Anytime he stopped crying, even momentarily, I would whisper praise and encouragement to him. If he became really disruptive, I would take him from the classroom, sit with him in the hallway, and firmly say, "No crying," not letting him go until he stopped. If he didn't stop, I took him home—which he didn't like, because in spite of his resistance, he still wanted to stay in school.

I knew I couldn't ask the teachers to be that mean. Especially these teachers. It went against all their training and all their loving inclinations.

One morning Patricia was singing "The Wheels on the Bus," I was holding crying, squirming Michel, and suddenly he began to give up. He quieted down and began to look at Patricia. His hands came up in the air. They began to make the circular motions her hands were making.

". . . go wownd and wownd . . ." came his childish voice.

"Good boy, Michel! Beautiful singing!" I whispered into his ear.

I looked up. Patricia kept on singing, but her eyes were filling up with tears. The other teachers sitting around the circle with the children exchanged glances. We all gave a collective sigh of relief and smiled a little giddily at each other.

"All thwoo da town!"

Over the next few months, I moved from holding Michel on my lap to sitting on the sidelines, to sitting out in the hallway.

And finally came the day, in December, when Patricia and I felt that he was fine in school and I could leave. He had begun to play a little with the other children, and his language was becoming more and more intelligible to the teachers. He wasn't throwing tantrums anymore. And he was following directions beautifully, even those given to the whole group of children.

Marc and I came back for one last meeting at Merricat's, in April of 1991.

We began our meeting at 8:15 A.M., as usual. Everyone was yawning sleepily and opening Styrofoam cups of coffee, trying to gear up for the day.

"Well," I began, "before we start what will probably be our last meeting, Marc and I wanted to say something to all of you."

There was an expectant silence.

"Dr. Cohen has just reevaluated Michel, and he's doing splendidly. He said Michel's progress was 'remarkable.' He has normalized in all areas now, and Dr. Cohen feels that he has only some residua left."

At the evaluation, I went on, Michel had interacted well with Dr. Sudhalter. In Dr. Cohen's words,

> . . . Michel seemed to enjoy the interaction and easily accepted Dr. Sudhalter's interaction with him. He was quite attentive, readily and accurately responded to most requests and evidenced good knowledge . . . of the concepts of people and their occupations; size, colors, food and action verbs. . . .

His interaction with me during the evaluation, I told the teachers, also showed how far he had come:

> During interaction with his mother, his affect was appropriate to the situation and his mood varied from curious interest to happiness. He exhibited good pretend play, appeared to understand the "silly" nature of a "Sesame Street" book by his affect, exhibited very good eye contact, imitation (both nonvocal and vocal) and interest in face-to-face interaction, and evidenced the ability to make inferences on the meaning of words and gestures.

There was a sigh of pleasure around the table. They had all ached through Michel's tears; now they were delighted to see him blossoming into happiness.

We talked for a while more, then finished the meeting by mapping out some goals for Michel for the rest of the semester.

We knew what his residua were: Michel's language might now fall within the "normal range," but it was still hard for him to pick up new syntactic and semantic concepts with the same facility and speed as other three-year-olds. There were some echolalia and high prosody left. His temperamentality was still an issue, especially when demands were placed on him.

But his social relatedness and his eye contact were quite good now. And he was speaking in ever more complex sentences and even beginning to ask some spontaneous questions. He was in a normal school, functioning well with normal peers. And he was only three years four months old. Moreover, he had been in therapy for just fourteen months.

Marc and I thought we had something to celebrate with his teachers. We thought we had something to celebrate with the whole world.

33

IT IS DECEMBER 18, 1991, four years to the day since Anne-Marie was diagnosed. I'm sitting in my kitchen drinking a cup of coffee as the sun slants in through the cold windowpanes. The children are in school, and I have a couple of hours to work again.

Today, I have some insights that I did not have back then, when any offer of help, any mention of a "cure," was a lifeline. Today, I know how many "miracle cures" are out there, and how few have any credible scientific basis, any proven efficacy.

It may be that at some time in the future there will be some medication or even surgical intervention that will indeed cure autism. Pharmacological research is going on all the time and probably will eventually yield a few safe and helpful drugs in the treatment of autism. Until then, we have only some rather poor alternatives: "poor" because none is a panacea; their effectiveness is sporadic at best; most are expensive; all require heroic efforts on the part of parents in terms of commitment and time; it is difficult to predict which children will respond well and which poorly to a given treatment modality.

Nevertheless, there is hope—for improvement, for progress, and, in some cases, for recovery. Even when there is no full recovery, autistic children can be helped—sometimes very significantly—through different therapeutic approaches. Parents today are seriously considering the benefits of vitamin B_6 and magnesium supplements, for instance, or of special diets to counteract severe food allergies. There is a growing body of research supporting the positive response on the part of *some* children to these different approaches.*

*Contact the Autism Research Institute (4182 Adams Avenue, San Diego, CA 92116) for information on these treatment modalities. Another group which may be of some help is the

An intensive, structured behavioral program, needless to say, is what Marc and I suggest to any parent who seeks our counsel. Such a program does not preclude trying any other approach that may seem promising. Many parents we know have tried two or more therapies simultaneously. But for us and for others, a behavioral program represents the core therapeutic approach for our children. We also stress to parents that although they may think they know what behavior modification is, they should probably keep an open mind for a while. Behavioral therapy includes a highly developed curriculum, a time-tested, thoroughly researched and proven method of teaching autistic children—one that has little to do with any simplistic notion of "punishment" for "bad" behavior.*

But there are a host of professionals in the field, with medical degrees and without, who consistently steer parents away from behavioral intervention, with sometimes tragic consequences. These people seem to reinforce parental fears about a difficult therapeutic approach: instead of helping them to see the long-term benefits that such intervention has been shown, over and over again, to provide, they often encourage parents' understandable reluctance even to attempt a behavioral program. I know of parents who have been informed, in categorical terms, that behavioral intervention will irrevocably harm their child.

Who are these antibehaviorists? What are their own methods and beliefs? Generally speaking, they are the proponents of the various psychodynamic approaches: holding therapy, the Option Process, most therapeutic nurseries, and play therapy. In addition to their antibehavioral stance, they all seem to share certain theoretical beliefs.

Psychodynamic approaches do not have to posit a failure in early parent-child relationships as causative of autism. They do not universally espouse the psychogenic origins of autism. Some, but not all, do concentrate on early childhood social/emotional wounds. The common thread in what I am calling psychodynamic approaches, the most recurrent theme, is this:

Autism Society of America. Although not a research organization, it can furnish information pertaining to legislative, educational, and advocacy issues. Contact the Autism Society of America, 8601 Georgia Avenue, Suite 503, Silver Spring, MD 20910. Tel.: (301) 565-0433.

*I am thinking of one mother who told me, "I *did* behavior modification! I punished my daughter when she acted inappropriately!" That, I believe, is analogous to claiming to have "done" France because you stayed overnight at Charles De Gaulle Airport.

Inside of the autistic child there is a little wounded self: intelligent, whole, aware, able to understand complex language. If the child does not talk, it is because he has *chosen* not to talk. This "hidden," normal child "inside" the autistic child is too afraid and upset to "come out." The word "breakthrough" appears so often in these psychodynamic approaches precisely because of that underlying concept of a whole, healthy child somehow "buried" or "imprisoned" in an autistic shell. A child "coming out of his shell" is a favorite image of this school of thought.

And how do you get him out? The most effective way of "reaching" that child is to convey total acceptance, understanding, and love. Furthermore, these psychodynamic approaches, without exception, assert that *any attempt to impose certain kinds of demands on that wounded, hidden self will only result in further emotional damage.*

Within the framework of this acceptance-respect-understanding approach, behavior modification, which insists precisely on imposing many demands on the child—insists on changing him—is universally despised. Parents who resort to it are castigated as manipulating the child for their own "convenience."

The psychodynamic concept has three thematic variations that crop up quite frequently:

The first emphasizes the necessity of entering the child's world, instead of forcefully bringing the child into our world. In a number of therapeutic nurseries—the ones that promise "caring," and little else—the teacher follows the child around—as much as is possible given a teacher-student ratio of one to ten—and respects his choices, rather than imposing anything on him.

When my friend Lucille went to see how her daughter was doing at one of these nurseries, she called me. "Alison stands at the sandbox and pours sand from one cup to another all day long," she said, sounding frightened. "What should I do? The director keeps telling me that that's her way of expressing herself." A father told me that in the therapeutic nursery his son attended, the staff permitted the boy to spin in place for extended periods. "Why?" I asked him. "They say he needs to do that," responded the father. "Why does he need to do that?" I persisted. "I don't know, but they must know! They're the experts!" he responded.

Holding therapy disciples, among the strongest believers in the "wounded, hidden child" concept, do allow forceful physical holding. But outside of the holding sessions, they continue to decry any attempt to subject the child to structured intensive learning programs. Forced loving is OK. Forced learning is not.

Of course, what some of these love-and-understanding therapies preach and what they practice can sometimes seem a bit at odds. One of the best known of the psychodynamic therapeutic programs is the "Option Process." According to Barry Kaufman, author of *Son Rise* (Harper & Row), an account of the recovery of his autistic son, Raun, the Option Process consists of

> a totally nonjudgmental approach to personal growth that helps people confront their problems and come to accept themselves as their own best source of solutions to those problems. It is based on an attitude of complete acceptance which we describe as "to love is to be happy with." This means you decide to love other people—and yourself too, of course—by being happy with them just as they are, without needing to change them in any way, although you certainly could want and try to help others to be all that they want to be for themselves.*

Currently, the Option Institute in Massachusetts charges parents $5,500 for a five-day training seminar on how to work with their autistic or other "special" child—something that I find puzzling when set against the imperative to "totally accept" such children "just as they are." Suzi Kaufman, Barry Kaufman's wife, has said, "It was totally OK with me for Raun to be autistic." She did, however, spend ". . . more than three years, twelve hours a day, seven days a week with Raun during every waking hour."† Why did she do this? How did the Kaufmans know their nonverbal child "wanted" to be anything different from what he was? Why did they want to "change" him?

The Option Process, as described in the thick packet of material sent to me by the Option Institute—"A Place for Miracles"—sounds loving and warm. Their literature has much talk of "nonjudgmental acceptance . . . self-understanding . . . unconditional loving . . . rechoosing. . . ." It *looks* loving and warm. There are idyllic photographs, in bucolic settings, of couples hugging each other, of groups seated in a circle on the grass, presumably communing together in a "totally nonjudgmental" way, of Barry ("Bears") Kaufman and Suzi Kaufman, holding each other and smiling lovingly into the camera.

---

*"An Interview with Barry Neil Kaufman; The Healing Power of Unconditional Love," by Ron Nelson, reprinted from *Science of Mind* Magazine and furnished by The Option Institute and Fellowship.
†Ibid.

But does the Option Process rescue children from autism? This is questionable. There are many ecstatic letters from parents included in the information package, but no objective evaluation of successes and failures from a disinterested psychologist or psychiatrist. Nor do any of these letters mention an autistic or formerly autistic child attending a normal school at peer level. Nor are there reprints of articles published in any psychological or medical journal backing the anecdotes of miracle cures. There are many testimonials of improvement, but no objective verification of recovery.

Option, like holding therapy, certainly seems to make parents feel better. Many of them, according to the letters furnished by the Option Institute, are apparently happier with their children, more accepting of their condition, after attending the institute. And surely there is something to be said for a philosophical stance that allows parents to believe that their child's autism is not an irremediable wound in their lives, but represents an opportunity for greater growth and more profound love.

But parents also have a right to know what to expect for their child when they choose Option. I find troublesome the frequent appearance of the words "cure" and "miracle" in their literature—especially when that literature mentions no downside, no failure rate, no instance, ever, of parental disappointment. I am also deeply disturbed by anyone's charging parents over $1,000 a day for the hope of a cure—a cure unsubstantiated by professionally recognized data in any mainstream scientific journal. The publicity material put out by the Option Institute rivals the advertisement brochure for the La Costa Spa: glossy photographs, advertisements for books, pamphlets, records, tapes, seminars, even special chairs—all at a price, of course, a price that many parents are more than happy to pay.

Predictably, as with all these approaches that counsel sensitive intuitive understanding of a hidden child, Option proponents tend to denigrate the "incredibly inhumane" behavioral approach. One morning, I decided to call the Option Institute myself. A very friendly young woman answered the phone, and I asked to speak with anyone who could give me information about their program for autistic children.

"You need to make an appointment to speak with Cindy Biaggi,"* said the person who answered the phone. "She can tell you about our program for special children."

Later, I spoke with Cindy.

*Not her real name.

I: "Can you tell me what is your success rate at the Option Institute? How many children have you helped recover from autism?"

Cindy: "Oh, success rate. It's a funny thing about success rates. I mean, what do you mean by 'success rate'? We have a lot of different children here with a lot of different problems. . . . I mean why do you want to know about a success rate? Because you want to prove that *you* can be successful . . . ?"

In spite of my probing, Cindy was unable to provide me with any concrete indications of the frequency of recoveries in the case of autistic children specifically. Indeed, she hedged and sidestepped the question when I tried to find out if she could tell me of *any* autistic or formerly autistic child who was currently functioning at peer level in a normal school—other than the Kaufmans' son, Raun.

I asked her what the Option Institute thought of behavior modification.

"Behavior modification is totally against the child. It turns the child into a robot."

"Have you read any of the recent literature about the recovery of some children through intensive behavior modification?"

"I don't have to read the literature. I know from my own experience that behavior modification is totally against the child."

The second recurrent theme of the psychodynamic approaches to autism centers around the concept of "therapist-as-seer."

The principal characteristics of the seer are his understanding, intuition, empathy, and ability to communicate in some mysterious higher-order mode with the wounded child. The seer is interpreter, analyzing the child's behaviors for their hidden meanings, declaring what those meanings are. The seer is calm and secure in his knowledge that he can "read" the secret life of the child in a way that others cannot. A friend of mine calls it the "herb tea and crystals" approach to autism.

Thus Bettelheim takes a series of drawings made by a little girl, Laurie. The drawings begin with round black designs and end with round white "holes." Round black designs are "bad breast/bad mother"; white holes are "good breast/good mother" (unattainable, absent).

Martha Welch takes as axiomatic the therapist's (learned? intuitive? mystical?—but in any case superior) understanding: the therapist's role, she writes, is "to observe and translate the signals mother and child give, but which each fails to understand."

Mothers I know have shared some interesting interpretations with me, pronounced by various psychologists and psychiatrists they have consulted:

> "Elizabeth's opening and closing of doors signifies her conflictual drives: should she let her anger out? should she keep it locked within?"

> "Michael's perseverative knocking on things signifies that he wants to be let into his parents' affections."

The seer not only understands the child; he names the affliction. His "diagnosis" of the child is often couched in seductively scientific or medical-sounding terms: "symbiotic psychosis," "pathology of the mother-child dyad," "attachment disorder," and that vague catchall, "emotionally disturbed." In these quasi-medical diagnoses, the seer's veneer of expertise is reinforced.

It is not only in the United States that the psychodynamic approach to autism is so firmly entrenched. In France, hidden messages of animosity are routinely read into parents' most mundane gestures toward their autistic children. One couple was accused of not having wanted their autistic daughter. The proof? They had named her Sylvie. In French, Sylvie sounds like *s'il vit*, which means "if he lives." The parents had *doubly* signaled their wish for their daughter's nonexistence by inserting the conditional "if" into her name *and* the masculine subject pronoun *il* ("he").

Another French couple was accused by their psychiatrist of "latent antagonism" toward their autistic son. Once again, this antagonism was evident in the choice of names. Their last name was Blanco (connoting whiteness); they had chosen to name their son Bruno (connoting darkness).*

And so it goes. Hidden meanings, coded messages—it's all there, but obvious only to the gifted few who can read the signs. "We choose to understand *why* this child is the way he is, rather than forcing him to change" is how one of Bettelheim's still-faithful disciples expressed the love-and-understanding approach. It sounds so kind, but lost forever in that purported understanding of what no one yet understands are the optimum years for bringing a child into the world of normalcy. While trying to explore the labyrinth of the child's supposedly wounded psyche, years are wasted. Time passes very quickly when you're struggling to hold on to a child who's slipping out of reach.

The third recurrent motif in the psychodynamic approaches is an

---

*Véronique Grousset, "La Fillette au Moi Dormant," *Figaro*, September 21, 1991.

emphasis on the therapist as savior and healer, in contradistinction to the parents, usually the mother, who is at best rather ignorant and obtuse, at worst a destroyer, contributing to, if not causing, her child's problems. The savior's role is not only to understand, but also to *heal the emotional wound*, rather than merely to teach the child some skills (or more pejoratively put, to simply "train" him).

It is in this rather narcissistic self-image of professional as emotional healer that the Bettelheimian theme of good doctor/bad mommy appears most markedly. For it must be pointed out that Bettelheim's *The Empty Fortress* is not only an attack on "cold, destructive" mothers, but an extended paean to himself and his staff at the Orthogenic School, which he founded at the University of Chicago to treat autistic and other "disturbed" children. Throughout, his and the staff's keen insight and caring, as well as the children's deep gratitude toward their therapist-saviors, are underscored at every turn:

> When I took Laurie back to the dormitory, she eagerly ran with me to return to her teacher, her counselors and the children. But a few minutes later, when I told her that she had to leave the School [with her father] . . . she collapsed into the total nothingness in which she came to us.

The Tinbergens similarly present themselves as possessed of a deep intuitive understanding of the needs of autistic children. They describe themselves as patient, unobtrusive, exquisitely respectful of the children. Longtime professionals and experienced clinicians stand in awe of them:

> One of us . . . has repeatedly demonstrated her way of assessing and adjusting to the "emotional age" of even severely autistic children. . . . The reaction of [clinic staffs] has invariably been: "I had no idea how cautious and patient your contact-making was, and how rapidly that child could be made to behave more maturely until I saw you do it. . . ." They assured us . . . that in one session of less than an hour the child had come out of his shell further than they had ever seen him do before.

This respectful caution, this sensitive and mysterious ability to draw children "out of their shells," is contrasted to the clumsiness of the parents—as the Tinbergens put it, ". . . insecure, sad, or inexperienced mothers or fathers [who] need to be taught how to be playful. . . ."

A psychologist I know once referred to those professionals who still espouse such psychodynamic intervention as "the lunatic fringe." They may be lunatic, but they are not fringe. On the contrary, they are pervasive, widespread, and contemporary.

A case in point is play therapy, launched in this country in 1947 by clinical psychologist Virginia Axline.

Axline's book *Play Therapy* (in 1992 in its twenty-eighth printing) supports and propagates the "understanding-respect-acceptance" concept. Her subsequent work *Dibs in Search of Self* (now in its *fiftieth* printing) applies the principles of play therapy to her work with a little boy, Dibs. Axline herself does not label Dibs as autistic, preferring to present him as emotionally disturbed. But there can be no doubt, to anyone familiar with the symptoms of autism, that Dibs is indeed autistic. The Tinbergens mention this book in their appendix, calling it a "gem" of a book, and adding that Dibs is "typical" of the class of children they are writing about.

In any case, the influence of the book appears to have been so powerful that play therapy is still routinely recommended for autistic children. In fact, some parents are initially told of no other option than play therapy—with a little speech therapy thrown in once a week.

Bettelheim had the literary skill to construct a mammoth heap of psychojargon to buttress his attacks on parents. Axline doesn't bother with that. From page one of both her books, her message is pure and simple. Parents are the enemy, coldly selfish, abusive of their children. Her books are veritable orgies of self-righteous wrath against the people who have so emotionally scarred these little ones. The children she describes are invariably "rejected, insecure, without love." Story after story of pathological parents is recounted. "Many of the children in this book are victims of parental neglect and rejection and mistreatment."

Through the experience of play therapy, however, her own brand of gentle acceptance, the emotional wounds are healed and the child finds the freedom to be himself. In the playroom the child is treated with dignity and respect. Gone are all "adult suggestions, mandates, rebukes, restraints, criticisms, disapprovals, support, intrusions." Instead, the child finds

> the presence of an accepting, understanding, friendly therapist . . . [who] is sensitive to what the child is feeling . . . she respects the child . . . she conveys to him the feeling that she is understanding him and accepting him at all times regardless of what he says or does. Thus, the therapist gives him the courage to go deeper and deeper into his innermost world and bring out into the open his real self. . . .

However, Axline cautions any therapist in training that it is often quite difficult to get rid of Mother. "Mama will enter into the structuring if the therapist doesn't look out." She suggests that the therapist say to the mother something like: "Don't you have an appointment to talk to Mr. X?" This often is enough for Mama to take the hint and stay out.

What happens inside the playroom, once that busybody is chased away, should follow some strict rules, says Axline. The therapist must accept the child exactly as he is:

> Any statements that she makes to him are *nondirective* . They reflect his feelings only. She guards against any criticism and reproof. . . . She avoids praise for actions or words. . . .

The child cannot be hurried or pressured in any way. After all, says Axline,

> When one stops to consider that the child has been brought to the clinic because the parent is seeking to change him, one concludes (and, it would seem, rightly*) that the parent is rejecting some part, if not all, of the child.

The savior therapist, on the other hand, knows just how to help the child. She establishes a feeling of complete acceptance and permissiveness so that the child can express his deepest feelings—feelings that invariably come down to deep-seated rage against the mother:

"Bill," in therapy, snatches a mother doll. "He turns her upside down. He takes her clothes off."

Bill: I'll beat her up.
Therapist: You feel like beating her up.
Bill: Now I'll bury her in the sand. She'll smother.
Therapist: You'll smother her in the sand now.
Bill: Nobody will ever see her again.
Therapist: You got rid of her. No one will ever see her again.

Whether or not this endless reflection of feeling helps normal children overcome their psychic wounds is debatable. But when this type of thing is recommended for autistic children, I see red. In *Dibs in Search of Self,* Axline reaches new heights in mommy-bashing, savior-therapist–stroking, and child-bonding.

Dibs has echolalia, pronoun reversal, extreme aloofness, stereotyp-

---

*Axline's words, not mine.

ical mannerisms. As an infant, he resisted his mother's embrace, stiffening and crying whenever she picked him up. He has many precocious splinter skills, such as early sight-reading and number recognition, but no normal interaction or communication. He throws tantrums whenever anyone tries to intrude on his routines.

Is he, could he be, autistic? wonders his mother.

No, says a psychiatrist quoted in the book. But he is "the most rejected child he has ever seen."

Axline concurs. In one wearying scene after another, she paints a picture of the mother as a cold, bitter, intellectual, repressed, foolish woman, "failing to relate to her son with love, respect, and understanding."

The mother is very wary and reticent around Axline, for she has already been through the inquisition. Psychiatrists have let her know what they think of her in no uncertain terms. The teachers at her son's school can barely repress their hostility and suspicion of her. One teacher erupts in rage during a conference to discuss Dibs (a conference from which the mother has been excluded):

> She'd rather believe he is mentally retarded than admit that maybe he is emotionally disturbed and maybe she is responsible for it!

But Axline believes she understands the mother's reticence and defensiveness. She wonders what this woman is hiding.

> What must this woman really think and feel about Dibs and the part she played in his young life to be so terrorized at the prospect of being interviewed and questioned about the situation?

Finally, in a cataclysmic scene, the mother confesses her sins to Axline:

> Suddenly [the mother] was in tears. "I don't know how I could have done this to him," she cried. "My intelligence seemed to have flown out the window. My behavior was compulsive and completely unreasonable. . . . I couldn't admit that I rejected him. . . ."

Needless to say, once Axline begins to work with this rejected child, he blossoms, emerges, breaks through, comes out of his shell, etc., etc. In just a few *hours* of her loving, nonintrusive, nondirective play therapy, she brings "this brilliant boy" to life and enables him to emerge a happy, well-adjusted, normal child, with a highly superior IQ.

At the end of the book appear the touching scenes of Dibs's parents thanking Axline for the miracle she has wrought, and Dibs himself thanking her, his "special friend," for giving him "the most wonderful time in his life." In fact, Axline spends a full chapter on the theme of her own monumental importance in Dibs's life. How thirsty are these saviors for worship and adoration!

Parental scapegoating did not begin with Bettelheim; it does not end with Martha Welch, the Tinbergens, the therapeutic nurseries which still treat autism as an "emotional disturbance," "a pathology of the mother-child dyad." It does not end with the fiftieth printing of *Dibs,* or because some more enlightened psychologists and psychiatrists have pronounced it passé. It goes on and on, appearing in more or less virulent strains and in various guises.

A few parents have shared their children's evaluations with me. In the beginning, I was disturbed to find, in these supposedly objective and scientific reports, constant criticisms, direct or veiled, of parental behavior. Now this doesn't surprise me in the least. I've come to expect it. It's completely in line with the habit of linking parental "pathology" to childhood autism; of reading life events as causative factors:

"Michael's parents arrived twenty minutes late."

"The parents did not seem to be appropriately concerned about their child's symptoms."

"John's mother presented as an anxious and domineering person."

"The parents utilized clinical jargon in their description of Timothy's behavior, seeming to deny their feelings of distress under a welter of pseudoscientific terminology."

"The parents took a vacation without their child when he was only a year old."

When I began to be aware of how widespread was this phenomenon of professionals attacking parents, I called Dr. Rimland. He laughed a little ruefully when I voiced my outrage. "I'm sorry to say," he told me, "that in my twenty-five years of reading thousands of autism evaluations, it's rare to find one that *doesn't* include some derogatory comment on the parents!"

If the proponents of these various love-and-understanding approaches are not recommending psychotherapy for parental pathology, they're advising "total, nonjudgmental acceptance" of the child. Often, the two recommendations go hand in hand. But the one type of treatment they strongly suggest that parents *not* pursue is a behavioral approach. It's so much easier, more lucrative, and more ego-gratifying to spout New Age psychobabble.

I accept the reality, in our troubled world, of abusive parents, negligent parents, incompetent parents. But I would submit that the vast majority of parents who seek help for their child's autism are none of these, and in fact are willing to do anything, sacrifice anything, to return their child to health.

I also accept the legitimate questioning of the possible misapplication of behavior modification—it is an imperfect therapeutic approach, far from a miracle cure, delivered by sometimes less-than-perfect therapists. But knee-jerk condemnation of the behavioral approach is another story—and condemnation is what parents are most likely to hear, still, today.

The behaviorist is often portrayed as Attila the Hun, while the psychodynamic therapist is the Guru Maharaji. The behaviorist is depicted as practicing a form of child abuse, while the healer-savior presents himself as an angel of love and acceptance, overflowing with mysteriously intuitive "understanding" of the child. And time goes racing by.

Too many therapeutic nurseries function, as one psychologist friend put it, "like expensive baby-sitting services, run by people who think their own personalities are somehow therapeutic to the children." In New Jersey there are several facilities serving the autistic population, facilities that have been using applied behavior analysis and discrete trial learning for years. I have grown to know the staff and students at one of these schools, and am continuously discouraged by the denigrating criticism they have to contend with. The director of "one of the best" therapeutic nurseries in New York came to see this particular school, and her response was sadly predictable. "I would invite you to come see our program," she said to the director of the New Jersey school, "but I know you would hate it as much as I hate yours." One can only imagine the number of parents this ideologue steers away from behavioral therapy. Her touchy-feely, warm-and-cuddly, love-and-understanding principles survive: the kids fall through the cracks.

As I review and update this chapter, Facilitated Communication (F/C) is currently being touted as the latest "breakthrough" in the treatment of autism. (Since my daughter was diagnosed in 1987, there has appeared on average one "breakthrough," "cure," or "miracle" per year in the autism world. Media attention is always feverish; controversy rages; parents desperately pursue every shred of hope.)

F/C is a method of assisting nonverbal autistic people—quite often severely impaired people—to communicate via handwriting, a typewriter, or a computerized device. Its proponents argue that close to 100 percent (yes, 100 percent) of such autistic individuals are actually capable of understanding complex language, and of communicating their quite sophisticated thoughts and feelings—provided that a facilitator sits next to them and supports but supposedly does not direct their hands as they tap out letters on a keyboard.

Can the technique be taught to parents or to other teachers? Only, F/C proponents assert, if such people have the proper sympathetic attitude for the facilitation to occur. One has to have "faith" and "a trusting attitude" to be an effective facilitator.

Are there objective data verifying the authenticity of the communication—verifying, for instance, that the communication truly does emanate from the autistic individual, and not from the subtle pressure of the facilitator's hand? The answer seems to be no. Robert Cummins and Margot Prior, writing in the *Harvard Educational Review* (Summer, 1992), note that

> On not one single occasion has a systematic investigation of assisted communication revealed consistent and valid evidence that such communications emanate from the client. Rather, all relevant investigations have revealed that in each instance studied the assistant has wittingly or unwittingly been responsible for the recorded response.

A rather puzzling, if not downright disturbing note: In September of 1992 *Newsweek* ran an article on F/C, which reported that not only were low-functioning autistic individuals said to be communicating in perfectly formed, grammatically correct sentences, but that even children from exclusively Hindi- or Spanish-speaking households were typing out statements in perfect English.

More alarming, however, is the near-hysterical multiplication of charges of sexual abuse brought by facilitators against the parents of autistic children. In the Syracuse area alone (Syracuse, New York, is the center of the American F/C movement), there have been no fewer than forty such allegations. In one case a young woman's father and two grandfathers were accused. After the father had been forced to move out of his home, it turned out that both grandfathers were, in fact, deceased. After dragging on for ten months, the case was finally thrown out of court for lack of evidence.

To sum up, it seems that this latest purported "breakthrough" in the treatment of autism shares certain disturbing characteristics with the various psychodynamic approaches:

• There exists within the autistic child a hidden child, cognitively sound, reflective, self-aware, misunderstood.

• The therapist alone knows how to reach the child, in some mysterious, intuitive way.

• The parents are often seen as the culprits: In the current climate some are accused not only of emotionally abusing their child but of sexually abusing him as well.

This does not necessarily mean that F/C is worthless. Dr. Rimland, whose objectivity I have always trusted, tells me that he has seen, over a thirty-year period, five or six autistic children who could write a little, in a limited way, but not speak.

What about the other approaches discussed in this chapter? I am convinced that there is a core of validity in each of them. But it seems equally true that the proponents of these approaches have vastly overstated the effectiveness of their methods, have seemed unable to bring the light of scientific objectivity to bear on their claims, and, in many instances, have continued to propagate the dangerous themes of hidden child/caring professional/abusive parent. Moreover, and most distressing, they encourage parents to focus on the one miracle method, discouraging them from persevering with the hard, relentless, boring, stressful regime of a behavioral approach.

Today, I have learned to recognize the dangerous words: words like "rebonding" instead of "teaching"; "emotionally disturbed" instead of "ill"; "psychotic mother" instead of "heartbroken mother"; "cure" instead of "recovery." I have learned to beware of anyone who sells a miracle, then explains away the failure to get one by implying that the *parent* does not have the proper mind-set, the right "attitude" for healing his child.

No matter how strong, intelligent, and objective we think we are, we can be seduced by any and every dubious claim when our children's lives are at stake. Again, the only scientifically documented, published study (based on statistical analysis rather than anecdote) that shows any autistic children to have recovered supports intensive behavioral intervention at an early age. Even then, the *majority* of children do not fully recover.

As one father who was running a home program for his son once said to me: "There's maintenance, and then there's Lovaas. There are holding tanks, and then there's behavior modification."

34

In June of 1991 Anne-Marie finished her year at pre-kindergarten.

A few weeks after school ended, we received her end-of-year report from her teachers, who had never been told of her history:

> ... Anne-Marie is friendly and caring. She continues to make contact more easily with her peers, and she is forming deeper relationships with them. ... Anne-Marie feels close to her teachers and is sharing more of her thoughts with them now. ... Anne-Marie is a cooperative, helpful group member who has learned to take her share of responsibility. ... Anne Marie is a capable child who is eager to learn. ... Her listening skills and her ability to follow directions have become much stronger. ... She is focusing more easily on a task and persevering with it. ... It's a pleasure to see Anne-Marie feeling comfortable and relaxed in her school environment and actively enjoying our various group activities with her classmates. ...

Not too bad for a "robot," her father and I thought.

Michel finished the year at Merricat's, then began fresh at a new school where, as with Anne-Marie, no one knows his history. At our first parent-teacher conference at this school, his teachers reported that "there's not a whole lot to discuss: he's doing very well."

"Is he communicating with you? I mean is his language OK?" I asked.

"Oh yes."

"Is he playing with the other children?"

"Yes. He has a couple of friends in the class."

"Is he aggressive? We used to have a problem with temper tantrums and aggression."

"We don't see that here."

We talked for a little while longer. I had to stop myself from grilling the teachers too much, lest they think there was something odd about *me*. Why does this mother keep asking us if there are problems?

Dr. Cohen saw both children again in the fall of 1991. Anne-Marie was five and a half, Michel was three years ten months.

> Anne-Marie enjoyed interacting with her mother and brother and appeared to be a happy child. Her vocal and nonvocal language was age-appropriate and she was very happy when she told stories and imaginatively played at a "tea party" with stuffed dolls. She was very good in waiting her turn and wanted to help her brother when he experienced difficulties with some questions.

In all areas of the Vineland Adaptive Scales, Dr. Cohen went on, Anne-Marie's scores were still "on target" and age-appropriate. And— at long last—he noted no residua of autism: "There was no evidence of autistic behavior."

As for Michel,

> . . . [he] interacted well with his mother and sister and patiently took turns when requested. He was quite attentive, asked and answered questions, imaginatively played with toys (both imitatively and spontaneously), told a story upon request (with prompted elaboration), and indicated when he did not understand something, e.g., "I forget what this is (and points to a toy roll)." His speech was not echolalic. . . .
> Michel's standard scores continue to improve and are well within the normal range. Over the past eight months, he has gained thirteen months in communication, twelve months in ADL [Adaptive Daily Living] skills, fifteen months in social skills and twelve months in motor skills. The language age-equivalent [four years, three months] is similar to that recently obtained by the speech-language pathologist.* . . . Michel no longer meets the criteria for Autistic Disorder. . . . He appears to be a healthy, happy, and contented child.

Residual deficits, as far as Dr. Cohen could see, were "very mild," and seemed to consist mainly of some articulation problems, and "some brief episodes of excited hand flapping." Dr. Cohen also noted that "his intonation was somewhat questionlike but this, too, was not consistent."

---

*Margery Rappaport had recently evaluated Michel's speech and language. In certain subtests, his language age-equivalent was very high, in others it was a few months behind his peers—his scores were very similar to those obtained by Anne-Marie at a similar age. His language was still "evening out." See Appendix II, p. 353, for a summation of this 1991 evaluation, as well as the results of a follow-up speech/language evaluation performed in February 1993, a few months before this book went to press.

No further follow-up visits were recommended. "Mr. and Mrs. Maurice have done a remarkable job for their children and would appear to be in the best position, at this point, for knowing how to 'fine-tune' any residual social or linguistic deficits (if needed) with the help of a good speech and language therapist."

The issue of residua is complex. Marc and I try to be honest with ourselves and vigilant about any remaining social or linguistic deficits our children may have. We know of more than one parent or professional who has claimed a child is "recovered" or "normal" when significant residua still remain: poor eye contact, sophisticated but echolalic speech, very little interest in initiating play with other children. We have tried to be our children's toughest critics as well as their strongest advocates.

But there comes a time when the distinction between "residual autism" and normal personality variation becomes quite fuzzy. In our experience, there has been no line of demarcation, clear and precise, denoting on the one side "autistic" and on the other side "totally normal." Rather, what we have seen is a gradual fading out of autistic symptoms, a gradual increase in social and linguistic competence, a gradual acceleration in our children's ability to learn normally from the environment. We look at our children today and we see that they are bright and happy. They are spontaneous, affectionate, sensitive to others' feelings, able to play cooperatively with each other and with other children. We see some linguistic immaturity in Michel, as we saw when Anne-Marie was roughly his age, but we are confident that the gap will close over the next year or so, just as his sister's did. Meanwhile, for sheer talkativeness he seems to be trying to outdo everyone in the family.

What of their future? I don't know. I can't predict what any of my children will be like at age ten, or fifteen, or twenty-five. Nor do I have an army of recovered kids out there to whom I can compare Anne-Marie and Michel. We hear that the handful that Lovaas has recovered continue to lead normal lives, but we have never met any of them.

I do know that Anne-Marie especially is at times emotionally fragile. Not that we believe she will ever become autistic again, but we still have to be somewhat protective of her, for she is prey to discouragement and anxiety. She needs that extra measure of love and reassurance before trying new experiences. We are working hard at "toughening her up." I give her more and more responsibilities around the house—

getting her own snacks, setting the table, dressing herself completely—because she needs more than anything now to know her own strength and intelligence.

Michel has none of that fragility and fearfulness. The simple act of getting some juice to drink illustrates one of the many differences between the two children:

Anne-Marie: Mommy, can I have some juice?
I: Yes, sweetie.
Anne-Marie: Should I get it myself?
I: Yes, go ahead.
Anne-Marie: Should I pour it now?
I: What do you think, Anne-Marie?
Anne-Marie (laughing): Oh, yes. I forgot. I can decide for myself!
I: That's right. Smart girl!

Whereas Michel, if he wants juice, will usually rush to the refrigerator, fling open the door, grab the juice, grab a cup, pour and drink without a second's hesitation.

One could conclude—as the antibehaviorists have no doubt already concluded—that the behavioral program rendered Anne-Marie overly dependent on authority, except for the fact that by the same token Michel should be even more timid! I think rather that this anxiety has always been part of Anne-Marie; it appeared in a pathological form when she was autistic and now manifests itself as a normal personality variation. In any case, she grows more self-confident and self-assertive with each passing month, and her kindergarten teacher mentioned in passing to me midway through the year that she can really hold her own if one of the other children tries to push her around. Having brothers helps her learn both how to stand up for herself and how to work out compromises. Every now and then, she shows true five-and-a-half-year-old defiance—jutting out her small chin, crossing her arms over her chest, stamping her foot as hard as she can on the floor, and letting fly with the angriest expression in her vocabulary: *"Pooey!"* (Marc and I find it hard to keep a straight face.)

But other than Anne-Marie's occasional lack of self-confidence, which any parent of any "normal" child might have to contend with, and which is waning anyway, we have no compelling reason now to fear the future. We have standard parental anxiety about the state of the world and of society; standard worries about how each of our kids will survive the perilous journey from child to adult. Bridget tells me that she wants to continue "tracking" them for the next few years, monitoring their progress every six months or so as they move through the school years. I told her that she would always be welcome in our home as a family friend, but that Marc and I needed to put some closure onto this story. We ourselves want to stop looking at our children clinically, stop putting them under a microscope. We want to savor their childhood, a childhood redeemed. We would like now to let go of the tears of the past and the anxieties for the future, and to follow our children into the present.

The present is fine. At home, on a Sunday in January 1992, the children's voices rise and fall. The topic of the day is dinosaurs. The topic of the past six months has been dinosaurs. There are more books on dinosaurs in this house than books on autism. Anne-Marie has decided that Michel is playing too many dinosaur games. She is lying on the couch with her arms around him. Daniel is playing nearby. Marc is doing the Sunday crossword puzzle. I am curled in an armchair writing. The sweet cadence of the children's conversation—childish, cheerful, profound, and simple—murmurs through the sunny afternoon, and, as always, fills their father and me with something quite piercingly close to reverence:

Anne-Marie: You know why you should stop playing dinosaur games?

Michel: Why?

Anne-Marie: You have to learn how to play other games. You will get bored-er and bored-er of dinosaur games. (Silence.) Did you learn the lesson?

Michel: Yes, but can I play dinosaurs three more times?

Anne-Marie: Yes, if you don't play it too much. (They pick up two dinosaurs.) I'll be long-neck. No, I'll be this little one.

Michel: I'll be monoclonius.

Anne-Marie: This one can go very fast.

Michel: Mine goes slow. Mine walks slow.

Anne-Marie: You can run faster than that.

Michel: Is monoclonius a meat-eater or a plant-eater?

Anne-Marie: I don't know. Ask Daddy.

Michel: Daddy, is monoclonius a meat-eater or a plant-eater?

Marc: They're plant-eaters.

Michel (to Anne-Marie): They're plant-eaters.

Anne-Marie: Oh. Daddy, what's this little one called?

Marc: Maybe an allosaurus.

Daniel: Allosaurus is a long-neck?

Marc: An allosaurus is like *Tyrannosaurus rex*.

Anne-Marie: Michel, guess what? I'm a meat-eater! And I can run faster than you!

Daniel: But you know what, Anne-Marie? He can't go faster than *Tyrannosaurus rex*. He can go as fast as a person and *Tyrannosaurus rex* walks faster than a person.

Anne-Marie: Michel, you know what? He really can't run faster than a *Tyrannosaurus rex*.

Michel: I can eat you *all* up!

(Peals of laughter all around.)

We walked through the valley of the shadow, and now we walk in light. Goodness and mercy now follow us. Sometimes I think that it is we who are guiding and teaching our children; at other times I look into their faces, I hear their voices, and what I am seeing and hearing is the fundamental holiness of all children. Sometimes I think it is they who are teaching Marc and me, they who are leading us back to the source of all holiness, of all light.

PART III

Catherine's Recovery?

October 1992

GETTING A BOOK into production can be, I have discovered, a lengthy process. Legal readings, copy-editing, "launch meetings," periods of intense activity interspersed with months of dead calm—almost a year has passed since I penned what I believed was my final chapter.

Life has gone on, of course, and the story has not really ended. How could it? These three children are still at the beginning of their lives. As each day passes, I want to keep writing, capturing forever their least gestures of love, their softest whispers in the night.

I know a mother whose son, Alex, almost five years old now, has just been reevaluated and found to have "no significant residua" of his once-autistic condition. He was instructed in a Lovaas-based program, partly at home and partly at school, and apparently all he has now are some linguistic lags. I called their home tonight, and Alex answered the phone.

"Hello!" he shouted. "Who is this?"

"This is Catherine. Is your mommy there?"

"Who?" he yelled, at a typical five-year-old decibel level. "Who is this?"

"This is Catherine. Who is *this?*"

"This is Alex! I'm Alex."

"Alex. Hello. Is Mommy there? This is Catherine."

"Mommy! There is Catherine on the phone!"

Alex's mother, Maureen, came to the phone. "Catherine? That's Alex. Isn't it great! Did you hear him?"

I knew how she felt. We never get used to this gift. Anything they do can still move us, thrill us, reduce us to tears. On more than one occasion I have made a fool of myself by clutching a near-stranger's arm and rhapsodizing about my children. "Oh my God, look at Mi-

chel!" I cry to a fellow parent at pick-up time at school. "What beautiful playing with the other children!" As she politely, though with
some perplexity, agrees, I tell myself to cool it a little; I'm trying to
remember what "normal" is supposed to mean in a mother.

And yet, coursing around and under and through that joy are lingering areas of vulnerability and sadness. In that last chapter, written
almost a year ago, I noted that Marc and I have the "standard" parental
anxieties about our kids' future. I think I spoke too soon. Marc
may have regained the peaceful equilibrium he had always possessed,
but I have found that I have significantly more than the "standard"
anxieties. Anything in the children's behavior has the potential to
throw me: negativity, timidity, aggression, forgetfulness, absent-
mindedness—it's very hard to refrain from overinterpreting and jumping to desolate conclusions. Especially when each of these traits or
tendencies can be seen as having its roots in what were once the characteristic (and extreme) behaviors of autism.

Anne-Marie has a tendency to forget her school bag. Every morning
I have to remind her, as she's halfway out the door, to go back and get
her bag. I try "fading my prompts." Instead of saying, "Did you remember your bag?" I ask her, "Do you have everything you need?"
Then I simply stand at the door and say, "Anne-Marie." Then I try
saying nothing, but just looking at her meaningfully as she walks out
the door empty-handed. She still forgets that bag. What's the matter
with her? She can't retain information. She can't learn from experience.
The teacher will have to repeat any direction she gives her three or
four times. She will fail first grade. She won't make it in a normal
school.

Anxiety gnaws away at me until two things happen. The first is that
I casually ask her first-grade teacher how things are going, and am told
that everything is fine. The second is that I suddenly realize, one morning, that Daniel forgets his bag just as often as Anne-Marie does! The
difference is that I'm so unconcerned about him that I don't even notice
how often I have to remind him to run back and get his bag.

I don't mean that the children are alike in all respects. Anne-Marie
is dreamier than Daniel or Michel. She still can take a while to warm
up to a group of people. She needs occasional help in focusing on a
task, especially when she doesn't find the task very interesting. But I
believe these traits may be found in any "normal" child, that they fit
within the spectrum of normal personality variation. Yet, even though
I know this, I keep having to remind myself to "cut the kids some

slack." I see that *at this point* it is harmful to Anne-Marie when I become overly anxious about her behavior. Harping at her, nagging at her, trying to push her too much, is not good for her, or for me. That same anxiety that propelled me to find out what was wrong, push for an answer, get an early diagnosis, and push her relentlessly until she was well—that anxiety served its purpose, but now the time has come to let it go, or, rather, to make an effort to overcome it. She is smart enough and aware enough to know when she is being criticized, however obliquely, and she is extremely sensitive. If I am relaxed and loving, so is she; if I become tense and worried, she begins to look sad.

One afternoon recently she was sitting on the playroom floor, staring off into space. I don't like that look. That look makes me nervous. "Anne-Marie!" I call, with an edge to my voice. "What are you doing?"

She turns to look at me. Her solemn Irish eyes are serious, then her face lights up with a soft smile. Her response is reasonable and calm: "I'm wondering if chipmunks have souls."

Oh. OK. Fair enough. Anne-Marie is my philosopher child. Sometimes she staggers me with her questions about being and life and time and God. Under the bubbling laughter and capriciousness of a typical six-year-old there lies a thoughtful and introspective nature. Her contemplative, meditative demeanor, in fact, adds to her charm. It is only when I link that demeanor to the time when she was *too* contemplative, *too* withdrawn, that I start to worry again. What if she daydreams too much in school, and doesn't pay attention to the lesson? The argument and the questions rage in my head. I talk it out to myself: Catherine, she did beautifully in kindergarten last year and in pre-K the year before that. She's holding her own very well so far in first grade. The first-grade teacher has specifically told you there are no problems. Obviously, even if she is daydreaming occasionally, the teachers do not look upon it as an aberration. Nor does it seem to be interfering with either her academic work or her ability to make friends. Please, remember how much you love her, treasure her, for who she is now: a contemplative, sometimes timid, daydreaming, tender, sweet, smart, and funny child.

I have similar difficulty in relaxing my guard over Michel. He ended the summer of '92 on another upsurge of aggression and inflexibility. Whenever anyone asked him to do something, such as putting on his pajamas or helping to pick up the toys at the end of the day, he almost invariably dug in his heels, whined, and resisted. In addition, he had a tendency to strike out whenever he got into a disagreement with his brother or sister.

Here again, as my irritation and anxiety mount, I have to be reminded that "normal" four-and-a-half-year-olds can be aggressive, inflexible, whiny, temperamental, resistant. The question is to what degree they are that way, and how quickly they can be distracted out of that mood through bargaining or compromising or ultimatums or whatever. I remember when, if a fork was placed in a "wrong" position on the table, Michel might have a tantrum of up to two hours; now, friends will often counsel me to "relax" about him. But it is not so easy to put aside, to forget, all the responses that kind of behavior once called forth in me: fear, worry, firm no-nonsense behavioral shaping. To say "All boys his age display aggression from time to time" is fine, if you are blissfully unaware of his history. But I lived his history with him, and acts of aggression and inflexibility can still set off alarm bells in my head. Will he be all right in pre-kindergarten? Will he fight with everyone constantly? Will he obey the teacher? Will the teachers be patient with him?

I have found that I am helped to trust in the children more when I trust in their teachers. Although happy to receive positive reports from the children's teachers, and grateful for their supportive attitude, I used to believe rather cynically that they were probably not observing the children closely enough to catch whatever subtle hints of pathology might remain. As I know from experience, it is hard to spot a "perseverative activity" unless you're attuned to it as something to watch for. Even infrequency of eye contact is not something a teacher would necessarily remark on, although she might vaguely feel some subtle lack of relatedness in a child who has such a behavior. For really objective evaluations, I used to rely more on Dr. Cohen, as someone who knew how to *seek out* signs of residual autism and maladjustment.

Now, however, the teachers' evaluations are more important to me. I'm starting to have more confidence in what these women say— especially those who have had years of experience, like the teachers from the children's classes last year. Anne-Marie's kindergarten teacher had been teaching for about twenty years; Michel's nursery school teacher for about ten. Their evaluations are replete with concrete observations of social and cognitive behavior. One has the impression that nothing significantly abnormal would have escaped their eye. As I begin to trust such professionals more, I take true consolation from their observations of my children:

Anne-Marie is a sweet and sensitive little girl and she brightens our day with her lovely face and endearing smile.

Anne-Marie enjoys playing in the "kitchen" with the girls. She also plays very well with the boys, building great Lego creations. The boys accept her as a play partner without question. They are very complimentary about what she builds in school and were awed by the Lego structure she brought in for Show and Tell.

Anne-Marie's art work is exceptionally good. She has a natural flair for painting and drawing lovely pictures. All the children steal a glance at her picture before they start drawing their own. She always adds something unusual to her artwork, color or designs. She always draws or paints what pleases her. She doesn't need to copy what her peers may be doing. Even when she is doing a class art project, she always adds the "Anne-Marie touch" to hers.

Anne-Marie has taken off like a rocket in reading and math. She can read all short vowel books and sight work books. She is reading well above grade level. I can always depend on her during a reading lesson. I ask her to read the first page and the other children are eager to follow her. A few days ago, she was given a sincere compliment by [one of her classmates]: "Anne-Marie is the smartest girl in the class."

Her math skills are good. She understands patterning and sequencing. She can add and subtract without the aid of rods. Anne-Marie never leaves a cognitive project until she has completed the assignment. Even if she is told she can finish it later, she always replies, "That's okay. I will do it now."

It is always a pleasure to read to Anne-Marie. . . . Anne-Marie will always say she is willing to give up free time to hear another chapter. We can always rely on Anne-Marie to remember what we have already read during review time.

We are so happy we have the pleasure of knowing Anne-Marie . . .

> —From Anne-Marie's kindergarten evaluation
> April 1992.*

Michel is such an enthusiastic little boy. He comes into class excited to start the day. Michel is self-motivated so he is content to play on his own and can become involved for long periods of time. He loves all the

---

*As the narrative of this book moves into the present, the necessity of documenting the children's health begins to conflict with the necessity of maintaining their anonymity. Marc and I decided, after having received Anne-Marie's evaluation and Michel's evaluation, to share our story with the children's teachers. We took them into our confidence and requested their understanding of our need to protect the children from public scrutiny. In this way we can reproduce their evaluations, which they will surely recognize if they see the book in print.

children in the class and has made progress in his social growth. Occasionally he will become frustrated when his attentions to a particular friend are thwarted, but he is learning to talk through his frustrations instead of striking out. He has made many friends and is so happy when one of them comes over to see what he is doing.

We are constantly amazed at Michel's ability to put on paper all of the ideas he has in his head. His fine motor skills are exceptional. He is persistent and a perfectionist at any task he attempts. He has high expectations of himself and he is always surprising us with his recall of facts and his understanding of his world around him. He takes great pride in his accomplishments and loves to show us what he has done. He is very creative both in drawing and in building. Drawing dinosaur scenes is a specialty of Michel's. He can draw in detail any of the dinosaurs and usually has it placed in a prehistoric scene with palm trees and erupting volcanoes. Michel's ability to write from memory or copy letters and numbers is amazing. Sometimes he likes to write his name "in script" and he often will make letters in a block-style format. Some of Michel's favorite things to do in class are drawing, playing with the dinosaurs and building with the Duplos and large wooden blocks. He loves to play outside, especially in the sandbox. He is interested in science, music and nature. Michel enjoys storytime and one can see he is totally absorbed in the story. He follows directions well and easily comprehends new information.

We have loved having Michel in class. With his enthusiasm for learning and his ability to absorb and understand any given facts, we know he will continue to flourish in the Pre-kindergarten next year.

—From Michel's Nursery Class evaluation,
April 1992

Perhaps a few more years of these reports and I will learn to let go of debilitating anxiety.

For anxiety does debilitate. It is as true for Michel as it is for Anne-Marie. Anxiety about him can begin to sap my joy in him, mute my breathless happiness in the child he has become: an exuberant and loving little boy who hero-worships his big brother and runs to kiss his sister if she falls; who dazzles strangers with his smile, and delights in "knock-knock" jokes. Michel, our golden child, our recompense, our delight.

Anxiety about how the children will perform in school is something I can at least grapple with, and analyze, and reason out. Late-night dread is another issue entirely. Most of the time I'm reasonably sane. If any minor illness threatens any of the children, however, I am prone to insomnia, nightmares, and expectations of catastrophe. Somehow, as I lie in bed in the darkness, faith and hope and logic and all normal defenses forsake me. All the world's ills come parading around my bed, all possible traumas and heartaches that could befall us loom as inevitable. And what good is thinking and praying and loving anyway, when that final catastrophe, death, will eventually claim us all? I can work myself into the most profound existential crisis. Marc helps a lot, simply by being himself: anchored in the present, leaving tomorrow's woes to tomorrow, knowing how to live on a less tortured plane.

Michel, as I am writing, is suffering from chicken pox. Last night I tossed and turned, periodically moaning and sighing until at last Marc took note.

"What's going on?" he muttered sleepily.

"I'm afraid Michel will develop Reye's Syndrome," I said.

"What's Reye's Syndrome?" he asked.

"It's some horrible complication that sometimes develops when kids are recovering from chicken pox. It can be fatal."

He propped himself up on one elbow. "Well, what are the chances he'll develop it?"

"Not very high, I think."

"Now that I think of it, I did read about that disease, and there's supposed to be some link between it and aspirin. Just don't give him aspirin."

Strangely enough, this conversation calmed me. Not because of the factual discussion over the frequency of the condition or the possible link with aspirin, but just because I had been able to let the fear out, put it into words, and have Marc listen to me, as he always does, seriously.

Letting go of sadness is more complicated than I expected. I can't stand on the mountaintop and exult completely when I am so often reminded of how dark and fearful was the valley. I have heard parents weep for their children, and too often I am helpless before them. I can give them information, but I can't find them therapists, can't tell them what the future holds, can't guarantee them anything. A mother calls me for information, and upon hearing Anne-Marie in the background asking me a question, suddenly falters. Her voice breaks, and the sound of her quiet sobbing fills the space between us. I know her terror, and her longing. A father calls from JFK Airport, stopping between business flights to put in a desperate call to an unknown woman. He starts to describe his two-year-old son, just diagnosed as autistic. The airport loudspeakers blare behind him and I hear the cacophony of a frantic pub-

lic space. He speaks of how long he and his wife had waited for this
child. His strong, confident voice begins to sound strained. He stops.
He struggles to maintain composure. "We love him so much . . . ," he
starts to say, and then, clutching a pay phone in the middle of an
airport, he is crying. Tears sting my own eyes too, because I remember
it all. And because I know better than he does how hard is the struggle
before him. I know that I have no miracle cure to give these parents.
Far from it, I have hope, but no guarantee of anything.

"Don't mourn for us, Catherine," said another father to me once,
when I tried to speak with him of this pain. "My son hasn't recovered
as your children have, but we have joy here too. There *is* progress that
is meaningful. There is a point where the deficits are not devastating,
and you do begin to accept." I am happy he said that to me, but my
happiness will always be tinged by the guilt and grief of a survivor,
one who knows that others are still there, left behind.

"How can your story hurt me?" asked a mother whose daughter's
progress in a behavioral program was slow. She had called to ask me
about Anne-Marie in kindergarten, and I was loath to give her many
details. "I know the prognosis. I've heard the horror stories. I can hear
about failure or read about failure whenever I want. Right now I'd like
to hear about success!"

Sometimes, when I am speaking with parents, it helps all of us—me
with my guilt, them with their need—to stop thinking in black-and-
white terms. Things have changed. It seems no longer accurate to speak
of recovery/nonrecovery, when so many of these children have only
recently started early intervention. Rather, there appear to be fast progress and slow progress, and no one can make absolute predictions,
either positive or negative, about anyone's future. Intensive, early,
structured intervention is changing the terms of any discourse on autism. One child may achieve functional normalcy in under two years,
another will need four years of work to attain communicative language. Michael, a seven-year-old who has been in intensive behavioral
therapy for almost four years now, continues to move forward at a
slow but steady pace. This past summer he finally began to speak in
spontaneous multiword utterances. Will his progress stop at some
point? Will he be normal one day? I don't know the answer to those
questions, and neither do his parents, or Bridget, or anyone.

I don't believe that my guilt or anxiety or sadness helps anyone
now—not me, not Marc, not the children, not other parents of autistic
children. If I were a parent whose child had just been diagnosed with

autism, I might feel like strangling someone whose child had recovered yet who refused to rejoice. Sometimes we're a little too wary of celebrating, we're fearful of boasting, crowing, preening, tempting fate. But celebration does not have to be boastful. It can be nothing more complicated than a prayer of thanks, nothing louder than a soul's deep sigh of gladness.

I record the children's words, and in doing so I celebrate. I testify not only to the beauty of my children but to the graciousness of God. As always, their innocent discourse, their purity of heart, reflect that grace and graciousness far better than I.

Evening, one day after school. The children are gathering for supper. Seven-year-old Daniel, six-year-old Anne-Marie, and four-year-old Michel have come inside. After hastily throwing some token water over their hands, they converge on the table. Their faces are flushed, the clean white shirts they put on this morning are now streaked with brown hand prints, sweat mats their fine hair. They are hungry, talkative, animated, opinionated.

Michel: I don't *like* peas!

I: Mi-*chel!*

Daniel: Michel, you shouldn't say "I don't like" when we sit down for dinner.

Michel: I didn't say "I don't like." I said, *"Excuse me,* I don't like peas."

(More discussion of peas and politesse. Then we careen off into culture:)

Daniel: Mommy, there was this kid—you're not going to *believe* this—his name was "Artsnote"—and he was only four years old, and he could play the piano with his eyes closed! And he went around to all these castles and kings and queens, see, and they put a blindfold on him so he couldn't see, and he played the piano without making a single mistake!

I: Artsnote?

Daniel: Yeah, Artsnote.

I: And he played the piano really well?

Daniel: Uh-huh.

I: Maybe his name was Mozart?

Daniel: Oh yeah, Mozart.

Michel: Daniel plays the piano! He plays the piano with no thumbs! (Somewhere they have got the idea that playing the piano "with no thumbs" means you can play the piano "really fast," and "really fast" is "really good." They begin to talk about speedy piano playing, which eventually brings them around to the topic of numbers.)

Anne-Marie: Mommy, did God invent the numbers last?

Daniel: Anne-Marie, God did not invent numbers. People invented numbers.

Anne-Marie: People invented numbers?

Michel: Yes they did, Anne-Marie. Daniel knows.

Daniel: Yeah . . . (pause) . . . numbers are like . . . you know . . . there are all kinds of numbers, in different languages. . . . Hey! You know what? God and numbers are almost the same! You know why? God has no end and numbers have no end! (I swear I do not make up these conversations.)

I: Do you know what it's called, to have no end? Infinity.

Anne-Marie: Infinity? To have no end? (She pauses and puzzles for a while.) One day I'll understand that, right, Mom?

I: Right, darling.

Now we see as in a glass, darkly. Then we shall see face to face.

PART IV

*Some Further Thoughts on Recovery;
Some Practical Advice;
Some Other Parents' Voices*

Once when I sent a mother to one of the early-intervention programs in New York to try to recruit some therapists for her home program, she reported back to me that the director had informed her that it was "illegal and unethical" for "amateurs" to be attempting this kind of work.

We parents *are* amateurs, in the true sense of the word: amateurs are lovers. We are lovers of our children, and until the professional community can offer us more effective programs, we will often have to take matters into our own hands.

A few parents are lucky enough to find an established behavioral program that has room for their child. From what a number of these parents have told me, however, I gather that some of these facilities are better than others. A good behavioral program, I believe, includes these basic qualities:

• A knowledgeable therapeutic team who know how to vary reinforcements and programs, how to keep accurate objective data, until they are *reasonably certain* that the child is doing as well as he can. In other words, they know how to push the child, and when to ease up on the pushing.

• Daily data collection, individualized programs for each child, one-on-one therapy, therapists trained in the principles and techniques of behavior analysis. One therapist to two students is probably not good enough, at least not at the beginning. Later, if the child reaches a higher level of functioning, he or she will probably benefit from small-group teaching. But in the beginning, your child most likely needs concentrated, intense, individual sessions, where the focus is on him or her alone.

• A director and staff who are willing to confer with you—not once a month, not once a week, but whenever you feel like getting or giving information.

In any case, however, these behaviorally oriented programs, whether excellent or mediocre, are few and far between at this time. At least half the families I have met have had to set up, at one time or other, their own home program, since there was literally nothing available to them.

Who Will Recover?

Who will recover under this behavioral approach? I don't know. No one I've spoken to seems to know at this point. There seem to be no "markers" indicating which children have the capacity to recover and which do not. Autism is evidently a disorder of many different causes and a wide range of severity. I find analogous the words "autism" and "cancer" in that they both represent one general name for many different forms of the illness, some curable, some not. Our knowledge about autism is imperfect, and the best available treatment we have is imperfect; we are a very long way from any miracle cure. The data that Dr. Lovaas had published when our children started therapy showed that, at best, only about half the children receiving this kind of therapy at this level of intensity at this young an age reach "normal cognitive functioning." So much seems to depend on the child's capacity to respond. So much depends on how severe his condition is, how early he is diagnosed.

Nevertheless, it appears that virtually all children can make some progress, even though different children can show wide variation in their rate of response. Two mothers I know—equally passionate and committed in their struggle for their children—have agreed to share their stories. ("Sharon" has requested anonymity; Lucille Schoales writes under her own name.)

Sharon's Story

It seems so long ago that our little boy sat by the hour, in silence, lining up letters of the alphabet and numbers, with very little interest in anything or anyone else. At age two and a half he was diagnosed autistic and given a bleak prognosis. We didn't know a lot about autism, but we knew there must be something we could do that could make a difference. We immersed ourselves in books and articles and the name

Ivar Lovaas kept popping up in reference to a program at UCLA that had documented proof of recovery of forty-seven percent of kids that had been receiving behavior modification. With figures like that, there was no doubt in our minds where we would turn next. Our fears of not being able to get into the UCLA program were dispelled when we learned that they would come to us, give a workshop, and train us.

Eighteen months later we have a very different child. He has thrived on the structure that this therapy has provided. Initially it gave him a means to show us exactly what he did know. Now it has become a comfortable way to teach new and appropriate skills and behaviors. Our son is now age-appropriate and even above-average in his cognitive skills, speaks in full sentences, although he is still lacking the spontaneity he should have, and is fairly self-sufficient in self-help skills. He loves the company of other children. In fact he goes overboard with hugging now, and we're working on normalizing the frequency and intensity of his affection. Play skills are still difficult for him, but are improving.

It has certainly been hard work. We've devoted anywhere from twenty to thirty hours a week to therapy. We've learned a lot along the way. This mother learned the hard way that one person should not try doing it alone. Burnout is a very real probability that negatively affects everyone, especially the child. At least two therapists are needed (more are preferable) with no one person putting in more than twelve hours per week. We also found out that to maximize the program it's advisable to have the UCLA folks come and monitor progress (about every five months has worked well for us). An in-person consultation is far more complete than a video evaluation. We've discovered that colleges and universities are a good source for therapists, and we've even found that some kids make effective therapists for certain drills. Most recently we have achieved an unprecedented goal in having our city school system accept the program as an *appropriate education* for our child and supply us with two very talented therapists at the school system's expense.

On the negative side, we've found our most frustrating experiences have been with those people in a position to be of the most help—professionals. They seem to be set in their ways and closed-minded to any way unknown to them. The six professionals who evaluated and diagnosed our child were not only negative in their prognosis, but also negligent in steering us toward any help whatsoever. When we had our workshop, I invited them to come so that they could know the best program available, but they turned down the offer. I find that totally irresponsible. Other professionals and certain chapters of the Autism Society of America also tend to be judgmental. We've heard the word "controversial" in relation to Lovaas so many times that we've lost count. What we've discovered is that these people mostly pass judgment based on hearsay, old information, and misconceptions. Virtually none of them has actually witnessed the therapy or knows someone who has. It upsets us that parents are hearing such negative things and taking it as truth simply because professionals or their ASA chapter have given the information. We make it a point to invite parents and anyone else who may be in a position to help another child to observe our son's therapy. Those who have were all amazed at its positive nature and its astounding results.

. . . Early intervention is so important. . . . We've never regretted our choice to contact Dr. Lovaas. We know we've got two more years of hard work ahead, but we also feel sure our son will begin first grade indistinguishable (except as an individual personality) from his peers.

Lucille Schoales's Story

As I sit here and recall the day my son Michael was diagnosed as being autistic I can still remember the feelings of fear, sadness, and horror that raged through my body. I wanted so desperately for it not to be true. How could God let my child, or any child for that matter, be affected by such a disability? The hopes and dreams for my son's future were shattered by one word: "autism."

He was barely two at the time and he had the face of an angel, as most autistic children do. However, his behavior had changed. Withdrawn and alone in a world of his own, he was totally nonverbal and had no understanding of what was being said to him. The once "normal" child I thought I had given birth to was gone, and a stranger had taken his place.

Even though at first I denied my son's disability, unable to even say the word "autistic," I researched autism intensely. Day after day was spent reading books about autism and seeking out professionals who might be able to help me. There were no answers, and I found myself alone fighting desperately to find a way to reach my son.

The two years following Michael's diagnosis seemed like a lifetime. During that time a variety of autistic behaviors began to emerge and I began to accept that my son was truly autistic. My main goal was to find an early intervention program that was appropriate for Mike. Those two years were the most frustrating years of my life.

There was an assortment of preschool handicapped programs to choose from in the area where I lived, and Mike attended three different ones before the age of four. As he went from preschool to preschool I was assured by each one that they offered the appropriate interventions that he needed. It hardly turned out to be true. He made little progress, and I began to question if they knew how to teach him the skills he needed to learn. Because I was so unhappy with the services Mike was receiving, I was becoming labeled as "the mother who couldn't accept her son's disability." There had to be a better way.

When Mike was enrolled in his third preschool program I met a mother of another child with autism who introduced me to a different method to teach autistic children. She had been implementing the program in her home with her daughter on a daily basis.* The program was based on a book by Ivar Lovaas called *The Me Book*. Dr. Lovaas's book gave detailed instructions on how to teach developmentally disabled children. The program was totally behavioral, using the principles of behavior modification, positive reinforcement, discrete trials, and taking data on the child's progress. I was very curious to see the program in action, so my friend invited me into her home to observe.

The program was wonderful. As I watched her child attend to and engage in appropriate activities I began to feel hopeful that my son could learn the things that her child had learned. My friend explained to me how I could set up the same program in my own home; so I did. I used *The Me Book* as my guide and hired my friend's best trainer to help me get started. I will always be thankful to my friend for sharing her knowledge with me because the results over the next few months were incredible.

As I became more knowledgeable over the next few months I was able to hire more trainers to come to my home and teach them how to implement the programs. It was time-consuming and expensive but worth it. This type of therapy gave Mike the foundation to be able to learn. We taught him such skills as eye contact, sound production, following simple commands and completing simple tasks such as matching and puzzles. Even Mike's private speech therapist agreed to implement the principles of behavior modification during her sessions

---

*I think I should mention, just to keep things clear, that I am not the friend Lucille refers to here.

with him. I could not believe that these services were not available for my son.

As the months flew by, Mike's progress was moving rapidly at first and then began to slow down, especially in the areas of receptive and expressive language. I wasn't sure if we were implementing the programs incorrectly or if Mike's deficits were more severe than we had anticipated. I heard about a person named Bridget Taylor from the same friend who introduced me to *The Me Book*. Miss Taylor was going to my friend's home to evaluate her home program, so I asked her to also come to my home and evaluate Mike's programs and his progress.

When Miss Taylor made her visit she made some extremely helpful suggestions for my home program and left an enormous impression on my husband and me. She was very knowledgeable in the area of autism and told us about a school that she and Dr. Linda Meyer were opening in New Jersey. The school, called the Alpine Learning Group, would service children with autism and pervasive developmental disorders and implement the principles of applied behavior analysis. Miss Taylor also told us that ALG would provide highly structured, individualized and data-based educational services to each child. After meeting Miss Taylor and hearing about ALG, my husband and I knew we had no other choice but to get Mike into that school.

Even though we didn't know exactly when the school would open or if Mike would be accepted into the program we began to plan a move from our home in New York to New Jersey. We called Miss Taylor and Dr. Meyer and expressed our desire to get Mike into their program, and they told us what to do to begin the intake process. We rented our home to my sister and spent the next three months traveling back and forth to New Jersey to find a house to rent for us. Mike went for his intake evaluation and did get accepted into ALG, and we moved to New Jersey four months after we met Bridget Taylor.

Prior to our move to New Jersey, we had to meet with the members of the child study team in our new school district. They were surprised, to say the least, at this family with this autistic child who came from another state to have their child placed in a school that wasn't actually open yet. They wanted to place Mike in a program like the ones we had moved away from. My husband and I explained to them that Mike did not make progress in the previous preschool handicapped programs that he had been enrolled in but that he was making considerable progress in our home program. We came prepared with Mike's programs and data sheets to back up our statements. None of the team members were familiar with Dr. Lovaas's thirty years of research with autistic children, so it was difficult for them to understand why we felt that ALG would be the only appropriate placement for Mike. We also discussed the fact that they had to place Mike in a program that would maximize his potential and that this could be done at ALG. The team was skeptical but they finally did agree to place Mike at ALG after it got state approval.

All our prayers had been answered. Mike started school at ALG in July of 1989 and it was one of the happiest days of our lives. The school started out with four children and we felt it was a blessing that Mike was one of them. Dr. Meyer and Bridget Taylor were devoted to making ALG an excellent program, making sure each child's individual needs were met. Even the parents of the other children welcomed us with open arms, trying to make our transition from one state to another a little easier.

As Mike was adjusting to his new school, my family was adjusting to our new home. I found a new job at a local hospital; my husband continued to work at his job on Long Island, commuting daily; my oldest daughter was adjusting to her new school and trying to make new friends; and my eighteen-month-old daughter was handling things quite well. We missed our newly renovated home on Long Island, our family and friends. Even though we sacrificed everything we had, we knew it was our only chance to get Mike the education he needed. My husband and I talked at great length about the move before we did it, but I don't think we realized how stressful it would be.

Four months later some things happened that we didn't expect. I found out that I was pregnant with my fourth child, and my husband lost his job after being employed with his company for almost ten years. My husband and I were both numb at that point wondering how we were going to survive. We used all of our savings to make the move, so we didn't have any financial reserves to help us get through the next few months. The following year was a financial disaster for us. Since I was a registered nurse I began working full-time while my husband brought in as much money as he could from jobs that were paying him much less than what he had been earning. We worked opposite shifts so that one of us could always be home with the children. Everything that could have gone wrong that year went wrong. The stress was overwhelming. Our family and friends were giving us support from afar, but we still felt alone.

Although we had a lot of misfortune that year, we did experience much joy. I gave birth to a healthy baby boy, and Mike's progress was slow but steady. I believe that God watched over us that year. We made a lot of new friends who helped us get through the tough times and gave us the support we needed. There were times that we questioned whether we made the right decision by moving, but every time Mike made a little progress we knew we had.

It has been almost three years since our move, and we have decided to take one day at a time. My husband and I still lead a very busy, stressful life with a lot of financial pressures, but things are starting to look up for us, especially for Mike. When we first moved here we hoped that Mike would recover from autism, but he did not. His deficits in receptive and expressive language are severe. He just recently began discriminating objects and labeling them verbally. This has been the most difficult thing for Mike to accomplish, and we are so proud of him. He is learning to read and write, and he can work on numerous tasks for long periods of time independently. His self-help skills have improved greatly, and he is a happy child with a real warm personality. The staff at ALG and my husband and I are working very hard to teach Mike the skills he needs to know so he can function as an independent adult. I know that Mike will continue to progress as long as he continues to receive the same behavioral therapy that he is receiving now. Mike doesn't have to recover from autism to be successful; he is already a success. My husband and I find such joy in watching Mike grow and learn. We feel like we have found the son we thought we had lost.

ALTHOUGH I have encountered much quiet heroism in the world of autism, Lucille Schoales's story still always moves me to tears.

Who Will Pay?

Who will pay, especially if the parents are forced to find their own therapists to work in the home? The more qualified the therapist, the more expensive she is. Most parents simply can't afford the help they so desperately need.

With the aid of a good lawyer, Jayne Zanglein, we were able to win an appeal to our insurance company, and they eventually paid for both children's therapy. I have made a copy of that appeal available to parents through the office of Dr. Rimland. Write to

Dr. Bernard Rimland
Autism Research Institute
4182 Adams Avenue
San Diego, CA 92116

and ask for the "Legrand Appeal." Send $4 to Dr. Rimland to cover copying and postage costs.

Dr. Rimland has also published in his newsletter a summation of *Kunin* v. *Benefit Trust*, a case where parents successfully sued their insurance company and won reimbursement for their autistic son's program. Mr. Thomas Borcher, the lawyer who represented the Kunins, has given me permission to quote from his summation of this case, the facts and participants of which are now a matter of public record:

> Under the Benefit Trust policy, an insurer's maximum responsibility for claims was $10,000.00 for matters that were related to a "mental illness or nervous disorder."
>
> At trial the judge agreed with our contention, that autism was not a mental illness, and awarded full policy benefits without applying the $10,000.00 limitation.
>
> Benefit Trust Life Insurance Company appealed the decision all the way up to the United States Supreme Court, but in each step of the appeal their pleas were denied.
>
> Parents of autistic children may be affected by this case if they submit claims to their insurer and the claims are denied, or the amount paid is limited by a "mental illness" limitation, which is actually quite common in health insurance policies. The Court of Appeals sustained the trial court's finding that autism is not a "mental illness" and that it is instead organically based. . . .
>
> . . . Any parent whose insurance claims for treatment of autism are being denied or limited because of a "mental illness" limitation may do well to consult counsel to see if the insurer's limitations on payment are proper.

Insurance policies differ, however, and many parents will not be able to win anything from their companies. The other recourse is to convince the local school district that the child needs this therapy, and that the district should provide it under the *Education for All Handicapped Children Act* (Public Law 94-142).

"The law guarantees every child a free public education. This means that a child with special learning needs is entitled to free special services to meet those needs." That statement is taken from a very helpful pamphlet, published by the Children's Defense Fund, entitled *94-142 and 504: Numbers That Add Up to Educational Rights for Handicapped Children. A Guide for Parents and Advocates.* You can obtain the pamphlet by writing to

> Children's Defense Fund
> 122 C Street, NW
> Washington, D.C. 20001
> (202) 628-8787

The pamphlet takes you step by step through the process of obtaining a free and appropriate special education for your handicapped child. It is available in Spanish or English, and when I last checked, cost $5.75, which includes the cost of postage.

Be aware as well of two important amendments to the Education for All Handicapped Children Act: The *Education of the Handicapped Act Amendments of 1986* (Public Law 99-457) mandates services for *preschoolers* with disabilities. In addition, "the law established the Handicapped Infants and Toddlers Program (Part H). As specified by law, this program is directed to the needs of children, from birth to their third birthday, who need early intervention services."* The *Education of the Handicapped Act Amendments of 1990* (Public Law 101-476) "reauthorized and expanded the discretionary programs, mandated transition services and assistive technology services to be included in a child's or youth IEP [Individualized Education Plan], and added autism and traumatic brain injury to the list of categories of children and youth eligible for special education and related services."†

You may need the help of a good psychologist or social worker to convince the district that a behavioral program, rather than some generic preschool early-intervention program, is what your child needs. Try to help those in charge to see that if they pay for two or three years of good, intensive therapy now, the state may not have to foot the bill for a lifetime of special education or even custodial care.

Here is how one father I know—writing here under the name Grant James—successfully argued his case before his local school district (a psychologist once told me that parents of autistic children have a reputation in the professional community for being strong advocates for their children. Grant provides a case in point):

News Digest, National Information Center for Children and Youth with Disabilities (NICHCY), vol. 1, no. 1, 1991.

†Ibid. The IEP, or Individualized Education Plan, is the specialized plan mandated for each child concerned under the Education for All Handicapped Children Act.

Initially, funding was provided through the county. After the laws changed, our funding continued through the school district.

One must understand the conditions surrounding our initial appeal for funds:

1) Our child had already been enrolled for over a year in a "special school" for autistic children. His education was funded entirely through the state and the county. During that time, our three-year-old child made no credible progress. That was documented in his IEP.

2) We had already independently studied Lovaas's *The Me Book* and the corresponding videotapes. My wife and I had begun implementing the Lovaas techniques to successfully teach behaviors that the "special" school had not been able to teach. We used the video camera to document our son at his school, at home, and during the therapy sessions.

These are two important factors. We were able to present the committee with conclusive proof that the system had failed, and we were able to document a more successful way. There was no disputing the effectiveness of the Lovaas approach, or that we were capable educators. We knew that we had to convince the committee of the following:

1) That the system had failed and would continue to fail. This would cost the district hundreds of thousands of dollars over the course of our son's education (to age twenty-one or graduation).

2) That the Lovaas program worked.

3) That we were capable of running such a program (i.e. training teachers, etc.).

4) That the cost-effectiveness of this program was remarkable.

Before we met with the committee, we prepared every detail. All information pertaining to our son was presented in the standard recognized format required from any school. The committee was the jury, and we had to present our case in an effective, convincing manner. We had been allotted forty-five minutes to present our case. This meant *rehearsing* and *editing* our case with friends and family. We made certain that every minute was maximized and that all relevant points were covered.

We prepared a detailed report that included: an introductory statement, copies of all available articles regarding Lovaas, letters of recommendation from all credible sources, a copy of our son's old IEP, a copy of his new IEP, a breakdown of funds requested, copies of *The Me Book,* a concluding statement, and a videotape. A copy of this report was presented to every member of the committee.

The video was a key factor in presenting a successful case. It took our presentation out of the abstract and brought it to reality. We edited the video down to eight minutes. Video segments lasted between fifteen and sixty seconds. It was very important to show the following:

1) Our son displaying poor behaviors prior to the Lovaas therapy.
2) Our son at the "special" school. This reinforced the hopelessness of the traditional system.
3) Our son in Lovaas therapy, with parents and nonprofessionals as educators. We showed the best behaviors he had acquired.

The video created a necessary contrast, from the worst to the best. It made an impression that lasted long after our presentation had finished. It made the Lovaas therapy come alive, it made our son very real, and it made the issues concerning his potential very focused.

The combination of these outlined factors played a hand in convincing the committee to support our efforts with partial funding.

By chance, I spoke with one of the committee members in a parking lot a year after our presentation. She told me that one of the key factors in our receiving funding was the video. Even with all the other convincing information, the video made it very real, and motivated them to take a chance on a radically different approach.

LYNN ADAMS, another parent of a young boy diagnosed with autism, also writes of the necessity of bringing convincing evidence and documentation to the meeting with the local school district. I find her story somewhat different from the norm in that almost everyone she first spoke to—pediatrician, local professor of psychology, director of the local mental health center—was supportive of behavioral therapy. Nevertheless, she still had to marshal the evidence and the professional support to build a case for funding. Lynn also shares her experience with respect to the finding and training of therapists.

Our son was diagnosed at age two-and-a-half with infantile autism. As we began to research this disorder, many articles and texts mentioned the name Ivar Lovaas. His work indicated that a significant percent of children had made astounding progress using one-on-one behavioral therapy. The first two professionals we spoke to about Dr. Lovaas were our son's pediatrician and the director of our local mental health center. The pediatrician was not familiar with his work, but copied a section on autism from her text *Developmental Behavioral Pediatrics*. Dr. Lovaas was mentioned numerous times throughout this text as having found a viable intervention for young autistic children. When we spoke with the director of our mental health center he said, without hesitation, "Ivar Lovaas is the leading authority on autism in this country at this time."

We immediately set out to implement a Lovaas program for our child. We contacted educators, ministers, child care facilities, and our local community college in our search for therapists. Dr. Lovaas' clinical supervisor, who would later conduct our workshops, explained the criteria for a therapist. She told us that our priority for a therapist should not necessarily be an educational background, but a willingness and ability to learn behavioral methods. A friend came to visit during this time and listened as we discussed our search for a therapist. This friend had nearly twenty years' experience in the child care profession. She expressed an interest in doing this work with our child. It soon became very apparent that she would make an excellent therapist. She attended our initial workshop and everyone, including Dr. Lovaas' representative, was very impressed with her ability to learn and implement behavioral theory. . . .

Later it would become necessary to hire and train other therapists. We had made contact with a professor of psychology at our local community college, and he was very enthusiastic about helping us. He sent several students whom he had carefully selected to be interviewed. We found excellent therapists through this man's efforts, and they received college credits in addition to the pay for their work. We continued to have follow-up workshops [with the Lovaas Clinic personnel] to update our child's program and to insure that all people involved with our child were professionally trained soon after they were hired.

The reality of our financial situation was that our money, even our borrowing power, would soon end. My son was approximately fifteen months into his program when he became of age to receive services from our local school district. . . .

Formal negotiations with the school system began in April 1991. By this time we had provided school officials with much documentation of Dr. Lovaas' work, many informational articles, a letter of recommendation from our pediatrician, and, most importantly, Dr. Lovaas' clinical findings—statistics indicating that intensive behavioral therapy was not only a viable intervention, but the most appropriate educational program for a young child with autism.

During our first formal meeting to develop an IEP we were offered a placement for him with eleven other handicapped children [eleven students to one teacher] and an assurance that he would receive [appropriate] therapy. We stood our ground and told the school administrator that this was inappropriate for our child. We pointed out that we had carefully researched and documented the program we felt was appropriate for our child. We further stated that if there were any documentation of success with the type of program they were offering we would consider their offer.

Several informal discussions followed. . . . We located a local advocacy group sponsored by the Association for Retarded Citizens. The primary function of this group is to give advice and support to parents dealing with their school system. A representative from this group came with us to our final meeting. She acted as a buffer between all parties involved. This was a great help to us, and all parents should check to see if there is a similar group available in their area.

The meeting began with another offer of a classroom setting and the administrators were vague about how many other children would be present. We explained that saying you are implementing a Lovaas program in a classroom with several other children present is a contradiction in terms. The teacher designated to implement the program read the IEP that we had developed together (taken directly from our Lovaas consultation report). It soon became apparent to all involved that one-on-one therapy was the only way to meet these goals. The teacher expressed a willingness to work with our child individually and in natural settings, including our home. She believed in behavioral theory and had studied this concept while obtaining her special-education degree.

Suddenly we were sitting there listening to an offer consisting of everything we had asked for. We were offered thirty hours per week of one-on-one behavior modification therapy, two half hours per week of speech therapy and structured peer modeling using kindergarten children specially chosen for this program. We also have biweekly meetings to revise and update our child's program. He is now in the hands of competent, caring professionals, receiving the "free and appropriate education" to which he is entitled.

Who Will Take Charge?

Who will take charge of the child's education?

I believe strongly in the empowerment of parents. Most of the parents to whom I've spoken recognize the magnitude of the challenges they face. All of us need the support of good therapists and good psychologists. But rather than giving our child completely over to some program or institution, rather than giving up in despair, most of us want one thing: to be shown *what to do,* to be empowered. In the history of autism therapy, we have either been blamed for our children's condition or been patted on the head and told to leave everything to the professionals—many of whom haven't changed their ideas on autism therapy since their last psychology class, fifteen, twenty, or however many years ago. If we raise our expectations, demand the best and most effective teaching for our children, and demand that the professional community teach *us* as well, we are on our way to effecting a profound and far-reaching change in the way the majority of autistic children are educated in this country. Katherine, mother of a seven-year-old autistic boy, Gregg, writes of her frustration with what she perceives as a paternalistic attitude, even among the best-informed and most well-intentioned professionals. Her poignant letter to a local support group challenges the assumption that all parents need is a listening ear, a shoulder to cry on, a sympathetic sharing. Although the people who ran the group were well versed in behavioral strategies, they seemed reluctant to burden the parents with "too much" information:

Dear Mrs. Andrews,

My family has been a member of your organization, after re-locating from out of state, for over two years. In that time, my husband and I have attended your Seven Week Parent Training Workshop, your many "advanced parent workshops," and the Annual Conference.

A few evenings ago, I attended your parent workshop entitled "Teaching Social Skills" along with 50 other parents of children with autism. I was reminded that evening of a disturbing condescension I always encounter at these training sessions.

It doesn't seem to matter who is conducting the training workshop, or what is the subject matter. We are spoon-fed the information, and then discouraged from attempting to teach our children too much. As the instructor cautioned more than once that evening, "Don't try to take on too much and become overwhelmed." I can tell you that we parents do not appreciate such patronizing remarks. During the "Social Skills" workshop we were also instructed to "speak with your schools" every time the subject of implementing certain programs came up. In other words, leave it to the professionals. One mother asked, "There are so many social skills to teach my son. Where do I begin?" The instructor responded by saying, "Don't let yourself get overwhelmed. Try one skill when you can—even once a week. You don't want to get yourself too stressed out."

Mrs. Andrews, these parents are already stressed out. That is why they have given up an evening to learn how they can change their children's and families' lives. These are parents who are eager not only to advocate, but to implement at home what they are learning. They are motivated people who are strongly invested in their children, as no one else will ever be.

At the workshop I also witnessed excitement when a parent would share an idea or strategy they had tried on their own child. For example, I described some strategies that had recently been taught to me—strategies that were enabling my son to play with his sister for the first time. After I finished, ten hands shot up with questions for me. All the parents wanted to know how they could initiate this program with their own children. There was such enthusiasm in their questions and such a desire to try.

You have a captured and willing audience coming to your workshops. They want to change the way parents have been left out of the teaching process by the professional community. They understand the great impact they can have on their children's development. They are also painfully aware of the importance of time in carrying out the many therapeutic treatments. Teaching their children is always a race against time, trying to catch up. Time is being wasted when you are told to step back and remain uninvolved.

Mrs. Andrews, I am asking you to use your training sessions to give parents the necessary skills to effect real change in their children. They say "a bit of encouragement goes a long way." I have been fortunate, over the years, to receive great encouragement and practical advice from various sources. I believe that with raised expectation, training, concrete information and hard work—in school *and* at home—our children with autism can go very far. My experience with my son has reinforced this belief many times over.

I recognize your good intentions and thank you for your commitment to all of us. But please understand that our children's success depends on our ability as parents to make every known effort possible. To offer ourselves to them not only as a committed parent, but as a teacher as well, is essential to changing the quality of their lives. Perhaps one of the keys to recovering our children from autism will be in how early and how quickly parents can react to the disability with a well-planned and well-executed home/school program. In the future, I hope your organization will meet this challenge, by telling parents how important they are in the education of their children. Our children deserve this, and we parents today will accept nothing less.

Recently, a friend of mine heard a psychologist expressing the fervent wish that "parents wouldn't start demanding this 'thirty-to-forty-hours-a-week of therapy' business." Why not? he was asked. How can they pay for that? he fumed. "I don't want to see parents having to take out a second mortgage on their homes!"

I reflected on that comment for a long time. It is true that money is a very real issue, and poses a significant problem for many parents of autistic children. There are ways of funding the therapy, as I have tried to indicate, but even so, the struggle to obtain these funds can be very difficult. Nevertheless, I would respectfully submit to that psychologist that it is not his responsibility or right to make that decision for parents. I would ask that psychologist to reflect on one question only, when he is so vehemently "protecting" parents from knowledge of what is out there: Would he want someone protecting him in such a fashion if this were his own child?

All of these stories and comments from parents reflect the difficulties people often face in obtaining appropriate intervention for their autistic children. It takes organization, commitment, courage, time, money. And over and over again, the point must be made that, though powerful and effective, behavioral therapy is not a panacea, not a miracle cure.

But difficult as the current state of affairs may be, it is still better than the universal hopelessness or the inflated promises that held sway just a few years ago. Whether the result is full recovery or slow and steady progress, intensive behavioral therapy begun as early as possible can offer parents today a means of fighting autism and teaching their children. Let us work to provide this educational service to all autistic children, regardless of age or severity of condition, and to all families, regardless of income.

Afterword

by

O. IVAR LOVAAS, PH.D.

University of California,
Los Angeles

READING CATHERINE MAURICE'S *Let Me Hear Your Voice*, I am forcefully reminded that only parents can adequately describe the agony and despair of living with a child who seems born into another world, so enormously isolated that all efforts to reach for contact fail. These parents observe a child who engages in never-ending ritualistic bodily movements, does not play with toys or other children, and does not develop meaningful language. As days, weeks, and years pass by they watch their children gradually deteriorate, falling further and further behind. Then, when they seek help for their children, they are given contradictory advice. Some professionals deny the validity of the parents' concern ("It will go away"). Others authoritatively state that the child has a profound pathology which cannot be altered. Still others boldly claim that they have a program which will help, but cannot document their claims. Many play destructive games in which they blame parents for causing their child's condition. Catherine Maurice presents the clearest description that I have read of the abnormal development of autistic children and the problems one encounters in seeking treatment for autism. By reading this book, students and professionals will gain a better understanding of the problems these children present and the stresses that parents experience. This understanding will enable them to offer more effective help.

In addition to providing a firsthand account of living with and teaching autistic children, this book also demonstrates the importance of selecting treatments that are supported with scientific data. It is an embarrassment to clinical psychology, psychiatry, and special education that it has been parents who have insisted that professionals become accountable and prove that their treatments work. Bernard Rimland, author of *Infantile Autism* and himself the parent of an autistic child, presented evidence that helped stop the abuses of psychoanalytically derived treatments which harmed autistic children and their families. Catherine Maurice takes on more recent and equally destructive practices in which professionals advocate unproven treatments and often charge enormous amounts of money for their "services." Parents must have a great deal of courage to face such confusion and demand better. Once pressure is placed on professionals to document their treatments' effectiveness by objective, peer-reviewed data, the foundation will have been laid for progress. Science will generate effective treatments for autism, and parents will seek them out. The same has happened in other areas of inquiry, such as in medicine.

Behavioral treatment is presented in a very favorable light in this book, and it is appropriate to provide an evaluation of this treatment. It is based on research in the instinctive and learned behavior of animals and humans, and began with the work of Darwin and Pavlov in the nineteenth and early twentieth centuries. An enormous amount of research has been generated, and laws of learning have been discovered. These laws describe proven procedures for altering behavior. About thirty years ago, investigators began to apply these laws to the behavioral treatment of autistic and other developmentally disabled persons. In a relatively short period of time, behavioral treatment has become the treatment of choice for these persons.

The effects of behavioral treatment can be summarized as follows: On the positive side, all clients appear to learn some adaptive behaviors, including complex behaviors like imitation and language. Maladapative behaviors, like self-injury, can be reduced. Some children have responded dramatically to this treatment, as did the Maurice children, and have progressed to a point where they can be considered normal-functioning: their cognitive, linguistic, and social behaviors no longer show the deviance associated with the autistic condition. According to our data forty-seven percent of the autistic children we treated before the age of three and a half attained normal intellectual functioning and passed first grade in a normal school by the age of seven (O. Ivar Lovaas, "Behavioral Treatment and Normal Educational and Intellectual Functioning in Young Austistic Children," *Journal of Consulting and Clinical Psychology* 55 [1987], 3–9). Recent follow-up data, taken when the children we treated averaged thirteen years of age, showed that their treatment gains were maintained and that their cognitive, emotional, and social functioning still appeared normalized (John McEachin, Tristram Smith, and O. Ivar Lovaas, "Outcome in

Adolescence of Autistic Children Receiving Early Intensive Behavioral Treatment," *American Journal of Mental Retardation,* in press).

On the negative side, some children learn much more slowly than others. Many clients, even though treated early in life, cannot be successfully integrated with normal peers, and relapse if treatment is terminated—although some progress will resume if treatment is reinstated. Perhaps the most difficult questions in the treatment of autism remain to be answered.

Adding to these difficulties is the scarcity of adequately trained therapists. Training should ideally include academic course work on basic research in learning theory as well as six to twelve months of supervised practice in delivering one-to-one treatment. Once trained, a competent practitioner must stay up to date, as programs are continuously evolving and improving. While some parents and volunteers have managed to become effective therapists for an autistic child, such efforts are exceedingly taxing and daunting. Obviously, what is needed is a far greater number of academic programs offering both theoretical and practical formation in this field—academic programs adhering to rigorous and uniform certification requirements. Equally obviously, parents need to be able to afford such therapists once they can be found. As of now, most parents still face a serious struggle in funding treatment for their child.

While there is still a long way to go before resolving these problems and satisfying these needs, we can nevertheless take hope and comfort from stories such as Catherine Maurice's. *Let Me Hear Your Voice,* while recognizing these inadequacies and problems of behavioral intervention, still attests to the progress that some children can finally make in triumphing over autism.

APPENDIXES

Appendix I

DIAGNOSIS

The entire issue of diagnosis is a proverbial can of worms. Parents can take the same child to six different psychiatrists and get any one of these labels tacked onto him:

> Pervasive developmental disorder
> Pervasive developmental disorder with autistic features
> Pervasive developmental disorder with autistic tendencies
> Pervasive developmental disorder, autistic-like
> Emotionally disturbed
> Autistic

What is the difference among all these?

It's almost impossible to get a straight answer. But the first time one hears of any of these terms other than "autism," one does have the impression that "pervasive developmental disorder" means something qualitatively different from "autism."

I went to the source of this diagnostic terminology to find out for myself if there was any clear distinction among the terms. The standard reference is the *Diagnostic and Statistical Manual of Mental Disorders, Third Edition—Revised* (DSM, III-R).

Pervasive developmental disorders is a diagnostic category, like mental retardation, or delusional disorders, or personality disorders. Its primary criterion is that it begins in early childhood or infancy. Its characteristic features include:

> 1) Qualitative impairment in reciprocal social relations
> 2) Impairment in communication and imaginative activity
> 3) Markedly restricted repertoire of activities and interests

In addition, there is a long list of associated features—stereotypical mannerisms, sleep disorders, odd responses to sensory input, etc. "In general, the younger the child and the more severe the handicap, the more associated features are likely to be present."

And prognosis for PDD? "Manifestations of the disorder are, in almost all cases, lifelong."

Autistic disorder falls under the heading of pervasive developmental disorders. It is one of the subcategories. Autistic disorder is the most severe form of PDD and has to meet at least eight of sixteen criteria for diagnosis.

And finally there is *pervasive developmental disorder—not otherwise specified.* This diagnostic category again involves a "qualitative impairment in the development of reciprocal social interaction and of verbal and non-verbal communication skills, but the criteria are not met for autistic disorder. . . . Some people with this diagnosis will exhibit a markedly restricted repertoire of behaviors, others will not."

That's what the book says. How and in what cases the individual psychiatrists apply this information is pretty idiosyncratic. I have seen children who I felt were more severely impaired than Anne-Marie receive only the diagnosis of PDD, or "autistic tendencies."

Most parents I've come to know don't pay too much attention, at least after a while, to trying to figure out these various terms. They're smart enough to know that whether their child gets a "PDD" or an "infantile autism," they had better treat the problem with the same urgency. But other parents, unfortunately, are led to believe, or choose to believe, that PDD means "not very severe." I will never forget a mother's sigh of relief after three harrowing weeks of diagnosis for her young son: "He's OK!" she told me in a phone conversation. "All he has is PDD!" To her, it seemed to mean he was not autistic and therefore would be fine, that he was merely in some sort of passing phase. I suggest that any parent who hears the statement "He's not autistic, he's only PDD" ask the professional pronouncing these words to explain the difference in prognosis between the two labels.*

---

*Again, the Autism Research Institute, 4182 Adams Avenue, San Diego, CA 92116, can be helpful when there is confusion or contradiction concerning the diagnosis of a child. The ARI collects and disseminates information on the diagnosis, cause, and treatment of autism, and provides a diagnostic service to parents and professionals. Parents fill out a four-page questionnaire, the form E-2 Diagnostic Checklist, which is then returned to the institute for evaluation. The checklist is scored by computer and a report sent to the parent or professional. There is no charge for this service, which has been provided for nearly 14,000 children to date.

Appendix II

INSTRUCTIONAL PROGRAMS

Introduction

"Behavioral therapy" is somewhat of a misnomer. Some people have had the impression that Bridget worked exclusively on behavior while Robin worked on language. In fact, Bridget's behavioral program focused mostly on verbal and nonverbal communication: play, cognition, socialization. The word "behavioral" refers to a style of teaching: emphasis on discrete trials, breaking down tasks, the systematic use of reinforcement and praise, etc. "Behavioral therapy" is also the general term used to indicate an extensive curriculum for learning-handicapped children developed over the past twenty-five years by Ivar Lovaas and many other researchers in the professional community. As such, it has been used with children who have received a wide range of diagnoses—from autistic to mentally retarded, to language-delayed, to "disturbed," etc.

I have decided to give an overview of Michel's curriculum. Originally I had included the curricula for both children, but found that there was a lot of redundancy. Also, we were better organized for Michel's program, and our notes are more extensive and systematic.

These programs are *not* intended as a prescription for any child. Each child's needs will vary, and each child's progression will be different. They are outlined here for two reasons:

1) In order to give some idea of the work that was done in our behavioral sessions, without boring the general reader with too much technical and repetitive information. It is important to reiterate the point I have tried to stress throughout this book: there was no "quick fix" magic cure. There was a lot of tedious work. The actual program notes for both children comprise a file of over 1,000 pages.

2) In order to offer as much information and assistance as I can to parents of autistic children—especially those who cannot find a good therapeutic program in which to enroll their child. Even though the curriculum outlined here was developed specifically for Michel, there may be some

information that can be used, adapted, or reformulated
for other children.

I strongly recommend, however, that any parent attempting to set up a
home program read *The Me Book*,, where the teaching method is explained
and many of these programs can be found. In addition, the parent will need
the help of a trained behavioral therapist to demonstrate the teaching and
to help set up a curriculum for that particular child.

The Me Book may be obtained by writing or calling the Pro-Ed company:

> Pro-Ed
> 8700 Shoal Creek Boulevard
> Austin, TX 78758-6897
> Tel. (512) 451-3246
> Fax (512) 451-8542

Therapists are difficult to find. College students, especially those
studying special education, make good candidates for training. Recently,
a father who was setting up a home program informed me that the career
placement offices of colleges and universities yield more candidates than
psychology or special-education departments. When we were first looking,
we put up notices at several colleges and universities. The most important
step is to find one experienced person who will then be able to train and
supervise others. Supervision must be constant. Contact the Lovaas Clinic
and ask them to send a clinic supervisor to conduct an initial workshop
and to help train any people you find.

> Ivar Lovaas, Ph.D.
> Department of Psychology
> University of California, Los Angeles
> 1282A Franz Hall
> 405 Hilgard Avenue
> Los Angeles, CA 90024-1563

The pacing of the programs is extremely important, so that the child is
neither rushed nor bored nor overwhelmed.

Reinforcement should be very frequent at the beginning, and varied.
Experiment with many different forms of reinforcement and praise. Food
and drink are primary reinforcers, but tickling, hugging, and smiling can
be powerful reinforcers as soon as you get the child's attention.

Many teaching materials can be ordered through educational resource
catalogues. We found excellent emotion-labeling photographs, sequencing
cards, action-labeling cards, and much more through these catalogues.

Constructive Playthings
1227 East 119th Street
Grandview, MO 64030
(800) 255-6124

Kaplan School Supply Corporation
P.O. Box 609
Lewisville, NC 27023-0609
(800) 334-2014

There is obviously much more to say about behavioral therapy, and this appendix can presume to impart only the broadest idea of what the techniques and curriculum entailed in the case of Michel. Nothing written will ever approximate watching a good therapist actually working with a child.

I regret the summary format: space does not permit a detailed analysis of all the programs.

Glossary

baseline: the child's unassisted performance on a certain task. The therapist asks the child to do something or say something, and offers no prompts or assistance. One collects baseline data on a skill to assess how much the child already knows and can do on his own. For example, you "baseline" the prepositions "on" and "under" by asking the child to put something on or under a chair and seeing if he understands without assistance.

DRA: differential reinforcement of alternative behavior, the attempt to extinguish an inappropriate behavior by rewarding the child for another, more appropriate behavior (reinforcing that behavior). Let's say the child is perseveratively lining up blocks. Instead of saying "No lining up blocks," which might, in certain circumstances, simply increase the behavior, you give the child some other, easy task to do, one that you know he has already mastered, and then you praise him for completing that alternative task. You're looking to set up a situation where you can ignore the autistic or inappropriate behavior and reward an alternative behavior. When Michel was crying and whining in therapy, we used a DRA of "good quiet, good listening" every time he had a five-minute period of no whining.

expressive language: verbal use of language. The terms "expressive language" and "receptive language," or understanding of language, can be paired with any word you're trying to teach. For instance, if you're teaching "expressive his and her," it means you're trying to teach the child to *use* the words "his" and "her" appropriately. If you're teaching "receptive his and her" you're trying to teach him to *understand* the distinction. Receptive skills usually are taught before expressive skills.

fading prompts: gradually withdrawing physical and verbal cues. It is im-

Appendix II

portant that the child not become "prompt-dependent." See *The Me Book* for a full discussion of prompt usage and prompt fading.

modeling: the therapist's modeling (demonstrating) of the correct answer for a child. Modeling is used heavily and extensively at the beginning of expressive language, then faded as the child grows more proficient. Modeling differs from verbal prompting in that the therapist demonstrates the full word, not just the beginning sound of a word. "Juice" is a verbal model; "ju . . ." is a verbal prompt.

prompts: the therapist's physical or verbal assistance in the completion of a task. An example of a verbal prompt is saying "sh . . ." when you want the child to say "shoe." An example of a physical prompt would be shaping the child's fingers into a "point."

randomizing tasks: mixing previously learned tasks within the same drill. Example: First you teach receptive "Touch head," then "Touch leg," then "Touch arm." When the child has mastered them separately, you mix all three in the same drill.

receptive language: understanding of language. See *expressive language*.

Sd: "discriminatory stimulus" (I don't know why the initials are backward!), the particular stimulus, usually a verbal command, that the therapist gives to elicit a particular response. The Sd's are very consistent in the beginning—for instance, "Put with same," but then they become more flexible and varied: "Would you put all the red blocks together?"

Michel's Curriculum

GENERAL PRINCIPLES FOLLOWED:

1. Eye contact accompanied each trial of each drill.
2. Each discrete skill was mastered before moving on to randomization of commands.
3. We varied the reinforcements constantly to maintain their effectiveness.
4. We worked through tantrums and resistant behavior.

Note: Skills *within* a category are arranged in a hierarchical order, from easier to more difficult. However, during each session, skills from several *different* categories were taught.

Inst. refers to Instructor. M. refers to Michel.

FROM FEBRUARY THROUGH JUNE 1990

1. Attending

The "Look at me" program was crucial for teaching M. how to pay attention. M. is prompted to sit in chair, hands quiet. Inst. sits close, allows no slouching, falling to the floor, or turning away. Inst. consistent, firm, and demanding: praising, hugging, and stroking for any compliance. Getting M. to pay attention is a major first step.

i. Look at me
Face to face
   One second
   Two seconds
   Five seconds
From activity to adult (that is, setting him up with an activity, then teaching him to look up and make eye contact in the middle of that activity, when the adult says "Look at me")
(Inst. prompts by putting hand under chin and holding food or other reinforcer up to eye level.)

ii. Responding to his name
Making eye contact upon Sd: "Michel"
Face to face
Activity to adult

2. *Following One-Step Instructions*
   Commands:
      Sit down
      Stand up
      Come here
      Hands down
      Clap hands
      Arms up
      Give hug
      Turn around
      Stomp feet
      Wave
      Etc.
   Physically prompt, then fade.

   Body Parts
   Sd = "Touch ——
      Head
      Nose
      Feet
      Tummy
      Eyes
      Legs
      Etc.

   Action commands (receptive language)
   Sd = "Show me"
      Eating

Drinking
Clapping
Waving
Hugging
Turning
Standing
Sitting
Walking
Running
Etc.

3. *Motor Imitation*

Sd = "Do this"

Gross motor actions

Clap hands
Arms up
Tap legs
Tap table
Touch head
Indian noises (tapping mouth with hand)
Stomp feet
Stand up
Shake head no
Nod head yes
Etc.

Fine motor actions

Pointing
Opening and closing hands
Touching various body parts
Etc.

Block imitation

Inst. puts blocks into a certain configuration, prompts M. to imitate the pattern. Start with three blocks, work up to five.

Object imitation

Inst. teaches imitation skills by using objects. Prompts M. to put a spoon into a cup, wipe the dolly's nose with a facial tissue, put the toy car into the toy garage, etc.

Grapho-motor imitation (pencil grasp, lines, circles, etc.)

4. *Point Response*

Point response—hold up desired item, state Sd: "Point," prompt his hand to point directly to desired item (touching it), then give him item. Fade prompts and distance of item.

Point to items upon Sd: "What do you want?"
Point spontaneously

Point plus verbal approximation
Point plus "want" and label of object
Point plus "I want——"

5. *Matching*
    Object to object
    Picture to object
    Picture to picture
    Color to color
    Letters
    Numbers

6. *Verbal Imitation*
    Vowels
    Consonants
    Vowel/consonant
    Consonant/vowel
    Consonant/vowel/consonant
    Words
    Word combinations

(Accept any approximation at the beginning; gradually "shape" sound into more exact imitation.)

7. *Play*
    Shape sorter
    Beads
    Blocks
    Music (tape recorder with songs)
    Beginner books
    Jack-in-the-box
    Farm animal puzzle
    Clock puzzle
    Number puzzle
    Musical percussion instruments

(Inst. makes animal sounds and actions with farm animal pieces.)

8. *Object Discrimination*
    Sd: "Give me"
    Ball
    Cup
    Shoe
    Etc.

(Gradually increase number of objects on the table.)

9. *Picture Discrimination* (For Receptive Vocabulary)
    Sd: "Point to ——"
    Start with two pictures, work up to many.

10. *Object Labeling* (For Expressive Vocabulary)
    Sd: "What is this?" Use real objects or pictures. Accept any
    approximation at the beginning.

11. *Yes/No*
    Head shake no—undesired food
    Head nod yes—desired food
    Prompt, then fade.

12. *Action Labels* (Expressive)
    i. With reference to instructor
    Sd: "What am I doing?"
       Waving
       Jumping
       Standing
       Sitting
       Clapping
       Running
       Sneezing
       Kissing
       Laughing
       Walking
       Sleeping
       Opening
       Drinking
       Eating
       Crying
       Etc.

(Model response, and accept any approximation at the beginning.)

    ii. With reference to self
    Sd: "What are you doing?"

    iii. With reference to others (pictures)
    Sd: "What is he/she doing?"

(Require only the verb at the beginning, e.g., "jumping.")

13. *Colors* (First Receptive, Then Expressive)

    i. Sd: "Point to red/blue/yellow, etc."

    ii. Sd: "What color is the ——?" Hold up object.

    (Model, then prompt, then fade prompt.)

14. *Possession*
    Sd: "Point to Bridget's shoe."
    Sd: "Point to Michel's shoe."
    (Laying foundation for My/Your program)

15. Shapes (First Receptive, Then Expressive)

   Sd: "Point to square, circle, triangle, etc."

   Sd: "What shape is this?" Use appropriately shaped wooden or plastic blocks. Model correct answer, then fade.

FROM JULY THROUGH AUGUST 1990

Maintaining all programs, including eye contact.

1. Attributes

   Big/little (receptive)

   Sd: "Point to big car/little car."

2. Action/Object Label (Expressive)

   "Drinking juice"

   "Eating cookie"

   In pictures (Sd: "What is she/he doing?")

   With reference to self (Sd: "What are you doing?")

   With reference to instructor (Sd: "What am I doing?")

3. New Colors (Receptive/Expressive)

4. Possessives (Expressive)

   "Whose shoe?"—"Bridget's shoe/Michel's shoe."

5. Making Choices

   "Do you want —— or ——?"

6. Chaining Imitation

   "Do this and this." (Tap table and touch nose, etc.)

7. Continue Block Imitation

8. Giving/Retrieving Two to Three Objects

   "Give me —— and —— and ——." Start at table. Then have him retrieve objects from around the room. Good for short-term memory.

9. Two-Step Directions: Receptive Language

   "Stand up and turn around," etc.

(Each separate command has already been mastered.)

10. Yes/No (Negation)

   "Is this a ——?" E.g., hold up teddy bear and ask, "Is this a horse?"

11. Play

   Beginning doll play with small figures: Mommy, Daddy, boy, girl, baby. Modeling simple actions: eating, sleeping, singing row-row-row, etc.

Looking through books together. Pointing at pictures. Ball bouncing and rolling. Prompt for return of ball. Sit close at beginning. Singing together. Praise for making any sound to the music.

Mr. Potato Head toy. Incidentally reinforce body parts: eyes, nose, mouth, ears, etc.

12. *Making Verbal Requests in Short Sentences* (Expand Sentences)
     Model: "I want ——." "Can I have a ——?"

13. *Identifying Emotional States* (Receptive/Expressive)
     Happy/sad/angry
     Sd: "How does she/he feel?" Use pictures.

(Model response, then prompt, then fade, then generalize program to magazine photographs and storybooks.)

14. *"My/Your"* (Receptive)
     With shoe
     Sd: "Give me *my* shoe."/"Give me *your* shoe."

(This is probably the hardest of the linguistic programs to teach, even more difficult than the later expressive questions. "My" and "your" are, obviously, words that are nonfixed—speaker-dependent. First we had to teach it *receptively*. That is, Inst. had to teach it *as though* the word "my" always referred to Inst., and "your" always referred to M. Then, when we taught it expressively, we had to teach M. the opposite: that is, when M. is speaking, the word "my" refers to M., and the word "your" refers to Inst.

"I" and "you" are also frequently confused in autistic speech.

Various psychologists and psychiatrists of the love-and-understanding school have of course had a grand time constructing elaborate notions of the lack of self-worth and self-identity that leads to the pronoun reversal so common in autism. Anyone who is interested in a more plausible explanation should read Dr. Rimland's illuminating discussion, in *Infantile Autism,* of the overall difficulty that autistic persons have in making abstract leaps in language: in exercising that innate ability that nonhandicapped persons have to infer, to transform, to generalize, and to build upon the raw linguistic data that comes in, rather than merely repeating it.

It seems to me that Noam Chomsky's famous "Language Acquisition Device"—that something in the brain that enables us to "naturally" learn the changing referents of "I" and "you" and "my" and "your," etc.—is not lacking in children like Anne-Marie and Michel; otherwise they could never have mastered such abstractions through our clumsy programs. But it does have to be "jump-started," which is precisely what we were trying to do with our endless drills. Both children eventually got it.)

15. *Verbal Imitation*
    "f" plus vowel
    "b" words

16. *Receptive "Where?" Plus Expressive in, On, Under*
    Sd: "Where's the whistle?"
    Model: "In the box/under the box/on the box."

17. *Receptive "Who?"*
    Use photos to elicit Mommy, Daddy, Daniel, Anne-Marie, Patsy, etc. (other familiar people)

18. *Receptive "What Is —— Doing?"*
    Use photographs of familiar people doing specific things (e.g., drinking juice), as well as picture cards.

FROM SEPTEMBER 1 TO NOVEMBER 15, 1990

(There are many programs, so each therapist is doing about ten programs per two-hour session, usually targeting what the other therapist has not done that day.)

1. *Begin Toilet Training*

2. *Attributes*
   Hot/cold; long/short; heavy/light; etc.
   Sd: "Show me '*heavy.*' " Use educational picture cards specifically targeting these different attributes.

3. *Pronouns*
   Receptive my/your with shoe
   Expressive he/she
   Sd: "What is *he* doing?/What is *she* doing?" Model "He is ——/She is ——, then fade.

4. *Two-Step Directions* (Maintain)

5. *Prepositions* (Receptive and Expressive; Continued)
   Next to/behind/in front of

6. *Colors* (continued)

7. *Emotion Labeling* (continued)
   Pictures
   Face to face (Sd: "How do I feel?" Inst. makes a happy, sad, angry, etc., face.)

8. *Discrimination of Wh/Questions* (continued)
   Who is this/What is ——doing/Where is ——? etc.

9. *Subject/Verb/Complement Sentences*
   Describing action pictures of people with fuller syntax: At first accept "Boy eating apple," but *gradually* model fuller

syntax: "The boy is eating an apple." After a while, begin to vary the Sd: "Tell me about this picture./What's happening here?/What's the girl doing?" etc. Maintain expressive prepositions "he" and "she," attributes, action labeling, emotion labeling, and expressive prepositions with this program.

10. *Simple Sentences*
   "I see a ——."
   "It's a ——."
   (Construct an "I see" book. Paste pictures in notebook. One item per page for five pages; two items per page for five pages; three items per page for five pages; etc. Prompt for longer sentences as mastered: "I see a —— and a —— and a ——." Before increasing objects, make sure he says "I see a ball" instead of "I see ball.")

11. *Retrieving Three Objects on Request*

12. *Requests with Name of Adult*
   "Bridget, I want to color," etc. After a while, add *tapping* to this program. Prompt Michel to tap instructor to get attention.

13. *Yes/No Negation* (continued)

14. *Simple Social Questions*
   Name
   Age
   Brother/sister

15. *Play*
   Felt board. Placing felt objects on a felt board to create scenes.

16. *Verbal imitation*
   "r" endings
   "l" blends
   Word combinations
   Correcting M's labeling of objects

17. *Maintaining Attention/Switching Attention*
(It's hard to rank goals in order of importance, but this had to be one of the most important of them.)

   i. Maintaining attention:
   Instructor asks several questions on the same topic, e.g., "See the dog? What he's doing? What color is the dog? Where is he going?" This is not a drill program, it is rather one of our ongoing goals, to be emphasized *incidentally* throughout the sessions, especially during play and book-reading. (Much

later, "maintaining attention" would also come to mean keeping Michel focused on the topic at hand, and limiting silly talk and irrelevant digressions. Some children diagnosed as autistic can speak at length with normal syntax and vocabulary, yet do not readily focus on what their audience (friend, sibling, parent) has asked about or wants to talk about. Of course, a lot of people need help in improving their listening skills, but some "high-functioning" autistic children seem to be consistently off-topic or meandering or silly in their discourse. As this behavior may cause them difficulty in making and keeping friends and in social relations generally, I feel that actively teaching them, at a very young age, to focus and stay on topic is invaluable.)

ii. Switching attention:
   a) My turn/your turn games.

   b) Inst. sits farther away for some programs, yet continues to demand intermittent eye contact. Inst. moves around the room more frequently, or has M. move around the room, yet continues to request his attention.

   c) Inst. begins one program, then says, "Oh no, let's do this instead." Helps with both attention-switching and flexibility.

   d) Inst. sets up an activity, such as drawing, that requires M. to focus on the table, but she maintains conversation and questions throughout the activity, encouraging and praising him for continuing to look up at her and respond to her.

18. *Monitor Tuning Out, Tantrums, Whining, Aggression, Self-stimulatory Behavior*

Increase pace of material to counteract tuning-out behavior. Spend no more than five minutes at a time in chair. Use DRA for "Good sitting," "Good listening," "You're not whining," etc. Increase reinforcement schedule. Experiment with different motivators. "Time out" for aggression (hair pulling). *Note:* One way to unpry little fingers from your hair is to press firmly down on the knuckles: his fingers will open naturally. For hand-flapping, body-tensing, and toe-dancing, state "Quiet hands" at each occurrence, and hold his hands by his side for three seconds. Praise for being still.

19. *Maintain Eye Contact*

20. *Practice "Circle Time"*

Every session now includes "circle time," where Inst. sings songs and reads books, just as Patricia does at Michel's school. Circle time is about fifteen minutes long.

21. *I Don't Know*
    Use cards. Pictures of familiar objects. Sd: "What's this, what's this?" etc. Intersperse a few pictures of unusual objects, such as a spark plug. Model "I don't know." As soon as he has understood this concept, begin generalizing it with books, magazines, etc. When "I don't know" is mastered, prompt him to say "I don't know, what is it?"

22. *Begin Modeling Low Intonation in Speech*
    Michel has begun to speak in a high-pitched, squeaky voice.

23. *Where?* (Expressive)
    (*Note:* Foundation for all expressive questions has already been laid with receptive questions programs.)
    Put two items on floor. Have him get one of the objects twice. On third trial, hide the target object. As he begins to look for it, prompt him to say "Where is the ——?" Full sentence, including "is." Give him object and praise for asking the question.

24. *Begin Drawing with Crayons*
    Simple shapes: square, circle, triangle. Inst. draws face, has M. fill in features, hair, glasses, etc. Inst. draws simple objects, has M. identify ("flower," "ball," etc.). Correct hand position physically prompted. Eventually we graduate to drawing stick figures, then to the beginnings of "scenes" with more than one character in the drawing.

25. *Continue Pretend Games*
    Pretend you're an airplane, monkey, baby, lion, etc., with sounds and actions.

26. *Categories*
    Animals/clothing/food
    Put three category cards on table. Hold up another card from the pile. Sd: "What's this?" Response: "Cat." Inst.: "Good." Sd: What's a cat?" Response: "Animal." Inst.: "Good." Sd: "Match animal." He should then place the cat on the animal pile on the table. Prompt initially, then fade.

FROM NOVEMBER 15, 1990, TO JANUARY 15, 1991

1. *Maintain Animals/Food/Clothing Categories, Add Toys/Food/Drink*

2. *Maintain Prepositions Incidentally Throughout Session, Not in Drill*

3. *Begin Functional Use of Objects*
   Use real objects. three or four on table. Q: "What do you *cut* with?" A: "Scissors."

4. *Maintain "I Don't Know/What Is It?" Program with Real Objects*

5. *Continue Receptive "My/Your"; Begin Receptive "His"*
Use "Buddy" doll. Place Buddy in chair. Sd: "What's *my*
name?/What's *your* name?/What's *his* name?"

(The data show that Michel is still having a lot of trouble with the receptive
"my/your" program. We have to discontinue the "his" program because he
is confused. We then add a verbal prompt to help him with the distinction
between "my" and "your." We structure the program like this: "Give me
my Bridget's shoe/Give me *your* Michel's shoe" where the "my" and "your"
are said very loudly, and the possessor's name very softly. We try to fade this
prompt after a while to *my* Bri- shoe/*your* Mich- shoe, and then finally to fade
it altogether.)

6. *Maintain Yes/No Program*
Attributes: "Are you wet/dry/cold, etc.?"
Identity: "Are you a frog?/A boy?"
Actions: "Are you sleeping?/Am I clapping?"
Emotion labeling: "Is he happy/sad/etc.?"
Object labeling: "Is this a truck or a carrot?"

7. *Begin Reciprocation Programs*
(The aim is to have him reciprocate conversational overtures from others.
It's all very rote at first, as usual, but becomes more natural and childlike as
he gets the concept. This is one of the great programs given to us by the
Lovaas people. We used it very successfully with both children—as soon as
they got the concept, they seemed to enjoy giving information about themselves.)

Sd: *"I'm* coloring with a *blue* crayon." Inst. models response:
"I'm coloring with a *red* crayon."
Sd: *"I'm* wearing *white* shoes."
Sd: "I like *toast* for breakfast," etc.

8. *Model Expressive Who, Where, What Doing, What*
Color Questions Incidentally Throughout Sessions

9. *Introduce Concept of First, Last, Next*
Sd: "What comes first?/What comes next?/What comes last?"
Inst. uses the number puzzle with the numbers laid out in
sequence, so this program is feasible even if M. is not yet
grasping the basic mathematical concept that two is "greater
than" three. For the moment, first, next and last are taught
as a spatial relationship only. Next they will be taught as
temporal relationships:
Sd: "What do you eat first?" Response: "Breakfast." Sd:
"What do you eat next?" Response: "Lunch." Sd: "What do

you eat last?" Response: "Dinner." Etc. Vary questions, find
different examples.

1. Continue "My/Your" (Receptive Only)

2. Retrieving Three Objects
   Start with objects close to him. Fade distance.

3. Three-Scene Sequences with Sequence Cards
   Purpose: to begin teaching the concept of narrative sequencing and story-telling, as well as to facilitate the ongoing goal of expanding creative and spontaneous
   language. Emphasize "first . . . and then . . . the end." Start
   with very rudimentary concepts (a boy filling a glass at
   the faucet and drinking). Model correct verb forms for
   each card: "going to drink . . drinking . . . drank." As his
   language improves, the "story" becomes more syntacti-
   cally and conceptually elaborate. (This is a program that
   we used over many months.) "Sequence cards" can be
   found in educational toy stores or educational catalogues.
   The Ravensburger company, for instance, makes a game
   called "Tell-a-Story." The child must arrange a series of
   picture cards in logical sequence, and then construct a
   story around them. One card may show a girl holding a
   deflated balloon, the second shows her blowing up the
   balloon, the third shows the balloon very large, the fourth
   shows the balloon popping. We instruct Michel to "put
   in order," then assist him to "tell the story." As he grows
   more proficient, we fade our assistance. Sequence cards
   may be found in three-, four-, and five-scene sequences.

4. Begin Expressive Categories
   Sd: "What's a knife?" Model: "Something you cut with."
   (Etc.) Fade prompt as soon as he has the concept. Start this
   program by holding up a knife. After a while, drop all
   visual cues and simply ask, "What's a sweater? What's a
   car?" etc.

5. Functional Objects (Expressive)
   "What do you do with a knife?" "You cut with a knife."

6. Rooms and Furniture
   We use a game we found in a learning resources catalogue:
   a board with pictures of different rooms—bedroom, bathroom, etc.—and little cards with different types of furniture
   and fixtures. Michel has to put the appropriate cards into
   the appropriate rooms. Beginning of more real-world information.

7. *Verbal Imitation*
   Targeting difficult words and sounds.

8. *Why/Because*
   Beginning inferencing with storytelling. Therapist leads him through the reasoning at first: "*Why* is the dog barking? *Because* he sees the cat."

9. *Social Questions*
   Name, age, brother's name, sister's name, "Where do you live?" "How old are you?"

10. *Who, What, Where, What Doing* (continued)

11. *Beginning Comparisons*
    Which is bigger? taller? shorter? etc

12. *Continue Work on Pronouns*
    He/she/I/you/expressive
    For "I" and "you" Inst. asks "What am *I* doing," as she performs some action—jumping, writing, etc." The response should now be the full sentence "*You* are ——" Inst. elicits "I am ——" in a similar manner, by requesting M. to do something, then asking "What are you doing?"

13. *Temporal Markers* (Receptive)
    "After," "soon," "later," "then," "now," "before." Inst. emphasizes these markers contextually during storytelling and play.

14. *Continue Circle Time*

15. *Review Prepositions, Colors, Articles "A" and "The," Attributes*
    Inst. beginning to give more and more choices, both concrete and nonvisual. Many of the programs are now being done in a less formal, less structured way. Children's books are becoming the main teaching material, along with picture cards and games from educational catalogues.

16. *Begin Receptive Plurals*

17. *Begin Same/Different Program*
    Start with "same." Two blocks same, one different on table. Sd: "Give me same." Prompt. Praise and explain. "Good, you gave me the same. They're both the same *color*." Other examples: two spoons, one fork. Two plates, one cup. Etc.

18. *Begin Letter and Number Recognition*
    Start with 1, 2, 3 and A, B, C.

19. *Begin Receptive Number Concept*
    Give me one, two, three—out of a group of four.

20. *Begin More/Less*
    Receptive. Set up two groupings, one more, one less. Sd: "Give me more/give me less."

21. *Recall of Past Event*
    Model past tense of two or three selected verbs. Take M. to another room, have him do something simple that Inst. decides upon, return to session room and ask: "What *did* you do?" Model appropriate response: "I *saw* Mommy; I *got* a fork." It doesn't matter if the past tense is regular or irregular at this point. We're not teaching any grammatical rule. We're practicing language use *in context*, aiming for understanding of the general concept of past tense.

22. *Mine/Yours* (Expressive)
    Sd: "Whose shirt/shoe/nose, etc.?"
    (Trying a different tack to help him with the my/your distinction.)

23. *What's Missing? Game*
    Put out three objects. Have. M. identify. Stone, circle, heart. Prompt M. to cover eyes. Take one away. Sd: "What's missing?" Model response. M. catches on quickly.

    Another type of "What's missing?" game can be done with drawings. Draw picture of face; include nose, mouth, hair, etc., but only one eye. Draw a table, include only three legs, etc. Sd: "What's missing?"

24. *Whose Turn? Your Turn/My Turn Games* (Receptive and Expressive)

25. *Expand Reciprocation*
    Inst: I see a cat and he says "meow."
    M.: I see a cat and he's drinking milk. (M. must continue to add new information.) Model at first, then prompt with "and . . ."

26. *When "I Am" Is Mastered, Move on to "You Are"* (Expressive)

27. *Beginning Reasoning with Common Situations and Storybooks*
    "Why is the girl eating?" "Because she's hungry." "Why do we go to the doctor?" "Why is the boy sleeping?" "Why is the daddy going to the grocery store?"

28. *Incidental*
    Limit verbal perseverations and silly talk. Prompt for varied sentence structures throughout session. Practice different ways of talking about the same thing. (Example: "You got a boo-boo. You hurt your hand. It has a scratch on it. It

hurts. I'll give you a Band-Aid. There. We're taking care of the scratch.")
Continue to redirect jumping and hand-flapping. "No jumping."

FROM APRIL I THROUGH MAY 30, 1991

1. *Emphasize Pronoun Programs*
   i. My/your receptive. Sd: "Touch ——"

   ii. His/her receptive. Two photos of boy/girl on table.
   Sd: "Touch her (nose, etc.)"
   "Touch his ——"

   iii. Randomize above when mastered.

   iv. Mine/yours expressive. Sd: "Whose shirt?"

   v. Your turn/my turn expressive.
   Use "Bambino Lotto" game.

2. *Responding "What" When Someone Calls His Name*

3. *Stop Echoing with Verbal Cue and Finger on Mouth*
   "No echo."

4. *Continue Same/Different Program*
   "What's the same about —— and ——?" "What's different about —— and ——?" Use visual aids.

5. *Use as Normal Language as Possible; Throw in Some Age-Appropriate Slang*
   "Cool," "neat," "wow."

6. *Concept of Absurdity*
   "What's silly about this picture?" Model answer, emphasize word "silly."

7. *Review Prepositions/Shapes*

8. *Which One Doesn't Belong? Why?*
   Use books with series of pictures: three items of food and a car, three people and an animal, etc.

9. *Begin Receptive Concept of "How?"*
   "*How* does this work?" "*How* do you play this game?" "*How* do I open this?" Teach incidentally mostly.

10. *More Symbolic Play*
    Role playing and sequencing. Use "community helpers": firemen putting out a fire, policemen chasing a robber, Daddy making dinner for the kids, etc.

    Pretending: pretend a neutral item, like a block, is a car, plane, sandwich, frog, drink, boat, etc. Acting each word

out. Emphasis on the word "pretending" itself, to help M.
understand meaning.

11. *Continue Verbal Reasoning and Inferencing*
Help M. to begin telling his own stories. Three-part stories.
Main character who goes someplace, does something, or
sees something, then goes home. Example: "Once there was
a little boy who went into the forest and saw a black dog.
He took the dog home. The end." Ask questions after each
story. "Who went into the forest? What did he see? Then
what happened?"

12. *Continue Preacademics with Letters and Numbers*

13. *Getting Information from a Third Party*
Three people in room, e.g.: Inst., Michel, Mommy.
Inst.: What did Mommy have for breakfast?
M.: I don't know.
Inst.: *Ask* Mommy. (Model how to do this)
M.: "Mommy, what did you have for breakfast?"

Practice until he has the concept, then generalize with many
more questions.

14. *Begin Asking "When" Questions with Storybooks;*
Continue Emphasizing "Why" and "How"
Inst. introducing more and more practical, real-world information: times of day, seasons, holidays, names of towns
and cities.

15. *Tell Me About*
Use pictures or photographs or magazines. Sd: "Tell me
about this picture." Then we say, "Tell me more." We are
using more open-ended questions to promote conversation.
This program receives great emphasis over the next couple
of months.

16. *Begin Working with Anne-Marie or Daniel in Room*
When we can interest Anne-Marie or Daniel in one of the
games or stories or pretend scenarios or activities, they furnish wonderful role models for Michel. He is becoming
more interested in them than in us, so we try to use that
interest to further facilitate his learning.

FROM JUNE 1 THROUGH AUGUST 31, 1991

1. *Continue Drawing*

2. *Continue Storytelling and Sequencing*

3. *Emphasize Why/Because*

4. *Emphasize Inferencing from Stories*

5. *Who/What/Where/How/When/Why Questions with Stories*

6. *Observational Learning and Peer Integration*
   Continue working with Anne-Marie or Daniel. Set up one
   play date a week with friend Eric, Evelyne's son. Supervise
   play date and assist sharing and turn-taking. Model getting
   information from and giving information to each other.

(M. is learning new syntactic structures on his own at an ever-faster rate.
Therapy is progressively more relaxed. There are almost no more drills now.
Eye contact continues to be emphasized.)

7. *Continue Role Playing and Sequencing*

8. *Begin Concept of Defining Some Words* (Metalinguistic Concept)
   Model "What does —— mean?" Use a harder word, then
   model asking what it means. Keep definitions clear and simple. Example: "It's really muggy today. . . . What does
   'muggy' mean? . . . 'Muggy' means 'hot and sticky.' " When
   he has the concept, encourage *him* to ask the question.

9. *Continue Working on Flexibility*
   Move easily from one activity to another. Ignore any crying
   or resistance. Keep up the variety of programs and activities.

10. *Verb Tenses* (Expressive)
    At first separately, then randomize:
    What are you doing?
    What did you do?
    What are you going to do?

    "What are you doing?" can be asked in the middle of any
    activity.

    "What did you do?" is asked after Inst. has taken M. to
    another room and done something very specific with
    him—for example, taking M. into the living room, look-
    ing out the living room windows at the traffic below,
    coming back.

    "What are you going to do?" is structured in the following
    way: Inst. tells M. to go do something: "M., go to the li-
    brary and get me a book." Just as M. is leaving the room,
    Inst. stops him and asks, "Michel, what are you going to
    do?"

    Obviously, the program is complicated and each question
    must be mastered receptively and each response mastered
    expressively before attempting to randomize them. Inst. as-
    sists with expressive syntax of all responses until she is able
    to fade back.

11. *Creative Building*
    Making things with Legos, Play-Doh, clay.

12. *Maintaining Topic*
    Maintain one topic of conversation over several turns. Bring in past or future events. Talk about phenomena not present. Use a concrete object to begin conversation if M. needs it.

13. *Look for Syntax Difficulties and Try to Extrapolate Patterns*
    For instance, is M. always leaving out the auxiliary verb? If so, make a game out of emphasizing it. Use Playskool "wee people." Model: "He *is* jumping," "She *is* sleeping," etc. Then ask: "What's *your* person doing?"

    Pay attention to syntax throughout. Emphasize words like "so," "if," "then," "both," etc.

14. *Continue to Work on All Questions, Receptive and Expressive*
    For "how," target all meanings. "How does it taste?" "How do you do that?" "How do you feel?" "How does it work?"

15. *Elicit Spontaneous Questioning of Inst.'s Activities*
    Example: Say, "I'm going to make something." Prompt for "What?"

    Say, "Oh, no!" Prompt him to say "What?" or "What's wrong?"

    Say "Hmm, look at that," while looking at a book away from him. Prompt him to come over and ask, "What is it?"

    Inst. pretends to write, dance, hunt for something, etc. Teach him to say, "What are you doing?"

16. *Keep Reminding Him to Acknowledge Adult During Free Play*
    Keep reinforcing eye contact. Never give him anything unless he prefaces his request with your name or with eye contact. Tell jokes to each other, sing songs to each other, etc.

17. *Continue Work on Categorizing*
    What belongs, doesn't belong? What goes in a circus, a school, a farm, a store, a bedroom, bathroom, etc.?

18. *Guessing Game*
    "I'm thinking of something that swims in the water and has fins," etc.

FROM SEPTEMBER I UNTIL DECEMBER 31, 1991

Continue work on observational learning, peer integration, reciprocal conversation, questioning skills, interactive games and expanded sentence structure.

Work with Daniel or Anne-Marie in room. Preschool letter and number activities, dot-to-dot books, mazes, simple beginning board games like "Candy Land," the "what's missing?" game, pretend play, the "tell me about" program, storytelling, drawing—virtually any of the programs at this point can be shared with Daniel or Anne-Marie or friend Eric. Encourage turn taking and mutual sharing of information and questions. The possibilities for observational learning with another child are endless, and require mostly that the therapist structure a fun activity for both children, then monitor and assist their participation and verbalizations to each other. By this point, other children have become the most important aspect of M.'s therapeutic program.

Speech/Language Reevaluation of Michel
February 1993

After Michel turned five, and as we were looking forward to his entering kindergarten in the fall of 1993, we decided to have his speech and language reevaluated by Margery Rappaport, who had performed an initial speech/ language evaluation in September 1991. We asked her for some objective measurements to determine if his language was still on track, progressing, and truly communicative. Here are her findings:

Michel Maurice was originally seen in this office in September 1991 when he was three years and ten months of age. Mild to moderate speech-language lags were noted at that time. Currently Michel attends preschool five afternoons per week where he was reported to be doing very well. Mrs. Maurice reports that his current teacher describes Michel as "gifted." He is receiving no formal therapy at this time.

RESULTS OF THE EVALUATION

Observations. Michel continues to present with an excellent attention span and no distractibility. He was well related and presented eye gaze that was typical of a child of his age. Michel was highly cooperative for considerable testing, demonstrating cheerfulness and delight in the proceedings, and enormous and rare persistence on questions that were challenging. Michel displayed his creativity and sense of fun by anticipating a task and actually making up questions for the examiner herself to answer.

HEARING: Hearing, based on clinical estimate, appeared to be within normal limits.

PERIPHERAL SPEECH MECHANISM: . . . no abnormalities . . .

ARTICULATION: The Goldman-Fristoe Test of Articulation was readministered. Many errors noted at the initial evaluation have resolved fully. Presently, in addition to age-appropriate substitutions such as th/s, Michel presents a mild lateralization of sh and ch and an occasional intrusive schwa vowel, ə, after plosives. Mild decrease in intelligibility was noted when topic was unknown. This was rectified consistently by a second repetition. Michel was stimulable for correct production of the ch and deletion of the ə, a good prognostic sign.

The Goldman-Fristoe Test of Articulation can also be used to assess naming skills (verbal retrieval) as pictures are flashed in front of the child and confrontation naming skills are required. Michel had no difficulty in the rapid retrieval of these nouns and verbs.

FLUENCY: No clinical dysfluencies were observed.

PHONATION: Vocal pitch, resonance, quality, volume and prosody are currently judged to be within normal limits. Michel now presents good variety and expression in the melody of his speech.

LANGUAGE: Michel's receptive/expressive language progress was evaluated by the readministration of the standardized instruments used at the original evaluation as well as analysis of a current spontaneous language sample. Scores from the present (2/93) and the original evaluation (9/91) will be contrasted.

The Peabody Picture Vocabulary Test–Revised (PPVT–R) was readministered. On this instrument, which evaluates vocabulary comprehension, Michel presents a 28-month increase in his age score over the 14 months since his original testing. This indicates that Michel's semantic knowledge is growing at a rate which well exceeds average expectations.

	9/91	2/93
Standard Score	114	122
Percentile Rank	82	93
Age Score	4–6	6–10

The Test of Auditory Comprehension of Language–Revised (TACL–R) was readministered. On this instrument, Michel jumps from the 69 %ile to the 86 %ile on his total score over the 14 months since his original testing. He currently received a remarkable 97 %ile score on his comprehension of elaborated sentences. His score in comprehension of grammatical morphemes is above average, but not as strong as his other language skills. Considering Michel's overall rate of recovery, this relative weakness is expected to even out over the next six to twelve months, with some particular attention.

	9/91	2/93
TOTAL SCORE	69 %ile	86 %ile
World Classes and Relations	46 %ile	64 %ile
Grammatical Morphemes	74 %ile	58 %ile
Elaborated Sentences	80 %ile	97 %ile

Two subtests from The Illinois Test of Psycholinguistic Abilities were readministered. These tests assess comprehension of noun-verb pairs and skill at completing verbal analogies. Once again, Michel presents increases which exceed the 14 months growth expected since the original evaluation and are well above age-expectancy.

	Age Score 9/91	Age Score 2/93
Auditory Reception	4 years, 7 mos.	6 years, 3 mos.
Auditory Association	5 years, 0 mos.	6 years, 6 mos.

The Preschool Language Assessment Instrument (PLAI) was readministered. This test assesses a young child's ability to cope with the language demands of the classroom. On previous testing Michel presented weakness in Group IV questions involving reasoning about perception. On current testing, all scores on this profile of a child's discourse skills fall in the Strong range. Michel's present ability to use language to offer explanations and rationales typifies what he was weak in 14 months ago: Examiner: Why did you pick that one? Michel: Because that doesn't have any holes.

	Qualitative Score 9/91	Qualitative Score 2/93
I. Matching Perception	Strong	Strong
II. Selective Analysis of Perception	Moderately Strong	Strong
III. Reordering of Perception	Moderately Strong	Strong
IV. Reasoning about Perception	Weak	Strong

Informal Assessment of Michel's current language skills corroborates above standardized scores in that he presents a rich expressive vocabulary and is able to use language in a spontaneous, flexible, and highly creative manner. His vocabulary is well developed, with no retrieval difficulty; Michel will create the name of a word if he does not yet know it. Mean length of utterance is markedly above age expectancy. (Mean length of utterance, MLU = 6.6 words for a five- to six-year-old.) Michel presents many examples of 12-word utterances. The content of his language, reflecting advanced world knowledge, is clearly precocious, as seen in the following language sample.

Michel: The sperm whale is fighting with a giant squid, like sperm whales do. The sperm whale won.
Examiner: What happened to the giant squid?
Michel: Down the ocean floor lying dead! Sperm whales eat giant squid. Didn't you know that? They eat—they only eat one of the tentacles. And do you know what also?
Examiner: What?
Michel: They breathe like—the water comes out their mouth, then it comes out their sgills (sic).
Examiner: Gills?
Michel: Gills.

Examiner: How do you know so much? Where did you learn that?
Michel: The gill part?
Examiner: Yes.
Michel: Oh, in a book with sharks and whales. Isn't that neat?

This example reveals not only Michel's precocious semantic knowledge, but the true communicative nature of his language as he consistently refers back to the listener to include her—i.e., "Didn't you know that?," "And do you know what also?" and "Isn't that neat?" This is precisely the development we are looking for in a child with Michel's history and it is more than well-demonstrated here. In other examples Michel demonstrates that his syntactic development needs to even out with his other advanced language abilities: irregular verbs ("swimmed," "bited,") are in error at times, as is occasional verb conjugation ("Every fish were" and "Know why he done that?") It was noted that Michel had some difficulty with first/last in the spatial modality although he did not have difficulty with first/last when used temporally.

IMPRESSIONS

Michel presents an impressive advance in his communication skills since his last evaluation. All formal test scores fall above age-expectation. Progress is presented in speech, voicing (melody of speech) and receptive/expressive language. The reevaluation reveals the flexible, spontaneous and truly communicative nature of Michel's present language skills. Occasional articulation and syntactic irregularities are noted. The enormous joy, perseverance and enthusiasm which he brings to his work are rare.

RECOMMENDATIONS

It is suggested that Mrs. Maurice, who is experienced in facilitating language in the home, listen for occasional grammatical (usually conjugation) errors and model the correct usage. As Michel was stimulable for correct speech production in most cases, spontaneous improvement may occur and may be reevaluated in six to twelve months.

Educational placement for children who are precocious in language, world knowledge, and enthusiasm for learning is recommended.

Margery F. Rappaport, M.A., CCC
Speech-Language Pathologist

Examples of Data Collection and Charting Progress

In the following charts, "session 1" refers to the start of a particular program, not to the first day of the global curriculum. In other words, "session 1" for one program could be February 5; "session 1" for another program could be July 16.

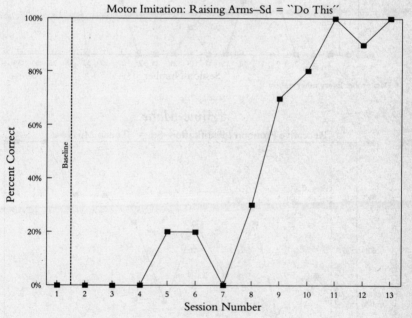

Anne-Marie

Motor Imitation: Raising Arms—Sd = "Do This"

Michel

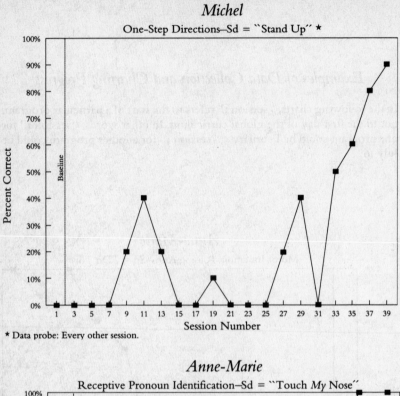

One-Step Directions—Sd = ``Stand Up'' ★

★ Data probe: Every other session.

Anne-Marie

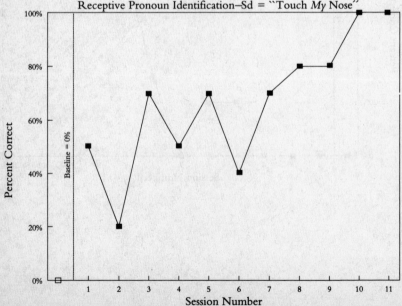

Receptive Pronoun Identification—Sd = ``Touch *My* Nose''

Anne-Marie
Frequency of Echolalia During Two-Hour Time Period

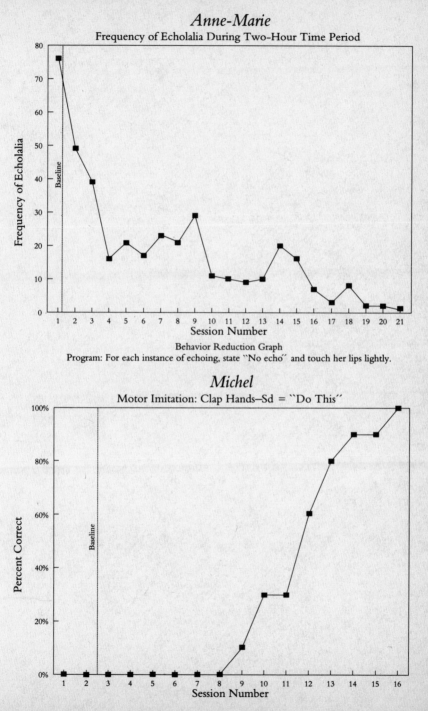

Behavior Reduction Graph
Program: For each instance of echoing, state ``No echo´´ and touch her lips lightly.

Michel
Motor Imitation: Clap Hands–Sd = ``Do This´´

Index